MOVING SHAKESPE

CW01657503

Shakespeare's Company, the King's Men, played at the Globe, and also in an indoor theatre, the Blackfriars. The year 2014 witnesses the opening of the Sam Wanamaker Playhouse, based on seventeenth-century designs of an indoor London theatre and built within the precincts of the current Globe on Bankside. This volume, edited by Andrew Gurr and Farah Karim-Cooper, asks what prompted the move to indoor theatres, and considers the effects that more intimate staging, lighting and music had on performance and repertory. It discusses what knowledge is required when attempting to build an archetype of such a theatre, and looks at the effects of the theatre on audience behaviour and reception. Exploring the ways in which indoor theatre shaped the writing of Shakespeare and his contemporaries in the late Jacobean and early Caroline periods, this book will find a substantial readership among scholars of Shakespeare and Jacobean theatre history.

ANDREW GURR has taught at universities in New Zealand, England, Kenya and the USA. He spent twenty years as Director of Research at the Shakespeare Globe Centre, London. His academic books include *Playgoing in Shakespeare's London* (Cambridge, 1987); *The Shakespearean Stage 1574–1642* (Cambridge, 1992); *The Shakespearian Playing Companies* (1996); *The Shakespeare Company 1594–1642* (2004); and *Shakespeare's Opposites* (Cambridge, 2009).

FARAH KARIM-COOPER is Head of Higher Education and Research at Shakespeare's Globe, and Visiting Research Fellow of King's College London. At the Globe, she is leading the research into the Sam Wanamaker Playhouse, the new indoor Jacobean theatre. She is the author of *Cosmetics in Shakespearean and Renaissance Drama* (2006); *Shakespeare's Globe: A Theatrical Experiment* (co-edited with Christie Carson, Cambridge, 2008); *Shakespeare's Theatres and the Effects of Performance* (co-edited with Tiffany Stern, 2013); and *Shakespeare and the Hand* (forthcoming).

MOVING SHAKESPEARE INDOORS

Performance and Repertoire in the Jacobean Playhouse

EDITED BY

ANDREW GURR

and

FARAH KARIM-COOPER

CAMBRIDGE
UNIVERSITY PRESS

CAMBRIDGE
UNIVERSITY PRESS

University Printing House, Cambridge CB2 8BS, United Kingdom

One Liberty Plaza, 20th Floor, New York, NY 10006, USA

477 Williamstown Road, Port Melbourne, VIC 3207, Australia

4843/24, 2nd Floor, Ansari Road, Daryaganj, Delhi - 110002, India

79 Anson Road, #06-04/06, Singapore 079906

Cambridge University Press is part of the University of Cambridge.

It furthers the University's mission by disseminating knowledge in the pursuit of education, learning and research at the highest international levels of excellence.

www.cambridge.org
Information on this title: www.cambridge.org/9781108438759

© Cambridge University Press 2014

This publication is in copyright. Subject to statutory exception and to the provisions of relevant collective licensing agreements, no reproduction of any part may take place without the written permission of Cambridge University Press.

First published 2014
First paperback edition 2017

A catalogue record for this publication is available from the British Library

ISBN 978-1-107-04063-2 Hardback
ISBN 978-1-108-43875-9 Paperback

Cambridge University Press has no responsibility for the persistence or accuracy of URLs for external or third-party internet websites referred to in this publication, and does not guarantee that any content on such websites is, or will remain, accurate or appropriate.

Contents

Colour plates section can be found between pages 50 and 51

Figures and plates

FIGURES

PLATES

The plates are located between pages 50 and 51

Notes on contributors

John H. Astington is Professor of English and Drama at the University of Toronto, and is the author of numerous books and articles on the early modern English theatre. He is author of *English Court Theatre, 1558–1642* (Cambridge, 1999) and *Actors and Acting in Shakespeare's Time* (Cambridge, 2010).

Eleanor Collins completed her Ph.D. at the Shakespeare Institute and is now a commissioning editor at Oxford University Press. She reviews theatre for *Cahiers Elisabéthains*, is a contributor to the *Year's Work in English Studies* and the *Lost Plays Database*, and is writing a book on the repertory of Queen Henrietta's Men for Manchester University Press.

Bart van Es is Lecturer in English Literature at the University of Oxford and a Fellow of St Catherine's College. He is the author of *Spenser's Forms of History* (2002) and *Shakespeare in Company* (2013) and is the editor of *A Critical Companion to Spenser Studies* (2006).

Sarah Dustagheer is Lecturer in Early Modern Literature at the University of Kent. She is currently preparing her first book, *Shakespeare's Playhouses: Repertory and Theatre Space at the Globe and the Blackfriars, 1599–1613* for publication. Sarah reviews regularly for *Exeunt Magazine* and her articles have appeared in *Shakespeare Jahrbuch*, *Literature Compass* and *Around the Globe*.

Jon Greenfield is a practising architect. He was appointed Project Architect for the Globe reconstruction in 1986 and is currently Reconstruction Architect on the Sam Wanamaker Playhouse project. His research has appeared in several project-related publications, most notably *Shakespeare's Globe Rebuilt* (Cambridge, 1997), and he has presented papers nationally and internationally interpreting the archaeological remains of the Rose Theatre, found on Bankside in 1989.

He also contributed to the Museum of London's recent monograph *The Rose and the Globe, Playhouses of Shakespeare's Bankside, Southwark. Excavations 1988–90*.

ANDREW GURR is a graduate of Auckland and Cambridge universities, and has taught at universities in New Zealand, England, Kenya and the USA. He spent twenty years as Director of Research at the Shakespeare Globe Centre, London. His academic books include *The Shakespearean Stage 1574–1642* (Cambridge, 1992), *The Shakespearian Playing Companies* (1996), *Playgoing in Shakespeare's London* (Cambridge, 2004) and *The Shakespeare Company 1594–1642* (Cambridge, 2010).

MARIKO ICHIKAWA is Professor of English at the University of Tohoku, Japan. She is co-author, with Andrew Gurr, of *Staging in Shakespeare's Theatres* (2000), and is the author of *Shakespearean Entrances* (Cambridge, 2002) and *The Shakespearean Stage Space* (Cambridge, 2012).

OLIVER JONES is the Humanities Research Centre Postdoctoral Fellow in Theatre at the University of York and the Indoor Jacobean Theatre Postdoctoral Research Associate at Shakespeare's Globe. He recently completed his doctoral thesis on the Queen's Men and performance by touring companies in provincial guildhalls, part of which is published as 'The Queen's Men in Stratford and the Troublesome Reign of John, King of England' in *The Guild and Guild Buildings of Shakespeare's Stratford*, ed. J. R. Mulryne (2012).

FARAH KARIM-COOPER is Head of Higher Education and Research (Globe Education) at Shakespeare's Globe. She chairs the Globe's Architecture Research Group and has been leading the research into the construction of the Sam Wanamaker Playhouse. In addition to numerous articles and book chapters, she is author of *Cosmetics in Shakespearean and Renaissance Drama* (2012) and co-editor with Christie Carson of *Shakespeare's Globe: A Theatrical Experiment* (Cambridge, 2008), and with Tiffany Stern of *Shakespeare's Theatres and the Effects of Performance* (2012) and *Shakespeare and the Hand* (forthcoming). She is on the Theatre board for the *New Oxford Shakespeare*, ed. Terri Bourus, John Jowett and Gary Taylor, and is on the editorial board for the journal *The Hare*.

PETER MCCURDY studied architecture and cabinet making. His company, McCurdy & Co., which specializes in the repair and conservation of historic timber-frame buildings and the reconstruction of historic buildings, has been responsible for the detailed design and the building of the reconstruction of the Globe and of the Sam Wanamaker Playhouse.

PAUL MENZER is Professor and Director of the Shakespeare and Performance graduate program at Mary Baldwin College. He is editor of *Inside Shakespeare: Essays on the Blackfriars Stage* (2006) and author of *The Hamlets: Cues, Q's, and Remembered Texts* (2008). His plays include *The Brats of Clarence*, *Shakespeare on Ice* and *Invisible, Inc.* which have played at Staunton, Virginia's Blackfriars Playhouse and in Austin, Texas.

TIFFANY STERN is Beaverbrook and Bouverie Fellow in English and Professor of Early Modern Drama at University College Oxford. Her major publications include *Rehearsal from Shakespeare to Sheridan* (2000), *Making Shakespeare from Stage to Page* (2004), *Shakespeare in Parts* (with Simon Palfrey; 2007) and *Documents of Performance in Early Modern England* (2009), she is co-editor with Farah Karim-Cooper of *Shakespeare's Theatres and the Effects of Performance* (2012). She has edited the anonymous *King Leir* (2001), *Sheridan's The Rivals* (2004), Farquhar's *Recruiting Officer* (2010), and Brome's *Jovial Crew*. She is a general editor of the New Mermaids play series, and is on the editorial board of the journals *Shakespeare Bulletin*, *SEDERI*, *The Hare* and *Shakespeare Quarterly*.

MARTIN WHITE is Professor of Theatre at the University of Bristol and Visiting Professor in Theatre and Performance History at the University of London, Royal Central School of Speech and Drama. His publications include *Renaissance Drama in Action* (1998), editions of *Arden of Faversham* (1982) and Massinger's *The Roman Actor* (2007), book-length studies of *A Midsummer Night's Dream* (2009) and Ford's *'Tis Pity She's a Whore* (2012), and *The Chamber of Demonstrations: Reconstructing the Jacobean Indoor Playhouse* (2009). He has directed scores of plays at Bristol, works regularly as a consultant to the RSC and advises the Globe reconstruction in London on research matters.

PENELOPE WOODS is a Research Associate at the ARC Centre of Excellence for the History of Emotions 1100–1800, at the University of Western Australia. She completed a doctorate on Shakespeare's Globe and its audiences, and has a chapter on audiences in Stephen Purcell, *Shakespeare and Audience in Practice* (2013). She is a member of the Architecture Research Group at Shakespeare's Globe and the New Fortune Theatre Committee at the University of Western Australia.

Acknowledgments

The editors would like to thank Sarah Stanton for her support and advice throughout the process of putting this book together. Thanks also to Rebecca Taylor, Hilary Hammond and Anna Lowe. We would like to thank Shakespeare's Globe for the grant to publish the plates in the volume; particular thanks are due to Neil Constable (CEO, Shakespeare's Globe); thanks are also due to Dominic Dromgoole, Patrick Spottiswoode, Paul Russell, Paul Wills, Claire Godden, Oli Heywood, Claire van Kampen, Ruth Frendo and Shauna Barrett. We are also extremely grateful to the contributors to this volume for their patience, diligence and their inspiring chapters. This book is dedicated to our families.

Introduction

Andrew Gurr and Farah Karim-Cooper

In the winter of 2014, Shakespeare's Globe moves indoors with an opening season for the indoor Jacobean theatre, aptly named the Sam Wanamaker Playhouse. The title of this book is in part inspired by this endeavour, one that Wanamaker envisioned as part of his own two-playhouse plan when he sought to reconstruct the Globe Theatre; this book will go some way to reflect upon and examine the task of building, as Oliver Jones refers to it in Chapter 3, a 'Jacobean ideal'. This scheme, the completion of a project first envisaged by Sam Wanamaker in the 1980s, is meant to add what the Shakespeare company wanted as early as 1594, a winter playhouse to accompany the outdoor playhouse they already possessed. Sam's reason for wanting an indoor venue as well as the outdoor Globe was that the Shakespeare company, within three months of its being founded, tried to obtain an indoor playhouse they could use in the winter. In 1596 the Blackfriars was built for them, but sadly the locals blocked them from using it. In the event, their plan did not succeed until 1609, when Shakespeare himself was near the end of his writing career.

The new indoor theatre is somewhat based on drawings discovered at Worcester College Oxford in the 1960s and that were once considered to be authored by Inigo Jones. Since Shakespeare's Globe opened in 1997, subsequent scholarship has shown that the drawings might have been penned as late as the Restoration and by John Webb, a protégé of Jones. The Globe's aspirations for a 'Jacobean' indoor theatre are driven by these drawings, which provide a 'spatial map' upon which to construct a playhouse Shakespeare might recognize. But the Globe's Architecture Research Group have been tasked with investigating what is known about indoor performance, Jacobean decorative arts and architectural construction; the new playhouse is not the Blackfriars, however, though it will invoke a version of the indoor playhouse Shakespeare's company occupied from 1609 to 1642.

The idea of using the Worcester College drawings as the basis for the new indoor playhouse was agreed for a number of reasons. First, although James

Burbage built the indoor Blackfriars for the Shakespeare company in 1596, in the later years of Queen Elizabeth, it did not become available to the company for regular use until the plague year of 1608, and plays were not performed there until 1609 or 1610. Thus it became in fact and in character the first Jacobean venue used for plays by an adult acting company. Second, it is the best and indeed the only set of drawings for an indoor playhouse that we have. It shows a number of distinctive features that might fix it to the Jacobean period, most notably the priority it may give to hearing over seeing the plays (though this positioning does allow for privileged viewing), since nearly a third of the seats are positioned at the sides or rear of the stage in order to give the best proximity for hearing. It does not do what modern theatres normally do, which is maximize the best views of the stage by positioning all the audience to face the stage from what we think of as the front. Thirdly, like the Blackfriars, it was clearly intended as a wooden construct built independently, and probably intended to fit inside a given external shell.

The drawings do suggest the style of decor that Inigo Jones began to use in his various designs from about 1616 onwards, when he became the king's Surveyor of the Works. Since that was also the date when the first Jacobean playhouse was built, designed deliberately to imitate Burbage's Blackfriars, that is, Christopher Beeston's Cockpit, the Globe has set its own target date for the design of its new indoor playhouse at around 1616. While this book will examine the documentary and practical evidence for the construction of an indoor theatre, it will, in the main, analyze the material, social and economic conditions that made the Shakespeare company invest in two playhouses, and will assess the effects this had on the repertory after 1608. The importance of Shakespeare's indoor theatre has been overshadowed by the attention to and focus upon the amphitheatres in the last twenty years of scholarship. Drawing upon established expertise and the new research emerging from the Globe's academic enquiry into indoor Jacobean performance and playhouse architecture, this book will examine the ways in which the indoor theatre affected the King's Men and their performance practices, the dramaturgy of Shakespeare and his contemporaries who created plays for the company, and its refashioning of and impact upon the playgoers. Despite the increasing critical interest in early modern performance history, apart from Irwin Smith's still highly rated *Shakespeare's Blackfriars Playhouse: Its History and Design* (1964) and the more recent collection from Paul Menzer, *Inside Shakespeare: Essays on the Blackfriars Stage* (2006), there have been very few considerations of the conditions at Shakespeare's indoor playhouse and the wider context for seventeenth-century indoor performance. Examining the past through the lens of the Globe's current construction of an indoor Jacobean theatre, this book will chiefly cover the Blackfriars, but will necessarily extend to both of the subsequent indoor playhouses (the Cockpit and Salisbury Court), and will look broadly at the evident material and ephemeral differences between the indoor and the outdoor repertories and the effects of the move indoors on dramatic style and content as playwriting developed through the Jacobean and Caroline periods.

Why indoors?

In October 1594 the company that included Shakespeare as a player, the Lord Chamberlain's Men, asked their patron to get them the use of an inn with a roofed upper room to perform in through the winter months. He specified the Cross Keys Inn, located in Gracechurch Street in the centre of the city. It had been used in previous years as a winter playhouse, and several members of the new company had performed there. Clearly the company wanted to continue their tradition when the weather was bad of performing indoors inside the city. This traditional view seems to have been maintained in striking contrast to the company's opposites, the Lord Admiral's Men, who seem to have been content to continue through both summer and winter at their assigned venue, the Rose on Bankside. This contrast between the two leading companies' policies had massive long-term effects.

However we read the limited evidence for this difference of attitude between the two companies to the changing seasons, it had drastic effects on the finances of the Lord Chamberlain's Men. The Lord Admiral's always sustained their use of their outdoor venues, first the Rose on Bankside, and then after the Globe was built barely forty yards away from the Rose, at the Fortune in Clerkenwell. They and their successors remained there until the total closure of all playing in 1642. The Lord Chamberlain's Men had a much more varied set of experiences. Whether they did get access to the Cross Keys or not that October we cannot tell, although in our view it was extremely unlikely, because the Lord Mayor who took office at the end of that month (at Michaelmas) was a notoriously severe enemy of all playing. What we do know is that in the following winter of 1595/6 the Chamberlain's Men's financier and playhouse owner James Burbage purchased the freehold of a property in the Blackfriars precinct, inside the city and close to St Paul's Cathedral (see John Astington's Chapter 1 below). There he built a new playhouse for his company.

This (second) Blackfriars venue eventually became the most famous and most fashionable theatre in London. But its first years were a disaster for the Burbages and their company. Their crisis may well have provoked the invention of Shylock as a well-disguised figure for London's moneylenders. On 6 February 1596 Burbage bought the freehold of the hall, originally the monastery's Upper Frater, tore down the tenements that filled it, and spent in all over a thousand pounds building the new playhouse inside that great chamber, which had once been used for meetings of Parliament under Richard II. But in November of the same year thirty-one senior residents of the Blackfriars precinct petitioned the Privy Council to forbid its use as a playhouse. The first signatory on this petition was the dowager Lady Russell, sister-in-law to Lord Burghley, who chaired the Privy Council. The second signatory was the new Lord Hunsdon, the company's own patron, who had inherited the title and the company upon his father's death five months earlier.

The petition was of course approved immediately, and old Burbage, less than three months from death, was immediately besieged by his creditors. They could see that he had lost any means to make money from it and repay their investments. This was when Shakespeare wrote *The Merchant of Venice*, depicting Antonio's problem with his bond, and its effect on his protégé Bassanio. That role was most likely played by Richard Burbage, who in February 1597 inherited the Blackfriars property and its debts from his father. While the play was first being staged, like Antonio, the young Burbage was suffering from London's moneylenders in the wake of his now deceased father. The play was written and staged just at the time when young Burbage found his father's creditors hammering on his own door. It is tempting to consider that the play may have been written and staged at least in part as a response to the financial position in which the company found themselves.

As with the Globe, almost all the sharers in the Second Blackfriars Playhouse were also sharers in the company. But unlike the £100 that each player contributed to buy their share in the Globe, none of the new Blackfriars sharers who were also players had to pay for their new property. It was Richard Burbage's gift to them, as leaders of the company team. This was a tricky deal, and is one that can be seen in various lights. It was distinctly old-fashioned, in that it relied on team spirit to run the operation. In practical and financial terms, to run the two playhouses as seasonal venues was potentially costly. To keep one playhouse closed while they played at the other deprived the sharers of any income from the one that was empty. That may explain Burbage's generosity in not asking the players to pay for their new shares in the Blackfriars. If the new deal had been a plan for the two playhouses to work at the same time throughout the year, they might have been expected to pay a lot for the privilege of doubling their income. Nothing is on record to explain why they adopted their new policy of using their two playhouses seasonally.

For a playing company's sharers to hold shares in their two playhouses was a substantial guarantee of security. They had the king as their patron, and they were far less likely than the boy company to suffer trouble with the authorities. What they chose to do with their new playhouse was, nonetheless, quite remarkable, and utterly unprecedented. In a time when playhouses were in notoriously short supply, with the king's two younger children each having a new company to be patron of, the King's Men chose to revert to the policy they had first tried to adopt back in 1594, and play outdoors in summer and indoors in winter. They could easily have rented one of their two prized venues to another company, but instead, it seems, they chose to keep one empty while they performed in the other. This was extravagant and arrogant. No company had ever followed such a practice since the years up to 1594, before they lost the use of the city inns. In later years they did sometimes let out the Globe for special performers such as acrobats, but they never allowed (as far as extant evidence tells us) another playing company to use either of their playhouses.

This brief summary of the King's Men's unique position as owners of two extraordinarily popular playhouses lays some foundation for the chief aim of this collection: to examine the motives and the conditions that provoked the move theatre companies – namely the Shakespeare company – made indoors. In doing so, this book will address several questions. When, fourteen years after it was originally built for them, the Shakespeare company finally started using their indoor playhouse at the Blackfriars, did they develop a new repertory of plays for it? What were the material, visual and acoustic conditions at the Blackfriars and how did these influence the early modern repertory? Who attended these indoor venues and what were the effects of the indoor conditions on audience reception? In Part I: The Context of Hard Evidence, we examine the appeal of the indoor playhouse and assess practical and documentary evidence for constructing a version of a Jacobean indoor playhouse now. In Chapter 1, John Astington examines why the theatres changed. For Astington, the acquisition of the Blackfriars playhouse by the King's Men in 1608 profoundly influenced subsequent theatre ventures: the Phoenix or Cockpit playhouse in Drury Lane (1616), the projected theatre at Porters' Hall (1613–17), and the Salisbury Court playhouse (1629–30). The change was driven by entrepreneurship on the part of the actors and by taste on the part of audiences. Playing indoors within a converted hall was an old practice, well known to actors and audiences of all kinds from the medieval period onwards, but it was the commercialized playing of the chorister children's troupes in the 1570s and 1580s that initiated an alternative option for playgoing within London: instead of mixing in the large crowds at the outdoor playhouses, wealthier members of society could join a smaller, select audience indoors, where plays were performed on smaller stage platforms illuminated by candlelight. Astington also explores the big question of whether or not the change in venues altered the ways in which actors approached the performance of plays, indoors and out. In Chapter 2, Practical Evidence for a Reimagining of an Indoor Jacobean Theatre, architect Jon Greenfield and timber craftsman Peter McCurdy show how the construction of an indoor Jacobean theatre is possible by applying an understanding of contemporary Jacobean construction technology, together with knowledge gained from an examination of contemporary building accounts and surviving Jacobean interiors. This process, they argue, has generated a reinterpretation that captures both strong similarities with the designs expressed in the Worcester College drawings and significant differences. The result is a Jacobean archetype that promises to yield important new discoveries in seventeenth-century indoor performance. We have chosen to leave some technical detail in this chapter to demonstrate the different sorts of evidence available and to draw attention to the historic methodology that accompanies 'reconstruction' projects. In the chapter that follows, Documentary Evidence for an Indoor Jacobean Theatre, Oliver Jones, who served as Research Associate on the Globe's indoor theatre project, suggests that clues about the construction and decoration of a seventeenth-century indoor theatre have to be teased from documents such as Burbage's purchase contract for his Blackfriars site and from inferences in surviving play texts, but that these do not offer a ready blueprint for modern reproduction. However, when casting the net wider to include a broader survey of Jacobean buildings, several examples emerge containing features similar to those present in an indoor theatre. Jones reflects that by investigating the accounts of work undertaken at elite estates such as Hatfield House, or at Whitehall during the construction of the pre-Inigo Jones Banqueting House, we can more fully understand the Jacobean building process and what ramifications this has when attempting to replicate an indoor theatre of the early modern period.

In Chapter 4, Continuities and Innovations in Staging, Mariko Ichikawa considers how the physical features of the stage and auditorium of the Blackfriars Theatre and what is known of performance practice might have influenced the plays acted there. The Blackfriars stage, being much narrower than that of the Globe, and the presence of stage-sitters would have reduced the width of the playing area, affecting actors' positions on the stage. By examining the entrances and exits in these plays, the width of the playing area in relation to a scene's location and the intended use of stage facilities, Ichikawa makes a convincing case for the Blackfriars having a significant atmospheric advantage over the open-air theatres where the actors played in broad daylight.

Part II examines the materiality of the indoor venues, and indeed many chapters in this volume take up the question of the visual and acoustic effects of this materiality on performance, audience response and repertory. In the first chapter of this section, Tiffany Stern starts with Blackfriars as a place of nostalgia, redolent of its past, with audiences who repeatedly draw attention to the space's previous manifestations: to the monastery once there, to the parliament and legatine court that shared its buildings, to the choirboys that typified its previous theatre. She asks how the prehistory visible in the entrance, stairway and outer shell of the Second Blackfriars Playhouse contributed to its haunted atmosphere. She also takes into account what theatrical accoutrements – such as boxes, latticed and otherwise, galleries and stage-stools, as well as audience effects (cloaks and bejewelled gowns) – may have been added to the Second Blackfriars Playhouse to make it simultaneously current as well as an echo of something lost. Stern asks if a yearning for being elsewhere – in court – also shaped the experience of attending the Second Blackfriars Playhouse. She considers how plays were affected by the combination of nostalgia and modernity that visually, aurally and sensually infused the space.

Following on from Stern's consideration of the look and feel of the Blackfriars, in Chapter 6, Martin White draws on a wide range of sources in order to try to understand how lighting technology was employed. White covers techniques of lighting the stage, the contribution that may have been made by daylight, and offers new insights into the number, nature and deployment of the candles used, their operation before and during performances, the possibility and impact of changing lighting states to match or create particular moods, and the ways hand-held instruments helped articulate and focus the general lighting. He consults a range of sources, including records of staging plays at court and at the professional commercial playhouses before and immediately following the Restoration, as well as accounts of the purchase and maintenance of the wide range of equipment required to light those performances. White also draws evidence from the texts of plays known to have been written for, or performed, indoors, and from the author's extensive experience of staging early modern plays under candlelight. This chapter explores how the nature of candlelight was a key factor in deciding the decor of the interior of the playhouses and examines its effect on the clothes worn by actors and their audiences, concluding with an analysis based on experiments undertaken in a temporary 'reconstructed' indoor playhouse with John Webster's tragedy, *The Duchess of Malfi*. In Chapter 7, Acoustic and Visual Practices Indoors, Sarah Dustagheer examines further the material constituents of indoor performance. Her chapter analyses the ways in which music was a dominant and integral aspect of the dramaturgy of indoor plays, as seen particularly in the work of Marston and Shakespeare. In the first part, she shows how, rather than just an incidental or discrete presence, music was woven into narrative and character development; in the second part, her focus turns to the visual aesthetic of Blackfriars. She notes, along with other contributors to this volume, that contemporary accounts of the Blackfriars indicate that the audience 'glittered' and 'glistened' under the candlelight, using the playhouse to display the latest London fashions. In response to this distinct visual environment, Dustagheer argues that playwrights deployed props and costumes deliberately to create a rich, 'material-laden vision' for their stage.

In the next chapter, The Audience of the Indoor Theatre, Penelope Woods considers the nature of the Jacobean audience at the indoor theatres by examining 'the ecology of performance effects' and audience responses to them that were produced by the professional adult company performing indoors. The Blackfriars was a commercial but expensive, and consequently, elite theatre with a much smaller auditorium than the outdoor performance space at the Globe used by the King's Men. Its seating arrangements and audience distribution brought actors and audiences into different physical relationships to one another, and since it was brightly illuminated with candles, and permeated with a different musical soundscape, this theatre produced a different audience experience and response to that previously examined in considerations of early modern reception history. Woods argues that these changes 'choreographed the audience's physical and emotional relationships' and its relationship to the actors in significant ways that were distinct from performance and its reception in the outdoor theatres. Drawing on the critical work of historical phenomenology, Woods considers what happened *in-between* performance, theatre and its reception. Her chapter takes the cases of 'pity' and 'wonder', key responses produced by indoor Jacobean audiences. Examining three moments of performance, from *Othello*, *The Lady's Tragedy* and *The Winter's Tale* and three corresponding eyewitness accounts, Woods considers what happens in these scenes between actor, audience and theatre space.

In Chapter 9, In the Event of Fire, Paul Menzer argues that the Blackfriars 'reset western theatre's disposition towards time and place' by articulating a commitment to intimacy and an investment in loss that permeates the protocols of playmaking, then and even now. In strictly material terms, Menzer argues, it is easy to think of Burbage's indoor playhouse simply as an 'inverted amphitheatre: private not public; coterie not populist; intimate not rowdy'. The Blackfriars, in these terms, compromised the Globe. The Blackfriars was simply the Globe turned outside in. Yet, to imagine the Blackfriars as an 'inverted Globe' underestimates its historical significance. For the Blackfriars did not just invert the Globe, Menzer suggests; it ultimately supplanted it. Menzer observes that, in fact, the Blackfriars struck the 'death knell' not just for the Globe, nor for early English outdoor playing, but for a nearly two thousand-year-old theatrical tradition of outdoor theatre. Menzer argues that the opening of the Blackfriars marked the beginning of the end to a long chapter in western theatre history, revising the 'sensory norm' for theatrical attendance, in which the experience of assembly has been thoroughly domesticated. He suggests emphatically that in fact the 'sensory norm of inside playing', as he calls it, of 'institutionalized intimacy', reconfigured 'not just what it meant to be live in 1610, but what it still means to be live today'.

The final chapter (Chapter 10) in Part II considers how faces might 'glisten in a playhouse'. Here, Farah Karim-Cooper examines the aesthetic implications of using cosmetic face paint in a candlelit indoor playhouse. Focussing on Ben Jonson's *The Devil is an Ass*, Thomas Middleton's *The Lady's Tragedy* and Shakespeare's *The Winter's Tale*, Karim-Cooper argues that the indoor repertory shows a markedly different type of engagement with cosmetics and cosmetic metaphors than the outdoor repertory (meaning plays written with outdoor spaces in mind – though not necessarily performed just in those spaces), which is, in part, a response to the different architectural, proxemic and lighting conditions of the indoor playhouses. In addition to imagining the visual aesthetic created by facial cosmetics on the indoor stage, Karim-Cooper's chapter explores the social and ideological questions raised by representations of cosmetic spectacle in Jacobean drama and the dialectical resonances the effects of makeup create for the female spectators in the space.

The final part of this book focusses on the influence that indoor theatres might have had on shaping repertory, re-examining what is meant by 'late Shakespeare' and looking forward to the Caroline repertory. Andrew Gurr, in Chapter 11, sees a radical shift in Shakespeare's own work as he developed the new, so-called 'romances' in the later part of his career. Gurr asks, what might have prompted this innovation? And how far did the Shakespeare company's acquisition of Blackfriars in 1608 influence the kind of plays that Shakespeare went on to write, such as *Cymbeline*, *The Winter's Tale*, *The Tempest* and *Two Noble Kinsmen*? Did the addition of Beaumont's and Fletcher's work to the company's repertoire influence Shakespeare's own writing, or did it work the other way round? Gurr suggests that calculating how far this set of innovations relates to the Blackfriars might either heighten the impact of the indoor theatre or shrink its distinctive value for the company.

In Chapter 12, Eleanor Collins explores the genres of tragicomedy and romance that were developed and revived on the Caroline stages of the hall playhouses, genres which have become, in many critical accounts, characteristic of drama in this later period. Collins focusses in particular on the figure of the heroic woman in 1630s drama, and the means by which male dramatists negotiated the representation of female characters. She argues that this was a period that witnessed a sea change in attitudes towards women, their cultural status and agency, in the light of Queen Henrietta Maria's interventions into drama, her influence on the courtier playwrights, and the idealization of women through the politicized doctrine of Neoplatonic love that she promoted at court. The discussion traces the development of the theatrical fashion for heroic women which emerged across the London repertories and was taken up by professional playwrights including James Shirley, Thomas Heywood and Philip Massinger, who all contributed to the debate over female autonomy and further established the appeal of strong female roles. It goes on to explore how these representations of women were enhanced and complicated by revivals from older periods and from the amphitheatre traditions. Finally, helping to draw together some of the other chapters in this book, Collins considers how heroic women in the Caroline repertory might have appeared on stage to audiences of the indoor theatres, taking into account the unique performance conditions, which include the portrayal of women by boy actors; the intimacy of the indoor theatres; and the uses of cosmetics, costuming, and lighting in the representation of women.

In the final chapter in this collection, Reviving the Legacy of Indoor Performance, Bart van Es questions the argument that 1608 was a turning point for Shakespeare's habits of composition. This chapter considers the Shakespearean late style in the light of the existing repertory of the indoor playhouse. On the surface, it seems that stylistic evolution was directly adapted to the physical qualities of the new venue, as some of the chapters in this volume argue. As several chapters here maintain, the greater control over sound and light, combined with the intimacy of the smaller space, align well with the qualities of the final plays. Yet the match between the new repertory and the demands of the indoor stage is less close than at first appears, van Es argues. The opening storm of *The Tempest*, for example, is little suited to what we know of performance conditions at Blackfriars. In terms of fashion, it was humoural comedy, satire and politic history that had been most successful in the private halls. Most importantly, many features of the late style are found in plays such as *Pericles*, which pre-date the acquisition of an indoor venue for the King's Men. Thus, while change occurs, van Es suggests, the case for strategic adaptation is harder to make. He argues that Shakespeare's dramaturgy had long been set against the elite tastes of the private theatre, and even after the acquisition of the new playhouse the playwright's commitment to the Globe's amphitheatre tradition remains strong. Yet the legacy of indoor performance is important. Van Es's chapter argues that although it is more complex than simple adaptation, a gradual merging of the indoor and outdoor repertories did occur in the final years of Shakespeare's career. Poets such as John Fletcher had made indoor production a speciality. What we see in the late years is Shakespeare's absorption of this influence, but we also see men such as Fletcher adapting to the 'Globe style', as Gurr's chapter in this volume likewise argues. The late plays, then, show a combination of adaptation and resistance to Blackfriars. Attention to the legacy of indoor performance from 1599 onwards provides insight not only into Shakespeare's final productions but also into the plays that he produced before the company made a commitment to the new theatre in 1608. In the last half-decade of his career, Shakespeare collaborated closely with a set of contemporaries who had made their reputations by writing for the children. Van Es concludes that co-authorship, imitation and rivalry, at least inasmuch as physical staging requirements are concerned, thus help to account for the playwright's 'Blackfriars style'.

The chief aims of this collection are to consider what prompted the move indoors; how an indoor theatre can be 'redolent of its past'; what knowledge is required when attempting to build an archetype of such a theatre; the effects the physical environs of the theatres might have had on performance and repertory; the impact of intimacy in these indoor urban spaces; audience behaviour and reception; and the ways in which the move indoors might have shaped not only Shakespeare's writing but also that of his contemporaries in the late Jacobean and early Caroline periods. This book opens with Astington's sense that the move indoors did not necessarily require a new type of repertory, and closes with van Es's notion of 'adaptation and resistance'; the chapters within argue for a more attentive consideration of the complex material features and architectural conditions of these playhouses, but all suggest bold ways of reading these spaces and the plays performed within them, and all agree that the move indoors redefined theatre practice for centuries to come.

PART I

The context of hard evidence

CHAPTER I

Why the theatres changed

John H. Astington

SIR EDWARD FORTUNE I sawe the Children of *Powles* last night,
And troth they pleasde me prettie, prettie well . . .
NED PLANET Ifaith I like the Audience that frequenteth there
With much applause. A man shall not be choakte
With the stench of Garlicke, nor be pasted
To the barmy Jacket of a Beer-brewer.
BRABANT JUNIOR . . .'Tis a good gentle Audience . . .'[1]

Thus the playwright John Marston, via his dramatic characters, suggests one reason for a change in the places where the performance of drama might be experienced in early modern London. The play in which these words were spoken was performed by Paul's Boys themselves, at their usual venue within the precincts of the great city cathedral, roughly a year after the Globe had opened on the opposite bank of the river, in 1599. The architectural model on which the Globe was based, indeed from which it was assembled, was the wooden O, as it is called in *Henry V* (Prologue, 13). Illustrated in the famous contemporary sketch of the Swan playhouse by Jan de Witt and Arend van Buchell, such places had possibly been inspired by arenas for animal baiting, and similarly had a large polygonal plan, with three storeys of wooden galleries surrounding an open central yard. Placed against one of the interior angles of such a building, the players' tiring-house (or in de Witt's Latin, '*mimorum aedes*') formed a rear façade behind a rectangular platform stage that projected well into the yard space, and which could be surrounded by a standing audience of those who paid the cheapest admission price of a penny.

On busy days, particularly the common holidays when working people were at liberty to go to the playhouses for an afternoon performance, standing in the yard or even sitting in the galleries might involve some discomfort in the form of being rather too closely jammed up against other

[1] John Marston, *Jack Drum's Entertainment* (London, 1601), sig H3v. (Speech prefixes expanded.)

people's bodies, as in a rush-hour train or bus, and hence encountering the smells of those bodies, likely to have been more detectable in Shakespeare's day than in our largely sanitized present. Planet complains about the prevailing smell of garlic, an item of common diet that has rather reversed its indicative class meaning in England in the intervening four hundred years. Moreover, he has encountered people at the public playhouses who have gone to the theatre without dressing up, straight from work, as they might, in certain quarters today, go to a bar. The beer brewer, possibly from a local Southwark brewery, still wears his sticky, yeasty, working clothes, also providing a characteristic smell. The democratically mixed, large, jostling crowd at the outdoor playhouses is evoked in some contemporary satirical verses by Sir John Davies, comparing the confused thoughts of 'Cosmus' to the rush for the exits at the end of the show:

> For as we see at all the play house dores
> When ended is the play, the daunce, and song:
> A thousand townesmen, gentlemen, and whores,
> Porters and serving-men togither throng[2]

(So does Cosmus allow a random flow of miscellaneous impulses to carry him away.)

Audience figures in the thousands, featuring all social classes as well as the socially deviant, belonged to the large outdoor playhouses; one of the attractions of the Paul's Boys' performances for those wanting a rather more intimate experience was the considerably smaller size of the auditorium and hence the audience it held. It seems unlikely that the audience at Paul's could have been made up of more than a couple of hundred people even under the most packed conditions: Paul's was one of the smallest of contemporary playing venues. We shall come to a fuller consideration of the kind of space of which the Paul's playhouse was representative, but a further attraction for the nervous or the pretentious was that the audience was 'gentle': that is to say not only more refined and considerate in manners but of a social rank above the common ruck, with money in inherited landholdings, one step short of the nobility. How universally true that may have been about audiences at Paul's might be doubted, but one filter on admission was commercial. The brewer could find a place to watch the play at the Globe for a penny; it would have cost him six times as much to see a performance at Paul's. So one might today, on the right evening, find a good

2 Robert Krueger (ed.), *The Poems of Sir John Davies* (Oxford University Press, 1975), 'In Cosmum', lines 5–8, p. 136.

seat at the National Theatre for fifteen pounds, but could never hope to attend an opera at Covent Garden on similar terms.

The mutual congratulation of groups whose members can afford to belong is not an attractive human trait, but is common enough, and is likely to have something to do with what Planet has detected about the audience at Paul's. The boy troupes who performed plays in London during the reign of Queen Elizabeth were never professional actors: their principal role was as treble singers in the choirs of St Paul's cathedral and the royal chapel. Their choirmasters had found favour with the queen early in her reign, and she encouraged the educational enterprise of extending choral training into the performance of spoken drama and had sponsored frequent appearances by the boys at her holiday courts, particularly during the 1580s. Nor were they alone; the queen also encouraged the masters of leading London schools to present plays at court in the Christmas and Shrove seasons. Boy players, in short, had the fashionable cachet of being 'by appointment to Her Majesty the Queen', while the adult players who bore the queen's name and livery from 1583 onwards never seem to have been particularly ambitious about their profile in London. Sebastian Westcott, the choirmaster at Paul's, by contrast, struck on the idea of opening, to a paying audience, rehearsals for the court, as it were, for a limited time at the turn of the year. Those who liked to imagine themselves suitably qualified to be members of the royal court, in rank and social accomplishments, were thus admitted to an exclusive entertainment, destined in its final form to be for the eyes and ears of the queen and her immediate entourage. Westcott was selling not only theatre but a restricted luxury – an atmosphere that simply reeked with class. The profits either compensated him for a responsible but not particularly well-paid job, or went to the coffers of the dean and chapter of St Paul's. His 'playhouse', sometimes so called in histories of the theatre of the time, was actually a fairly small hall in the house where he lived, immediately to the south of the cathedral, used most of the time as a schoolroom and rehearsal space for singing, annually adapted for a week or two each winter to accommodate a modest tiring-house, stage and audience.

Such conditions corresponded to a long tradition of playing in adapted indoor chambers, the social conditions of which were not notably exclusive. Henry Medwall's hilarious two-part play *Fulgens and Lucrece* was written for performance on a feast day in the Great Hall of Lambeth Palace before the household of Cardinal John Morton in 1497. Its conception suggests that its audience saw it in the same space in which they ate, a large roofed hall of the kind in which Oxford and Cambridge college communities still gather to eat, and further that the entire household, from serving staff on upwards, were gathered to watch it. It is from among the household servants that the otherwise anonymous A and B step through the fourth wall to take roles in the play.[3] The annual feasts of the London livery companies, held in each company's hall within the city of London, frequently featured visiting players, as did the similar ceremonies of the law societies of the Inns of Court.[4]

Public access to plays performed indoors was common in places where there were no playhouses: the provincial towns and cities of England visited by touring players, as well as in London itself before the later 1560s. A vivid memory of being at such a performance is provided by a man who had been raised in Gloucester, where visiting players performed in the Bothall, or town hall, a roofed stone building used principally for the administration of civic business, and a typical principal architectural feature of large towns and cities throughout England.

> In the City of Gloucester the manner is (as I think it is in other like corporations) that when Players of Enterludes come to town, they first attend the Mayor to enforme him what noble-mans servants they are, and so get licence for their publike playing; and if the Mayor like the Actors, or would show respect to their Lord and Master, he appoints them to play their first play before himselfe and the Aldermen and common Counsell of the City; and that is called the Mayors play, where every one that will comes in without money, the mayor giving the players a reward as he thinks fit to shew respect to them. At such a play, my father took me with him and made me stand betweene his leggs, as he sate upon one of the benches where wee saw and heard very well.[5]

The memoir continues with a fascinating account of watching a morality play, *The Cradle of Security*, in which a prince succumbs to sin and is carried away to hell; details of costumes, properties, music, and stage movement are all recalled. It is recorded in the spiritual autobiography *Mount Tabor*, published in 1639 when the author, R. Willis, was 75 years of age; the remembered performance must have happened in the earlier 1570s, when Leicester's, Sussex's and Worcester's players, among others, were visiting Gloucester regularly.

[3] See Alan H. Nelson (ed.), *The Plays of Henry Medwall* (Cambridge: D. S. Brewer, 1980).

[4] See Anne Lancashire, *London Civic Theatre* (Cambridge University Press, 2002); Alan H. Nelson and John R. Elliott Jnr (eds.), *Inns of Court* (3 vols.; Woodbridge: Boydell & Brewer, 2010).

[5] R. Willis, *Mount Tabor* (London, 1639). Quoted in Audrey Douglas and Peter Greenfield (eds.), *Cumberland, Westmorland, Gloucestershire* (University of Toronto Press, 1986), pp. 362–3.

The Gloucester Bothall does not survive, but several buildings like it, including the Guildhall at Leicester and St Mary's Guildhall at Coventry, next to the old cathedral, may still be seen today: both were used by visiting players in the sixteenth and seventeenth centuries. Such places varied somewhat in size, but as one of their chief functions was to serve as either or both market hall and court or council chambers, they were generally spacious; dimensions of 25–30 feet of width by 50–60 feet of length have been given as an average.[6] The space at the Blackfriars in London acquired by James Burbage in 1596, a 'great hall or room' in which he was to set up a playhouse,[7] had not dissimilar if rather more generous dimensions: 46 feet by 66. Like some of the guildhalls, the buildings at Blackfriars dated from the fourteenth century, and had substantial stone walls, large windows and high pitched roofs.

In the days before playhouses began to be built, then, players commonly performed indoors, in halls adapted to hold an audience – seated on benches, in Gloucester – and a performing space, whether a raised platform stage, which provincial accounts not infrequently mention as being provided for players, or simply on an area of the hall floor. We might ask why the hall model for permanent commercial playhouses was not adapted earlier than in fact it was: effectively about 1600. Indoor theatres were not at the mercy of adverse weather conditions, and they did not necessarily require lighting with candles, if the halls in which they were set up had suitable windows and performances took place at the traditional afternoon hours. Before the advent of playhouses, however, other spaces – specifically outdoor spaces – were used to stage and watch plays. The great civic dramas of the fifteenth and earlier sixteenth centuries were acted in town streets and squares, notably in York along an elaborate processional route, with shorter scriptural episodes moving from place to place on mobile pageant wagons. Commercial players also took up the medieval tradition of outdoor playing; although northern European weather was not as friendly to actors and audiences as was that in Italy, where *commedia dell'arte* developed partly as a popular street theatre, similar advantages to players might be had from natural bright and even lighting, and the chance to gather a large standing audience around a platform stage, within the confines of a town square or green. In certain English towns,

6 Peter Greenfield, 'Touring', in Richard Dutton (ed.), *The Oxford Handbook of Early Modern Theatre* (Oxford University Press, 2009), p. 298.

7 Quoted from the 1651 deed of sale, reprinted in *English Professional Theatre, 1530–1660*, ed. Glynne Wickham, Herbert Berry and William Ingram (Cambridge University Press, 2000), p. 529.

Shrewsbury for example, players could make use of traditional outdoor gathering places for public performances.[8] At Cambridge, the university authorities were exercised about undergraduates possibly misspending their time by attending plays at Sturbridge Fair, held annually outside the town in late summer.[9]

Yet if audiences could assemble in large public spaces, they could equally dissipate once the show was over, without paying anything for their entertainment. To address this problem the yards of inns, paved spaces large enough to accommodate horses and wagons and surrounded by outbuildings, seem to have been a reasonably popular choice for actors to adapt into temporary theatres. There are fewer surviving provincial records than one would like for us to claim confidently that the inn-yard was a commonly employed theatre space, but the Queen's Men were certainly playing in such a place at Norwich in June 1583, when an argument broke out between the players and certain members of the audience.[10] The incident seems to have arisen from someone trying to 'jump the turnstile', in modern terms, indicating that the inn-yard, like the hall, was favoured because the gate could be controlled. No one could observe the performance without paying admission, or being invited, as at 'the Mayor's play'.

Whatever the situation in the provinces, inn-yards were favoured places to stage and watch plays within London, even after the first playhouses were open for business. At least two playhouses, the Boar's Head in Whitechapel (1598) and the Red Bull in Clerkenwell (*c.* 1607) were adapted from existing inns and their yards, while the earliest playhouse we know of, the Red Lion in Stepney (1567), was constructed within an existing 'court or yard'.[11] Inns within the city of London, at Ludgate, Bishopsgate, and along Gracechurch Street, a major north–south thoroughfare connecting with London Bridge, also were adapted for theatrical performances.[12] They were rented by various playing companies, including the Queen's Men, as they also were by professional fencers, whose bouts were frequently played before a paying public. One stage, in such places, served both actors and sword-fighters. (The renowned Richard Tarlton was both.) The inn playhouses had their

[8] See J. Alan B. Somerset (ed.), *Shropshire* (2 vols.; University of Toronto Press, 1994), vol. II, pp. 387–8.

[9] See Alan H. Nelson (ed.), *Cambridge* (2 vols.; University of Toronto Press, 1989), vol. II, pp. 704–5.

[10] David Galloway (ed.), *Norwich 1540–1642* (University of Toronto Press, 1984), pp. 70–6.

[11] Wickham et al., *English Professional Theatre*, p. 292.

[12] On the inn theatres see ibid., pp. 295–305, and David Kathman, 'Inn-Yard Playhouses', in Dutton, *Oxford Handbook*, pp. 153–67.

heyday in the 1580s, when two large playhouses were operating immediately to the north of the city walls, and one of their advantages must have been their accessibility: they were surrounded by the densely populated streets of central London, as also were the two venues at which the boy troupes performed, St Paul's and Blackfriars.

The inn-yard model, so to speak, was therefore one influence on the building of dedicated playhouses. The shape of inn-yards, defined by the ranges of the buildings surrounding them, was most usually rectangular, or approximately so; the wooden playhouses embraced the O form, except that when in 1600 the Fortune was built to rival or surpass the Globe and to replace the smaller, ageing Rose, it was given a square plan, following the layout of the converted inn-yard playhouse of two years earlier, the Boar's Head. Square, round or rectangular, yard playhouses had the advantage of capacity. Any transportation engineer knows that the fewer fixed seats there are in a train carriage the more passengers it will hold at rush hours, packed up against one another without much comfort, but on their way. Popular desire to see a play (formerly), a rock concert (now), a football match or simply to get home comes with a certain trade-off of relaxation for anticipated pleasure. Such was the calculation about the open yard at ground level in the large outdoor theatres of Shakespeare's day. Standees in such places arguably had the best places, with a clear view of the stage, close proximity to the actors, and the acoustic advantage of the amplifying and distributive effect of the surrounding galleries and walls. At the Rose, excavation has revealed, the yard was raked, to allow a better view to those further from the stage. The yard audience, like football crowds, undoubtedly had some group spirit, probably more animated when the yard was absolutely full, although to assume that its members were predisposed to be noisy and disruptive, ignoring the excitements, tensions and surprises of the story being told on stage is to misread their motives for being at a playhouse in the first place. A large yard perhaps held a thousand people when jammed full; a modern experiment with the area of the smaller yard at the Rose yielded an estimate of 740 people, so jammed.[13]

A thousand heads filling the yard like a sea around the island of the stage entailed a thousand hands dropping pennies in the collectors' boxes, for a total take of slightly more than four pounds. If the galleries collectively held another thousand, at roughly twice the basic admission price, players at the Globe or the Fortune would have expected a total box office of about twelve pounds, at popular plays on busy days. This compares favourably

[13] Christine Eccles, *The Rose Theatre* (London: Nick Hern, 1990), pp. 134–6.

with the standard fee for a contemporary commissioned performance at court, ten pounds, which presumably did indeed bear a realistic relationship to the profit from a good day at the playhouse. Even allowing for higher prices, then, the considerably smaller audiences at Paul's plays were not bringing in sums comparable to the commercial playhouses, although the terms of the comparison are truly between an amateur and occasional theatre on the one hand and a professional operation on the other, playing as often as custom and authority allowed.

Whatever comparative calculations we might make, the enterprise of James Burbage in 1596 looks like a radical move in theatre business. Engaged in a dispute with the landlord of the site in Shoreditch where twenty years earlier he had built the Theatre, a large wooden O, he opted for a completely unprecedented plan; an indoor playhouse run commercially for performances by adult actors, within the city walls. The location of Blackfriars, his chosen site, on the slope of Ludgate Hill immediately to the south and west of Paul's churchyard, made it an immediate competitor for audiences with the playing space at Paul's, and a challenge to the boys. One chief reason the theatres changed was that an ambitious and determined man decided that they could; for Burbage, who had seen the Elizabethan theatre grow up, there was nothing essential or final about playhouses like the Theatre, the Curtain, the Rose and the Swan. Had his plans gone forward in 1596, the famous Globe of three years later might never have been built. The most renowned theatre of the period in subsequent legend was in fact something of an accidental compromise at the time. It would be rather more than a dozen years before Burbage's daring plan was put fully into action, long after his death in 1597. One corollary we might note is that Burbage was simultaneously capable of imagining the successful repertory of his son's company in the middle 1590s – such plays as Shakespeare's *Richard II*, *A Midsummer Night's Dream* and *The Merchant of Venice*, for example – as equally capable of success on a smaller indoor stage before a smaller seated audience. There would appear to have been no essential division in a contemporary actor's mind between 'outdoor' and 'indoor' plays.

The space Burbage bought from Sir William More early in 1596 constituted a substantial part of the 'Parliament Chamber' at Blackfriars, a large hall where parliaments had occasionally been held in the past. No plan or representation of it survives, but the sale contract mentions 'great stone walls' and the 'leads or roof' over the space, which was on the second storey, accessed by a 'great pair of winding stairs'.[14] Modern speculative

[14] Wickham et al., *English Professional Theatre*, p. 504.

reconstructions and sketches of the building show it as a gothic hall with a pitched timber-beam roof and pointed-arch windows flanking the side walls: similar, in short, to a medieval guildhall or church nave.[15] By the end of the year local residents petitioned the Privy Council to stop Burbage's plan 'to convert and turn the same [space] into a common playhouse', pleading the inconveniencies of unruly crowds, dangers of infection and noise, and adding the further point that the Lord Mayor had banned playing within the city limits.[16] By the time the new playhouse was stopped Burbage had presumably taken down the partition walls which had divided the old hall into seven rooms used for lodgings and set up within the resulting 'great hall or room' the 'stage, galleries, and seats' which were, four years later, rented to Henry Evans for use by the Children of the Chapel.[17] Thus a playhouse planned for an adult troupe reverted to the boys, who had occupied an earlier theatrical space in the Blackfriars for rather less than a decade from 1576 to 1584. The Burbages' enforced lease of their Blackfriars playhouse could only have furthered London playgoers' impressions of an indoor–outdoor divide between the performances of the child amateurs and those of the adult professional players. The new theatres of the adults at the turn of the century were the Globe and the Fortune, playhouses to hold thousands, with a large standing audience in the yard.

As to why a playhouse banned through local resistance in 1596 managed to open for business four years later, we can only guess that the Chapel children were seen as a less disruptive presence. They played only once or twice each week, rather than daily, and probably only through the winter months. They had the cachet of being in royal service, and of providing sophisticated music as well as drama, and they were not, at least on the surface, in the business of making money from public entertainment, although their adult managers and backers were increasingly pushing them in that direction. Otherwise we might imagine that the comings and goings of audiences, potentially as large as they might have been for the professional players, were exactly the same in their impact on the immediate neighbourhood. If that impact was not as bad as it had been painted, the boys perhaps softened up the resistance to the full-time use of the theatre after 1608.

15 See Irwin Smith, *Shakespeare's Blackfriars Playhouse* (New York University Press, 1964); Richard Hosley, 'The Second Blackfriars Playhouse (1596)', in Clifford Leech and T. W. Craik (eds.), *The Revels History of Drama in English*, vol. III, *1576–1613* (London: Methuen, 1975), pp. 197–226 (sketches by Richard Southern).

16 Wickham et al., *English Professional Theatre*, pp. 507–8. 17 Ibid., p. 508.

The gradual professionalization of the Chapel troupe, which finally became an independent playing company in 1604, was no doubt furthered by their tenure of the Blackfriars playhouse.[18] Never before had a troupe of chorister players worked in a dedicated playhouse – a space given over entirely to the performing and watching of plays. The Paul's 'theatre' was a temporarily converted singing school, and it seems likely that the first Blackfriars 'theatre' had been similar, despite the protests of its landlord that it had been made into 'a continual house for plays'.[19] Burbage's establishment, by contrast, was a permanent playhouse. The famous passage in the Folio text of *Hamlet* in which Rosencrantz recounts the success of an 'eyrie of children' (2.2.315) in competition with the adult players is usually taken to be referring to events in London after 1600, though there is otherwise not much to indicate that the boys affected the success of the adults adversely. The repertory, at both Blackfriars and Paul's, certainly seems to have offered something new, although Ben Jonson continued, between 1599 and 1610, to write similar plays both for the boys and for Shakespeare's troupe. Otherwise John Marston, George Chapman, Thomas Middleton, Francis Beaumont and John Fletcher all provided a rather different flavour of repertory, including tragicomedy, and plays that through tone, character and action offered what R. A. Foakes has called a 'challenge to the adult stage'.[20] A new kind of repertory, it might be thought, was calculated to appeal to a new kind of audience, one that was not only 'gentle' in Brabant Junior's terms – of suitably refined birth, education and manners – but that also prided itself on its 'wit', that crucial seventeenth-century counter of intelligent elegance and of what might now be termed 'cool'. Long before the Restoration drama, with its battles between true and false wits, Ben Jonson had brought on to the stage characters with such names as Truewit and Lovewit, inviting audiences to align themselves with their superior discernment and its attendant cynicism.

A taste for satire perhaps was also appreciated by such a 'smart' audience; certainly satirical plays landed the boys in trouble more than once and finally led to the end of their career at Blackfriars, but we should not overemphasize the distinction from the adult troupes in this regard. Nor was the audience at Blackfriars before 1608 necessarily more discerning than those at the Fortune and the Globe, since they famously failed to accept Francis Beaumont's theatre comedy, mocking popular taste in meandering

[18] For an up-to-date account of the company, its fortunes and its repertory, see Lucy Munro, *Children of the Queen's Revels* (Cambridge University Press, 2005).

[19] See Wickham et al., *English Professional Theatre*, pp. 401–2.

[20] R. A. Foakes, 'Tragedy at the Children's Theatres after 1600: A Challenge to the Adult Stage', in David Galloway (ed.), *The Elizabethan Theatre II* (Toronto: Macmillan of Canada, 1970), pp. 37–59.

romantic drama, *The Knight of the Burning Pestle* (*c.* 1607), missing its 'privy mark of irony', which is hardly buried deeply.[21] Beaumont's subsequent writing partner, John Fletcher, fared no better with his early play *The Faithful Shepherdess* (*c.* 1608). A fashionable spin-off from Italian pastoral tragicomedy, it was unrecognized as such by its first observers, who seemed to be looking for something broader and more knockabout; Fletcher's play is not without its own tongue-in-cheek humour, but it failed to work at Blackfriars. Divisions of taste, then, between the smaller audiences at the indoor theatres and the larger, more socially mixed audiences at the outdoor playhouses, have to be defined with suitable caution and qualification: during the boys' occupancy of the Blackfriars playhouse a difficult and challenging play like *Measure for Measure*, for example, was written for the audience at the Globe. If Blackfriars audiences were not necessarily more intellectually advanced or culturally aware, however, they were richer, better dressed and more socially select, perhaps becoming more exclusively so as their consciousness of being a 'set' developed, a phenomenon I have noted above. If James Burbage had calculated that there was a niche market, as it were, to be exploited through a smaller playhouse within the city of London in 1596, his son's troupe could not have brought the same conditions of performance to the theatre as did the Children of the Chapel. The deferral of the adult players' occupancy of Blackfriars provided a further decade of 'audience development', in modern terms: the establishment of a sector of the London playgoing public who regularly attended the theatre and enjoyed its ambiance. By 1608, when the children left, the 'goodwill' of the Blackfriars establishment must have been worth considerably more than in 1600. Meanwhile Richard Burbage and William Shakespeare's company had become the King's Men, and could represent themselves as continuing a tradition of public performance by royal servants in the same physical surroundings.

Had the Blackfriars children been governed by more astute managers, Richard Burbage, who had rented the theatre to them on behalf of the Burbage family, might never have seen it revert to his control. The lease to Henry Evans, the leading entrepreneur connected to the Chapel boys, ran for twenty-one years from September 1600; until after Burbage's death in 1619, that is to say.[22] Had the Children of the Queen's Revels, as from 1604 the troupe became, been more successful than in the event they were,

[21] See the dedicatory epistle by Walter Burre in the first edition of the play (1613); Sheldon P. Zitner (ed.), *The Knight of the Burning Pestle* (Manchester University Press, 1984), pp. 51–2.

[22] Wickham et al., *English Professional Theatre*, pp. 508–9.

perhaps metamorphosing into a more viable version of Lady Elizabeth's Men, then the Blackfriars would probably now have quite a different significance in the history of the theatre. Whether the crisis over the burning of the Globe in 1613 would have driven the King's Men to look for another indoor space in that year is another speculative matter of alternative history. There was nothing inevitable or determined about the change in 1608, however. What finally broke the rather rackety financial structure supporting the child players at Blackfriars was the ill-judged performance of two plays in March 1608 that drew the attention of the authorities.[23] The children were punished and their playing suspended; their managers, unable to meet the rent, surrendered the lease to Burbage in August of the year. Simultaneously a new lease to cover the management of the theatre, to run until 1629, was shared among the leading members of the King's Men, Shakespeare included.[24] The appearance of the troupe in their regained playhouse, however, is likely to have been delayed for at least twelve months because of bad plague conditions from 1608 to 1609. James Burbage's original project, then, took thirteen years to be realized.

If the Blackfriars project between 1600 and 1608 was not a notable success for those who had put money into it, running one crisis away from failure, as it happened, why might the King's Men have been persuaded that they would do better? Theatre business generally 'never is, but always to be blessed', and seventeenth-century conditions were similarly tough. Yet the King's Men, it has often been remarked, were distinguished from other troupes by their remarkable cohesion and astute organization, with some collective wealth in property, costumes and playbooks. Two things followed: they were able to afford the new commitment of running two theatres, and they saw no unusual risk, more than that attending any theatrical venture, of opening at Blackfriars; its opportunities were no worse than they had been in 1596, and were probably better, for the reasons discussed above.

The changing social and cultural conditions of Stuart London continued the expansion of the city and the disposition of its human inhabitants that had marked the Elizabethan years. Civic wealth and power arising from foreign trade reached new heights, and a consequent retail trade in luxury goods was reflected in the opening of the New Exchange in

23 The first, now lost, parodied the Scottish followers of King James, and the second, Chapman's *The Conspiracy and Tragedy of Charles Duke of Byron*, offended the French ambassador. Questions of how or whether these plays had been approved for performance are taken up by Richard Dutton in the seventh chapter of *Mastering the Revels* (University of Iowa Press, 1991).

24 Wickham et al., *English Professional Theatre*, pp. 515–16.

the Strand in 1609, designed by Inigo Jones, and for the opening ceremonies of which Ben Jonson wrote an entertainment; the venture was backed by the leading statesman and courtier Sir Robert Cecil. The place was, in effect, an early seventeenth-century shopping mall, catering to the rich who increasingly populated the western edge of the city, in the areas between the old city walls at Ludgate, Newgate and Aldersgate to the east and Whitehall and St James's palaces to the west.[25] The established legal communities of the Inns of Court – Gray's Inn, Lincoln's Inn and the Middle and Inner Temple – stood and still stand within the centre of this district, and their young gentleman students, mostly from the families of the rich, were one index of the prosperity of the area: they were patrons of the leisure culture of the seventeenth-century city, including its theatres. In the 1630s the new development of Covent Garden would give a particular focus to the superior social and cultural character of the area. Both the lawyers and the richer residents of the district followed a season, defined by the legal terms, running from the autumn to the early summer following, and by the similar calendar of the court's residence in London. Landed gentry with estates spent their summers in the country, and their families and servants accompanied them.

Of the new theatres built in the first half of the seventeenth century, three were in this 'west end' of London and all were modelled on the Blackfriars, which lay only just outside it: smaller, covered theatres, with seats for the entire audience, which was charged higher prices. The economic calculations of the King's Men in 1608 would have been based on the capacity of the theatre and its history of attracting audiences, so far as they knew it. Once there had been a rationalized plan or account of the place; the lease of 1600 mentions 'a stage, galleries, and seats of a quantity specified in a schedule annexed', a document that has since disappeared.[26] Richard Burbage would have known the numbers; historians can only guess at the precise layout of an auditorium built within a hall 46 feet wide by 66 feet long. Such modern guesses generally arrive at a capacity of five to six hundred people, a third of the likely size of the audience at the Globe. Six hundred sixpences, however, would have yielded a total of fifteen pounds, a sum favourably comparable with either

[25] See Norman G. Brett-James, *The Growth of Stuart London* (London: Allen & Unwin, 1935); Roger Finlay, *Population and Metropolis: The Demography of London 1580–1650* (Cambridge University Press, 1981).

[26] Wickham et al., *English Professional Theatre*, p. 508.

the fee for a court show or the income from a full day at the Globe. Playing at the Blackfriars was a profitable proposition, if the new residents could attract audiences.

Calculations about adjustments to repertory to do precisely that have consistently interested readers of Shakespeare: simply put, were the late plays 'Blackfriars plays'? One might ask the same question of any of the new plays the King's Men acquired after 1608–09. *Philaster*, for example, a collaboration between John Fletcher and Francis Beaumont, has been thought of as a deliberate acquisition of a piece by 'Blackfriars' writers, and as representing a new style of tragicomedy likely to appeal to a sophisticated audience. The first edition of the play (1620), however, proclaims that it was acted '*at the Globe*' (the second edition adds 'and Black-Friers'); a successful play that was periodically remounted could be shown at either theatre.[27] Jonson's *Volpone* was first acted at the Globe (1605), but was certainly performed on indoor stages later in its repertorial career; *The Alchemist* of some years later (1610) perhaps plays a joke about the location of its house of illusory wonders, 'here, in the Friars' (1.1.17),[28] but there is otherwise nothing about the play which would not work at least as well before a larger audience at the Globe. Both *The Tempest* and *The Winter's Tale* were performed in the winter of 1611/12: they were presented at court in early November of that year, and had probably therefore appeared at the Blackfriars beforehand, in the last weeks of October. In the preceding summer, however, *The Winter's Tale* had been staged at the Globe, as had *Cymbeline*. There seems, in short, to be very little about the character of the repertory in the first years of the King's Men's occupancy of Blackfriars to suggest that plays were 'playhouse specific', or that the different composition of the audience radically affected either writing or playing. Certainly the statue scene in *The Winter's Tale* or the storm in *The Tempest* would have looked and sounded different at the company's two theatres, but variability of venue for given plays had long been a condition to which actors adjusted themselves.[29]

Moreover, the strength of the King's Men's repertory up to 1608, which we now think of as having been provided by Shakespeare (lacking anything like a view of the company's plays similar to that demonstrated by Philip Henslowe for the Rose and the Fortune), had already proved itself with 'the

[27] Andrew Gurr (ed.), *Philaster* (London: Methuen, 1969), p. lxxiv.

[28] G. A. Wilkes (ed.), *The Complete Plays of Ben Jonson* (4 vols.; Oxford University Press, 1981–2), vol. III, p. 233.

[29] See Andrew Gurr '*The Tempest*'s Tempest at Blackfriars', *Shakespeare Survey* 41 (1989) 91–101.

Blackfriars set', as it were. In 1602 *Twelfth Night* had been played in a privately commissioned performance to an Inns of Court audience in Middle Temple Hall. The actors also held a commanding position in court performance: in the winter of 1604/5 they had played six distinct Shakespeare plays at court, *The Merchant of Venice* encored at the king's request, as well as three other plays, for a total of ten occasions between November and February. In that same season, by contrast, the Blackfriars company, the Children of the Queen's Revels, performed at court merely twice.[30] If court taste to a degree set the standard for what audiences at the indoor theatres went to see, then there is little doubt that Shakespeare's company could count on its credentials by 1609.

Evidently the company's commitment to Blackfriars entailed a change in company practice which their old rivals, the Admiral's/Prince Henry's Men at the Fortune, never seem to have sought: the old form of theatre still paid those willing to work for its audiences. If the Globe was closed in the winter months, not all of its audience could have been accommodated at Blackfriars, even if they had been prepared to pay; the Fortune and the Red Bull were perhaps the beneficiaries of the surplus. Audiences for the King's Men year round thus became smaller in number, and, overall, more representative of the London elite. The company did not abandon their democratic traditions, playing at the Globe in the summer, but as the Blackfriars became increasingly successful and socially fashionable, the queen attending performances there in the 1630s, they increasingly became associated with the higher ranks of London society, and, arguably, with royalist politics. Whether the theatre itself ever became simply regarded as 'royal' territory seems doubtful, however; at least one of its players and one prominent member of its audience supported Parliament in the civil wars.[31]

The landlord of the Fortune playhouse, the famous former player Edward Alleyn, was briefly involved in a scheme to open a second indoor playhouse in the Blackfriars precinct, at Porters' Hall, somewhat to the east of the Burbages' theatre. Alleyn inherited Philip Henslowe's theatre investments at the latter's death early in 1616; Henslowe had joined a consortium led by the musician and entrepreneur Philip Rosseter to establish a new playhouse for the combined companies of the Queen's

30 John H. Astington, *English Court Theatre 1558–1642* (Cambridge University Press, 1999), pp. 238–9.

31 Eilert Swanston and Bulstrode Whitelocke. On Swanston, see John H. Astington, *Actors and Acting in Shakespeare's Time* (Cambridge University Press, 2010); for Whitelocke, see *The Oxford Dictionary of National Biography* (Oxford University Press, 2004).

Revels and Lady Elizabeth, beginning in 1613. Apparently an entirely new building was erected, and may have housed a few performances, but the project was stiffly opposed by the local residents and the city authorities, who eventually prevailed in closing the playhouse by early 1617, when Alleyn's property holdings in the Blackfriars were undoubtedly turned to other purposes. Simultaneously, a younger actor had more success. Christopher Beeston, who had trained within the ranks of the old Chamberlain's Men, broke from his colleagues in the Queen Anne's company at the Red Bull in 1616, adapting the site of an old cockpit just off Drury Lane, in the heart of the fashionable moneyed suburbs and outside the immediate control of the Lord Mayor and aldermen of London, into a new indoor theatre of the same size and general character as the Blackfriars. It was called the Cockpit but was often referred to as the Phoenix playhouse. Beeston developed his theatre into a conspicuous success, attracting leading companies, players and playwrights, making it the rival playhouse to the Blackfriars in the 1620s and 1630s and cultivating similarly stylish and select audiences from the surrounding district. A third theatre of a similar kind – small, roofed and lit by candles – was set up in 1629–30 at Salisbury Court, between St Bride's church and the river (and thus not far from Blackfriars).

The theatres changed, then, but the change was not universal: the market represented by the audiences at Blackfriars was limited, and there was still money to be made from playing in the larger, cheaper, more socially mixed outdoor theatres right up to 1642 and beyond that date.[32] The change came about through entrepreneurship: first that of James Burbage, then of his sons and their associates, followed and copied by Christopher Beeston, William Blagrave and Richard Gunnell, the latter two the builders of the Salisbury Court theatre. Burbage, Beeston and Gunnell had been actors, and had the interests of actors in mind: to find good spaces in which to perform to an audience, and to be well rewarded for doing so. The change was also, evidently, accidental, in being a phenomenon now identified with Shakespeare's last years in the theatre, and with the afterlife of his plays in repertory. The Blackfriars theatre was substantially complete and 'very shortly' to become 'a common playhouse' in November 1596.[33] Had the 'not in my back yard' outcry from the local inhabitants and neighbours failed to convince the Privy Council, we would now think of the great

[32] Both types of playhouse are mentioned in the intermittent attempts to revive playing surreptitiously during the Interregnum, and at the Restoration the outdoor Red Bull was reused for a season or two.

[33] Wickham et al., *English Professional Theatre*, p. 507.

Shakespearean tragedies of 1601–08 as Blackfriars plays, solely; the Globe investment would surely not have been made three years later had Blackfriars gone forward. Finally, the change was both new and not new: never before had an adult troupe appeared at an indoor playhouse; elsewhere, however, on provincial tours and on visits to court, noble households and the inns of court, adult players had for some time performed indoors within halls to seated audiences, often at night beneath stage and auditorium lighting provided by candles. The forms of the early stage and theatre space were multiple; the change effected at the Blackfriars playhouse was to select one of those older forms and apply it to a new social and commercial setting.

CHAPTER 2

Practical evidence for a reimagined indoor Jacobean theatre

Jon Greenfield (with assistance from Peter McCurdy)

This chapter is an account of the challenges and decisions made during the design and construction phases of the indoor Jacobean theatre project at Shakespeare's Globe. It is intended to show how research informed the design and to what extent current knowledge of indoor playhouses of the period can inform a physical re-creation of an early seventeenth-century private playhouse. Research from documentary sources, starting with drawings 7b and 7c held in Oxford's Worcester College library (Figure 1), was crucial, as Oliver Jones's chapter in this volume shows, but perhaps the most applicable sources for creating an archetype of an indoor Jacobean theatre can be found among surviving practical Jacobean buildings and interiors (see Plates 8 to 16 inclusive).

What to build?

Writing in *Rebuilding Shakespeare's Globe* (1989), John Orrell, who along with Andrew Gurr was chief academic advisor to the Globe theatre reconstruction, introduced plans to build an indoor theatre:

> In proposing to reconstruct the Globe on Bankside the International Shakespeare Globe Centre quite rightly sees as its central task the building of the great amphitheatre itself, but in recent years it has also undertaken to include in the project some representation of the Blackfriars side of Shakespeare's working world.[1]

The 'great amphitheatre itself'[2] was completed and opened in 1997, and now, fifteen years on, the focus is on the second objective; a 'representation of the Blackfriars side of Shakespeare's working world'.[3]

[1] John Orrell, 'The Inigo Jones Designs', in *Rebuilding Shakespeare's Globe* (London: Weidenfeld & Nicolson, 1989), pp. 128–9.
[2] Ibid., pp. 128–9. [3] Ibid., p. 129.

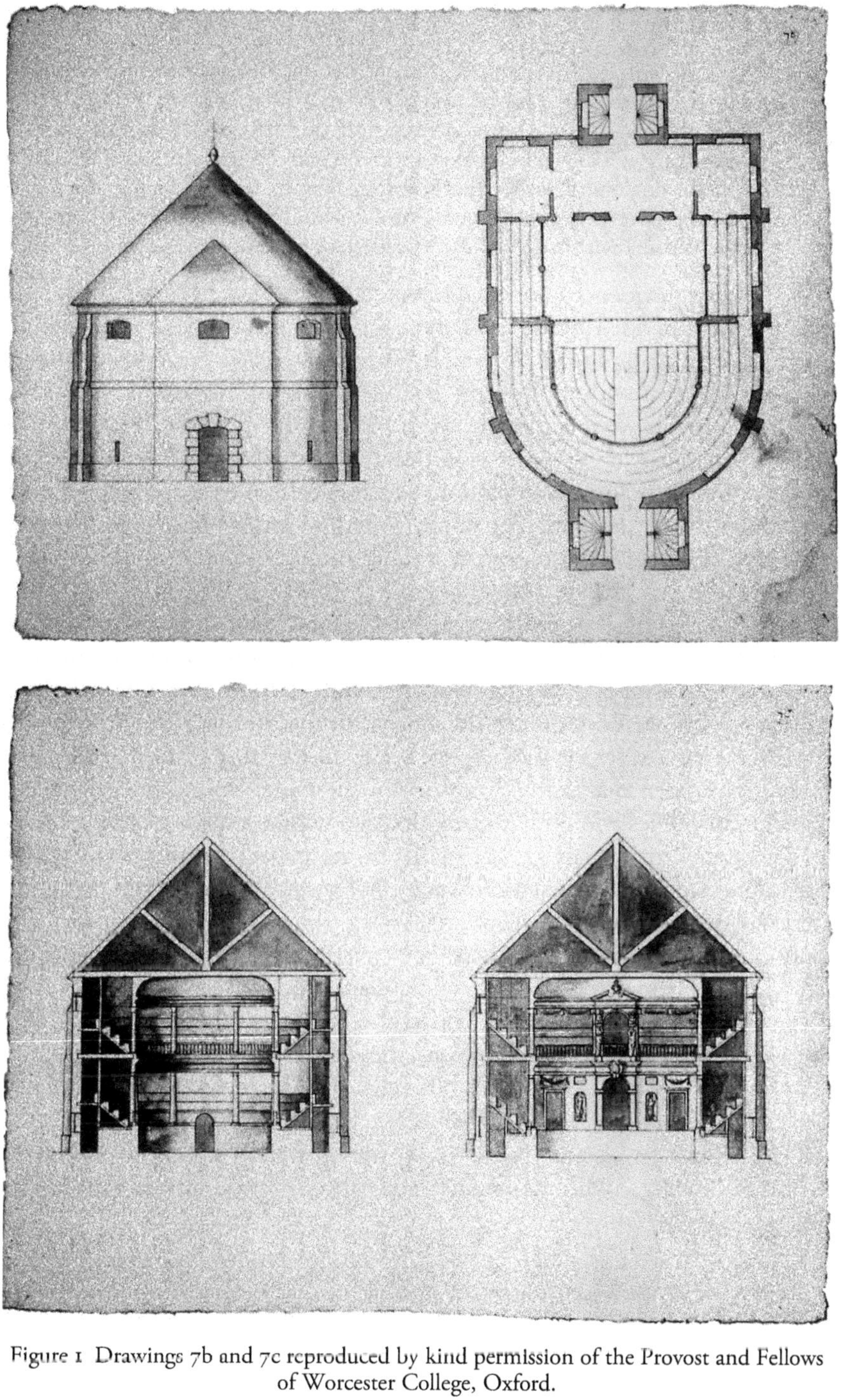

Figure 1 Drawings 7b and 7c reproduced by kind permission of the Provost and Fellows of Worcester College, Oxford.

Orrell continued:

> The ideal would be a reconstruction of the upper frater (of the Blackfriars) itself, complete with vaulted undercroft and thick masonry walls. But the speculative nature of the reconstruction outlined above makes such an undertaking a risky affair. Almost every part of the structure would be based on analogical rather than direct evidence, and of course the whole would be extremely expensive because it would be necessary to recreate the medieval shell within which the Elizabethan playhouse was erected.[4]

Orrell's 'direct evidence', and that adopted by the Shakespeare Globe Trust (SGT), was provided by designs, then thought to have been generated by Inigo Jones in around 1616, shown on Worcester College drawings 7b and 7c. Brought to the attention of theatre historians by Don Rowan in 1971,[5] these drawings provide what is thought to be indisputable practical evidence of an indoor playhouse, although it is not clear which one. They have been the subject of near forensic examination, as scholars have tried to discover every secret that may be hidden. The drafting method for architects and surveyors was very different in the seventeenth century compared to today, even ignoring the sea change brought about by the use of computers. Paper available at the time would have been made by hand in a variety of non-standard sizes, and the draughtsman would have chosen a unique drawing scale to fit the sheet of paper, rather than using a standard ratio marked out on a scale rule, as we do today. A drawing instrument, called 'dividers', would have been used to set up the bespoke scale; measured positions on the sheet would have been marked with a prick in the paper from the dividers, and 'construction lines' would have been formed with a stylus – a sharp pointed leadless pencil that creates score marks in the paper, making near invisible 'ghost lines' for inking-in at a later stage. Stylus score marks and divider pricks observable in the paper of Worcester College drawings 7b and 7c provide an unquestionable five foot scale; stage, pit, galleries and *frons scenae* are all clearly delineated. There was no need to reimagine an indoor Jacobean theatre. The Worcester College drawings provided the answer to the question of what should be built. In construction terms, these drawings provided a 'quick win', an unquestionable 'blueprint' for building, or so it seemed in 1989; and so it seemed in 1995, too, when the shell of the indoor theatre was constructed.

The exterior was also built to the designs shown on the Worcester College drawings, with reimagined external neoclassical elements in the

[4] Ibid.

[5] Andrew Gurr, *The Shakespearean Stage, 1574–1642* (4th edn; Cambridge University Press, 2009), p. 197, n. 69.

places not covered by the original elevations. Specially fired handmade bricks were carefully bonded with carved Portland stone trims, giving the enclosing wall an immovable thickness of half a metre. The space enclosed by these perimeter walls was bigger than that shown on the seventeenth-century drawings, as it was enlarged to accommodate the addition of a perimeter fire escape zone. In all other respects construction was based faithfully on the theatre described in Worcester College library drawings 7b and 7c. At that time, funds were not adequate to construct the interior of the theatre, so the empty shell was provisionally converted to provide rehearsal and education studios on three levels, creating temporary space in place of the indoor playhouse. These were in continuous heavy use for the following fifteen years.

During these intervening years, specialists in the work of Inigo Jones, Gordon Higgott in particular, examined the Worcester College drawings more closely, and many of the conclusions once thought to be secure were unpicked. Significantly, it can no longer be believed that Worcester College drawings 7b and 7c provide safe blueprints to follow when 'some representation of the Blackfriars side of Shakespeare's working world'[6] is the primary aim. Gordon Higgott's careful investigation of the drawing style now places the Worcester College drawings at a much later date, the early 1660s, and convincingly ascribes the drawing work to John Webb, Jones's pupil who later became his assistant and collaborator.[7] The drawings are not from 1616, and were not drawn by Inigo Jones.

Before discounting Inigo Jones entirely, it is necessary to examine the extent of the influence he may have had on an indoor Jacobean theatre, as his work was both contemporary and strongly associated with theatre architecture. Although not impossible, it was perhaps hopeful to believe that Inigo Jones could have produced such an accomplished architectural playhouse design in 1616, only months after he had returned from his watershed second trip to Italy with Thomas Howard, 2nd Earl of Arundel. Indeed, understanding Inigo Jones in these transitional few years is difficult since our view of his work is so defined by his later neoclassical architecture and by his earlier masque designs. Architectural historian John Summerson comments on 'the immaturity of Jones's designs before 1615',[8] and notes that his first architectural designs embrace a rich Jacobean

[6] Orrell, 'Inigo Jones Designs', p. 129. [7] Gurr, *Shakespearean Stage*, p. 197.
[8] John Summerson, *Inigo Jones* (Harmondsworth: Penguin, 1966), p. 41.

eclecticism[9] not visible in the Worcester College drawings. Jones' architectural works after this time are no longer exercises but the work of a man treating architecture as his main profession. As Surveyor of the King's Works, his designs became more assured and his architectural output quickly coalesced into the new and revolutionary neoclassical style that was to become so strongly associated with the Caroline era. Timothy Mowl explains why Jones and his followers after 1616 become the ones *not* to follow if the objective is to create 'some representation of the Blackfriars side of Shakespeare's working world',[10] a world so firmly rooted in the Elizabethan and Jacobean:

> Inigo Jones was to live well into Oliver Cromwell's Commonwealth, so it is easily forgotten that in artistic upbringing he was an Elizabethan, already in his thirtieth year when the old Queen died. If the reigns of Elizabeth and James are to be seen as a stylistic continuum, then Jones, whose scholarly study of Roman remains and Venetian Palladian villas was to end that continuum, was an integral part of it, lurking like a design traitor at the heart of the Jacobean court.[11]

The style of Inigo Jones is atypical of Jacobean design. He became the champion of a startlingly new and different style that provides the architectural end-stop to the Jacobean period. Given that Shakespeare retired to Stratford-upon-Avon in 1613/14, it is arguable whether 1616 should be seen as the upper limit for formative influences associated with Shakespeare's working world. So, when reviving the indoor theatre project at the Globe, it became clear that the neoclassical style represented with such assurance on Worcester College drawings 7b and 7c did not wholly pass the test of 'some representation of the Blackfriars side of Shakespeare's working world'.[12] The drawings beguile because they provide a link from playhouse to proscenium arch auditoria; they gesture towards the next chapter for theatre historians, but that is something different from a wholly Jacobean theatre. When considering the SGT's aim to build a theatre of Shakespeare's time, the notion of 'reconstruction' from the Worcester College designs required some serious rethinking, without Inigo Jones.

9 Ibid., pp. 25–34. It should also be noted that in this section Summerson defines Jacobean architecture as 'still substantially in the medieval tradition but modified by successive waves of fashion through the reigns of the Tudors' (pp. 25–34).

10 Orrell, 'Inigo Jones Designs'.

11 Timothy Mowl, *Elizabethan and Jacobean Style* (London: Phaidon, 1993), p. 125.

12 Orrell, 'Inigo Jones Designs', p. 12.

The changing status of Worcester College drawings 7b and 7c

Despite the problems with Worcester College drawings 7b and 7c, they have not been put to one side and ignored. They can no longer be taken as 'direct evidence'[13] for reconstruction, but they remain the best available representation of an indoor playhouse of the seventeenth century and remain formative in the reimagining of an indoor Jacobean theatre. There are a number of possible explanations of what Webb's drawings may represent, although theatre historians have not yet reached a consensus as to which is the most credible. Some of the theories include the possibility that the drawings show plans for a stylistic makeover of a much earlier playhouse; others that they are an early Restoration attempt by the ageing Webb to win a new commission when theatre building started again, but that he made the mistake of basing his ideas on the pre-civil war 'playhouse' model. Webb can be pictured as an older designer in 1660 missing the new influences that were flowing in from the Continent and looking back to the kind of theatre space he had known forty or more years before, perhaps even Christopher Beeston's Cockpit of 1616.[14] But this is a supposition and a diversion from the central aim of finding material that will inform the construction project. Regardless of their true provenance, the Worcester College drawings nevertheless provide valuable evidence of the size, shape and interrelationship of features characteristic of an early seventeenth-century indoor playhouse. There is no reason not to adopt the arrangement of spaces – galleries, pit, stage, *frons scenae* and tiring-house – directly from the Worcester College drawings, and this conclusion became the first decisive step in reimagining the indoor Jacobean theatre.

Demoting Webb's drawings from the status of 'blueprint' to that of 'useful guide' means it is true, in Orrell's terms, that the end product will be a more speculative reimagining, 'based on analogical rather than direct evidence'.[15] The new design brief is to create a *simulacrum*, an *archetype* of an indoor Jacobean playhouse. In the new designs the arrangement of space is given by the Worcester College drawings, the look and feel of the space by accounts of the Blackfriars, and all other details by knowledge gained from surviving contemporary examples, such as buildings and decorative interiors of the period, and by documents drawn and written. This reimagining relies heavily on finding surviving examples – prototypes of elements of the theatre that can be copied in exact detail. The search for the best prototypes became the most important endeavour. Of course, the new design has to fit

[13] Ibid., p. 129. [14] Gurr, *Shakespearean Stage*, p. 197, n. 69. [15] Orrell, 'Inigo Jones Designs', p. 129.

into the existing shell built in 1995, not 'the medieval shell'[16] that Orrell had called for, but this is a constraint which has the unanticipated advantage of making this project much more like the project undertaken by James Burbage when he was faced with converting the Blackfriars monastic hall into a commercial indoor theatre in 1596. Forgetting the stylistic oddity of 'inherited' neoclassical detailing on the exterior, there are strong parallels with the Blackfriars project undertaken four hundred years ago: a late Elizabethan/early Jacobean set-up of galleries, *frons scenae* and stage in a pre-existing mediaeval interior; a neo-Jacobean set-up of galleries, *frons scenae* and stage in a pre-existing masonry interior.

Close examination of the Worcester College drawings 7b and 7c

Although in stylistic terms Webb's drawings are a generation ahead of the Jacobean, building technology was not moving so quickly and the techniques used by craftsmen in the neoclassical period during the reigns of kings Charles I and II were much the same as had been used by craftsmen during the earlier reigns of James I, Elizabeth I and before. Of course Webb's drawings can be overinterpreted. It is tempting to read every mark as having great significance, when in fact the drawings were intended as 'concept' presentation drawings and show building construction only to set the scene and give the drawings some vicarious authority. In modern terminology, these are RIBA (Royal Institute of British Architects) Design Stage C 'Concept' drawings, so it is a little unfair, and potentially misleading, to analyze them as if they were RIBA Design Stage E 'Technical Design' drawings.[17] As concept drawings they were intended to convince a client of a strategic idea, were not the product of careful and thorough building construction design, and should not be read as such. Unsurprisingly, examination of the details shown on Webb's drawings reveals some frustrating inconsistencies.

A close examination of the drawings reveals a number of discrepancies, which are summarized in Figure 2. The most obvious are the plan features, as Webb has conflated elements from the upper and lower levels on to one drawing, upper level windows and lower level stage and tiring-house, for example. He also shows large articulations of masonry within the galleries on either side of the stage front, cutting through the galleries and creating impossible viewing obstructions if they are intended to rise through the

[16] Ibid., p. 129.

[17] See RIBA, 'Plan of Work'. It should be noted that the numbering of design workstages was due for revision in May 2013.

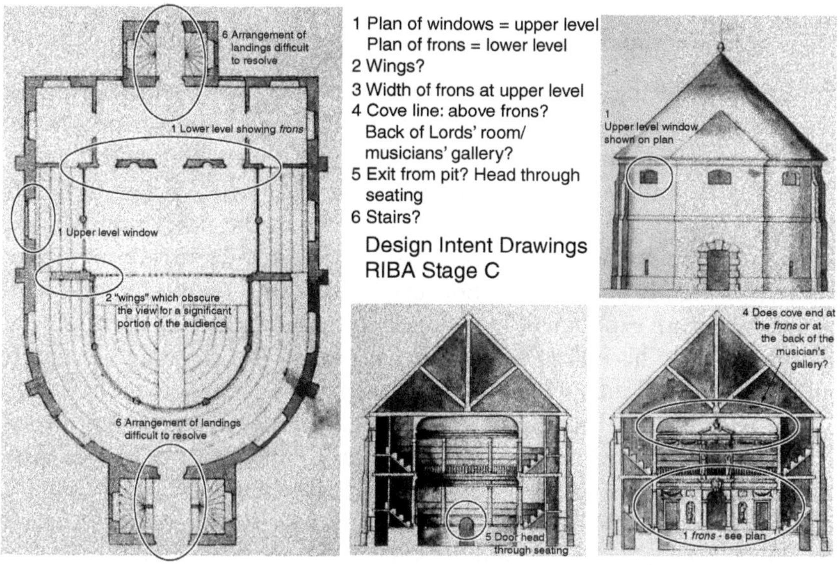

Figure 2 The Worcester College drawings marked up to show drafting inconsistencies.

building, which they may not. These large masonry elements may indicate that the drawings were an adaptation of a pre-existing building, while the other inconsistencies confirm the drawings as early concept designs, probably presentation drawings. Viewed side by side with John Webb's drawing of the Cockpit-in-Court (*c.* 1660) and his two studies for adapting Palladio's Vicenza Teatro Olimpico into a given space (dated later than 1635), drawings 7b and 7c are revealed to be very different in drafting style from the other drawings.[18] Drawings 7b and 7c are rendered in pen and line wash, and the comparison drawings in pen with pen hatching. It is understood from Gordon Higgott that Webb's style changed through his professional life, but the care taken with his draftsmanship on 7b and 7c, the balanced way the sheets are arranged and the lack of grime on the paper (usual if a design has been taken forward) strongly suggest that these drawings were intended to impress a client at an early stage in a project and that the designs may never have been built. It is very likely that they were presentation drawings and if they helped turn Webb's client pitch into a live project then they would have served their purpose. With a commission, Webb would have been able to spend more time working up detailed aspects of the design.

[18] Gurr, *Shakespearean Stage*, p. 197.

Understanding the underlying geometry of the plan

Noting the drafting inconsistencies, the difficulty faced when trying to understand the underlying geometry of Webb's plan and particularly his positioning of columns at the curved end can be understood. Webb's plan shows the columns on the inner ring set out on half of a seven-sided geometry (septagon); in contrast, the windows in the outer ring defined by the outer wall are set out on an eight-sided figure (octagon) with the same centre (see Figure 3). This does not seem particularly significant, and may just have been an experiment in geometry by Webb, until we think of how the interior may have been built. The galleries would certainly have been built as a timber frame, which in simple terms is an arrangement of beams supported on posts. Using two opposing geometries in his design means that Webb is not providing structural support to the timber beams where it is needed. Particularly when constructing galleries on a curve, the geometry has to be consistent with the structural frames. Furthermore, a trawl through surviving Jacobean buildings has failed to find a building of any type, in any location, that has curve-fronted timber galleries. Over seven hundred surviving Jacobean buildings have been identified and not one has a curved gallery. All Jacobean galleried structures identified are rectangular in plan and have straight galleries running parallel to the enclosing walls. Of course the outdoor playhouses are an exception, and it should be remembered that 'the wooden O' is in fact a polygon in plan, and the curved effect

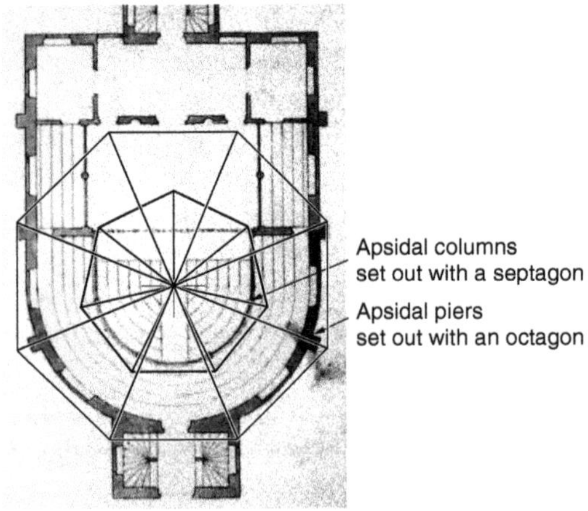

Figure 3 The geometry of the Worcester College plan.

is created by a series of straight facets. It is possible that examples of curve-fronted galleries have simply been lost, or there may even be evidence to be found in studying early modern shipbuilding (ships being intrinsically curvaceous). However, the lessons from a similar exercise for reconstructing the Globe, based on the target date of 1599, are still useful in this exercise of examining the construction technology of just seventeen years later.

Constructional knowledge of historic timber work reveals how difficult it would be to make the curved beams and handrails of sufficient strength and precision to deliver the galleries as they are shown by Webb. It would not be possible to select a large straight timber and cut a curve from it as the straight grain of the timber would run out across the curve, providing an unacceptable structural weakness in the timber (see Figure 4a). Steaming and bending large structural timbers is out of the question; this is a technique used in shipbuilding for bending thin section planks around the curve of ships' hulls, not for large section structural timbers used in building. In order to maintain structural strength it would be necessary to select a tree that had naturally grown to the desired curve, as is the case with structural braces (see Figure 4b). Finding a number of trees that had grown to the same, geometrically true shape would have been prohibitively time-consuming and costly.

It is not surprising, then, that it has not been possible (as yet) to find any examples of curved-fronted galleries. The closest example is Oxford's Sheldonian Theatre, an early English baroque building of 1664 that was constructed forty-eight years after our target date for the indoor Jacobean theatre at Shakespeare's Globe and is coincidentally roughly contemporary with Worcester College drawings 7b and 7c on Higgott's dating. Although the Sheldonian's architect, Christopher Wren, would have followed the same process as Webb of handing his designs to a master craftsman for structuring, detailed design and realization, he was famously a 'Man of Science' and perhaps had a better grasp of the limitations of a particular construction technology than did Webb, even when developing his conceptual designs. Understanding that the Sheldonian's galleries would be made from timber, Wren drew the galleries as *straight* fronted, even in what are believed to be his earliest designs. Wren forms his Sheldonian 'curves' as series of *facets*, and forms wedge-shaped structural bays, just as with the Globe reconstruction – an 'O'-shaped open-air playhouse (see Figure 5).

It seems most likely, therefore, that if Webb's 7b/7c designs had been realized, they would have been built containing galleries whose structure was a series of facets and, based on the evidence uncovered so far, an indoor Jacobean theatre made in timber in 1616 is also most likely to have had faceted galleries (see Figure 6). A faceted layout dictates the position of posts

A The problems with forming large curved timbers by cutting are (i) the timber has to be very large to take account of the curve and (ii) the straight grain sets up lines of weakness in the timber where splitting is likely to occur.

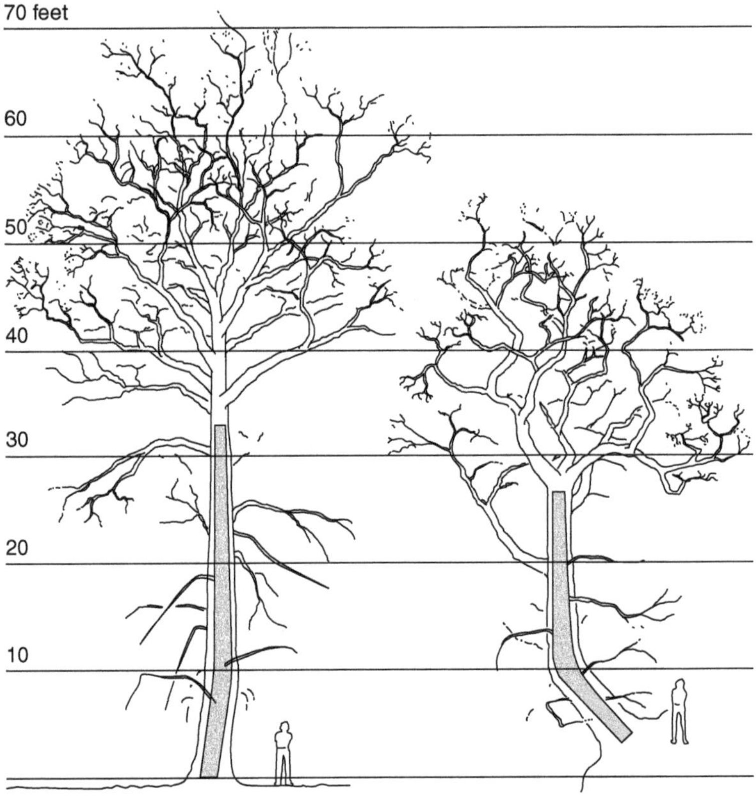

B To get the grain growing around the desired curve it is necessary to find a tree with limbs that are already growing to shape. It is very difficult to find timbers that naturally grow to a segment of a circle. (Apologies to F.B. Charles)

Figure 4 The difficulty of creating curved structural timbers.

Figure 5 An early drawing of the Sheldonian Theatre by Christopher Wren showing polygonal bays. Reproduced by kind permission of the Warden and Fellows of All Souls College, Oxford.

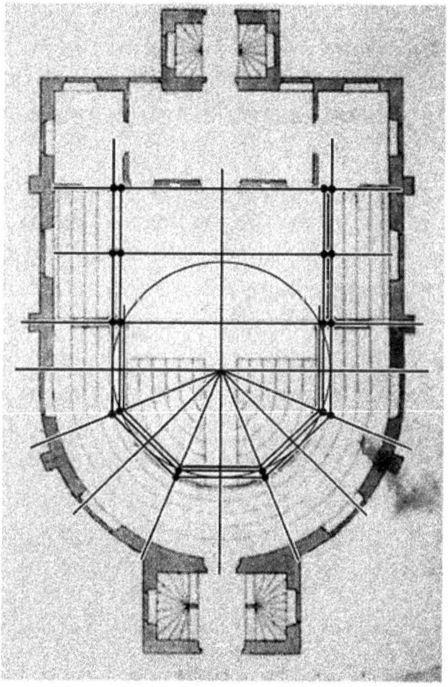

Figure 6 The new plan of the reimagined indoor Jacobean theatre overlaid on the Worcester College plan.

(or columns), which have to be on the 'point' of adjoining facets, not on the 'flat' of the facet itself. To achieve this with a galleried structure the inner ring must have the same geometry as the outer ring. Webb's geometry of a septagon within an octagon was therefore unrealizable in timber. Construction logic dictates that the geometry would have had to be septagon within septagon or octagon within octagon.

At this point, it is useful to reflect on John Orrell's thoughts on the Blackfriars auditorium shape:

> The shape of the auditorium is unknown, though various academic reconstructions have favoured a rectangular plan with three levels of galleries following the right angles of the room. Ben Jonson, in the Introduction to his Blackfriars play The Magnetic Lady (1632) brings a snobbish spectator on stage to complain to one of the theatre employees about 'the faces, or grounds of your people, that sit in the oblique caves and wedges of your house, your sinfull sixe-penny Mechanicks . . .' 'Caves and Wedges' are odd words to find in a description of an auditorium, but they correspond in a rather pedantic way to the cavea and cunei into which the round of an ancient Roman theatre was divided. This suggests that the Blackfriars galleries were segmental or U-shaped in plan, perhaps in imitation of the theatre scheme published by the Italian architect Sebastiano Serlio, whose work profoundly influenced Elizabethan designers.[19]

A number of studies have been carried out to see how the geometry of the galleries could be resolved (Figure 7). Each highlights two recurring issues: (i) Webb does not show a column on the springing of the curve; and (ii) 9 foot 6 inch bays on a gallery front setting-out radius of 10 foot 6 inches is an uncomfortable ratio. These issues lead to a crude series of facets if Webb's columns are simply joined with straight lines, and this is at odds with the refinement of the drawings. Webb masks the problem by showing curved gallery fronts. He may well have been more concerned with making reference to Sebastiano Serlio than with solving the construction geometry.

Joining a polygonal structure to a rectangular one, as Webb has drawn, is more difficult than would first appear. Wren's geometry for the Sheldonian is instructive in this, too. Although Wren was designing a much bigger building, in which he had to resolve the junction of a twenty-sided polygon with a rectangle, he found a geometry that provides a smooth and pleasing junction. It is best described in a diagram (see Figure 8), where it can be seen that a faceted version of the Worcester College drawings had to be based on the combination of a square and an octagon. Reapplying this setting-out to

[19] Orrell, 'Inigo Jones Designs', p. 127.

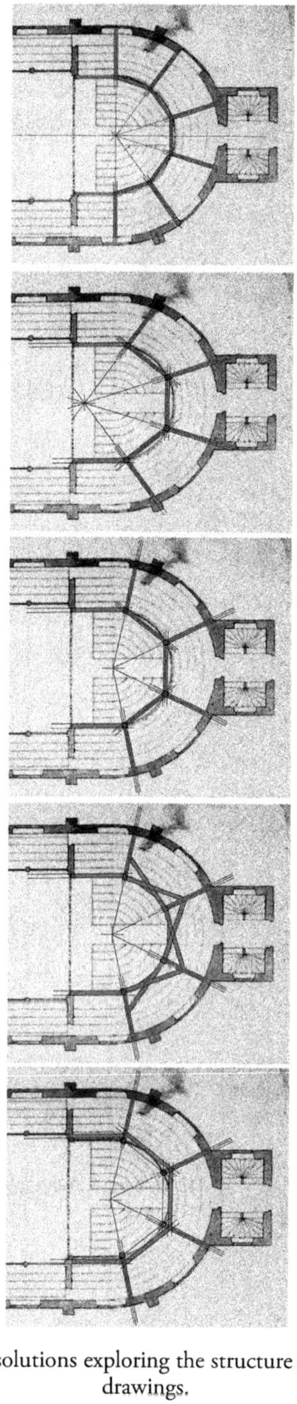

Figure 7 Trial and error solutions exploring the structure of the Worcester College drawings.

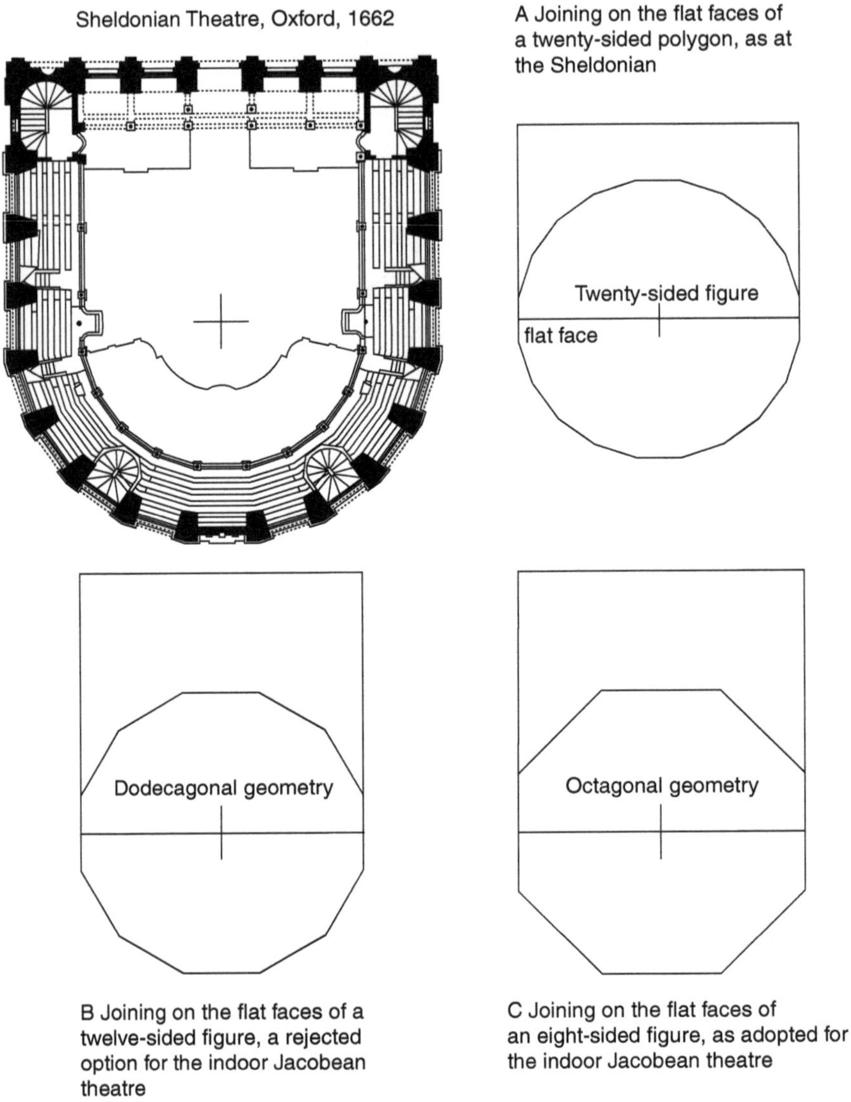

Figure 8 The geometry: joining a polygon with a rectangle, and the lessons from Wren at the Sheldonian Theatre.

Webb's plans, with the incorporation of a jetty, gave a close match to the number and location of columns drawn by Webb. The result is a design that is credible in comparison with known Jacobean examples of galleried interiors, and which closely matches drawings 7b and 7c in the arrangement and proportion of the auditorium space (see Figures 14 and 15). This was the second decisive step in reimagining the indoor Jacobean theatre.

Carpentry and timber framing

Craftsmen in the early seventeenth century would not have looked to the architects' drawings for instructions on how to build, as they do today. Indeed there were very few who could call themselves 'architects' in 1600, and even the term 'architect' was barely established. John Summerson explains:

> 'Architecture', in England of this time, was a rare word, at once invoking architectura, the Roman science of building. 'Architect' was no more common and was a rather grandiose and literary appellation for somebody who designed buildings. Nearly all the building work of James I's reign was designed by those who built it, and they were masons, bricklayers or carpenters, working in with other trades which might include carvers for exterior ornament and joiners and plasterers for interiors. These were the people who built the kind of buildings which we naturally call 'Jacobean'.[20]

When looking at the design of the indoor Jacobean theatre (see Plates 2, 3 and 4), we are therefore not examining the work of engineers, architects or surveyors, but primarily looking at the intellectual contribution and secondly at the handiwork of highly accomplished craftsmen. Investigation of the geometry has shown the importance of understanding the method of construction that would have been used, an understanding that influences every aspect of the project details. The construction method would have been derived from the craft skills, and, although our imagined indoor commercial playhouse would have been a civic building, the craft skills and methods would have had their basis in the vernacular building tradition, pushed a little out of its comfort zone to meet the particular needs of the prevailing fashions and the status of the building. Craft skills would have been learned from a young age by an apprentice, honed as a journeyman, and reinforced with many years of experience as a guild member. For a Jacobean, unless you were a gentleman, your trade would have defined you as a person.

The essential elements of an Elizabethan/Jacobean timber framer's method are summarized for the general reader in chapter 5 of *Shakespeare's Globe*

[20] Summerson, *Inigo Jones*, p. 25.

Rebuilt.[21] Building the gallery structure for an indoor Jacobean theatre would have been very similar to building an open-air playhouse, if a little more refined and on a smaller scale. Key documents studied for the Globe reconstruction, such as the Fortune contract of 1600[22] and the Hope contract of 1613,[23] have also provided essential information for the indoor Jacobean theatre project, as has the craft knowledge developed by McCurdy & Co. over many years of surveying, repairing and fabricating historic timber frames (see Plates 7a, b, c, d). The practical evidence for this reconstruction is therefore drawn from many examples, not just through study but through the practice of dismantling and rebuilding many vernacular timber frames. Capturing all the practical evidence that has informed the timber tradition is material for a different publication, but it is useful to be reminded of the key principles as this account moves to the more detailed issues. The essential elements of the historic carpenter's method would have been:

1. Very careful selection of timber, usually English oak, sometimes even ensuring that the trees will produce sound and consistent wood by examining them while they are growing.
2. Resolution of the three-dimensional 'space frame' into a series of component two-dimensional flat frames. Timber framing is a little like constructing a 'flat pack' piece of furniture, but on a much larger scale and assembling flat oak frames rather than flat particle-board panels. After fabrication each flat frame in the workshop is dismantled for transport to the site.
3. When constructing the individual flat frame (the 'flat pack' furniture equivalent of the particle board panel), it is generally jointed to give one 'good' face on which the timber faces are set flush with one another. This is best imagined if one has a series of timbers of different cross-sectional size (scantling), laying them on a flat floor and jointing them as they lay. If one then stood the resulting frame upright, one would see that the frame had one side on which all the timbers were in line (the face that had been on the floor) and one face on which all the timbers protruded to different depths. Historic oak frames are not constructed on the floor, but the effect is the same. The exception to this is a radial frame, which is set out from the centre line of each timber. These frames do not have one 'good' face and have the timbers protruding on both sides equally.

21 Jon Greenfield, 'Timber Framing, the Two Bays and After', in J. R. Mulryne and Margaret Shewring (eds.), *Shakespeare's Globe Rebuilt* (Cambridge University Press, 1997), pp. 97–120.

22 R. A. Foakes and R. T. Rickert (eds.), *Henslowe's Diary* (Cambridge University Press, 1961), pp. 307–10.

23 W. W. Greg (ed.), *The Henslowe Papers* (London, 1907), pp. 19–22.

4. Prefabrication of the two-dimensional flat frames in a carpenter's yard – generally on trestles, so that the craftsmen are working consistently at 'table top' height.
5. Measuring and cutting of individual joints ('scribing') so that the individual angles and shapes of each particular timber are accommodated. For this reason it is not possible to swap similar timbers around within a frame – each joint is individual.
6. In order to avoid placing a jointed timber in the wrong place in the frame during site erection, a careful numbering system is used to ensure that each joint can be referenced to its three-dimensional location (e.g. frame three, top level, tie-beam to back post junction).
7. The tools available, and the craftsman's skill, define what is technically achievable. Tenon saw, pit saw, side axe, draw knife and chisel are the basic tools which cover most operations. Lathes and augers are also needed for the indoor Jacobean project, to create the shaped and centre-bored columns.
8. Site construction uses a 'piece on piece' method, with each timber being assembled in sequence. Continuing the flat pack furniture analogy, the problems encountered by the purchaser of Ikea self-assembly packs are in some ways the same as those encountered when building a historic timber frame – each piece must fit together perfectly, it must be assembled in the right order, and it must be strong enough in its half-completed state to avoid self-inflicted damage. The significant difference is that historic English timber-framing does not involve the prefabrication of whole flat frames for raising as one preassembled element, like American frames (as brilliantly documented in the film *Witness*).[24] Historic English frames are site-assembled one piece at a time, slowly building up the frame into a complete three-dimensional network.

The inner frame jetty, the outer frame and the upper gallery columns

Having established the essential two-dimensional plan layout, it is necessary to move on to the three-dimensional aspects, starting with the section drawings by Webb. Close inspection of the sectional design on Worcester College drawing 7c raises three key issues when reconciling the construction methods that would have been used for making a timber-framed Jacobean indoor

[24] Dir. Peter Weir, Paramount Pictures, 1985.

playhouse. The first is the vertical positioning of the gallery columns one above the other. Webb's section shows the two levels of columns completely in line, one column directly above the other. Indeed, from the way the section is drawn, it could almost be that the two columns are cut from the same two-storey continuous timber. This is very unlikely for many practical reasons, such as finding such long, defect-free timber, 'turning' such a timber to form the round column shafts, and the difficulty of incorporating a two-storey member into the frame, which is particularly difficult if both front and back frame timbers are continuous. It is much more likely that the upper columns were offset from the lower columns, even if only slightly, and offset inwards towards the auditorium, and that it was only the outer columns that were continuous. The result is that the inner gallery columns at the two different levels are each separate storey-height pieces, and that a 'jetty' is formed as the upper gallery protrudes in front of the lower gallery. A jetty is very common in timber framing, and is in the popular imagination for historic 'black and white' high streets. It has the great advantage that jointing of timbers at the head and base of the inner columns is simplified, and site erection is much less complicated, but it has the disadvantage that the viewing angle from the upper level is made a little worse, as the audience has been moved slightly closer to the stage compared to seating at the lower level. To mitigate this, the jetty has been kept to a minimal 5 inches (125 millimetres), which is just enough to separate the upper and lower column tenons where they come together at the upper gallery floor level.

With the inner frame resolved, the next issue was to examine the galleries' outer frame. On drawing 7c, Webb does not show a frame member at all but clearly shows cross-beams (summer-beams) *built into* the masonry outer wall. In Webb's mind the outer masonry wall has replaced the outer frame, a strategy which introduces more constructional difficulties. Although building timbers into masonry walls was commonplace during the period, and was for centuries afterwards (it's not considered to be good practice now), these were usually timber 'grounds' (timbers incorporated to provide a medium for fixing rather than large structural sections), which do not need particularly careful positioning. For constructing the indoor Jacobean theatre's galleries as Webb has shown, all the columns and beams would have had to be very precisely positioned. The galleries would have been prefabricated frames as described above, and it would have been very difficult to co-ordinate this prefabrication with the work of the mason or bricklayer. It is much more likely that a different method would have been used by Jacobean carpenters, as exemplified by Robert Lyminge's two great staircases, one at Hatfield in Hertfordshire, built in 1611 for the Cecil family, and

1 (a–c) Visualizations: To help the design team understand the auditorium space viewing angles, the effect of decoration and candlelight, various visualization techniques were used including: (a) white card architectural models made by Jon Greenfield (NPS); (b) a full-size mock-up of two structural bays made in softwood at McCurdy's yard at Stanford Dingley; and (c) computer modelling by Allies & Morrison.

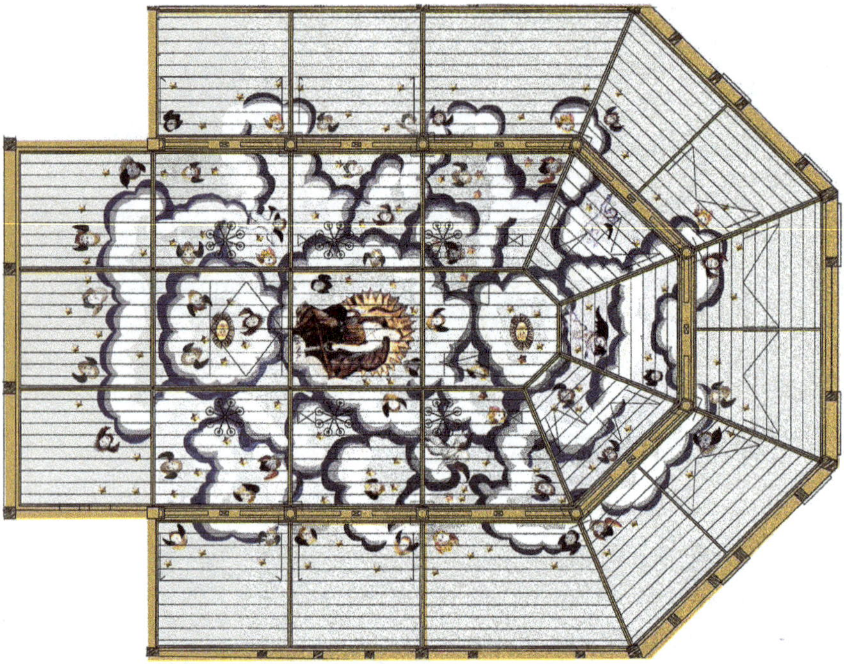

2 A reflected ceiling plan of the auditorium showing the scheme for painted decoration and gilding by Jon Greenfield (NPS).

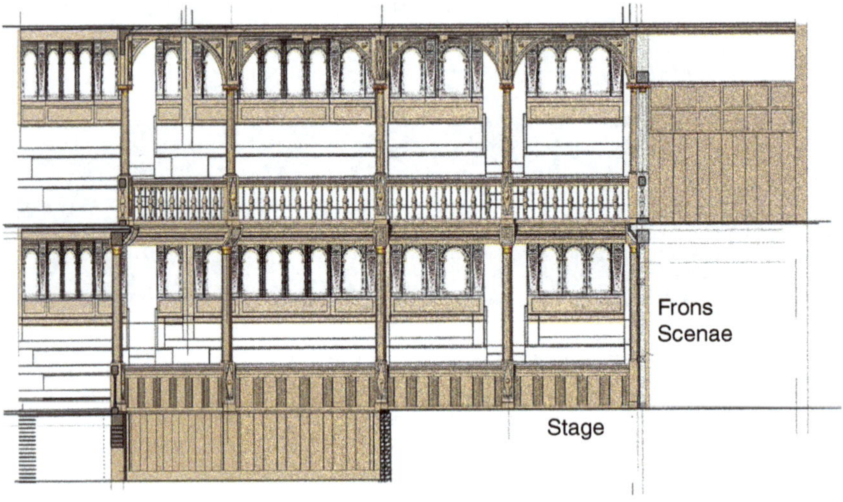

3 A section through the auditorium pit and stage showing the gallery construction, seating beyond and painted 'blind arcading' on the back wall by Jon Greenfield (NPS).

4 (a–d) Experimental options for the *frons scenae* showing different combinations of oak carving and painted decoration by Jon Greenfield (NPS).

5 A carved oak ionic capital at Chilham Castle dating from 1616.

6 A carved oak ionic capital made for the Sam Wanamaker Playhouse.

7 (a–d) The workshop process at McCurdy & Co.: (a) carefully laying out timbers for jointing; (b) scribing a new timber into a frame, ensuring that the unique variations in shape of the timber are accommodated in the jointing – this way a timber has a unique location within the frame and cannot be swapped; (c) inspecting and hand finishing inner gallery columns after they have been turned on a lathe; (d) an oak frame in the workshop showing that the three-dimensional building frame is resolved into two-dimensional component frames.

8 An oak and plaster hall screen at Burton Agnes dated 1601–10.

9 A stone hall screen at Montacute dated 1598.

a

b

10 (a–b) Oak arcading at Chilham Castle fronting the galleried stair landings dated 1616.

11 Oak panelling in the hall at Exeter College, Oxford dated 1618.

12 Strapwork cresting at St John the Evangelist Church, Leeds dated 1632–4.

13 Detail of hall screen panelling and guardroon moulding in the screen at Wadham College, Oxford dated 1613.

14 Typical sunken geometric decoration from Burton Agnes dated 1601–10.

15 Detail of an arch-headed door and carved spandrel in the hall screen at Wadham College, Oxford dated 1613.

16 Typical elements of Jacobean decoration: string course, fluted pilasters and panelling at Montacute, early seventeenth century.

the other at Blickling in Norfolk, built in 1618–29 for the Hobart family (although the Blickling staircase was moved and altered in 1767). Lyminge is perhaps the one exception to Summerson's rule about Jacobean architects; he was a carpenter who became that rare Jacobean beast, an architect.[25] Both his houses have main staircases that are very grand and ornate affairs, but it is their underlying structure which is instructive.

Both the staircases are composed of a series of stair flights and landings, articulated at the junction between flight and landing with a large, solid (and ornately carved) post (the 'newel'). However, for every post on the inside of the flight, there is a corresponding half-post on the outer line, hard against the masonry wall. These staircase 'newel posts' correspond with the inner and outer gallery columns in the indoor Jacobean theatre. Lyminge's framers were therefore able to fully frame up the staircases off site in their workshop, and bring them to site as one entity confident that they would fit together, even if the mason/bricklayer had not worked to similarly accurate tolerances. The staircases were assembled on site and fixed in position by securing the half-posts flat against the masonry walls. Large 'lost-headed' wrought-iron nails spike the half-posts into the masonry walls, and the heads of these nails can still be found at Hatfield, among the decorative carving on the posts.

It is believed that this is the way the gallery frames would have been made by Jacobean craftsmen (see Figure 9b), so that they could be prefabricated and

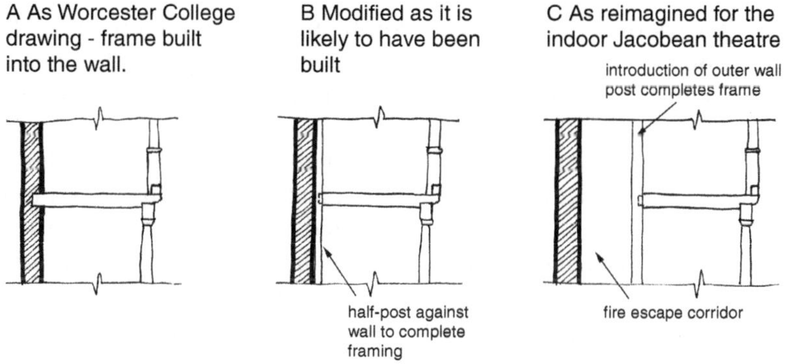

Figure 9 Timber framing – the importance of the outer frame columns.

[25] Summerson notes in *Inigo Jones* that Robert Smythson and Robert Lyming, the two men who could call themselves 'architects' at the time, were 'men (who) came, for the most part, out of the building trades, but could draw and write well and often knew some Latin' (p. 26).

installed within a pre-existing mediaeval structure such as the 'great Hall or Rome' at the Blackfriars.[26] Turned, carved and ornamented columns would have constituted the inner gallery line, but the corresponding position on the outer line of the frame would most probably have been only lightly decorated and was only there to complete the timber frame and provide a tidy and easily constructed interface with the masonry wall. These timbers would have been laid flat against the inside face of the masonry walls, and would have been carefully adjusted and then spiked very accurately into position with wrought-iron nails, as at Hatfield. Timber joints (mortices) to receive all beams would have been prefabricated in the half-columns so that the frame structure could be assembled on site in the traditionally English 'piece on piece' sequence.

The reimagined indoor Jacobean theatre faced an additional issue with the outer line of the gallery timber frame, as it is necessary to accommodate a perimeter fire escape corridor, needed by the authorities as part of the strategy for permitting candlelit performances (see Chapter 6 below). The junction of the inner face of the masonry wall and the half-column outer frame is where the escape corridor is required, so it has been possible in the reimagining to enlarge the half-column to a full column and create a space between timber frame and masonry wall of the required 1100 mm escape corridor dimension (see Figure 9c). So, where a Jacobean gallery frame would have spanned to the masonry, albeit to a timber fixed to the inner face of the masonry wall, in the new designs a full timber frame has been constructed, standing in space and set away from the enclosing masonry walls by the width of the escape corridor. In turn, the corridor is formed by a separate simple span between timber frame and masonry wall. It is possible that the reimagined galleries could have been designed to span from the inner column line all the way to the masonry wall, but this would have been a much larger gallery span than is associated with historic examples and would have meant that a modern addition had been incorporated into the layout of the timber frame. It was considered to be much better to use the timber frame as the conceptual demarcation line between the construction based on historic research and the construction arranged to meet modern requirements (see Figure 13, which shows the full timber frame that was constructed to sit separately within the existing masonry enclosure).

A third curious feature of the Worcester College architectural section drawings shown on 7c is the very existence of columns on the upper gallery

[26] Irwin Smith, *Shakespeare's Blackfriars Playhouse, its History and Design* (New York University Press, 1964), pp. 471–5.

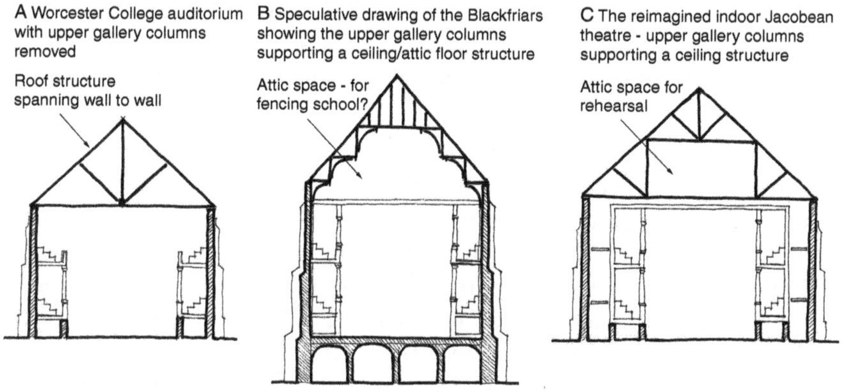

Figure 10 Timber framing – the significance of the upper gallery columns.

level at all, and it was necessary to investigate these in order to inform our reimagining. It would be easier and cheaper, although perhaps aesthetically less pleasing, to create two galleries using only the lower columns (these provide the important structural function of supporting the upper gallery). The Sheldonian Theatre in Oxford is configured in this way; the lower columns support the upper gallery, and only continue high enough to form the upper gallery balustrad (see Figure 10a). Removing obstructions from the upper gallery sight lines is a distinct improvement. Webb shows upper gallery columns that rise to the ceiling and in his layout shows a high proportion of the upper gallery audience seated at what could be called backstage, as at Burbage's Blackfriars, a layout in which a reduction of visual obstructions would be welcome. So the question is, what did Webb intend these columns to support? It seems very unlikely that they were just decorative, so they must have had a more integrated function (see Figure 10).

One element of the Inigo Jones work and the subsequent neoclassical movement was the gradual introduction of scientific principles to roof designs, enabling roof structures to span further with less timber than the vernacular English counterparts. This may seem curious, given that the architectural term 'neoclassical' is usually associated only with architectural decoration, but it is characteristic of the nascent 'Age of Reason' that science and aesthetics were advancing simultaneously. The earliest of the new, innovative structures was the king-post roof-truss, based on an Italian innovation, which looks much like the roof structure drawn by Webb on Worcester College drawing 7c. Historian of historic timber structures David Yeomans explains:

> The earliest uses of trussed roofs in Britain are to be found in the work of both Inigo Jones (1573–1652) and Christopher Wren (1632–1723) . . . For each, their inspiration for the use of the form can be clearly traced to Italian sources: either to Italy itself, in the case of Jones who visited the country, or Italian books.[27]

Yeomans also explains the common confusion, as vernacular triangulated roof structures (i.e. Jacobean and before) are commonly referred to as 'roof-trusses', when they would better be referred to as 'roof frames',[28] whose span is largely limited by the distance that a tie-beam can span. The configuration of timbers in a traditional roof frame is not able to work in combination and therefore does take account of tension and compression forces in the efficient way that can be found in a truss. In a scientific 'trussed roof', a long span can be achieved by using a multitude of short lengths of timber. Webb's drawing 7c shows one of the new Italian trusses, with a metal strap at the mid-span 'propping' the tie-beam by truss triangulation, making it what Yeomans would define as a 'trussed roof'. Webb shows quite a large span for his roof structure, from masonry wall to masonry wall. As drawn, the upper columns of the galleries also prop the span of the tie-beam, thereby using the upper gallery columns prudently to help mitigate the risks of using an innovative roof-truss design that he may have feared would have a sagging or otherwise failing tie-beam. In a Jacobean example the roof would have been of a traditional 'frame' type and would have been close to the limit of its spanning capabilities, so the propping effect of the upper gallery columns would have been essential. At the Sheldonian, Wren had the confidence to span from masonry wall to masonry wall, much further than the span required in Webb's small theatre, and he achieved this without help from the gallery structure, which explains why there are no upper gallery columns at the Sheldonian. But this was fifty years later than our reimagined indoor Jacobean theatre.

Of course, the Blackfriars had a pre-existing mediaeval roof, and it is not known whether it had upper gallery columns, but it is known that there was a fencing school above the auditorium, presumably in the roof space. There is a poetic image of the mediaeval roof being open to the auditorium, but this would have introduced a number of acoustic problems to the indoor playhouse, as the additional roof-space volume would have lengthened the reverberation time of the auditorium, possibly making speech unacceptably indistinct (not the preference of an actor) and losing sound energy into

[27] D. T. Yeomans, *The Trussed Roof: Its History and Development* (Aldershot: Scholar, 1992), p. 30.
[28] Ibid., p. 28.

the large roof space, thereby reducing the apparent volume of what was being said on stage. These would have been good reasons for introducing a ceiling in the Blackfriars and separating the auditorium from the mediaeval roof volume.[29] Strengthening this ceiling structure to be a full floor would have had the additional advantages of creating useful attic space for property storage, for accommodating a windlass and other stage machinery associated with flying, and of accommodating rehearsal space or a fencing school, as is presumed. A floor structure spanning across the Blackfriars hall at ceiling level would certainly have needed the inner gallery columns to act as props (see Figure 10b). In the current designs for SGT, the gallery frame has been extended to include a ceiling–floor structure over the auditorium, which provides a kind of lid to the frame and a useful structure for supporting show equipment. The ceiling structure therefore gives purpose to the upper-level columns, as they reduce the free span of the ceiling by 46 (13 metres) to 23 (6.5 metres) feet, and help to create a more naturally rigid timber frame structure (see Figure 10c).

Reimagining Jacobean decoration

Looking at Webb's drawings through half-closed eyes to obscure the obviously neoclassical features, one can get a good sense of an archetypal indoor playhouse of the earlier, Jacobean generation. The only feature that is still strikingly neoclassical, however, is the coved ceiling, particularly where it runs around the curved end of the auditorium. There are examples of coved Elizabethan ceilings, such as the long gallery at Montacute House in Somerset (1598), subsequently thoughtlessly modified by the Georgians,[30] and the Jacobean great hall at Hatfield. All known examples of a coved ceiling are on a rectangular plan, commonly with the cove running down the two long sides of a hall or large room. None show an apse, or have anything like a cove following around the edge of a curved ceiling as shown on the Webb drawings. Complex ceiling shapes in surviving Jacobean examples, even ones with ornate fibrous plaster decoration, generally have flat, coveless ceilings, so this is the design that has been adopted for the indoor Jacobean project. However, omission of the ceiling cove particularly compromises the proportion of the inner galleries, and the refined proportional relationship between the Doric lower

[29] Smith, *Shakespeare's Blackfriars Playhouse*, p. 167.

[30] The long gallery roof at Montacute House was modified by cutting through the tie beam. The weight of the roof has since pushed out against the side walls, causing structural problems that remain to this day.

columns and the Ionic upper ones. To overcome this formal problem of proportion, arcading has been introduced around the inner line of the auditorium, to the depth of the omitted cove. The inner line of the auditorium, or gallery front, has therefore become a two-storey arcade, as can be found in several notable Jacobean examples, such as Oxford's Bodleian Library, where a large book-stack follows a gallery layout, around the great staircase at Knole in Kent, built 1605–08 for the Sackvilles, at Chastleton Hall, built 1607 to 1612 for Walter Jones, and at Chilham Castle, built by Sir Dudley Digges in 1616 (see Plate 3).

Columns, carving and Jacobean ornament

Having established the basic geometry, form and configuration of the reimagined Jacobean auditorium, applying the detail is a little more straightforward when considered element by element; column, arcade, handrail, baluster, balustrade and panelling (see Plates 3 and 4). The most important decision for these is finding the right surviving Jacobean model to follow, in terms of the date, jointing method, decoration and finish. The most difficult has been the design and detailing of the shaped classical columns of the gallery front.

Before looking at the detail of the columns, it is useful to understand the difference between *carvings* and *mouldings*. Classical and neoclassical design has a very strong visual grammar and syntax – it is a language of shapes, and there are many rules. These rules were understood and precisely followed in neoclassical design, but the Jacobeans did not fully understand the visual language, and were getting information mostly from woodcut publications produced in Flanders and the Low Countries, not Italy. Jacobean ornament is a distorted version of classicism, overlaid on a base of traditional English Gothic influences. In replicating Jacobean ornament, it is necessary to capture a 'wrongness' in the replication of classical detailing that came because there was little direct knowledge transfer from Italy to England, all of it being circuitous and using crude representations. Woodcut printing can be distorted and it struggles to convey the fine lines and elegant proportion needed to capture the essential features of classical and neoclassical decoration.

Many of the complicated shapes associated with classical ornament can be seen to be made up from a relatively limited set of fairly simple shapes, such as *cyma, cyma reversa, corona, ovolo, cavetto, astragal, scotia* and *torus* (see Figure 11). As neoclassical design grew in popularity and established itself as the most basic architectural grammar for the next three hundred and fifty years or so, many profiles became produced as standard components in

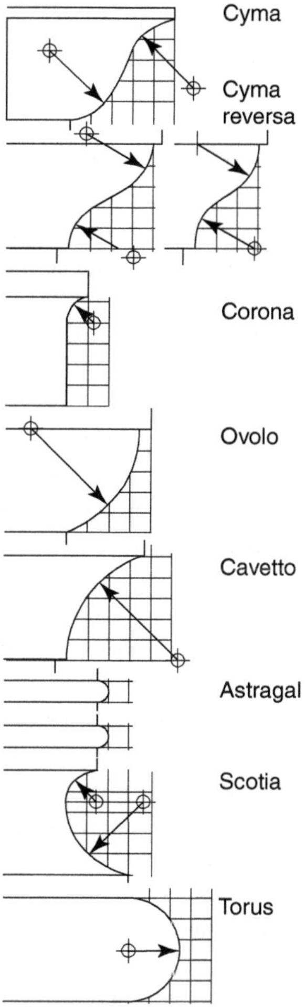

Figure 11 'Canonical' classical profiles.

plaster and timber, and it became the norm to build up complex shapes from these standard components. This process is essentially *additive*, meaning that several standard profiles could be used in combination to make a complex shape, such as cornice or entablature, particularly when using timber or plaster. In contrast, the Jacobean timber carver often used a *subtractive* method, starting with a large block of timber and cutting into the material until the desired shape was achieved. It is a subtractive process that involves a great deal of effort on behalf of the craftsman, and a great deal of material wastage.

A similarly subtractive method was used for making the indoor Jacobean theatre's circular gallery columns, with their carved capitals and carved bases. These columns are both structural and decorative, and are shaped by cutting down from solid structural timbers. The raw material for these columns has had to be carefully chosen for straightness and lack of defects, and for which the sequencing and processes of jointing and decorative carving have to be carefully considered. In simple terms, the timbers sourced for the gallery fronts are 10 inch (250 mm) square, and all of the shaping had to be contained within this dimension – including the more expansive shape of an Ionic capital (see Figure 12c). The circular column shafts were turned on a lathe, as was shaping of the Doric capitals, Ionic capitals, and decoration on the bases and heads, hand-carved into the structural timber. The result is columns that are very constrained in their width proportions: they are slender and clipped in their overall effect, as the decorative sections have small projections, the column bases are narrow, and the capitals are squeezed. Although non-canonical when compared with neoclassical examples, this constraint has helped to make the columns look very Jacobean, and to capture the 'right kind of wrongness' described above. The slender proportions can be found in a number of examples, notably the prints that show Stephen Harrison's designs for temporary gates used for James I's entry into London, in surviving examples of inn gallery fronts, and colonnaded staircase newels, such as those found at Knole and Chilham Castle, as well as base and head decoration found on staircase newels at Chastleton House. Replicating Jacobean design has been achieved in these tightly constrained columns, deduced from a detailed understanding of how they would have been made four hundred years ago.

Our shortage of Jacobean galleried and arcaded structures that fit the layout of the indoor Jacobean theatre has led research again to staircase structures, some of which range over two storeys and are very similar to the gallery front columns under consideration. The main staircases at Knole and at Chilham Castle in Kent are the most informative (see Plate 10). Dimensions derived from a logical progression through the major determinants, as described in this account, have been found to match the dimensions surveyed at Chilham Castle so closely that these columns, and the arcade that goes with them, have been adopted as the principal prototype for the reimagined indoor Jacobean theatre. Mouldings and carvings, as well as sunken strapwork and other carved decoration from these prototypes, are being used as the principal source for the auditorium. The Ionic capitals are a direct copy of the ones found in the grand staircase at Chilham Castle (Plates 5 and 6).

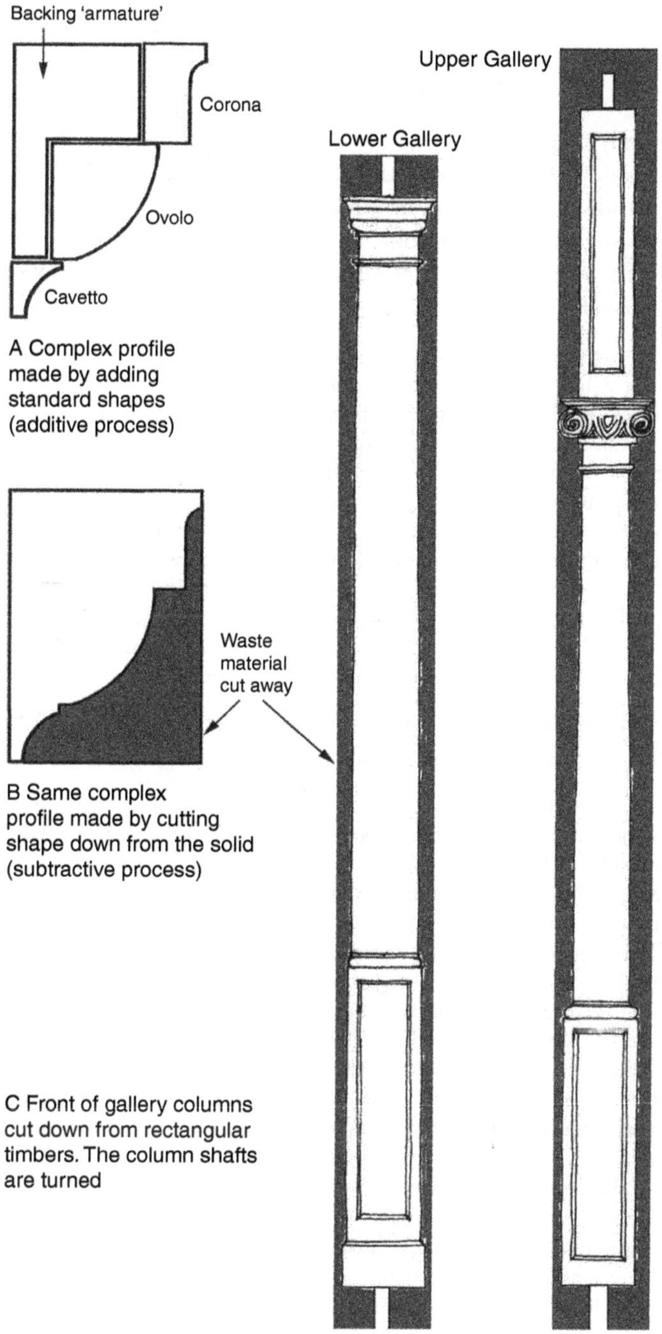

Figure 12 Columns and cornices – 'additive' and 'subtractive' methods of creating complex shapes.

Reimagining the *frons scenae*

Unfortunately, there are no equally useful surviving examples of the *frons scenae* available to be adopted as the basic construction model for an indoor theatre. Although taking the argument in a different direction, Frances Yates,[31] writing about the Globe in 1969, highlighted the lack of really usable information, and no new discoveries have been made that countermand her conclusion:

> The Swan stage, as depicted in the De Witt sketch, does not give an adequate idea of what the frons scenae or tiring house wall in an Elizabethan theatre, designed solely for acting, may have been like. The unsatisfactory nature of the Swan's evidence in this respect has been a constant worry to theatre historians, for the features are difficult to reconcile with the needs of the Shakespearean drama ... If theatre historians have longed to see a ground plan of the Globe, they have longed still more to see its stage. C. W. Hodges, who in his reconstruction of the Globe leaves the stage wall a blank and inscribed with the words 'details not known', has imagined a large company of Shakespearean scholars sitting in the Globe theatre in darkness, waiting for the dawn to break to reveal the stage, the nature and arrangement of its exits and entrances, what was on the upper level.[32]

Timothy Mowl has offered a more certain direction, drawing inspiration from hall-screens found in Jacobean country houses and Oxford colleges:

> If, as some authorities claim, these halls had begun to sink in status and become a dining room for upper servants it is difficult to explain why the most splendid internal features of such houses continued to be their hall screens, topped with ornate overhanging galleries and pierced by either one or two impressive archways.
>
> The explanation is that the screens were designed as permanent stage scenery for performances of actors on their summer perambulations away from the plagues of London and for amateur masques. Much time and money has been spent scouring the South Bank for the foundations of Shakespeare's Globe Theatre, when up to twelve authentic Elizabethan or Jacobean theatres survive intact with their backdrops in great houses like Hatfield. Palladio's Teatro Olimpico stands in Vicenza with its scenery still fossilized as for the first performance of Sophocles's Oedipus Rex in 1585. How much more interesting to have, as in Audley End, an infinitely flexible

[31] Interestingly, Robert Fludd's drawing that Yates argued depicted the Globe actually contains all the features that can be seen in Webb's *frons*. Yates argued for five stage entrances – three at the lower level and two at the upper level, with an architectural feature in the centre at the upper level. This also describes Webb's design.

[32] F. A. Yates, *The Theatre of the World* (London and New York: Routledge & Kegan Paul, 1969), pp. 136–7.

> screen and stage set ready to double as Juliet's balcony, the battlements of Elsinore, a cave for Macbeth's witches, Timon of Athens's den, Cleopatra's palace or later her Pharos.[33]

Dampening Timothy Mowl's enthusiasm a little, there is some difficulty in reconciling the evidence from hall-screens with our primary source, the Worcester College drawings. Drawing 7c clearly depicts the *frons scenae*, showing it with *three* openings, one in the centre and two at the sides, and with the screen ranging over *two* storeys. None of the surviving hall-screen prototypes have three doors or are two storeys high; they all have one or two doors and are only one storey high (see Plates 8 and 9 for typical examples). The solution has been to 'Jacobeanize' Webb's design. If Webb's drawings do indeed show a scheme to update and makeover an earlier interior, then this is the reverse process. Consequently Webb's split pediment has been translated into strapwork capturing a coat of arms (for which there are many Jacobean examples), the twisted lower body of Webb's herms have been translated into architectural bases (for which there are many Jacobean examples), swags, panels and niches have been incorporated into a timber wainscot panel solution, and the columns and arch orders of the central opening have followed Jacobean doorcase prototypes. References have been drawn from Montacute, Hatfield (hall and chapel), Burton Agnes, Dore Abbey Church, Audley End, Exeter, Wadham, and Jesus College Halls in Oxford (see Plates 8 to 16 inclusive). It is a necessary disappointment to have had to 'cherry pick' from so many sources, but it was necessary to rank the evidence available, and the *frons scenae* arrangement shown by Webb took priority (see Plate 4).

Similarly, the musicians' gallery, upper-level seating, one central arched door and two rectangular-headed smaller side doors were a theatrical necessity. Documentary evidence from Stephen Harrison's arches, Serlio's 'Four Books', and the small number of well-known depictions of *frons scenae* have reinforced the conclusion.[34] In execution, the *frons scenae* will be made to a higher 'joinery' standard of finish than the auditorium and painted. The staircase at Chilham Castle has provided a compelling example of an

[33] Mowl, *Elizabethan and Jacobean Style*, p. 146.

[34] A vignette from the title page of Nathanael Richards' 'Messallina' (1640), in Jean Wilson, *The Archaeology of Shakespeare* (Stroud: Allan Sutton, 1997), p. 150. The frontpiece from 'The Wits', by Francis Kirkman (1662), ibid., p. 151. The 'Roxana' title page (1632), in Andrew Gurr and John Orrell, *Rebuilding Shakespeare's Globe* (London: Weidenfield & Nicolson, 1989), fig. 17. John Speed's title page (1614), in C. Walter Hodges, *The Globe Restored* (London: Earnest Benn, 1953), plate 42. Ben Jonson's title page (1616), ibid., plate 43. The Swan Theatre (1596), by Arend van Buchel/Johannes de Witt, ibid., plate 7. Stephen Harrison's 'The Triumph of James I' (London 1604), a series of illustrations including 'The Flemish Arch' (plate 29), 'The Temple of Janus' (plate 30), 'The Arch of London' (plate 31), 'The Garden of Plenty' (plate 32), 'The New Arabia Felix' (plate 33) and 'The Arch of the New World' (plate 34).

appropriate finish for the auditorium, where the carving is relatively roughly hewn, as if worked in double-time by a carpenter rather than a joiner or carver. Sunken strapwork decoration is relatively simple and repeating and is ubiquitous in surviving Jacobean examples. The screen will provide a contrast to the auditorium embellishment, and will be to a more refined standard of finish, with more ornate carving, appropriate to the focus of theatrical attention (see Plates 2, 3 and 4).

Conclusion

John Orrell would describe a departure from the Worcester College drawings as a 'risky affair',[35] but the focus of attention is not on one particular

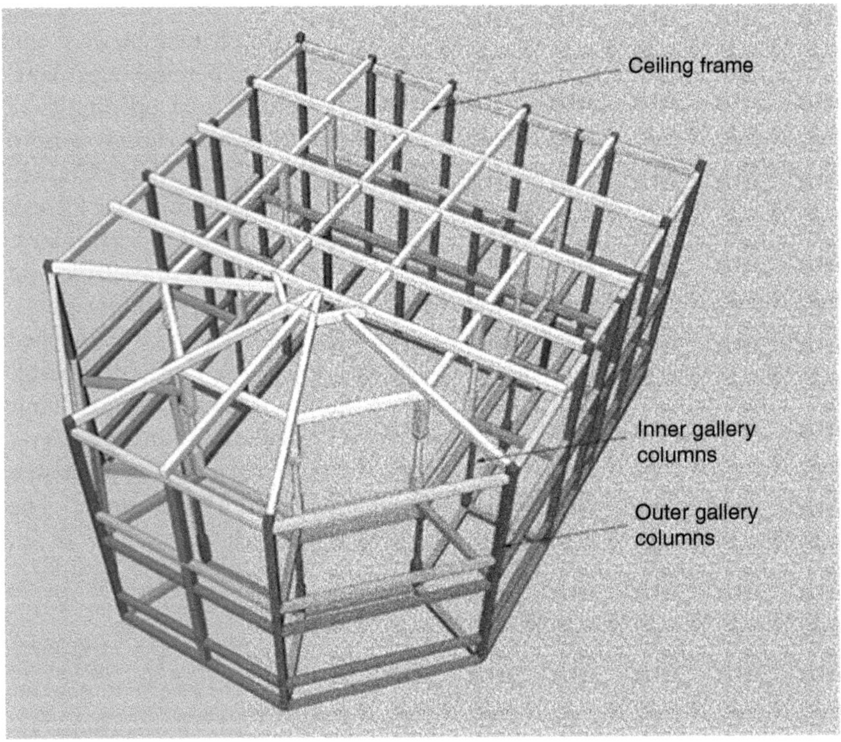

Figure 13 The full, self-contained timber frame that sits within the theatre's masonry shell.

[35] Orrell, 'Inigo Jones Designs', p. 129.

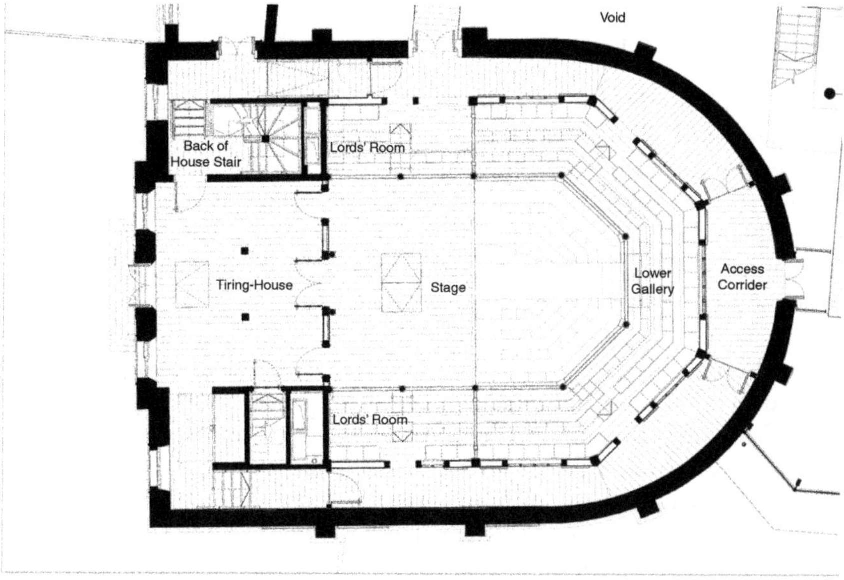

Figure 14 Pit and lower gallery architectural plan for the Sam Wanamaker Playhouse, Allies & Morrison.

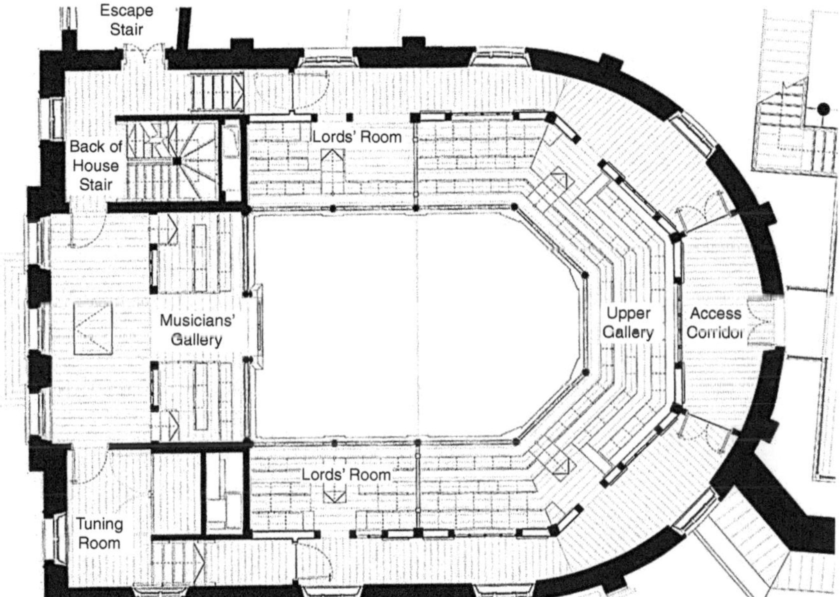

Figure 15 Upper level architectural plan for the Sam Wanamaker Playhouse, Allies & Morrison.

indoor Jacobean theatre, and the outcome intended is an analogue of one. All re-creations tell more about the age in which they are built than about the age they are trying to capture, but this does not diminish the principles behind the attempt. In order to mitigate the risks, considerable care has been taken with this reimagining to ensure that there is a footnote to every element of the indoor Jacobean theatre, why it has been incorporated, and which source informed it. During the design stages each part of the theatre has been drawn, computer-modelled in 3D, physically modelled and mocked up in full size (see Plates 1a, b and c). Much knowledge has been applied to the theatre, and much new knowledge gained during the design in all fields, from the interpretation of texts to the formation of Jacobean joinery. There is no other theatre space quite like this one, in size, configuration and sheer density of humanity in the auditorium. The test, however, will be in performance, when the space will become the vehicle for making new discoveries about what works dramatically and what does not, testing some of the theories posed in this collection. As with the building phase, many preconceptions will be reinforced and many more challenged. Once the building work is completed, the real work will begin.

CHAPTER 3

Documentary evidence for an indoor Jacobean theatre

Oliver Jones

> We amused ourselves by admiring the decorations and beauty of the house, with its two orders of columns, one above the other, their distance from the wall equalling the breadth of the passage, that of the second row being upheld by Doric pillars, while above these rise Ionic columns supporting the roof. The whole is of wood, including even the shafts, which are carved and gilt with much skill. From the roof of these hang festoons and angels in relief, with two rows of lights.[1]

On 6 January 1618, Orazio Busino, almoner in the entourage of the Venetian ambassador to King James, attended the opening performance of *Pleasure Reconciled to Virtue*, a court masque written by Ben Jonson and designed by Inigo Jones. Busino's detailed observation of the event not only offers us a colourful vignette of courtly entertainments, but has left one of the few eyewitness descriptions of the interior of a building that housed Jacobean plays. The building he describes is not, however, one of the indoor playhouses occupied by professional companies, but the Jacobean Banqueting House, which stood at Whitehall for ten years before burning to the ground on 12 January 1619 after an ill-placed candle set oil-painted scenery, and the hall, ablaze.

For all that drama flourished during the reign of James I, explicit evidence for the buildings in which plays were performed is slight. Records are rarely detailed and often incidental, and, as with the outdoor amphitheatres, there are few surviving images of indoor playhouses to guide how we might envisage their construction, organization or decoration. However, while there may be insufficient evidence to aid the reconstruction of a specific Jacobean theatre, there is a greater wealth concerning Jacobean building and

[1] *Calendar of State Papers: Venice*, 188. Allen B. Hinds (ed.), 'Venice: January 1618, 21–31' in *Calendar of State Papers Relating to English Affairs in the Archives of Venice, Volume 15: 1617–1619* (1909), pp. 108–26. British History Online, accessed 22 October 2012, www.british-history.ac.uk/report.aspx?compid=88670

decoration more widely that offers strong analogues for a theatre that might have been built in the period.

We should begin by looking at the evidence for the theatre buildings themselves. Four indoor theatres operated at one time or another during James I's reign: the Blackfriars, the Whitefriars, Porter's Hall and the Cockpit, later known as the Phoenix. Only two, Blackfriars and the Phoenix, enjoyed any sort of lasting success. Porter's Hall hosted a single performance before it was closed down and has left no useful documentary evidence for its design,[2] while the Whitefriars theatre lasted a brief and turbulent eight years and left no further evidence for its design beyond the dimensions of the hall in which it stood.[3] It wasn't until Salisbury Court opened four years after James' death that a third rival theatre was established. The documents the playhouses engendered are on the whole of a legal nature, whether describing the purchase or lease of property, arbitration between stakeholders, or the catalogue of minor and more serious misdemeanours of the playgoing public. These have been published comprehensively elsewhere and there is little need to repeat them in full, but it is useful to review them for as much information on the buildings' size and construction as can be extracted.[4]

Blackfriars

The association of Blackfriars Playhouse with Shakespeare and the King's Men has ensured its place at the centre of theatre historical discussion.[5] While not technically a Jacobean building – it was an Elizabethan conversion of a medieval monastic hall – it nevertheless deserves consideration. The theatre's role in the development of Jacobean drama is undeniable, hosting plays not only by Shakespeare but also by Jonson, Marston, Middleton and many more, and the success of the King's Men residency undoubtedly prompted

[2] See G. E. Bentley, *The Jacobean and Caroline Stage* (7 vols.; Oxford: Clarendon Press, 1940–68), vol. VI, pp. 77–86.

[3] Andrew Gurr, *The Shakespearean Stage: 1574–1642* (3rd edn; Cambridge University Press, 1992; 4th edn 2009), p. 160.

[4] Herbert Berry, 'Playhouses, 1560–1660', in Glynne Wickham, Herbert Berry and William Ingram (eds.), *English Professional Theatre, 1530–1660* (Cambridge University Press, 2000), pp. 287–674; pp. 501–30, 547–63, 623–37, 649–74; E. K. Chambers, *The Elizabethan Stage* (4 vols.; Oxford: Clarendon Press, 1923), vol. II, pp. 472–517; Bentley, *Jacobean and Caroline Stage*, vol. VI, pp. 77–86.

[5] Irwin Smith's *Shakespeare's Blackfriars Playhouse* (New York University Press, 1964) remains the most substantial work on the playhouse's history and design, and along with articles by Richard Hosley and Herbert Berry it continues to shape discussion of the playhouse. See Herbert Berry, 'The Stage and Boxes at Blackfriars', *Studies in Philology* 63 (1966), 163–86; Richard Hosley, 'A Reconstruction of the Second Blackfriars', in David Galloway (ed.), *The Elizabethan Theatre II* (Toronto: Macmillan of Canada, 1970), pp. 77–88; Richard Hosley, 'The Second Blackfriars (1596)', in Clifford Leech and T. W. Craik (eds.), *The Revels History of Drama in English, 1576–1613* (London: Methuen, 1975), pp. 197–226.

competing companies to attempt to open their own indoor venue. More importantly, the playhouse boasts the greatest extent of documentary evidence for its dimensions and configuration.

An indenture dated 4 February 1596 documents the sale of the playhouse site to James Burbage by Sir William More.[6] In it is described the 'seven great upper rooms', 'middle storeys' and 'vaults' that formed the monastic hall, known as the Parliament Hall, which Burbage would go on to convert into his playhouse. An earlier survey of 1548 gives the external measurements of the hall as 107 feet long by 52 feet wide, while in a later 1609 deposition Alexander Hawkins[7] estimates the internal measurements of the playhouse as being 66 feet by 46 feet.[8] The range in whose upper storey the hall was situated stood on a steep slope, so that while at the north end it had a single storey beneath it, at the south there were three. Access to the hall was given by a 'great pair of winding stairs' situated at the northern end.[9] Of how tall the Parliament Hall stood, how it was roofed or lit, we have no record. Irwin Smith's suggestion that it is likely to have had a hammer-beam roof is based on comparison with four halls of a similar size and status elsewhere in London – Westminster Hall, the Guildhall, the Great Hall at Hampton Court and Middle Temple Hall.[10] However, there is solid evidence against a hammer-beam roof at Blackfriars. Firstly, the internal measurements for the inner cloister, which sat immediately east of the range, were recorded as being only 5 feet 6 inches,[11] leaving no room for the buttresses necessary to support the weight of a hammer-beam construction. Moreover, Smith's examples of hammer-beam roofed halls all post-date Blackfriars by at least a hundred and twenty years. The earliest example, Westminster, did not have its hammer-beam roof installed until *circa* 1395, by the carpenter Hugh Herland.[12] At the time of the Blackfriars' construction in the 1270s, the

6 See Berry, 'Playhouses', pp. 504–7.

7 Hawkins was the son-in-law of Henry Evans, who had leased the Blackfriars from Richard Burbage in September 1600 after the Lord Chamberlain's Men were prevented from establishing themselves there. Evans and Hawkins, along with Edward Kirkham and (briefly) Nathaniel Giles, ran the Chapel Children and subsequently the Children of the Queen's Revels boy companies until they were forced to disband in 1608.

8 Smith, *Shakespeare's Blackfriars Playhouse*, pp. 431–2 and 516–19. The discrepancy in width suggests walls approximately three feet thick at the upper levels; we would, however, expect the walls to be thicker at ground level, measuring perhaps five feet. See pp. 93–4.

9 Berry, 'Playhouses', p. 504.

10 Smith, *Shakespeare's Blackfriars Playhouse*, p. 102.

11 Nick Holder, 'The Medieval Friaries of London: A Topographic and Archaeological History Before and after the Dissolution', Ph.D. thesis, University of London, 2011, fos. 51, 376; see P. Mills and J. Oliver, *The Survey of Building Sites in the City of London After the Great Fire of 1666* (5 vols.; London Topographical Society, 1962–7), vol. v, p. 123.

12 L. T. Courtenay and R. Mark, 'The Westminster Hall Roof: A Historiographic and Structural Study', *Journal of the Society of Architectural Historians* 46 (1987), 374–93.

Westminster roof would have been a much simpler and technically less sophisticated design, needing the support of timber or stone columns.[13] While it is possible a similar construction may have been used at Blackfriars, a building with a roof that needed central supporting posts is unlikely to have appealed to Burbage, a trained carpenter, when he came to select a site for his new playhouse. It is therefore more likely that the Blackfriars roof used an aisled construction, perhaps similar to that surviving at Prior's Hall Barn, in Essex,[14] and that the supporting posts and bay divisions would have had to be incorporated into Burbage's design when he came to fit out a new theatre in 1596.

For further evidence of the arrangement of the auditorium we have to turn to literary sources, which are often rather more open to interpretation, as aside from four generic mentions of galleries, boxes and seats, legal documents are largely silent.[15] While Smith and Hosley both assume a square-ended auditorium, there is some evidence for a rounded – or, more probably, faceted – auditorium. In Ben Jonson's *The Magnetic Lady*, Probee talks of the 'oblique caves and wedges of your house',[16] which John Orrell linked to the Latin terms *cavea* and *cunei* used to describe the segmental seating and sectors of seating in Roman auditoria.[17] In the prologue to *The Wits*, William Davenant also describes the playhouse as a 'Hemispheare',[18] which must refer to the auditorium.

How the auditorium was arranged is less clear. There were at least two levels of galleries, as the testimony of Hawkins and colleagues refers to them in the plural,[19] but whether there was a third depends on our interpretation of Cocledemoy's address to 'my very fine Heliconian gallants, and you my / worshipful friends in the middle region'[20] in Marston's *The Dutch Courtesan*. The middle region may refer to the second of three galleries, or to an indeterminate middle area, perhaps the pit.[21] Evidence for the zoning of seating comes from numerous references to ticket prices in Blackfriars plays

13 Ibid., pp. 376–7, n. 5.

14 See D. Sherlock, *Prior's Hall Barn, Widdington, Essex* (London: English Heritage, 1991).

15 Hawkins describes the hall as being 'cum Theatro Anglice a Stadge porticibus Anglice Galleries & sedibus' (Smith, *Shakespeare's Blackfriars Playhouse*, pp. 290 and 516–19).

16 Ben Jonson, *The Magnetic Lady*, ed. P. Happé (Manchester University Press, 2000), Induction, 29.

17 John Orrell, *The Human Stage* (Cambridge University Press, 1988), p. 196.

18 W. Davenant, *The Wits*, sig. A5, Early English Books Online, accessed 01/02/2013, http://gateway.proquest.com/openurl?ctx_ver=Z39.88-2003&res_id=xri:eebo&rft_id=xri:eebo:citation:99844961

19 See note 15 above.

20 John Marston, *The Dutch Courtesan*, ed. D. Crane (London: A&C Black, 1997), 5.3.157–8.

21 Henry Fitzgeffrey also speaks of 'the middle Region' in his 'Notes From Blackfryers' (London, 1617); Smith, *Shakespeare's Blackfriars Playhouse* (p. 291), and Gurr, *Shakespearean Stage* (p. 157), both favour the three-gallery argument, but the evidence does not favour either option.

and commentaries, but it does not give us a clear picture.[22] It appears that sixpence gained entry to the galleries, 1s 6d provided a bench in the pit and for a further sixpence gallants could hire a stool and sit on the stage. Boxes could be hired for half a crown.[23] The boxes' location has been made clearer since Herbert Berry's discovery of correspondence concerning a quarrel at the Blackfriars between Lord Thurles and Captain Essex in January 1632:

> Their lo[rds] [i.e. the Star Chamber] made my lord Thurles of Irland also to doe the like satisfaction to Captaine Essex. The occasion was this. This Captaine attending and accompanying my Lady of Essex in a boxe in the playhouse at the blackfryers, the said lord coming upon the stage, stood before them and hindred their sight. Captain Essex told his lo[rd], they had payd for their places as well as hee, and therfore intreated him not to depriue them of the benefitt of it. Wherevpon the lord stood vp yet higher and hindred more their sight. Then Capt. Essex with his hand putt him a little by. The lord then drewe his sword and ran full butt at him, though hee missed him, and might have slaine the Countesse as well as him.[24]

That a standing gallant could both obscure the box-holder's view and be physically pushed to one side suggests the boxes were adjacent to and at the same level as the stage.[25] An argument between the Duke of Lennox and the Lord Chamberlain gives rare evidence for physical features in the playhouse, namely that the boxes had keys and could be locked.[26] It is not clear whether the boxes comprised a single level of boxes at the side of the stage, or whether they were repeated immediately above. While most scholars have favoured the former proposition, Andrew Gurr has more recently suggested that the Blackfriars 'probably' boasted two levels of boxes.[27] His conclusion is drawn from his analysis of the earliest graphical representation of a seventeenth-century playhouse interior, a design held in Worcester College's collection of drawings by Inigo Jones and John

22 For a discussion of pricing and evidence for seating, see Smith, *Shakespeare's Blackfriars Playhouse*, pp. 297–301, and A. Potts, 'The Development of the Playhouse in Seventeenth-Century London', Ph.D. thesis, University of Cambridge, 1998, accessed 23/10/2012, http://playhousehistory.co.uk/part1-blackfriars.html

23 Gurr, *Shakespearean Stage*, pp. 157–9.

24 Berry, 'Stage and Boxes', p. 165.

25 This view is shared by Gurr (*Shakespearean Stage*, p. 159) but not by Smith, who did not know about the Thurles–Essex argument and who placed stools for gallants at stage level but set back under the galleries, pushing the first boxes back in front of the stage and continuing down the length of the auditorium. See Smith, *Shakespeare's Blackfriars Playhouse*, pp. 307 and 310.

26 See Smith, *Shakespeare's Blackfriars Playhouse*, p. 294.

27 Berry, 'Stage and Boxes'; Hosley, 'Reconstruction'; Keith Sturgess, *Jacobean Private Theatre* (London and New York: Routledge, 1987), pp. 38–44. Gurr makes the suggestion in his revised 4th edition of *Shakespearean Stage*, p. 195; cf. 3rd edition, p. 159.

Webb,[28] and one which seems to demonstrate many close similarities with the descriptions of the Blackfriars interior. Whether these later drawings of the 1660s do in fact show two levels of boxes is a matter of some debate, however, and further investigation conducted by Jon Greenfield has raised a host of complications and problems for their interpretation.[29] While the drawings may hint at a possibility that the Blackfriars contained more than the single level of boxes, the evidence is not strong enough to insist as such.

Further hints can be gleaned from Blackfriars plays, but few offer extensive detail. The playhouse had a central trap where Envy could arise 'in the midst of the stage' in Jonson's *Poetaster*.[30] In addition to trap machinery, several plays call for descents from the heavens, such as Jupiter's entrance in *Cymbeline* where he '*descends in Thunder and Lightning, sitting upon an Eagle. He throws a thunderbolt*'.[31] Smith suggests that the Citizen's Wife's reference to a painted cloth in *The Knight of the Burning Pestle* and a description by one of the boys of a 'silke cortaine, come to hang the stage here' in the induction to *Cynthia's Revels* are evidence of a cloth hung centre stage that concealed a 'rear' stage; this space, he argues, also contained a second trap needed for the staging of *The Wonder of Women*.[32] Smith envisages two main doors, with a third at the back wall of the 'rear' stage. Gurr notes that *Eastward Ho!* explicitly demands three doors – '*Enter* MAISTER TOUCHSTONE, *and* QUICKSILVER *at several dores ... At the middle dore Enter* GOLDING *discovering a Goldsmiths shoppe*' – and suggests that this indicates the need for three doors, the central one of which should be large enough to conceal a shop.[33] However, beyond acknowledging the need for a third door or central alcove for the staging of many Blackfriars plays, we cannot do more than speculate over the *frons scenae*'s construction or decoration.

The Cockpit, or Phoenix, Drury Lane

The Phoenix[34] has been the subject of much discussion by theatre historians due in large part to Don Rowan's discovery in 1969 of designs for an

[28] For more on the drawings in the Worcester College Oxford collection, see Chapter 2 above.
[29] See ibid. [30] Gurr, *Shakespearean Stage*, 3rd edn, p. 159.
[31] For a discussion of stage machinery, see John Astington, 'Descent Machinery' and 'Counterweights', *Theatre Notebook* 41 (1987), 18–24.
[32] Smith, *Shakespeare's Blackfriars Playhouse*, pp. 343–52, 358–65.
[33] Gurr, *Shakespearean Stage*, 3rd edn, pp. 159–60.
[34] For the sake of clarity I will refer to the Phoenix, in order to avoid confusion with the Cockpit-in-Court at Whitehall.

unnamed theatre in the collections of Worcester College, Oxford.[35] Subsequently identified as being the work of Inigo Jones by John Harris, the drawings were then linked to the Phoenix by Iain Mackintosh, who observed how a design for William Davenant's *The Siege of Rhodes* fitted exactly the dimensions of the theatre stage.[36] The argument for the drawings representing the Phoenix and being the work of Inigo Jones became widely accepted,[37] but the association of either theatre or architect has since been disproved.[38] While the drawings appear to share many of the features associated with Jacobean theatres, and may offer many useful clues for the organization of an indoor playhouse, we cannot rely on them as a true depiction of a playhouse of this period.

In the absence of the Worcester College drawings, the remaining documents that give evidence for the Phoenix building itself are somewhat depleted. Graham Barlow is persuasive in his argument that the playhouse is depicted as the square, three-gabled structure shown in Wenceslas Hollar's *View of West London*, and working from tenement records he shows that the building measured 40 feet square.[39] The plot was leased by Christopher Beeston from John Best on 9 August 1616, and consisted of 'all that edifices [*sic*] or building called the cockpits and the cockhouses and sheds thereunto adjoining'.[40] Beeston quickly sought the support of Queen Anne's Council to

35 Donald F. Rowan, 'A Neglected Jones/Webb Theatre Project, Part II: A Theatrical Missing Link', in David Galloway (ed.), *The Elizabethan Theatre II* (Toronto: Macmillan of Canada, 1969).

36 John Harris, Stephen Orgel and Roy Strong, *The King's Arcadia: Inigo Jones and the Stuart Court* (London: Arts Council of Great Britain, 1973); Iain Mackintosh, 'Inigo Jones – Theatre Architect', *TAB* 31 (1973), 99–105.

37 John Orrell was the strongest advocate, and his arguments were widely taken up and continue to be reaffirmed (John Orrell, *The Theatres of Inigo Jones and John Webb* (Cambridge University Press, 1985); see Gurr, *Shakespearean Stage*, pp. 160–4, and Sturgess, *Jacobean Private Theatre*, pp. 30–55). Correspondence held in the archives of Shakespeare's Globe records that Glynne Wickham preferred the argument that the designs showed Salisbury Court, while Richard Hosley and Don Rowan believed the drawings represented an unrealized project (Academic Committee records, Shakespeare's Globe Archives).

38 The dating and authorship of the drawings has been reassessed several times by Gordon Higgott, who now believes them to be the work of John Webb in around 1660. Higgott has outlined his reasoning in two papers given at the International Shakespeare Conference in Stratford in 2005 and at the Jacobean Indoor Playing Symposium at King's College, London, in 2012. A full article is in preparation, but the key points are outlined in a discussion with Martin White in the *Chamber of Demonstrations* DVD (Bristol: Ignition Films for the University of Bristol, 2009); see also John Harris and Gordon Higgott, *Inigo Jones: Complete Architectural Drawings* (New York: Drawing Centre, 1989). It should be noted that Graham Barlow had already provided evidence that the building shown in the Worcester College drawings could not have fitted on the plot occupied by the Phoenix (Barlow, 'Wenceslas Hollar and Christopher Beeston's Phoenix Theatre in Drury Lane', *Theatre Research International* 13.1 (1988), 30–44).

39 Barlow, 'Hollar and Beeston's Phoenix', p. 39.

40 Berry, 'Playhouses', pp. 626–7.

convert 'the cockpit in the fields into a playhouse'.[41] His company, the Queen's Men, moved to their new home sometime between a performance at the Red Bull on 23 February 1617 and Shrove Tuesday on 4 March, when during a performance rioting apprentices burnt the new playhouse to the ground.[42] Beeston immediately rebuilt his playhouse, and in doing so changed its name from the Cockpit to the Phoenix, a new playhouse having risen from the ashes of the old. The building was made of brick – in Middleton's *Masque of Heroes* Dr Almanack describes it in derisive terms: 'ruin the Cockpit, the / Poor players ne'er thrived in't: a my conscience, some/ Quean pissed upon the first brick'[43] – and its roof was tiled.[44]

Fewer plays written for the Cockpit seem to acknowledge the building in the manner of those at Blackfriars, but it appears the playhouse retained the circular form of the old cockpit. In Heywood's *Loves Maistresse* (1636), Apuleius describes a 'sphere spangled with all these stars', while the female prologue to *The Coronation* (1640) by Shirley or Fletcher tells the ladies in the audience how they 'make a harmony this sphere of love'.[45] However, the only clue to the design of the stage and *frons scenae* comes from Thomas Nabbes' *Covent Garden* (1638), which suggests the stage had three doors and a balcony.[46]

Towards a Jacobean ideal: classicism vs. 'Jacobethan'

The long-held belief that the Worcester College drawings were for a Jacobean theatre and in the hand of Inigo Jones was beguiling, not least as it seemed to connect a visionary architect, already closely involved with the theatrical world through his court masques and relationship with Ben Jonson, to an act of theatre design that anticipated the birth of a new classical architecture he encapsulated in 1619 with the Whitehall Banqueting House. That the Worcester College drawings have been reassigned to John Webb and the early 1660s has not diminished Jones' stature as the man who brought classicism to England. Yet Jones was a late convert. In the same year in which he embarked on his tour of Italy with the Earl of Arundel, aged just short of 40, he had devised designs for a masque by Thomas Campion for the marriage celebrations of Princess Elizabeth and the Elector Palatine which were a far remove

41 Ibid., p. 627.

42 Ibid., pp. 627–8. Shrove Tuesday was a traditional holiday for apprentices. Bentley notes that rioting and destruction on the occasion were common enough, but the holiday in 1616/17 was 'particularly distinguished' (*Jacobean and Caroline Stage*, vol. VI, p. 54).

43 Berry, 'Playhouses', p. 630.

44 Report by Edward Sherburne, 8 March 1617. Ibid., p. 629.

45 Ibid., p. 630.

46 Ibid.

from the 'correct form' he would return to impose. Campion's account of Jones' design conjures something far more decadent:

> The wood was insensibly changed with ornaments of architecture which filled all the end of the house and seemed to be all of goldsmiths work. The first order consisted of pilasters all of gold set with rubies, saphyres, emeralds, opals and such like. The capitals were composed and of a new invention; over this was a bastard order with cartouches reversed coming from the capitals of every pilaster, which made the upper part rich and full of ornament.[47]

While Jones returned from Italy a convert to the teachings of Palladio and Scamozzi, it took many years for his ideas to be taken up more widely, and during the first half of the seventeenth century few buildings were commissioned in the classical vein.[48] James I's reign was an era of great house-building, yet not one of them complied with classical ideals. Instead, they built on a tradition of design and construction that had flourished during Elizabeth's reign, and which employed a 'Jacobethan' decoration aesthetic that was ornate, excessive and full of life.[49] Robert Smythson, the architect who made his name during Elizabeth's reign with designs for houses such as Wollaton Hall, Nottinghamshire, and Hardwick Hall, Derbyshire, maintained his popularity well into James' reign, particularly in the north of the country. Burton Agnes Hall, near Driffield in the East Riding of Yorkshire and built for Sir Henry Griffith in 1601–10, reflects Smythson's 'perfect' expression of 'the Jacobean paradox of intense decorative richness ... contained within a native simplicity of outward forms'.[50] Griffith's craftsmen worked with wood, plaster and alabaster to produce decoration that Sir Nikolaus Pevsner deemed 'crazily over-crowded',[51] but which to Sir Henry was richly allegorical, depicting Heaven, Hell, and countless biblical references that served to underpin the patron's religious beliefs and his conduct in life.

The design and decoration of houses like Burton Agnes offer a different vision of Jacobean style from Jones' classicism. That such an aesthetic might inform the interior of an archetypal Jacobean theatre is underscored by two

[47] Timothy Mowl, *Elizabethan and Jacobean Style* (London: Phaidon, 1993), p. 125.

[48] See Mowl's discussion of Jones' influence (or lack thereof), ibid., pp. 125–57.

[49] See Malcolm Airs, *The Tudor and Jacobean Country House* (Stroud: Allan Sutton, 1995); Mark Girouard, *Robert Smythson and the Elizabethan Country House* (New Haven and London: Yale University Press, 1983); *Elizabethan Architecture: its Rise and Fall, 1560–1640* (New Haven and London: Yale University Press, 2009); John Summerson, *Architecture in Britain 1530–1830* (New Haven and London: Yale University Press, 1993).

[50] Mowl, *Elizabethan and Jacobean Style*, p. 129.

[51] Nikolaus Pevsner and David Neave, *Yorkshire: York and the East Riding* (2nd edn; New Haven and London: Yale University Press, 1995), p. 368.

great houses built by two of James' most senior advisors: Hatfield House, built in 1611 by Robert Cecil, 1st Earl of Salisbury and chief minister to the king, and Audley End, built in 1603–14 by the 1st Earl of Suffolk and Lord Treasurer, Thomas Howard. Both houses contain extravagant halls which are decorated in the height of Jacobethan decadence, despite the status of halls having started to decline as Jacobean aristocratic families retreated into private quarters. Each hall boasts a spectacular screen, topped with ornate, overhanging galleries and with either one or two grand doorways, and in these halls masques and plays were performed for the entertainment of the family and their visitors. Timothy Mowl has argued that the screen at Audley End 'should be considered as a permanent stage set for it has all the extrovert qualities that were soon to become standard in the interior of the theatre'.[52] Mowl is somewhat hyperbolic, given how little is actually known about theatre interiors, but the halls and their screens certainly offered many of the features that a company of players might have required for a performance. It is not difficult to imagine that a company might want to replicate a similar space and aesthetic in their own playhouses.

We can take a step closer to a building that housed performance by returning to London, and to the Jacobean Banqueting House at Whitehall visited by Orazio Busino and the Venetian ambassador in 1618. On his arrival at Whitehall in 1604, James I embarked on an extensive and expensive programme of new building and renovation, and the surviving records offer a wealth of information about the materials used to construct and decorate the palace complex. The old Banqueting House, built by Elizabeth in 1581 as a temporary structure, had survived a quarter of a century but was by now decrepit. James appointed the architect Robert Stickells to design a new edifice on the site of the Elizabethan building, making it suitable for the courtly masques and entertainments it was likely to host. It may not have been the wisest choice. Stickells was a devotee of architectural theory and based his design on his understanding of the 'Egyptian' hall described by Vitruvius. As Vitruvius' text was not illustrated, Stickells may well have been inspired by a Dutch engraving by the designer

[52] Mowl, *Elizabethan and Jacobean Style*, p. 143. Alan Nelson's seminal work *Early Cambridge Theatres* offers a direct counter to this argument, where he shows that stages erected for the performances of college plays were situated at the high end of the hall, away from the hall screen and service rooms at the low end of the building. However, as I have argued in my doctoral thesis, while Nelson's observations are sound for the specific cases of the university colleges, there is equally strong evidence for players using the low ends of halls, and the hall screens situated there, in civic corporation guildhalls across the country. As such, there is no reason why we should not look towards surviving hall screens, in guildhalls or in high-status buildings such as Audley End, as examples of what might have been constructed in the London indoor playhouses.

Hans Vredeman de Vries, 'Ionica super Dorica', which shows a large open space surrounded by colonnades and galleries in classical orders. However, what should have been a light, spacious room well suited to the masques and entertainments it was to host was transformed into a dark, cluttered space, where a forest of columns obscured not only sight-lines but windows. The king was furious, and Stickells never worked for the crown again. Nevertheless, the first masque was held in the completed Banqueting House in January 1608 and it continued to be the focus of courtly entertainments until it was destroyed by fire eleven years later.[53]

The Jacobean Banqueting House has always been overshadowed by Inigo Jones' replacement, and has received less attention from architectural historians in pursuit of classical architectural merit.[54] However, the catalogue of expenditure for the building project contained in the account of works offers a wealth of information to supplement the observations recorded by Busino. The accounts describe an elaborate building of wood and stone, with turned wooden Ionic and Doric columns with carved and gilded capitals and bases. The hall was decorated with detailed carvings of the royal arms and other badges, depictions of 'Artillarye and Muiscke',[55] and of an elaborate architrave frieze running around, set about with 'diverse kinds of beastes armes pendaunte and roses'.[56] At some point a great stage was constructed 'all the height of the Banquetting house', with mechanisms that operated 'greate gates and turning doores belowe and a globe and sondry seates above for the Queen and Ladies to sitt on and to be turned rounde aboute'.[57] It is difficult say how permanent a feature the stage was – but the description of a great quantity of railed degrees set up on each side of the hall and their later dismantling suggests an occasional, rather than permanent, presence.

These records provide useful descriptions of decoration, and are coupled with lists of materials that are invaluable when thinking about the materials for an indoor theatre. Frustratingly, the accounts do not distinguish between tools and materials used for the Banqueting House itself and those used elsewhere for other Whitehall works – at the same time workmen were replacing the floor of the oven in the great 'bakehouse', renewing battlements, reflooring the tennis court floor and erecting degrees for the wedding of Lord Haye, rebuilding the stables and tilt-yard, and renovating rooms for the Earls of Salisbury and Warwick, to name just a few of the

53 S. Thurley, *Whitehall Palace* (London: Merrel Publishers and Historic Royal Palaces, 2008), pp. 48–9.

54 Howard Colvin's *History of the King's Works* (6 vols.; London: HMSO, 1963–83) remains the most comprehensive documentary survey of the palace.

55 PRO E 351/3242, fo. 4r. 56 PRO E 351/3243, fo. 5r. 57 Ibid.

projects.[58] Even so, the range of materials is considerable. Stone is divided in Oxfordshire, Yorkshire, Gloucestershire, Dorsetshire, Purbeck marble, Rigatestone, Caveston, Ragstone and paving stone,[59] while timber is sorted by how it is to be used – planks, boards, quarter joists and rafters, and so on.[60] There are frequent references to payments made to John Decreete, Sergeant Painter, for 'pryming and layering in leade coloure in oyle',[61] and for the wherewithal to make the paint itself – ochre, black, white and russet pigment is ordered by the pound, and oil to mix it in by the pint.[62]

However, it is the account of the payments to the craftsmen that must give us pause. Different levels of craftsmanship were rewarded according to the difficulty of the task and, presumably, the time it took to complete it, and it soon becomes evident that the delicate jobs of carving and joinery cost substantially more than carpentry. Thomas Stiff, carpenter, was paid 33s for making three frames and pendants, and his colleague Robert Hall was paid 23s for his work on three more. In comparison, the carver Sebastian Vickers was paid £45 for 'the garnishment of the dorricke freeze in the Banquetting house and for his dilligent attendunce in ordering the Ionick freeze'. The two joiners, Clement Chapman and Samuel Jeniver, were paid £312 for 614 yards of wainscoting. A similar, though less extreme, discrepancy is seen in the payments for plasterwork. The King's Plasterer, Richard Dungan, is paid 5s the yard for plastering 677 square yards of the Banqueting House roof 'being wrought with deepe pendauntes and compartiments', but only 3s 6d the yard for 388 yards of the upper ceiling of two galleries and the lower end of the Banqueting House 'with a plaine frett'.[63]

This kind of expenditure is matched in the records for Hatfield House. The accounts do not go into much detail, nor is it clear exactly what work was accomplished when. However, these records serve to give us an idea as to the scale of what was being undertaken. To take as an example the accounts for one year, Michaelmas 1611/12, we can see that the carver John Bucke charged £162 17s 10d for his work, while the painter Rowland Bucket charged £417 9s 1d for painting and gilding, and Samuel Jeniver, having finished his work at Whitehall, charged £642 13s 8d for his joinery.[64]

[58] PRO E 351/3242, fo. 4r; PRO E 351/3243, fos. 4v–5r.
[59] PRO E 351/3242, fo. 5v; PRO E 351/3243, fo. 6v. [60] PRO E 351/3242, fo. 5r.
[61] PRO E 351/3243, fo. 10r. [62] PRO E 351/3242, fo. 7r. [63] PRO E 351/3243, fo. 12v.
[64] Accounts G/13 BHH/157–179. I am grateful to Vicki Perry, head of archives at Hatfield House, for allowing me access to transcripts of the relevant documents. It is notoriously difficult to convert early modern finances into their modern equivalent: the period was one of rapid inflation and changing prices. Labour was cheap while raw materials were expensive, in direct contrast to what we might expect today. According to the National Archive currency converter (www.nationalarchives.gov.uk/

It is clearly not fair to compare strictly the relative costs of different crafts from such examples. But what is clear is that to build on the scale of the Banqueting House, Hatfield or Audley End, and to decorate them as sumptuously as they were, required an eye-watering sum of money. Only the richest aristocrats, and the king, could afford such buildings. Audley End cost Thomas Howard £200,000 to build, which he financed through bribes collected as Lord Chamberlain[65] and four years of embezzlement during his tenure as Lord Treasurer (for which act he was sent to the Tower, although he was subsequently released and fined a mere fraction, only £7000, by King James).[66]

But theatre companies were not in possession of a royal fortune. If we are to imagine a Jacobean theatre built to a more modest standard, we must also consider the means of those who might have originally built it. What kind of financial outlay would a company or impresario make? We have little evidence for the kind of expenditure made by Burbage or Beeston when converting the Blackfriars and Phoenix. Burbage paid £600 for the purchase of the Blackfriars site, but how much he spent turning it into a playhouse is not clear. However, it is hardly likely that either man had the same resources to build something as ornate as the Banqueting House or Hatfield.

We must consider that a Jacobean theatre was a less ornate affair, although we can only speculate to what level it was decorated. It seems unlikely that such a space was heavily ornamented with carving and wainscoting throughout; instead the most elaborate decoration might be reserved for the most significant visual aspects of the building, such as the *frons scenae*. The auditorium, and particularly the galleries, may well have been altogether plainer affairs, with a strong resemblance to such as those we see at the reconstructed Globe, or in the photos of the many galleried coaching houses which survived until the late nineteenth century.[67] For the *frons*, the elaborate

currency), £1 in 1590 is the equivalent to £125.29 in 2005; the same sum in 1610 drops to £97.88. By one measure, then, Bucke, Bucket and Jeniver received around £15,944, £40,860 and £62,906 respectively. However, it is perhaps more useful to compare the relative buying power of such sums, and the annual salaries of various professions. Jeniver's fee equates to a single craftsman working 12,853 days, or 36 years' salary. A minor parson or a schoolteacher might expect to earn between £10 and £30 a year: it would take them anywhere between 21 and 64 years to earn Jeniver's fee for his work at Hatfield. If a modern teacher were on a salary of, say, £30,000, Jeniver received a sum nearer £1.9 million in today's money. See also J. L. Forgeng, *Daily Life in Elizabethan England* (Santa Barbara, CA: ABC-CLIO, 2010), pp. 99–104.

65 Howard gained the position following the death of George Carey, 2nd Baron Hunsdon and the patron of Shakespeare's company; he held it until 1613.

66 Mowl, *Elizabethan and Jacobean Style*, p. 140.

67 The photos, many taken by the Society for Photographing Relics of Old London in the 1880s, are housed in the collections of the London Metropolitan Archive, SC/GL/PHO/C/023/1/2–7, SC/GL/NOB/C/023–023/1, SC/GL/NOB/C/023/1–9. Some may be accessed through http://collage.cityoflondon.gov.uk/collage/app

hall screens suggested by Hatfield and Audley End may be less appropriate than something similar to the church screens found at Dore Abbey, Herefordshire, and St John the Evangelist, Leeds. The Dore Abbey screen, constructed by John Abel, the king's carpenter, a few years after James' death, demonstrates the kind of ornamentation that can be achieved through carpentry alone, while the 1634 carved and gilded screen at St John's demonstrates a focus of design without the overwrought excess of the greater houses.

Building a Jacobean ideal

It is the goal of the modern Shakespeare's Globe to build an indoor theatre that is a simulacrum of a Jacobean playhouse, and to produce a space that Shakespeare would have recognized. To do so is an exercise that demands a careful appraisal of the wider evidence for Jacobean buildings, and a willingness to draw on examples that contain analogous features, but are not in themselves theatres or built with theatrical pursuits primarily in mind. It is clear that the Jacobean 'ideal' remained firmly vernacular, and that we should not expect an indoor playhouse of the early seventeenth century to have followed the classical inclinations Inigo Jones would later impose on his architecture. Rather, a Jacobean theatre would express the culmination of the aesthetic tastes of the sixteenth and early seventeenth centuries. The extent to which such an aesthetic was realized in a playhouse's decoration, however, hinges on what we believe a company might have been willing to spend. Nevertheless, we can see from the £600 sum that Burbage originally spent to acquire the Blackfriars, and the repeated attempts by other theatre impresarios to open indoor venues, that indoor playhouses represented at least the potential for a good investment, and one from which their owners stood to make a good return. Even if Burbage and his competitors would not have been able to stretch as far as the royal purse, they nevertheless would have aspired and strived towards the kind of work found in the elite buildings, and may well have achieved an interior that was similar in effect, if not in substance.

The resulting spaces clearly differentiated themselves from the outdoor amphitheatres, and the move indoors engendered significant changes in repertory and performance. The architectural decadence seen in the Jacobean Banqueting House – with its golden pilasters set with precious stones – chimes with Epicure Mammon's dream of splendid food and comforts in Ben Jonson's *The Alchemist*, whose food 'shall all come in, in Indian shells, / Dishes of agate set in gold, and studded / With emeralds, sapphires, hyacinths and rubies'. It is on the indoor stage, with its highly ornate and decorated interior, that so much of the Jacobean repertoire begins to make sense.

CHAPTER 4

Continuities and innovations in staging

Mariko Ichikawa

Taking into account what we know in general terms about contemporary performance practice, this chapter considers how the physical features of the Blackfriars theatre might have influenced the plays acted there.[1] It will involve a concentration in particular on its stage and auditorium. I will deal mainly with plays written by Shakespeare, Fletcher and their fellow dramatists for the King's Men after the company's acquisition of the Blackfriars in 1608, though I will refer also to earlier plays written for the Theatre or the Globe.[2]

Although we do not know the precise size and design of either the Globe or the Blackfriars stage, we can work back from such information as we do have. The Fortune playhouse had a stage 43 feet (13.1 metres) wide and 27 feet 6 inches (8.4 metres) deep, if the generally accepted interpretation of the Fortune contract is correct;[3] the Globe stage, on which it was modelled, would probably have been about the same size. In a legal deposition of 1609, the Blackfriars theatre is said to have measured 66 feet (20.1 metres) by 46 feet (14 metres). This space would probably have contained a tiring-house and a stage, flanked with boxes, at one end, as well as galleries and seats in front. Given these various requirements, Richard Hosley proposes a

I wish to thank Andrew Gurr, Franklin Hildy and Raymond Powell for their kind help and useful advice at various stages of this chapter.

[1] In this chapter I refer to the theatre built by James Burbage in the Blackfriars precinct in 1596 simply as the Blackfriars, and not as the second Blackfriars.

[2] Quotations from Shakespeare are taken from *The First Folio of Shakespeare: The Norton Facsimile*, ed. Charlton Hinman (2nd edn; New York: W. W. Norton, 1996) and *Shakespeare's Plays in Quarto: A Facsimile Edition of Copies Mainly from the Henry E. Huntington Library*, ed. Michael J. B. Allen and Kenneth Muir (Berkeley: University of California Press, 1981). Folio texts are cited by the through-line numbers (TLN) provided in the *Norton Facsimile*; Quarto texts are cited by signatures. Act–scene–line references are those of the New Cambridge Shakespeare editions (Cambridge University Press, 1984 onwards). Citations from non-Shakespearean plays, either in facsimile or in the original printed form, use signatures; references to Malone Society Reprints use the TLN provided in the editions.

[3] This estimate has been questioned by some scholars. See John Orrell, 'Beyond the Rose: Design Problems for the Globe Reconstruction', in Franklin J. Hildy (ed.), *New Issues in the Reconstruction of Shakespeare's Theatre* (New York: Peter Lang, 1990), pp. 95–134 (pp. 111–16); Franklin J. Hildy, 'Reconstructing Shakespeare's Theatre', in *New Issues*, pp. 1–37 (pp. 13–17).

possible stage size of 29 feet (8.8 metres) across and 18 feet 6 inches (5.6 metres) deep, while Keith Sturgess suggests a stage 30 feet (9.1 metres) by 23 feet (7 metres).[4] These suggestions would imply that the Blackfriars stage was about half the size of the Globe stage. There were, nevertheless, certain similarities. Although the Blackfriars stage had no roof supported by posts, the other stage facilities were broadly the same; the requirements of plays performed at the Blackfriars suggest that its stage had two doors in the façade, a discovery space between them, a balcony above, a trapdoor to the space below and a descent machine.

In private theatres such as the Blackfriars and the Cockpit, gallants sat on the stage itself, thus reducing the players' acting space.[5] As to where exactly they were on the stage, the account of a quarrel that took place at Blackfriars in 1632 between Lord Thurles and Captain Essex appears to suggest that they sat in front of the boxes flanking the stage, that is, on the sides of the stage.[6] In indoor playhouses, pauses in the performance were essential to give time for stage attendants to trim the candles. The acquisition of the Blackfriars theatre led to a great change in the company's performance practices: the King's Men adopted the practice of *entr'acte* music for performances at both the Blackfriars and Globe. The question we need to address here is: in what way did the smaller size of the stage and auditorium, the presence of stage-sitters and the use of act intervals influence the presentation of plays acted at Blackfriars?

In early modern commercial theatres, whether public or private, the stage was almost entirely surrounded by the auditorium, and so actors

4 Richard Hosley, 'A Reconstruction of the Second Blackfriars', in David Galloway (ed.), *The Elizabethan Theatre II* (Toronto: Macmillan of Canada, 1970), pp. 74–88 (p. 80); Keith Sturgess, *Jacobean Private Theatre* (London: Routledge & Kegan Paul, 1987), pp. 39–40. Earlier, Irwin Smith had assumed that the length of 66 feet referred only to the stage and auditorium and did not include the tiring-house. In addition, he took the view that there were no boxes at the sides of the stage but instead two rows of stage-sitters at each side. As a result, he had proposed a possible stage depth of 22 feet and a 'usable platform width of 34 feet'. Irwin Smith, *Shakespeare's Blackfriars Playhouse: Its History and its Design* (London: Peter Owen, 1964), p. 309.

5 It should be noted that some public playhouses including the Globe may have, at least occasionally if not regularly, allowed gallants to sit on the stage. See Glynne Wickham, *Early English Stages, 1300–1660* (3 vols.; London: Routledge & Kegan Paul, 1959–1981), vol. II, part 2, pp. 178–82; Leslie Thomson, 'Playgoers on the Outdoor Stages of Early Modern London', *Theatre Notebook* 64 (2010), 3–11.

6 'This captain attending and accompanying my Lady of Essex in a box in the playhouse at the Blackfriars, the said lord, coming upon the stage, stood before them and hindered their sight. Captain Essex told his lordship they had paid for their places as well as he and therefore entreated him not to deprive them of the benefit of it. Whereupon the lord stood up yet higher and hindered more their sight.' Glynne Wickham, Herbert Berry and William Ingram (eds.), *English Professional Theatre, 1530–1660* (Cambridge University Press, 2000), p. 527. Herbert Berry's earlier interpretation of this incident, to the effect that the boxes were not merely contiguous and level with the stage but actually behind it, is extremely hard to accept. See Herbert Berry, 'The Stage and Boxes at Blackfriars', *Studies in Philology* 63 (1966), 163–86 (169–77).

would have used the front part of the stage as the main acting area. Most entrances and exits were made through the flanking doors in the tiring-house façade. When entering or exiting, major characters, therefore, usually walked the distance between a stage door and front stage. In Shakespeare's plays, most of which were written for open-air theatres, characters with important speaking parts are generally allowed about three or four lines to complete the move.[7] *Othello*, a Globe play, offers an instance where Iago expresses his malicious intentions towards Othello in three and a half lines, filling the time needed for the entering Othello to join him.

> IAGO . . .
> *Enter* OTHELLO.
> Looke where he comes: Not Poppy, nor Mandragora,
> Nor all the drowsie Syrrups of the world
> Shall euer medicine thee to that sweete sleepe
> Which thou owd'st yesterday.
> OTHELLO Ha, ha, false to mee?
> (F1, TLN 1970–5; 3.3.330–4)

The smaller stage of the Blackfriars theatre would have caused Shakespeare to reconsider his habit of writing three- or four-line speeches to allow for characters' entrances and exits.

Andrew Gurr observes that *The Tempest* is Shakespeare's first play indubitably written for the Blackfriars rather than the Globe,[8] and the characters' arrivals and departures in this play show that Shakespeare continued to take the depth of the stage into consideration; it was merely a matter now of reducing the amount of time needed for entrances and exits. Consider, for example, the concluding passage of 2.1:

> ALONSO Lead off this ground & let's make further search
> For my poore sonne.
> GONZALO Heauens keepe him from these Beasts:
> For he is sure i'th Island.
> ALONSO Lead away.
> ARIEL *Prospero* my Lord, shall know what I haue done.
> So (King) goe safely on to seeke thy Son.
> *Exeunt.*
> (F1, TLN 1030–6; 2.1.321–5)

[7] For a full discussion of this matter, see Mariko Ichikawa, *Shakespearean Entrances* (Basingstoke: Palgrave Macmillan, 2002), ch. 3.

[8] Andrew Gurr, '*The Tempest*'s Tempest at Blackfriars', *Shakespeare Survey* 41 (1989), 91–102 (93).

Despite the stage direction '*Exeunt*' marked at the end of the scene, Alonso, Gonzalo and other shipwrecked people would begin to leave the stage after Alonso has ordered Gonzalo to 'Lead away'. Shakespeare's intention would seem to be that Alonso should make his heavy-hearted exit with the others while Ariel is delivering his sympathetic scene-closing couplet. This example and others like it suggest that Shakespeare was developing a new practice of allowing about two lines, rather than three or four, for entrances and exits.

A reduced time for entrances may have become the norm in writing for the Blackfriars, but Shakespeare, as always, treated the matter flexibly, not least because plays written primarily for the Blackfriars were very often also put on at the Globe. An example of a very leisurely arrival can be seen in the next scene of *The Tempest*. While Caliban is cursing Prospero, Trinculo makes his first appearance:

> CALIBAN . . .
> Lo, now Lo,
> *Enter* TRINCULO.
> Here comes a Spirit of his, and to torment me
> For bringing wood in slowly: I'le fall flat,
> Perchance he will not minde me.
> TRINCULO Here's neither bush, nor shrub to beare off any weather at all: and another Storme brewing, I heare it sing ith' winde: yond same blacke cloud, yond huge one, lookes like a foule bumbard that would shed his licquor: if it should thunder, as it did before, I know not where to hide my head: yond same cloud cannot choose but fall by paile-fuls. What haue we here, a man, or a fish?
> (TLN 1053–64; 2.2.14–23)

Trinculo's role in the play is essentially comic, and his arrival marks a shift of tone from the emotional intensities of the opening scenes. Instead of the usual three lines before he notices Caliban, he is allowed a total of about ten. As a result, the actor playing the part is given scope to introduce comic business as he looks around and maybe gestures languidly at the sky while making his slow approach to the front of the stage where Caliban lies face down in an ineffectual attempt at self-concealment. An alternative staging possibility, however, is that, following Shakespeare's usual practice, Trinculo reaches Caliban by the end of Caliban's speech. A comic effect is instantly created before he even opens his mouth by his failure to notice the fearful Caliban at his feet, and this is then reinforced by the rambling, self-absorbed meteorological discourse of his first six and a half lines. Shakespeare regarded entrances and exits as significant actions in the Blackfriars, no less than at the Globe, but his handling of these moments always allowed for the possibility of fresh and inventive variations.

The Blackfriars stage was much narrower than the Globe's, and the presence of stage-sitters would have reduced the width of the playing area, since they sat at the sides of the stage. This would have affected actors' positions, especially in those scenes where a character or group of characters had to remain at a distance from another character or group. But since indoor theatre plays, including Blackfriars plays by Jonson, Massinger and Davenant, contain quite a few instances where a character is directed to step or stand aside,[9] it looks on the face of it that we should take '*aside*' literally and accept that dramatists used side positions despite the presence there of gallants.

There is, however, one example where, despite a stage direction for a character to step aside, the character would have moved to the upper level. In an eavesdropping scene (4.2) in Massinger's *The Renegado*, performed by the Lady Elizabeth's Men at the Cockpit in Drury Lane, Asambeg tells Paulina to go to the upper level: 'Aboue you shall obserue all' (Q1, I1r). The stage direction for her at this point reads 'PAUL. *steps aside*' (I1r). Since, however, at the end of the scene Asambeg orders her to 'descend' (I3v), the clear implication is that she must have moved to the upper level. On the discrepancy between dialogue and stage direction, Michael Neill cites John Jowett's view that 'a change of intention about the staging of the scene may have been involved, and that the abruptness of Asambeg's commands indicates that they may have been tacked on once it was decided that it was preferable to have Paulina observe the remainder of the scene from above – perhaps in a deliberate recollection of Asambeg's and Mustapha's eavesdropping from this position in 3.5.68ff ["*Asambeg and Musta. aboue*" (G4v)]'.[10] One reason for locating the eavesdroppers '*aboue*' in 3.5 and 4.2 may have been that, in indoor theatres, the upper playing area was simply a better location for observers than a side position on the stage where gallants were sitting.

This fact may have influenced the staging of *The Tempest* 3.1. In this scene, Prospero observes the meeting of Miranda and Ferdinand. Although the stage direction only says '*Enter* MIRANDA *and* PROSPERO' (F1, TLN 1250–1; 3.1.15), Prospero would enter second and position himself at a distance from the young couple. Had the first performance been at the Globe, he could have stood behind a stage post, but the Blackfriars stage had no roof supported by pillars. It is possible but unlikely that he would

9 Examples include: 'Madrigal *steps aside with* Broker' (Jonson, *The Staple of News* F2, D2r); '*Parthenius goes off the rest stand aside*' (Massinger, *The Roman Actor* Q1, K3r); '*They step aside, whilst he cals betweene the Hangings*' (Davenant, *The Wits* Q1, B2r).

10 Michael Neill (ed.), *The Renegado* (London: A&C Black, 2010), p. 190, n.

eavesdrop from behind the curtains covering the central discovery space. He might enter after Miranda and remain near the entry door. But he has to speak the speech at the end of the scene, as Miranda and Ferdinand exit separately, most probably by opposing doors:

> MIRANDA And mine, with my heart in't; and now farewel
> Till halfe an houre hence.
> FERDINAND A thousand, thousand.
>
> *Exeunt.*
>
> PROSPERO So glad of this as they I cannot be,
> Who are surpriz'd with all; but my reioycing
> At nothing can be more:
>
> (TLN 1342–7; 3.1.92–6)

Unless he is dressed in a special coat so as to suggest that he is invisible to the other characters, he would have avoided taking a position near the tiring-house façade. As some editors suggest, therefore, Prospero might have appeared on the upper playing level and observed the young couple from there.[11] Although his presence would not draw the audience's attention until his first words sixteen lines after his entrance ('Poore worme thou art infected, / This visitation shewes it' [TLN 1272–3; 3.1.32–3]), the upper location would have constituted an appropriate symbol of his superior relation to Miranda and Ferdinand.

In Blackfriars plays, the distribution of different characters or groups of characters is frequently not across the stage from the centre to the side, or from one side to the other, but rather from the front to the back. One likely reason for this is that the area from front to back is visually uncluttered by the gallants lounging on the sides, where they might prove a distraction. Plays written or co-written by Fletcher offer many instances where an entering character does not come forward but remains either just behind or on the threshold of the stage door, as indicated by the following stage directions:

> *Enter to the doore* JULIO and ANGILO.
> (Fletcher [with Beaumont?], *The Captain* F1, 2H2r)
>
> *Enter* JUDAS *and his people to the door.*
> (Fletcher, *Bonduca* F1, 4H3v)
>
> *Enter* LA-WRIT, *and a* GENTLEMAN *at the dore.*
> (Fletcher and Massinger, *The Little French Lawyer* F1, I3r)

11 See Virginia Mason Vaughan and Alden T. Vaughan (eds.), *The Tempest* (Walton-on-Thames: Thomas Nelson, 1999), p. 219, n.; David Lindley (ed.), *The Tempest* (Cambridge University Press, 2002), p. 157, n.

The third direction, which indicates that only the second character remains '*at the dore*', is in a scene commonly ascribed to Fletcher.[12] Most of Fletcher's plays, written for the King's Men, would have been performed at both the Blackfriars and Globe, but they might have been written with the Blackfriars primarily in mind. This does not imply that positions around the threshold of stage doors were not used in performances at the Globe and other outdoor theatres; in fact outdoor theatre plays also offer quite a few instances where actors would or should take such positions.[13] But the specific examples just cited nevertheless appear to suggest that, in writing for the Blackfriars, Fletcher and his co-dramatists were particularly keen on keeping characters around the threshold of stage doors, and its effect would have been to favour a front-to-back stage distribution of the various characters rather than one from side to side.

In order to see how the smaller, indoor stage might have influenced both the establishment of a scene's location and the use of stage facilities (especially the use of stage doors), let us compare two tomb scenes in which a young woman is falsely believed to be dead. The first is from *Romeo and Juliet*, acted by the Lord Chamberlain's Men, probably first at the Theatre and then at the Curtain, and the second is from *The Knight of Malta*, written by Fletcher, Field and Massinger and acted by the King's Men at Blackfriars.

The last scene of *Romeo and Juliet* (5.3) is very long, lasting over three hundred lines. It appears to take place in a churchyard in which there is a tomb belonging to the house of Capulet. Paris and his page are the first to arrive, followed by Romeo and Balthasar, and finally Friar Lawrence. Paris, Romeo and the Friar would proceed to the central part of the stage, because either the discovery space or the stage trap or, perhaps, a curtained bed thrust out from the discovery place, would have been used as Juliet's tomb.[14] They treat the central and marginal areas of the stage as different parts of the churchyard, as indicated in the Friar's words to Balthasar:

> Blisse be vpon you. Tell me good my friend
> What torch is yond that vainly lends his light

[12] For the authorship of the play, see Robert Kean Turner (ed.), *The Little French Lawyer*, in Fredson Bowers (gen. ed.), *The Dramatic Works in the Beaumont and Fletcher Canon* (10 vols.; Cambridge University Press, 1966–96), vol. IX, pp. 329–30.

[13] For a detailed discussion of this and related matters, see Mariko Ichikawa, *The Shakespearean Stage Space* (Cambridge University Press, 2012), ch. 2.

[14] For useful discussions of the staging of Juliet's tomb, see Leslie Thomson, '"With patient ears attend": *Romeo and Juliet* on the Elizabethan Stage', *Studies in Philology* 92 (1995), 230–47 (240, 242); Alan C. Dessen, *Recovering Shakespeare's Vocabulary* (Cambridge University Press, 1995), pp. 176–95; Andrew Gurr, 'The Date and the Expected Venue of *Romeo and Juliet*', *Shakespeare Survey* 49 (1996), 15–25 (24).

To grubs and elylesse sculles: as I discerne,
It burneth in the *Capels* monument.
. . .
Go with me to the Vault.

(Q2, L3v; 5.3.124–7, 131)

Since there is nothing that marks the boundary between the central and marginal areas, the division of the stage space would be more theoretical than actual:[15] when the Friar approaches Juliet, the whole stage might now in effect represent the vault. For the stage space to have this degree of flexibility, the flanking doors would need to be kept open throughout and to remain entirely neutral; that is, they would have no realistic function within the world of the play. They would, however, contribute in both a practical and symbolic way to the start and end of the scene. Paris's entry with his page and Romeo's arrival with his man would have been made through different doors. Capulet's entrance with his wife later in the scene and Montague's entry with the news of his wife's death would also have been made through different doors. The structural correspondence of both sets of arrivals is, of course, overshadowed by their inevitable contrast, the former erupting into conflict and death, the latter offering a muted hope for the future.

The tomb scene in *The Knight of Malta* (4.2; a Fletcher scene)[16] is almost as long as *Romeo and Juliet* 5.3, but a major difference is that all the entrances and exits are made through only one of the stage doors. The reason for this is that, unlike the tomb scene in the earlier play, the door has a realistic function; it represents the entrance to the Temple of Saint John where Oriana has been laid to rest in the family monument. At the beginning of the scene, the knights Miranda and Norandine, accompanied by Miranda's servant Collonna, come to pray at the temple.

Enter MIRANDA, NORANDINE, COLLONNA.
COLLONNA Here sir I have got the Key, I borrowd it
Of him that keeps the Church, the door is open.
MIRANDA Look to the horses then, and please the fellow.
After a few devotions, i'le retire.
Be not far off, there may be some use of ye,
Give me the light: come friend, a few good prayers
Were not bestowd in vaine now, even from you sir.

(F1, 5L4v)

[15] Stage posts could have served as boundaries between the main and subordinate acting areas, but there is no evidence for a stage roof supported by posts either at the Theatre or at the Curtain.

[16] For the shares of the three dramatists in the play, see George Walton Williams (ed.), *The Knight of Malta*, in Bowers, *Dramatic Works, Beaumont and Fletcher Canon*, vol. VIII, pp. 347–8.

Despite the stage direction, '*Enter* MIRANDA, NORANDINE, COLLONNA', they do not enter at this point. The audience hears Collonna's voice from behind the door that represents the door of the temple; the door is then opened; Miranda dismisses his servant, and only he and Norandine come forward. They hear groans and find Oriana alive in the tomb. They summon Collonna, and the three men carry off the already awake but still faint Oriana, leaving the key in the keyhole of the door. Scarcely have they left the stage when the villainous knight Mountferrat and his servant Rocca arrive with Oriana's maid Abdella in order to steal Oriana's supposedly dead body. The leaving and entering characters use the same door, but the entering characters' speeches make it clear that although the two groups passed each other off stage, in the darkness they did not recognize each other:

> ROCCA The door's already open, the Key in it.
> MOUNTFERRAT What were those past by?
> ROCCA Some scout of Souldiers, I think.
>
> (5M1r)

Later in the scene, when Oriana's husband Gomera arrives with his page, he also identifies the door as that of the temple: 'Looke to the doore Boy: keep it fast' (5M1v).

In Shakespeare's tomb scene the setting is not that of an enclosed space; its status remains characteristically fluid and changeable, with the result that Paris at the beginning refers casually to the topography of the churchyard ('Vnder yond young Trees lay thee all along' [Q2, L1v, 5.3.3]), while a little later the entering Friar identifies Juliet's tomb and a torch over the Capulets' monument as being somewhere in the central part of the stage. In the second tomb scene, on the other hand, the stage space is both consistent and identifiable: the tiring-house wall serves to demarcate the inside of the temple from the outside. The former scene uses the two stage doors neutrally, making it possible for opposing characters to enter by both, while the latter uses only one of the doors, clearly representing the door of the temple. Whether in public or private theatres, dramatists were of course free to use one or both doors, realistically or neutrally, in whatever combination they chose. Fletcher's tomb scene appears to have been influenced, consciously or not, by the smaller size of the Blackfriars stage and the indoor theatre's distinctive atmosphere. In a scene located in an enclosed space such as this, the roofed candlelit Blackfriars would have had a significant atmospheric advantage over the open-air theatres where the actors played in broad daylight.

As Bruce Smith has persuasively argued, the acoustic environment of indoor theatres was altogether different from that of open-air theatres.[17] Evidence suggests that after the acquisition of the Blackfriars, the King's Men began to use quieter musical instruments such as cornets and recorders, following indoor theatre tradition (see Chapter 7 below). *The Two Noble Kinsmen*, a tragicomedy by Shakespeare and Fletcher, was most probably written specifically for the Blackfriars during the period between the burning of the Globe in 1613 and the completion of its reconstruction in 1614.[18] This play employs cornets frequently and some stage directions for fanfares ('*flourish*') specify the use of them: '*This short florish of Cornets*' (Q1, E4v; 2.5.0); '*Florish of Cornets*' (K3v; 5.1.5).[19] A fanfare of trumpets would have been too loud in the smaller, roofed theatre.

Many stage directions calling for '*still*', '*soft*', '*sad*' or '*solemn*' music can be found in plays written for performance at indoor theatres. This may be related to the size of the theatres as well as the genres of the plays. An analysis of stage directions shows that '*still*' or '*solemn*' music would often have involved recorders, as specified in the following examples:

> *Still Musicke of Records.*
> (*The Two Noble Kinsmen* Q1, L1v; 5.1.136)

> *Recorders: Sadly. / She dies. still Musicke aboue. / Cease Rec.*
> (Davenant, *The Cruel Brother* Q1, I1v)

> *Recorders or other solempne Musique playes them owt.*
> (Middleton, *The Second Maiden's Tragedy* MS, TLN 2454–5)

> *They sleepe, and a sweet solemne Musicke of Recorders is heard, then enter an Angel.*
> (Burnell, *Landgartha* Q1, I1r)

The first three examples are from Blackfriars plays. In the second example, the direction '*She dies. still Musicke aboue*' is most probably authorial and the two instructions mentioning recorders must be annotations marked by the company bookkeeper. As the third example suggests, other instruments would occasionally have been used for performing solemn or still music.

In *The Tempest*, music is an important element of the play's action, mostly related to the exercise of Prospero's magic power. This play offers three stage directions calling for '*solemn*' music and two for '*soft*' music. One of them invites particular comment:

17 Bruce R. Smith, *The Acoustic World of Early Modern England: Attending to the O-Factor* (University of Chicago Press, 1999), pp. 206–17.

18 See Lois Potter (ed.), *The Two Noble Kinsmen* (Walton-on-Thames: Thomas Nelson, 1997), p. 59.

19 For a comment on the use of cornets in the play, see Robert Kean Turner and Patricia Tatspaugh (eds.), *The Two Noble Kinsmen* (Cambridge University Press, 2012), p. 216.

> *Solemne and strange Musicke: and Prosper on the top (inuisible:) Enter seuerall strange shapes, bringing in a Banket; and dance about it with gentle actions of salutations, and inuiting the King, &c. to eate, they depart.*
>
> (F1, TLN 1535–8; 3.3.17)[20]

We should not be disconcerted by the reference to '*Solemne and strange Musicke*'. The phrase is not unique and crops up elsewhere, for instance in *A Warning for Fair Women*, acted by the Lord Chamberlain's Men, where we are told, '*Here some strange solemn musicke like belles is heard within*' (Q1, D1r). Despite the reference to '*belles*', there is no need to assume that some unusual musical instrument was used to provide the '*Solemne and strange Musicke*' in *The Tempest*. The precise phrasing of the stage direction may well be that of the F1 scribe Ralph Crane rather than Shakespeare,[21] and if so, he may have derived the strangeness of the music from Gonzalo's description of it as 'Maruellous sweet Musicke' (TLN 1541; 3.3.19). I therefore think that the heavenly music could have been played on nothing more exotic than recorders. As to where Prospero appeared while the music was being played, it has been suggested that '*the top*' referred to a further level above the stage balcony where the music room was situated.[22] But there is no evidence for a third level in the Blackfriars tiring-house.[23] Since the phrase seldom occurs in early modern stage directions, it seems unlikely that it was a technical term for a special location. More plausibly, Prospero, in an 'invisible' coat, would have appeared on the balcony in front of the musicians. It is true that he does not speak until about twenty lines after his entrance ('Honest Lord, / Thou hast said well' [TLN 1559–60; 3.3.34–5]), but from the moment he appears there, the music would draw the audience's attention to him and make them share his awareness of what is taking place below.

The use of the smaller theatre might well have affected the style of acting. As quieter instruments were fit for the venue, so quieter delivery of lines might have been adopted there. Jonson's *Epicoene*, written for the indoor theatre at Whitefriars, provides an interesting scene (2.5), where Morose meets Epicoene for the first time.

20 For the other four directions calling for solemn or soft music in *The Tempest*, see F1, TLN 862, 1616–18, 1716, 2008; 2.1.180, 3.3.82, 4.1.58, 5.1.57.

21 See John Jowett, 'New Created Creatures: Ralph Crane and the Stage Directions in *The Tempest*', *Shakespeare Survey* 36 (1983), 107–20 (114).

22 See Sturgess, *Jacobean Private Theatre*, p. 91; Stephen Orgel (ed.), *The Tempest* (Oxford University Press, 1987), p. 164, n.; Vaughan and Vaughan, *Tempest*, p. 235, n.

23 See Andrew Gurr, *The Shakespearean Stage: 1574–1642* (4th edn; Cambridge University Press, 2009), p. 195; Andrew Gurr, '*The Tempest*'s "Top"', *Notes & Queries* 257 (2012), 550–2.

MOROSE . . . Can you speake lady?
EPICOENE Iudge you, forsooth. *She speakes softly.*
MOROSE What say you, lady? speake out, I beseech you.
EPICOENE Iudge you, forsooth.
MOROSE O' my iudgement, a diuine softnes!

(F1, 2Z5r)

Morose cannot hear her very well and makes her speak the same words again. This pattern is repeated three times in the scene. She would probably speak all her six speeches in a very quiet voice so that she could charm Morose. Jonson knew that the audience could hear her speeches in the Whitefriars theatre. In indoor theatres a low-key, naturalistic mode of delivery was possible.

A similar point may be made about visual expressions. As Tiffany Stern notes, in the Blackfriars theatre minute elements of this kind may have become more important. Shakespeare and Fletcher's *Henry VIII* provides several stage directions for the face: '*The* CARDINALL *in his passage, fixeth his eye on* BUCK[ING]HAM, *and* BUCKINGHAM *on him, both full of disdaine*' (F1, 176–9; 1.1.114); '*Exit* KING, *frowning vpon the* CARDINALL, *the* NOBLES *throng after him smiling, and whispering*' (TLN 2080–1; 3.2.203).[24] High-paying spectators, seated either on or nearest the stage, could fully appreciate this kind of emotional expression. However, directions for the face can be found in earlier outdoor theatre plays as well: '*She reads the letter, frownes and stamps*' (*King Leir* Q1, E1r);[25] '*she wringing her hands, in teares departes*' (*A Warning for Fair Women* Q1, E3v); '*Exeunt.* GRIS. *and* BA. *grinning at him*' (Chettle, Dekker and Haughton, *Patient Grissil* Q1, K3r). In *Hamlet* 2.2, when reciting the 'rugged Pyrrhus' speech to Hamlet, the First Player might well have actually had 'teares in's eyes' (F1, TLN 1561; 2.2.477–8), as Polonius describes it, and the effect was sufficiently convincing for Hamlet to allude to it again at the beginning of his 'Hecuba' soliloquy: 'Teares in his eyes, distraction in's Aspect' (TLN 1595; 2.2.507). Even if very few members of the Globe audience could have seen actual tears, the First Player would have realistically communicated the effects of grief both in his face and in his movements. It is possible that the smaller size of the Blackfriars auditorium made a difference in allowing a

[24] Tiffany Stern, 'Taking Part: Actors and Audience on the Stage at Blackfriars', in Paul Menzer (ed.), *Inside Shakespeare: Essays on the Blackfriar's Stage* (Selinsgrove, PA: Susquehanna University Press, 2006), pp. 35–53 (p. 46).

[25] Henslowe lists performances of a 'kinge leare'/'Kinge leare' in 1594, when the Queen's Men and Sussex's Men were acting together at the Rose. See R. A. Foakes (ed.), *Henslowe's Diary* (2nd edn; Cambridge University Press, 2002), p. 21.

subtler mode of acting, but we must not assume that this would have been significantly different from what had been practised before, and continued to be practised, in the open-air theatres.[26]

Throughout most of his career, Shakespeare wrote his plays to be performed continuously, from start to finish, with no breaks between acts or scenes. Shakespearean scenes generally conclude with the exit of all the on-stage characters, the new scene opening with the entrance of new characters. This was essential for smooth scene changes: an immediate re-entrance of the same characters would give the wrong impression that the previous scene still continues, unless a fairly long pause comes between their exit and entrance. The adoption of the practice of *entr'acte* music naturally affected the structure of plays. In *The Tempest*, Prospero and Ariel leave the stage together at the end of Act 4 and enter together at the start of Act 5: '*Exeunt*' (F1, TLN 1944; 4.1.260); '*Enter* PROSPERO (*in his Magicke robes*) *and* ARIEL' (TLN 1946; 5.1.0). Shakespeare made use of the interval between the acts, which could give the impression that some length of time has passed in the fictional world between their exit and entrance. At the beginning of Act 5, Prospero asks, 'how's the day?' (TLN 1949; 5.1.3), and Ariel replies, 'On the sixt hower' (TLN 1950; 5.1.4). The act break also gave Prospero time to put on his magic robes off stage.

The interval between acts did not mean the disconnection of the audience from the dramatic world, and it was sometimes used to present in musical terms the event taking place in the play world during the time between the acts. In the Folio text of *King Lear*, which represents a post-1609 version, a stage direction marked near the end of Act 2 calls for '*Storme and Tempest*' (F1, TLN 1584; 2.4.277), and the opening stage direction of Act 3 reads '*Storme still. Enter* KENT, *and a* GENTLEMAN, *seuerally*' (TLN 1615; 3.1.0). It is very likely that sound effects representing strong winds, rain and thunder would have filled the interval between Acts 2 and 3.[27] Furthermore, act intervals were occasionally used to present fictional events in abbreviated form by means of a dumb-show device, as in the following example from a Blackfriars play: '*Here a passage ouer the Stage, while the Act is playing for the Marriage of* CHARALOIS *with* BEAUMELLE, *&c.*' (Field and Massinger, *The Fatal Dowry* Q1, F1r).

[26] For a similar view, see Daniel Seltzer, 'The Staging of the Last Plays', in John Russell Brown and Bernard Harris (eds.), *Later Shakespeare* (London: Edward Arnold, 1966), pp. 127–66 (pp. 139–41).

[27] For a useful comment on this example, see Gary Taylor, 'The Structure of Performance: Act-Intervals in the London Theatres, 1576–1642', in Gary Taylor and John Jowett, *Shakespeare Reshaped: 1616–1623* (Oxford: Clarendon Press, 1993), pp. 3–50 (pp. 49–50).

It is notable that the act divisions in *The Two Noble Kinsmen* match the intervals. In Act 3 all the scenes take place in the woods near Athens. In scenes 1, 3 and 6, Palamon's entries read as follows: '*Enter* PALAMON *as out of a Bush, with his Shackles*' (Q1, F2v; 3.1.30); '*Enter* PALAMON' (F4v; 3.3.1); '*Enter* PALAMON *from the Bush*' (G4r; 3.6.0). Despite the variations of the direction, he would make these entrances from the same place referred to as a 'bush'. Gary Taylor observes that 'Act 3 is . . . given a visible unity of place by the bush from which Palamon emerges in the first, third, and sixth scenes' and suggests that this property bush would be brought on stage during the interval between Acts 2 and 3 and removed during the interval between Acts 3 and 4.[28] Stage keepers would occasionally have placed or removed props during act intervals, but in the present case I am somewhat dubious about the use of a property bush. A major reason is that in the stage direction '*Enter* PALAMON *as out of a Bush*', which is in a Shakespeare scene, the inclusion of '*as*' implies that the bush was imaginary and not a real property.[29] As for the direction '*Enter* PALAMON *from the Bush*', from a Fletcher scene, the '*as*' may be implicit and so the direction may have been understood as '*Enter* PALAMON *as from the Bush*'.[30] Similarly, Beaumont and Fletcher's *Philaster*, performed at the Globe and Blackfriars, offers 'PHILASTER *creepes out of a Bush*' (Q2, I1v) in a Beaumont scene.[31] Suzanne Gossett notes that throughout Act 4 the scene moves about the woods and suggests that some representation of shrubbery might have been put on the stage.[32] Although the illustration on the title page of the Q1 text of *Philaster* shows Philaster creeping into the bushes, it appears not to derive from actual performances.[33] I think that in each instance Palamon/Philaster would have emerged from the curtained discovery space, which could well have represented the bushes. The use of a property bush remains a possibility but on the whole does not seem to be necessary in either play.

Since the stage was bare of scenery, at both public and private playhouses, the stage hangings could be useful in creating a specific mood or atmosphere. Several plays contain references to the practice of using black hangings for performances of tragedies. *A Warning for Fair Women*, for example,

28 Ibid., p. 42. See also Eugene M. Waith (ed.), *The Two Noble Kinsmen* (Oxford University Press, 1989), p. 131, n.; p. 166, n.

29 For the authorship of the play, see Turner and Tatspaugh, *Two Noble Kinsmen*, pp. 1–6.

30 For an important discussion of the function of '*Enter [as] in* . . .' and '*Enter [as] from* . . .' directions, see Dessen, *Recovering Shakespeare's Theatrical Vocabulary*, ch. 7.

31 For the two dramatists' shares, see Suzanne Gossett (ed.), *Philaster* (London: A&C Black, 2009), pp. 14–20.

32 Ibid., p. 199, n.

33 For a comment on the woodcut, see R. A. Foakes, *Illustrations of the English Stage: 1580–1642* (Stanford University Press, 1985), pp. 118–19.

has an induction in which History says to Comedy: 'Looke Comedie, I markt it not till now, / The stage is hung with blacke: and I perceiue / The Auditors preparde for Tragedie' (Q1, A3r). Andrew Gurr argues that 'this tradition of signalling how a play would end seems to have vanished when tragicomedy entered the repertory'. As he observes, 'Fletcher's plays, starting with *Philaster* at the Globe in 1609, depended on their ability to hold the audience in suspense until the surprise revelation of the ending.'[34] We have evidence that the hangings were occasionally changed during the performance. The quarto text of Massinger's *The City Madam* reproduces several instructions by the King's Men's bookkeeper, and one of the instructions reads '*Whil'st the Act Plays, the Foot-step, little Table, and Arras hung up for the Musicians*' (Q1, K1r). Although the musicians do not play music behind the arras until the third scene of Act 5 ('*Musick*' [L2v]; '*Sad musick*' [L3r]), it is hung up for them during the interval between Acts 4 and 5. Frederick Kiefer considers why such an instruction was needed if the central discovery space was already covered by hangings, and offers his view that 'The arras newly hung up probably portrays a figure or scene or colors in keeping with the dramatic action: the wondrous animation of the statues.'[35] To return to *The Two Noble Kinsmen*, it is tempting to speculate that during the interval between Acts 2 and 3 of the play, the stage keepers changed the hangings, fitting new ones that suited the forest setting more obviously.

In *The Tempest*, the curtained space would have been used at least twice, but the context and dramatic purpose for each use are so different that it is likely that the hangings were changed. In 1.2, Caliban makes his first appearance as if from his den ('*Enter* CALIBAN' [F1, TLN 458; 1.2.321]), and describes it as 'this hard Rocke' (TLN 482; 1.2.344). A cave could have been represented by either a discovery space or a trapdoor, but the fact that he speaks from '*within*' before making his entrance ('There's wood enough within' [TLN 451; 1.2.315]) confirms that the location of his rock-den is within the tiring-house. Although the play is full of spectacular events and shows, one of the most important takes place in 5.1, when 'PROSPERO *discouers* FERDINAND *and* MIRANDA, *playing at Chesse*' (TLN 2141–2; 5.1.171). The shift from Caliban's cave to Prospero's cell might well have involved a replacement of hangings that are nondescript, maybe even ragged and filthy, by more elegant and elaborate ones appropriate both to Prospero himself and to the virtuous natures of Ferdinand

34 Andrew Gurr, *The Shakespeare Company, 1594–1642* (Cambridge University Press, 2004), p. 46.

35 Frederick Kiefer, 'Curtains on the Shakespearean Stage', *Medieval and Renaissance Drama in England* 20 (2007), 151–86 (171).

and Miranda. Webster's *The Duchess of Malfi*, acted by the King's Men at both the Blackfriars and Globe, also has at least two scenes that require the use of hangings, and, once again, they serve very different purposes. In 1.2, Cariola hides 'behind the Arras' (Q1, C2v) at the Duchess's command and serves as a witness of her secret marriage with Antonio. When in 4.1 Bosola reveals the wax bodies to torment the Duchess, the stage direction reads '*Here is discouer'd, (behind a Trauers;) the artificiall figures of* ANTONIO, *and his children*; *appearing as if they were dead*' (I1v). The hangings in 1.2 would be neutral in character. By the fourth act, however, the play is moving to its tragic climax. The Duchess is imprisoned in almost total darkness, and so when the supposed dead bodies of Antonio and the children are revealed, it would be entirely fitting that the curtains concealing them should be black.

Although the stage facilities at the Blackfriars were not very different from those at the Globe, the smaller stage and the presence of gallants on the stage itself affected the structure of scenes, especially the arrangement of entrances and exits. Unlike at the Globe where three or four lines were the norm, Shakespeare appears to have usually allowed about two lines for an entering or exiting character to complete his move. In scenes involving two characters or two groups of characters, such as eavesdropping scenes, a front-to-back distribution of characters worked better than a centre-to-side distribution, while the upper playing area became a more useful location for potential eavesdroppers. Fletcher and his collaborators were keen on making use of the visibility of the positions behind the threshold of stage doors. The fundamental difference between the larger, outdoor stage and the smaller, indoor stage would sometimes have influenced the establishment of a scene's location and, therefore, the use of the stage space and stage doors as well. In the smaller theatre, the use of music was much more sophisticated and generally quieter, and the reduction in size made possible a low-key, more naturalistic mode of delivery by the actors. The adoption of act intervals influenced the structure of plays and also the use of facilities and properties. The *entr'acte* music and even the physical time filling the interval itself were made integral to the structure of the play. During intervals stage hangings could have been changed in order to provide the new act with an appropriate background or atmosphere. These various new staging devices, ranging from the subtle to the conspicuous, represented a departure from what was practised at open-air theatres and would have significantly shaped the audience's experience of a play at the Blackfriars.

PART II

Materiality indoors

CHAPTER 5

'A ruinous monastery': the Second Blackfriars Playhouse as a place of nostalgia

Tiffany Stern

A standard character in Restoration comedies is the boring old man who drones on about the lost wonders of yesteryear. Sometimes he is obsessed with Charles I, sometimes the Civil War, sometimes obsolete fashion. When his focus is outdated drama, he refers to the long demolished playhouse, the Blackfriars. So there is the 'paltry Old-fashion'd Wit', Oldwit, of Thomas Shadwell's *Bury-fair*, who claims 'to have seen Plays at the *Blackfryers*', and the 'grave fool' of Aphra Behn's *The Rover* who continually refers to the plays of his 'young days' and who now 'seldom sees a Play, / Unless it be the old Black Fryers way'.[1] Snarl, in Shadwell's *Virtuoso*, meanwhile, is obsessed with recalling the wonderful actors he has seen 'at Black Fryers', Joseph Taylor, John Lowin and Elliard 'Swanstead' (Swanston). 'I can never endure to see Plays since Women came on the Stage,' he maintains, denigrating the contemporary drama of which, in a metatheatrical joke, his character is a part; 'Boys are better by half.'[2] Snarl's focus on boy players suggests he cannot fully remember which manifestation of the Blackfriars he is claiming to love – the playhouse of the adult players, for which Shakespeare wrote, or one of its predecessors, occupied exclusively by boy companies and described in salacious terms by contemporaries. Collectively, what these references show is that any remembered Blackfriars playhouse was, by the Restoration, a locus for all-purpose nostalgia.

As this chapter will argue, however, 'Blackfriars nostalgia' is by no means exclusive to the Restoration. What the old men of the late seventeenth century were remembering, and mirroring, was not just a playhouse but a site, Blackfriars, that constantly brought its past to mind. Unlike the purpose-built Globe playhouse, constructed for Shakespeare's company in around 1600 and rebuilt afresh after a major fire in 1613, the Second

[1] Thomas Shadwell, *Bury-fair* (London, 1689), p. 2; Aphra Behn, *The Rover* (London, 1677), p. 84.
[2] Thomas Shadwell, *The Virtuoso* (London, 1676), p. 14.

Blackfriars Playhouse was slotted into an ancient space built for another purpose entirely. By the time Shakespeare's company were given rights to perform in it, in 1608, it had been not just upper frater (refectory) to a Dominican friary, but also a lawcourt, parliament and a theatre for choristers (1600–08). This chapter will explore the extent to which the prehistory visible in the entrance, stairway and outer shell of the Second Blackfriars Playhouse contributed to its haunted atmosphere. Turning to what was added to the old space in terms of contemporary theatrical accoutrements (boxes – latticed and otherwise – galleries and stage-stools) and audience effects (cloaks and bejewelled gowns), it will ask how yearning for being elsewhere – in court – also shaped the experience of attending the Second Blackfriars Playhouse. Throughout, it will suggest that Shakespeare's plays were moulded by and to a wistful space that continually recalled other places.

The plays covered in this chapter will generally be those Shakespeare wrote after 1608: plays penned anticipating performance at the Globe, which his company continued to use, *and* at the Blackfriars, which served as an 'exclusive' alternative space. 'Blackfriars' plays are conventionally said to be *Henry VIII*, *The Tempest*, *Pericles*, *The Winter's Tale*, *Cymbeline* and *The Two Noble Kinsmen*. But I will also, sometimes, refer to Shakespeare's earlier works. That is because popular 'stock' plays by Shakespeare were revived for Blackfriars performance. One nostalgic seventeenth-century text, *Historia Histrionica*, for instance, states that the 'Old Black-friers Men' of the 1620s, Lowin, Taylor and Swanston, played, among other characters, Falstaff (Lowin), Hamlet and Iago (Taylor) and Othello (Swanston), concluding 'these' – perhaps the actors, perhaps the plays – 'were of the Blackfriers': *Hamlet*, *Othello* and presumably *Henry IV Part 1* were, *Historia Histrionica* maintains and other accounts also make clear, Blackfriars staples.[3] A poem written by Leonard Digges in 1640, meanwhile, refers to lesser poets whose productions 'at / Blacke Friars . . . suffer' when compared with Shakespeare's plays (presumably performed in the same space): *Julius Caesar*, *Othello*, *1 Henry IV*, *Much Ado About Nothing* and *Twelfth Night*.[4] Indeed, Shakespeare's *oeuvre*, not merely his late plays, came to be associated with the Blackfriars stage. In 1642, James Shirley's

[3] James Wright, *Historia Histrionica* (London, 1699), p. 4. John Greene's 1635 diary records a trip to Blackfriars to see 'Ffalstafe'; see E. M. Symonds, 'The Diary of John Greene (1634–57)', *English Historical Review* 43 (1928), 385–94 (386). Henry Herbert, Master of the Revels, received payment for a winter 'Blackfriars' benefit of *Othello* on 22 November 1629. See N. W. Bawcutt, *The Control and Censorship of Caroline Drama* (Oxford: Clarendon Press, 1996), p. 169.

[4] Leonard Digges, 'Upon Master WILLIAM SHAKESPEARE, the *Deceased Authour, and his* POEMS', in William Shakespeare, *Poems* (1640), 3a–4a.

'Prologue at the Black-Fryers' to *The Sisters* asks 'what Company / *To* Shakespear *comes*'; Fleckno, passing by the empty Blackfriars theatre during the Interregnum, bemoans the closure of the 'Poor House . . . where . . . We have seen so many of *Shakspears* Playes'; 'pray Sir,' asks Lovewit in *Historia Histrionica*, 'what Master Parts can you remember the Old Black-friers Men to Act, in . . . Shakespear . . . Plays'.[5] Too great a focus on dating Shakespeare's plays to their first performance has blinded us to the versions of his plays that actually survive. If, as is often maintained, we possess several of Shakespeare's texts in revised form, then those texts are probably haunted by the Blackfriars space too; indeed, as this chapter will suggest, some of them seem to have been reshaped with Blackfriars performance in mind.

Monastic nostalgia

The word 'Blackfriars', to an early modern Londoner, never automatically indicated a theatre: it was the name of an entire area. From 1276 onwards a monastery had occupied the space, constructed by the Dominican friars whose black 'cappas' originally gave their building its name. When Henry VIII had, as part of the dissolution of the monasteries, shut the Blackfriars priory in 1538, the resultant area had retained its monastic rights of independence. Not bound by the usual London laws, Blackfriars became what was known as a 'liberty' within London: a space that was legally independent of the City authorities. Blackfriars, then, was distinctly different from the city that encompassed it. A recognized safe haven, it was a stylish and popular area, popular among the gentry but also receptive to 'outsiders': Catholics, Puritans, foreigners, composers, artists, players.

The one detailed picture we have of 'Blackfriars', printed shortly after Shakespeare's death, gives a sense of the mixed nature of the area, and the kind of buildings to be found there (see Figure 16). It shows an upper chamber in 'Hunsdon House', a residence within the gatehouse of the old monastery. On the occasion represented by this picture, 5th November 1623, Hunsdon House, home to the French ambassador, had hosted a sermon by the famous Jesuit preacher, Robert Drury. Many Blackfriars residents, excited by the promise of foreign and dissident entertainment, had flocked to hear the charismatic speaker. As the picture shows, tragedy ensued. The main girder that supported the ancient floor of the room in which Drury was speaking, overloaded by the weight of the collective

[5] James Shirley, *The Sisters* (London, 1652), A3a; Richard Flecknoe, *Miscellania* (London, 1653), p. 142; Wright, *Historia Histrionica*, p. 4.

Figure 16 Frontispiece to Richard Hord's *Black-Fryers* (1625), depicting the 'fatal vespers'.

audience, snapped. The preacher, and many of his three-hundred listeners, fell through the floor to the room below, and thence to the room below that; about ninety-five of the congregation, including Drury, died, in an episode that became known as the 'fatal vespers'.

Terrible as is the story of the fatal vespers, it is revelatory about the nature of the buildings in the Blackfriars precinct in the first half of the seventeenth century. As it reveals, major structures in the precinct were still made up of old bits of the monastery, which had been reappropriated rather than pulled down. Hunsdon House and the Second Blackfriars Playhouse were immediately compared, and so they were presumably similar structurally – for why, wondered commentators, would part of Blackfriars collapse during a sermon, albeit a Catholic one, when a similar part, given over to theatrical performance, stood firm. 'Observe' wrote Thomas Scott shortly after the disaster, 'the Play-House stands in that place unshaken, though too often laden with sin-full multitudes of all sort, sexes, and sects . . . But this House [Hunsdon House] . . . the Lord makes . . . a spectacle of his Judgement'.[6] A few years later, 'R. C.' congratulated Alexander Goughe on publishing his play *The Queen*, pointing out that 'blackfriers . . . in this age / Fell when it was a church, not when a stage'.[7] The suggestion is that the Second Blackfriars Playhouse ought by rights to have fallen too, not only because it was wicked but because, like Hunsdon House, it was likewise reliant on its ancient fabric. Might it, then, also have resembled part of a monastery in appearance?

There is, indeed, every suggestion that the Second Blackfriars Playhouse visually recalled its heritage. Unlike the Globe, a purpose-built theatre with an entrance leading into its pit, the entrance to Blackfriars was a floor at least below the playhouse – the theatre itself being located upstairs – as William Davenant describes in the epilogue to his Blackfriars play *Love and Honour*:

> Our Poet waits below to heare his destiny;
> Just in the Entry as you passe, the place
> Where first you mention your dislike or grace.[8]

That means the audience had to approach the Second Blackfriars Playhouse by walking through the old monastery courtyard before entering a door and then climbing up a flight of stairs to the theatre proper. Sir John Harington wrote, in about 1602 of the lady who goes to see an interlude, seemingly at Blackfriars, 'Through a great preasse, up a darke paire of staires'; and T. M. depicted one 'Nim' who attends a Blackfriars play in the hope of seducing a woman. Spying his prey, he decides to 'discover a good-will to her' when the play is over by 'following her down the Staires', where he believes he will be able to whisper to her without other people noticing.[9]

[6] Thomas Scott, *Exod. 8.19. Digitus Dei* (London, 1623), pp. 24–5.

[7] R.C., 'To Mr Alexander Gough upon his publishing The excellent Play call'd the Queen', in Alexander Goughe, *The Queen or the Excellency of her Sex* (London, 1653), A3a.

[8] William Davenant, *Love and Honour* (London, 1634), E3a.

[9] Sir John Harington, 'Of the Lady that lookt well to her borders', in *The Most Elegant and Witty Epigrams* (London, 1618), I6a; T. M., *The Life of a Satyrical Puppy Called Nim* (1657), pp. 105–6. Harington's epigrams, written between 1585 and 1603, are hard to date; manuscript evidence, however, suggests that their order is roughly chronological. 'Of the Lady that lookt well to her borders' is written in the late tranche dated 1600–03 (I am grateful to Gerard Gilroy, the epigrams' latest editor, for supplying this information).

As there is a reference, in the documents of sale for the buildings adapted into the Second Blackfriars Playhouse, to 'all that greate paire of wyndinge staires *with* the staire case thereunto belonginge *which* leadeth upp . . . oute of the greate yarde', the very Blackfriars staircase appears to have been a leftover from the monastery. As a result, entering the theatre, said in the same document to be enclosed in 'greate stone walls', meant confronting its architectural past.[10]

Once inside, the interior, too, seems to have reflected what the building used to be. 'Playes and Interludes' are said, in one legal document, to be put on in the 'great Hall in the ffryers', suggesting that the space in layout recalled its past life as a dining hall.[11] Quite how many other internal features it will have retained from its monastic past are unclear, but its fabric – in particular, its floor and roof – was, for practical reasons, likely to have remained substantially unaltered.

Certainly spectators attending the Second Blackfriars Playhouse continually recalled its earlier historic manifestation – and not only because the title 'Blackfriars', of course, brought the monastery to mind. John Stephens, writing in 1617 to commend Henry Fitzgeffrey's poem 'Notes from Black-Fryers', compares modern contemplations brought about by the theatre with the monkish thoughts that must have occupied the space's earlier manifestation:

> Had the Black-Fryers beene still un-suppressd,
> I cannot thinke their Cloysters had bin blessd
> With better contemplations: Seeing now [what] you
> Have gathered from the Play-house.[12]

Richard Flecknoe, meanwhile, walking past the Second Blackfriars Playhouse after it had been shut for the English Civil War, lamented equally the absence of the place's theatrical life, and its religious life before that:

> Poor House, that in dayes of our Grand-sires,
> Belongst unto the *Mendi[c]ant Fryers*:
> And where so oft in our Fathers dayes
> We have seen so many of *Shakspears* Playes . . .

[10] Malone Society, *Collections Vol. II, Part 1*, 'Blackfriars Records', ed. Albert Feuillerat (Oxford: H. Hart, 1913), p. 61.

[11] Henry Evans, lawsuit against Richard Burbage, John Heminges and others, 1600, quoted in Frederick Fleay, *A Chronicle History of the London Stage, 1559–1642* (London: Reeves & Turner, 1890), p. 248.

[12] John Stephens, 'To his worthy Friend, H. F. upon his Notes from Black-Fryers', in Henry Fitzgeffrey, *Satyres and Satyricall Epigrams: The Third Booke of Humours: Intituled Notes from Black-Fryers* (London, 1617), F8a.

He concludes by hoping the space can revenge its two pasts: that, as puritans have dragged it down, 'To comfort the *Players* and *Fryers* not a little, / Thou' – the ex-playhouse/monastery – 'mayst be turn'd to a *Puritan* spittle'.[13] There is every reason to think that going to the Second Blackfriars Playhouse was like going to a monastic hall.

The interest in old monasteries, and in ruins, that Shakespeare showed throughout his writing career may relate to his encounters with and in the Blackfriars precinct even before his company played there – for, as the precinct housed his Stratford printer friend, Richard Field, Shakespeare probably became familiar with the area soon after he arrived in London. At any rate, in *Comedy of Errors* the Duke comes to the melancholy vale 'Behind the ditches of the abbey here' (5.1.122); in *Titus Andronicus*, Second Goth strays 'To gaze upon a ruinous monastery' and hears a child cry underneath the wall of 'the wasted building' (5.1.22–4).[14] Shakespeare had likewise long been drawn to the trappings of monastic life, giving substantial parts to 'Friars' – and people who disguise themselves as friars – in *Romeo and Juliet* and *Measure for Measure*. Acquiring the use of a familiar ex-monastery for performance, then, will have been creatively appealing to Shakespeare – Blackfriars will have provided a space in which he and other Londoners could explore their conflicted feelings about past and present, Catholicism and Protestantism.

Shakespeare's post-1608 'Blackfriars' plays, however, focus not on actual monasteries but on secular monasteries: 'temples'. Sometimes the temples hover off stage, as though a functioning religious site is just behind a wall, on the other side of the *frons scenae*: in *Cymbeline*, the King proposes at the end of the play to 'quit this ground' and 'smoke the temple with our sacrifices' (5.5.398–9); Cleomenes and Dion go off to visit Apollo's temple in *Winter's Tale*, returning to describe it as 'much surpassing / The common praise it bears' (3.1.2–3). Sometimes, more daringly, the temple is located where the play itself is taking place. In *Pericles*, Pericles and Thaisa are, in a protracted recognition scene, reunited in the temple of Diana (5.3); in *Tempest*, the list of places that will dissolve and fade ranges from 'the great globe itself', seemingly a metatheatrical Globe reference, to 'the solemn temples' (4.1.153), seemingly a metatheatrical Blackfriars reference (raising the possibility, as Gordon McMullan points out, that other references in the speech are metatheatrical too, the 'towers'

[13] Richard Flecknoe, *Miscellania* (London, 1653), p. 141.

[14] All Shakespeare quotations are taken from Richard Proudfoot et al. (eds.), *The Arden Shakespeare Complete Works* (London: Bloomsbury, 2001).

perhaps an ironic gesture at the Tower of London, the 'gorgeous palaces' an equally ironic reference to Bridewell).[15] Drawing attention to the theatre's religious aura, while making it secular, allowed Shakespeare to exploit the atmosphere of the place without suggesting he felt affiliation with it.

There is one play, however, that will have been profoundly affected by performance in the Second Blackfriars Playhouse. *Measure for Measure*, first penned in 1604, survives only in its 1623, revised, folio manifestation. Act breaks and songs have been added to the play, probably, John Jowett argues, by Thomas Middleton.[16] But act breaks and songs are features indicative of Blackfriars performance – Globe plays were written in continuous scenes and used comparatively little music; there was, as Burbage is made to say in the Globe's induction to John Marston's *Malcontent*, a 'not received custome of musicke in our [Globe] Theater'.[17] *Measure for Measure*, in the form in which we have it, then, seems to be a Blackfriars play. But the effect of placing a novice, and what appears to be a friar (actually Duke Vincentio in disguise) on the Blackfriars stage will have been startling: performance of *Measure for Measure* in the Second Blackfriars Playhouse would have rendered almost the entire play a metadramatic reflection on the place that housed it. This will have been highlighted by scenes actually set in a nunnery and monastery – though, threateningly, other scenes, in a prison, and a palace, suggest all four are equatable. As with the 'secular' monasteries, however, the play will have been made more, rather than less, ambiguous by location. *Measure for Measure*'s questions about the competing claims of holy orders and secular life will have been confused by a performance space that had (forcibly) given over the one for the other.

Parliamentary nostalgia

A later aspect of the past life of the Blackfriars influenced Shakespeare even more directly. The Upper Frater that became the Second Blackfriars Playhouse had been used, since the fifteenth century, for events of national importance: major court cases and, on occasion, Parliament, had been held there, hence its alternative name of Old Parliament, or Parliament Chamber. In 1529 the Upper Frater, as a legatine court, had been used for Henry VIII's trial of Katherine of Aragon; the failure of that court to secure an

[15] Gordon McMullan, private email, 21 November 2012.

[16] See John Jowett's introduction to *Measure for Measure* in *Thomas Middleton: The Collected Works*, ed. Gary Taylor and John Lavagnino (Oxford University Press, 2007), pp. 1542–7.

[17] John Webster, 'Induction' to John Marston, *The Malcontent* (London, 1604), A4a.

annulment had led to the downfall of Cardinal Thomas Wolsey. Shakespeare's *Henry VIII*, which stages Katherine of Aragon's 'trial scene', crowbars an unnecessary 'Blackfriars' reference into *Henry VIII* to ensure 'nobody misses the connection' between play and place:[18]

> KING Deliver this with modesty to th'Queen.
>
> *Exit* GARDINER.
>
> The most convenient place that I can think of
> For such receipt of learning is Blackfriars:
> There ye shall meet about this weighty business.
> My *Wolsey*, see it furnished . . .
>
> (*Henry VIII* 2.2.135–9).

True, we know most about the Globe, rather than Blackfriars, performance of *Henry VIII*, for the play, under the title *All is True*, was in performance when the place burned down in 1613.[19] This, however, merely raises more fascinating questions about Shakespeare's metatheatre. At the Blackfriars, a reference to the space would come with all the *frisson* of being there, so that 'All' really was 'True' – the urge to re-enact Henry VIII's divorce story in the very space where it happened is surely behind Shakespeare's choice to write a play on that subject in the first place. At the Globe, a Blackfriars reference would recall both the historical site of the play's action and the current site of the company's alternate theatre, combining metatheatre with something more knowing: advertising.

Theatrical nostalgia

Shakespeare seems, finally, to have been mindful of the earlier theatres that had also occupied the site of his dramas: the first Blackfriars Playhouse (1576–84) that had been located nearby in part of the monastic buttery, and that had housed plays by boy choristers; and the earlier manifestation of the Second Blackfriars Playhouse, which from 1600 till 1608 had also put on plays by boy choristers. Blackfriars, in performance terms, had had a long-standing reputation for beautiful-voiced, sexually alluring youths. In William Fennor's *Pluto*, a cross-dressed young man is described as performing 'in such quaint manner' that he 'seemed to surpasse the boyes of Blacke-fryars'; in Thomas Middleton's *Father Hubburds Tale* (1604), 'the

18 Gordon McMullan, *Shakespeare and the Idea of Late Writing: Authorship in the Proximity of Death* (Cambridge University Press, 2007), p. 98.
19 Gordon McMullan, introduction to William Shakespeare, *King Henry VIII* (London: Thomson, 2000), pp. 58–60.

Blackfriars' was said to provide 'a nest of boys able to ravish a man'.[20] Shakespeare, in *Hamlet*, written for the Globe in about 1600, had been acutely conscious of his adult company's failure to win audiences from the gorgeous Blackfriars boys. Hamlet is told that the adult city tragedians are no longer popular because 'children' are 'now the fashion'; he asks 'Do the boys carry it away?' 'Ay, that they do' is the response, 'Hercules and his load too' (2.2.361–3). As the sign of the Globe was Hercules with the world on his shoulders, Hamlet appears to be indicating that the compelling boys occupying the Second Blackfriars Playhouse were tempting the audience away from his own company.

When Shakespeare started writing for the Second Blackfriars Playhouse himself, then, he will have had to win round a ready-made audience used to boy performance. Perhaps that explains why Shakespeare's post-1608 plays are, in innuendo-filled fashion, repeatedly concerned with boys and girls on the sexual threshold (both of whom would have been played by boys, of course) – Ferdinand and Miranda (*Tempest*), Perdita and Florizel (*Winter's Tale*), Palamon/Arcite and Emilia (*Two Noble Kinsmen*); and with adolescents confronting sex and sexual threats head-on – Marina in a brothel (*Pericles*), Imogen violated in her sleep (*Cymbeline*). Yet, as these youthful characters are often also paired with members of the older generation – Miranda and Prospero, Marina and Pericles, Imogen and Cymbeline, Florizel/Perdita and Polixenes/Leontes – Shakespeare may, too, have been showing what made his company different from earlier Blackfriars ones. In boy companies, boys had to play old men; the repeated youth–age contrast of Shakespeare's later plays allowed him to showcase his talented older actors and celebrate the 'realistic' age range offered by an adult–boy ensemble.

Another memorable feature of boy performance that Shakespeare needed to subsume was use of music. The Children of the Chapel Royal, who had performed in the first Blackfriars under the auspices of the composer Richard Farrant, and in the second Blackfriars under the organist and composer Nathaniel Giles, had been choristers. They had also been, or acquired, instrumentalists. Frederic Gerschow had recorded, of the second Blackfriars during its 'boy' manifestation in 1602, that plays were preceded by a concert: 'For a whole hour preceding the play one listens to a delightful musical entertainment on organs, lutes, mandorins, mandolins, violins and flutes'.[21]

[20] William Fennor, *Pluto his Travailes* (London, 1612), 8; Thomas Middleton, *Father Hubburd's Tales* [1604] in Taylor and Lavagnino, *Collected Works*, p. 173.

[21] London diary of Frederic Gerschow, tutor and secretary to Philip Julius, Duke of Stettin-Pomerania, 1602, recorded in *Transactions of the Royal Historical Society*, n.s. 6 (1892), 26–81 (29).

Shakespeare's late plays, gratifying the audience, give haunting ditties to singing boys ('Full fathom five', *Tempest* 1.2.397–405; Marina's lost song in *Pericles* s.d. 5.1.80; 'Fear no more', a boy song changed to spoken verse presumably because the adolescents' voices broke, *Cymbeline* 4.2.258–81). They also, perhaps using the musicians who came with the space or perhaps acquiring their own, are full of instrumental music, which is used to enhance – and bring about – frequent 'magical' moments: the music of the spheres in *Pericles* (5.1.226), the '*Solemn music*' that ushers in the ghosts in *Cymbeline* (s.d. 5.4.29), the twangling instruments of the *Tempest*, an isle 'full of noises' (3.2.136), and the enchanted music that is required to 'awake' Hermione in *Winter's Tale* (5.3.98). Few of Shakespeare's other plays are so musical, with the exception of *Twelfth Night*, and that, too, is likely to have been revised with Blackfriars in mind. Beginning with a concert, and containing songs throughout, this play's most visible revision occurs around songs and music. It is often thought that *Twelfth Night* was updated to showcase the company's acquisition of a new clown, Robert Armin, to play Feste; it seems, however, to have been altered – or additionally altered – for the space whose interests it promotes.[22]

That said, the new fascination in music evinced by the Blackfriars plays was also reflective of the Blackfriars precinct more generally, for the area was home to many composers and instrumentalists – to whom, on a practical level, the playhouse could turn; by whom, on an artistic level, the playhouse was influenced; and for whom, on a financial level, the playhouse was writing. In Shakespeare's time, famous musicians living in the Blackfriars precinct included theatre composers Nathaniel Giles (*c.* 1558–1634), Philip Rosseter (*c.* 1568–1623) and Robert Jones (*fl.* 1597–1615); lutenist and composer John Dowland (1563?–1626), John Daniel (1564?–*c.* 1626) and Robert Johnson (*c.* 1583–1633); musician and composer John Adson (*bap.* 1587?, *d.* 1640); composer John Milton, father of the poet of that name (1562–1647); and musician Robert Dowland (*c.* 1591–1641). The musicality of Shakespeare's Blackfriars plays may, then, also be a broader statement about place (as well as a reflection of it) – composers living in Blackfriars, including Robert Johnson, seem sometimes to have provided music for the plays.[23]

Thus Shakespeare's plays seem to have negotiated with place on a number of levels. At playhouse level, they appear to have responded nostalgically to the location's earlier manifestations as monastery, lawcourt, parliament, and

[22] See Tiffany Stern, 'Inverted Commas around the "Fun"': Music in *Twelfth Night*', in Alison Findley and Liz Oakley-Brown (eds.), *Twelfth Night: A Critical Guide*, Arden Renaissance Drama (London: Bloomsbury, 2013).

[23] Tiffany Stern, *Documents of Performance in Early Modern England* (Cambridge University Press, 2009), pp. 139, 149.

theatre; at precinct level, they seem to have responded creatively to the artistic and inventive neighbourhood of which they were now a part.

Courtly yearnings

Generally, however, it is the second Blackfriars Playhouse *as a theatre* that is said to have affected the plays written for it. And, of course, that must also be the case. Despite the playhouse's nostalgia for the past, it was also shaped by its present. As is often pointed out (and by Martin White in Chapter 6 below), its artificial lighting seems to have brought about plays with a five-act structure, so that the candles could be trimmed in the four act breaks; its need for 'indoor' instruments rather than loud outdoor ones – like trumpets and drums – seems to have resulted in its concentration on gentler, less battle-filled dramas.[24] The Blackfriars' smoky atmosphere, too, may have encouraged plays about ghosts, spirits and people who have lost their way; while the playhouse's smaller stage and intimate audience may likewise explain why the late plays revolve around minute theatrical props – the telling moles in *Cymbeline* – or speaking facial expressions.[25]

Yet even the modern theatrical accoutrements of the second Blackfriars Playhouse had something nostalgic about them. An indoor theatre within an old dining hall was automatically reminiscent of court; it was the palace dining halls in Whitehall, Greenwich, Hampton Court, Windsor, Nonsuch and Richmond, which were fitted up to receive plays on special occasions. Blackfriars Playhouse seems, moreover, to have emphasized its courtly resemblances. At court, 'masks and playes' were put on 'in the night season (even crossing the Ordinance of God, which he hath appointed for people to rest, and in the day to travell)'.[26] At Blackfriars, productions were likewise pointedly mounted in the evening, by candlelight, though daytime production, exploiting the light from the windows, would have been cheaper. Horatio Busino, in 1617, was apparently taken to Blackfriars; he relates a jest played on him at a private indoor London playhouse during performance 'that very evening'.[27] Post-1608 Blackfriars plays habitually draw attention to their late performance time, differentiating themselves

[24] Andrew Gurr, *The Shakespeare Company, 1594–1642* (Cambridge University Press, 2004), p. 81.

[25] Tiffany Stern, '"Taking Part": Actors and Audience on the Blackfriars Stage', in Paul Menzer (ed.), *Inside Shakespeare: Essays on the Blackfriars Stage* (Selinsgrove, PA: Susquehanna University Press), pp. 35–53.

[26] David Brown, *The Naked Woman* (1652), p. 11.

[27] *The Journals of Two Travellers in Elizabethan and Early Stuart England Thomas Platter and Horatio Busino*, ed. Peter Razzell (London: Caliban Books, 1995), p. 121.

from outdoor, public, productions. Shakespeare and Fletcher's *Two Noble Kinsmen* even states its Blackfriars, rather than Globe, affiliation by ending its epilogue with 'goodnight!' (Epilogue, 18). William Davenant similarly refers to the second performance of his *Unfortunate Lovers* that will take place 'the next night'; Ben Jonson in the *New Inne* is 'sad' if you 'expect more then you had to night'; John Fletcher in *The Chances* maintains that 'Aptnesse for mirth to all, this instant night / Thalia hath prepar'd'; in his *Love's Pilgrimage*, he writes 'This night / No mighty matter . . . We must intreat you look for'.[28] John Price records in 1654 how 'wanton Courtiers' would go 'to Black-fryers' in order to see plays and 'offer up their evening sacrifices to the Devil', and evening performances at Blackfriars seem to have been a given until the closure of the theatres; they clearly also 'worked' as courtlike productions, encouraging an abandoned, courtly audience.[29]

Courtly people – or would-be courtly people – dressing for an evening spent indoors, could wear their finest clothes. That too became part of the look of the theatre. Here, then, was a huge difference between the Globe and the Blackfriars. At the Globe, outdoor clothing was necessary for warmth; at the Blackfriars, layer after layer of expensive clothes could be, during the evening's advancement, slowly revealed. Nim goes to Blackfriars after having spent 'Fifty Pounds' to dress himself in 'glorious Garments'; he then presents his cloak and what is underneath it, his 'Sute', which he shows 'to a more apparent view, by hanging the Cloak upon one Shoulder: or letting it fall (as it were) by chance'; Fitzdotterel likewise has a fifty-pound cloak which he plans to take to the 'Black fryers Play-house' – there he will 'Sit ithe view' on stage, and 'let fall my cloake, / Publish a handsome man, and a rich suite'.[30] Shakespeare plays written with Blackfriars in mind from the outset often seem to josh with this overly clothes-conscious audience. They focus on characters who do not know they are well born and so wear humble attire – through which their innate nobility shines through: Miranda (*The Tempest*) does not realize she is the daughter of a duke; Marina (*Pericles*) and Perdita (*Winter's Tale*) do not know that they are daughters to a king; Arviragus and Guidarius (*Cymbeline*) are unaware that they are princes.

The playhouse's extravagant use of candles also encouraged the well-dressed audience, always conscious of the effect that candlelight would have on their garments, to wear their richest colours and most

28 William Davenant, *The Unfortunate Lovers* (1643), p. 48; Ben Jonson, *The New Inne* (London, 1631), G7b; Francis Beaumont and John Fletcher, *The Chances in Comedies and Tragedies* (London, 1647), 3c3a; Beaumont and Fletcher, *Love's Pilgrimage, in Comedies and Tragedies* (London, 1647), 8db.

29 John Price, *Tyrants and Protectors Set Forth in their Colours* (1654), p. 16.

30 May, *Life of a Satyrical Puppy*, 103; Ben Jonson, *The Divell is an Asse* in *Workes* (London, 1631), p. 105.

sparkling jewellery: Francis Bacon reminds masquers that 'The *Colours*, that shew best by Candlelight, are; White, Carnation, and a Kinde of Sea-Water-Greene; And *Oes*, or *Spangs*, as they are of no great Cost, so they are of most Glory'.[31] Spectators, who might go to the theatre with 'Cloathes in seemly, & most sumptuous fashion: / Wearing a border of rich Pearle and stone' chose embellishments to pick up the artificial light.[32] Francis Lenton writes tellingly of the 'spangled . . . attires' in which a gallant 'glistred' in the 'Torchy Fryers'.[33] Hence, perhaps, Shakespeare's quiet insistence, in his late plays, on the gaudy and ridiculous nature of bejewelled gowns: it is the fools Trinculo and Stephano in *The Tempest* who gather up '*glistering apparel*' (s.d. 4.1.193), confusing mere outer-wear with kingship, while Time in *The Winter's Tale* will use his art to 'make stale' ('to age', but also 'to urinate on') 'The Glistering of this present' (4.1.13–14).

The playhouse itself, then, was filled with gorgeous textiles: though the details of the interior decoration of the second Blackfriars Playhouse are unknown, much of the colour palette, texture and gleam will have been created by the audience. Mr Damplay in the induction to Jonson's Blackfriars play *Magnetick Lady* even calls the spectators 'Plush and Velvet-outsides! that stick your house' ('house' meaning 'playhouse') 'round like so many eminences'.[34]

What the playing company added to the space in the way of theatrical furniture seems to have kept the audience's clothing in mind. It was furnished with benches, chairs and stools – as at court, there were no standing places – the most visible of which cost the most money. As those who had worn their best attire to the theatre would pay to display it, so the theatrical arena offered a space where social standing could, up to a point, be paid for.

Hence even the communal gallery seems to have been filled according to, or at least reflecting, (perceived) rank. It consisted of an area that Fitzgeffrey calls the 'Gallants Roe', and another area he calls 'the middle Region', because it was in the middle and, by analogy, filled with the middling kind; Marston too differentiates 'my verie fine *Heliconian* Gallants, and . . . my Worsh[ipful] friends in the middle Region' of the Blackfriars playhouse.[35] These, then, were spaces whose very titles suggested value judgements. There were, alternately, dark corners that, throughout Blackfriars' manifestation as a theatre, made

31 Francis Bacon, 'Of Masques and Triumphs', *The Essayes or Counsels* (1625), p. 225. (Cited elsewhere in this volume, pp. 128 and 192.)

32 Harington, 'Of the Lady that lookt well to her borders', I6a.

33 Francis Lenton, *The Young Gallants Whirligig* (London, 1629), p. 16.

34 Jonson, *The Magnetick Lady* in *Workes* (1641), p. 6.

35 Fitzgeffrey, *Satyres and Satyricall Epigrams*, F2a, E6b; John Marston, *The Dutch Courtezan* (1605), H4a.

negative comments on those who chose to occupy them. 'Behinde each post and at the gallery corners, / Sit empty guls, slight fooles and false informers'; 'the *Faeces*, or grounds of your people . . . sit in the oblique caves and wedges of your house'.[36] The connection between money and space with respect to seats provided in miniature what the comparison between the Globe and the Blackfriars made in large: the less one paid, the less private and exclusive – the less noble – would be one's experience; conversely, the more one paid, the more exclusive one would seem.

A particularly grand way to attend Blackfriars performance was to purchase a box: a private, elite space within which an exclusive group could be walled away from its neighbours. The very marketing of these boxes encouraged feelings of entitlement. Boxes might, for instance, be secured for named individuals. In Thomas Killigrew's *The Parson's Wedding*, the Captain observes, 'there's a new play at the Friars today, and I have bespoke a box for Mr Wild and his bride'; the narrator of a poem on the Blackfriars hopes to attract a woman who then simply walks past – he concludes, 'Sure shee's bespoken for a box before'.[37] The lockable doors of boxes furthered their possessors' sense of ownership. When James Stuart, Duke of Lennox, and Philip Herbert, Earl of Pembroke and Montgomery as well as Lord Chamberlain, had a quarrel about a box, it was one to which 'the Duke' claimed rights because he 'had got the Key'.[38] Combining exclusivity with visibility, these tiny spaces were triumphant social sites that presented clear rival interests to the stage itself. Richard Brathwait writes of a woman in a private theatre who 'desires to be observed' – 'Her Behaviour in a *Box*, would make any one thinke shee were a Bee in a box; shee makes such a buzzing and rusling'; 'who do you think I saw [at Blackfriars]?' asks Mr Jolly in Killigrew's *The Parsons Wedding*, finally offering:

> JOLLY Your Aunt and Mistriss *Pleasant*, and trusty *Secret*.
> WILD What man?
> JOLLY The Lovers onely, so close in a Box!
> CAPTAIN It will be a match, and there's an End.[39]

Boxes, their owners, and the gossip they encouraged, illustrate that the play was not necessarily what the theatre was about. Blackfriars provided a space

[36] John Day, *Ile of Gulls* (1606), G3b; Jonson, *Magnetick Lady*, pp. 5–6.

[37] Thomas Killigrew, *The Parsons Wedding* in *Comedies and Tragedies* (1664), 138; Fitzgeffrey, *Satyres and Satyricall Epigrams*, F1b.

[38] Letter from the Revd G. Garrard, 25 January 1636, in William Knowler (ed.), *The Earl of Strafforde's Letters and Dispatches* (2 vols.; 1739), vol. 1, p. 511.

[39] Richard Brathwait, *The English Gentlewoman* (1631), 53; Killigrew, *Parsons Wedding*, p. 122.

for spectators to watch one another and pay for the privilege; a play might have to fight to compete with the interests of a sumptuous audience.

This remained the case even with the boxes set aside for those who attended the playhouse incognito. Leonella in *The Lady's Tragedy* (1611) may relate to Bellarius how a 'private gallant' can sit 'for all the play, and ne'er be seen thyself',[40] but that shows how audience exchanges – trysts, or the telling of secrets – might be the focus of a trip to the theatre. John Davies likewise describes how one 'Rufus' decides 'at the Theater' to leave 'the ... most conspicuous place' and instead 'through a grate, doth show his double face'.[41] As this indicates, theatres might have special boxes fronted with a grate or lattice to hide the spectators within them: in *The Careless Shepherdess*, Landlord decides to follow Spruce and Spark into 'a Box', as ''tis better looking o're a Ladies head, / Or through a Lettice-window, then a grate'.[42] Such latticed boxes, still seen in Drottningholms Slottsteater in Sweden, and l'Opéra Royal in Versailles, provide privacy for the grandest members of the audience: early modern latticed boxes may, then, have been mimicking the court's desire for gossip-provoking privacy; they certainly pandered to the self-importance of those who sat in them.

There was one space, in particular, where one's own visibility outweighed the desire to see or encourage a decent performance: the stage itself. Paying an additional sixpence for a stool on stage allowed gallants to sit around – and practically within – the fictional world depicted beside them. Stool-sitters were thus rather like the king or queen in court, always a rival focus for the watching audience. Mirth, in Jonson's *Staple of Newes*, arrives at Blackfriars and demands a stool 'o' the Stage', because 'wee are persons of quality ... and women of fashion; and come to see, and to be seene'; in *Divell is an Asse*, Fitzdotterel will take a stool on the Blackfriars stage because, he explains, 'The Ladies ... come / To see us, *Love*, as wee doe to see them'.[43] Squashed for space, plays themselves might suffer as a result. In *Divell is an Asse*, the Prologue pleads with the audience for enough stage to act in, around the stools: 'Doe not ... force us act, / In compasse of a cheese-trencher ... / ... If you'll come / To see new Playes, pray you affoord us roome'.[44] Again, the audience's need to make statements about themselves was at the expense of the plays that, supposedly, they wished to see.

[40] Thomas Middleton, *The Lady's Tragedy* (the *Second Maiden's Tragedy*), in Taylor and Lavagnino, *Collected Works*, p. 892.

[41] John Davies, *Ovid's Elegies* (1603), F4b.

[42] Induction, probably by Richard Brome, to Thomas Goffe's *The Careles Shepherdess* (1656), p. 8.

[43] Jonson, *The Staple of Newes* in *Workes* (1631), 4; Jonson, *Divell is an Asse*, p. 106.

[44] Jonson, *Divell is an Asse*, p. 94.

Shakespeare's plays written for the Blackfriars both question and flatter this audience. They vary entertainments – masques, songs, processions, tricks, elaborate stage effects – perhaps to jolt or endear spectators all too ready to be deflected. That may even explain why Shakespeare and Fletcher became interested in the tragicomedic form: its varied style will have seemed suited to an audience with wayward or wandering attention.

One particular sop that Shakespeare and other playwrights at the Blackfriars gave their audience was direct experience of a court entertainment in the form of internal masques. Masques were beautifully dressed dances, performed to specially written music and put on for exclusive court occasions. Shakespeare's plays, however, contain fictional moments where recent court masques are called for, allowing his company to reuse entertainments they had learned already, and his audience to see a 'select' and privileged diversion. Thomas Campion's dance of knights with helmets in *Maske . . . in Honour of the Lord Hayes* (performed in Whitehall on Twelfth Night 1607) appears to be behind the dance of the knights 'in your armours' in *Pericles* (2.4.94); the satyrs' dance of Jonson's *Masque of Oberon* (performed on 1 January 1611), with music by Robert Johnson, seems to have become the '*Dance of twelve Satyres*' in *Winter's Tale* (s.d 4.4.344); the 'May dauance' of Francis Beaumont's *Masque of the Inner Temple and Gray's Inn* (performed on 20 February 1613 in the Banqueting House, Whitehall Palace) is thought to be the 'country pastime' morris in Shakespeare and Fletcher's *Two Noble Kinsmen* (3.5.101).[45] Other Shakespeare plays gather masques, though Shakespeare himself does not appear to have inserted them. The anti-masque of women 'in the habit of *hags*, or *witches*' from Jonson's 1609 *Masque of Queenes* made its way first into Middleton's play *The Witch* (written between 1609 and 1616), and seemingly thence, probably through Middleton's auspices, into *Macbeth*, as '*the Witches dance*' (s.d. 4.1.132).[46] *The Masque of Amazons*, prepared for performance at Sir James Hay's residence on Twelfth Night 1618, two years after Shakespeare's death, but not put on because 'neither the Quene nor King did like or allow of yt',

[45] Thomas Campion, *The Discription of a Maske, presented before the Kinges Majestie at White-Hall, on Twelfth Night Last* (1607), C4a; Francis Beaumont, *Masque of the Inner Temple and Gray's Inn* (1613), B2b–B3a. For more on masques in plays, see Stern, *Documents of Performance*, pp. 150–3. For more on music and Blackfriars revision, see David Lindley, 'Music and Shakespearean Revision', *Archiv* 249 (2012), 50–64.

[46] John P. Cutts, 'Robert Johnson and the Court Masque', *Music and Letters* 41 (1955), 110–25 (120). Ben Jonson, *Masque of Queenes* in *Workes* (1616), 945; Thomas Middleton, *The Witch*, ed. W. W. Greg (Oxford: Malone Society Publications, 1948 [1950]), p. 89.

appears to be called for as '*masque of ladies as Amazons, with lutes in their hands*' (s.d. 1.2.131) in *Timon of Athens*.[47]

These masques, in particular, show how problematic was, and is, nostalgia. Cut-down masques reprise aspects of a missed court production, but by so doing they also remind the audience that it is not actually at court – and that what it is seeing is a reduced and repositioned entertainment. Nostalgia, never satisfied, always has regret at its core, and things that assuage it make it deeper too. Perhaps, then, the yearning in Shakespeare's late plays is a response to the melancholy of the Blackfriars atmosphere. As ex-monastery, ex-parliament, ex-boy theatre and would-be court theatre, Blackfriars was always defined by being *not* somewhere or something else. The edge of dissatisfaction in Blackfriars plays may relate to that.

Wistful desire came, however, to affect more than simply the plays *written for* Blackfriars performance. Blackfriars' perceived superiority to the Globe – on the title pages of the plays performed by the King's Men between 1616 and 1642, the Blackfriars is mentioned forty-eight times, the Globe, only twenty-seven – allowed its pervasive nostalgia to dog Shakespeare's revision even after his death. During Shakespeare's life, this chapter has shown, the second Blackfriars Playhouse affected the way he thought; after his death, the second Blackfriars Playhouse affected the way his texts were rethought by his company. As many of Shakespeare's works, including the folio of 1623, were only published after performance at Blackfriars, so the second Blackfriars playhouse, its monasticism, its parliamentary echoes, its boys, its lighting, its seating, its well-dressed audience, its glamour, its unease, moulded the Shakespeare we know. The second Blackfriars Playhouse, then, is not just a theatrical site; it is a reviser and rethinker of 'Shakespeare' and hence a significant part of what our 'Shakespeare' is.

47 John Chamberlain, Letter to Dudley Carleton, 3 January 1618, in Norman E. McClure (ed.), *The Letters* (2 vols.; Philadelphia: American Philosophical Society, 1939), vol. II, pp. 125–6. Nan Cooke Carpenter, 'Shakespeare and Music: Unexplored Areas', in Stephen Orgel and Sean Keilen (eds.), *Shakespeare and the Arts* (New York and London: Garland, 1999), pp. 123–35 (p. 133) thinks this music relates to *Timon of Athens*; Andrew J. Sabol, *Songs and Dances for the Stuart Masque* (Providence, RI: Brown University Press, 1959), p. 168, disagrees, thinking this music is for Jonson's *Salmacida Spolia*.

CHAPTER 6

'When torchlight made an artificial noon': light and darkness in the indoor Jacobean theatre

Martin White

In 1609, when the King's Men eventually got their hands on the indoor playhouse in Blackfriars, they were, as others in this volume point out, returning to a familiar performance environment rather than embarking on a voyage of discovery. Both before and after the opening in 1567 of the Red Lion (so far as we know the first outdoor, commercial playhouse in London), professional actors had far more experience of performing indoors than out: in London at court, in the houses of aristocrats, at the Inns of Court and in city taverns (especially in the late 1580s–early 1590s); in guildhalls in cities and towns across the country when they toured;[1] at colleges of the universities of Oxford and Cambridge. Indeed, it was performing in the substantial outdoor playhouses in London that the actors must have needed to get used to.

Added to that, by 1609 the King's Men already had a decade of seeing how the companies of child actors, including the Children of the Queen's Revels who occupied the Blackfriars, used the indoor space they had now recovered. In 1601 at Paul's, for example, the boys performed John Marston's *Antonio's Revenge*, in which the use of light and darkness was so integral to both the mood and structure of the play that he 'may have been experimenting with lighting effects, at least to the extent of requiring the "tireman" to light and extinguish candles to set the mood for different acts'.[2] Now, firmly established in the Blackfriars playhouse, it was the adults' turn to explore more fully the opportunities offered by candlelight and for their writers to begin to embed those opportunities into plays designed primarily for indoor performance.

The quotation that forms part of the title to this chapter is taken from Thomas Middleton, *The Revenger's Tragedy*, ed. R. A. Foakes (Manchester University Press, 1966), 1.4.27.

[1] Alan Somerset, '"How chances it they travel?": Provincial Touring, Playing Spaces and the King's Men', *Shakespeare Survey* 47 (1994), 45–60.

[2] John Marston, *Antonio's Revenge*, ed. W. Reavley Gair (Manchester University Press, 1978), p. 35.

Documented evidence about the nature and operation of lighting in the early modern commercial theatre is scant, and descriptions of its effects and impact are even rarer.[3] The majority of writing on lighting in sixteenth- and seventeenth-century performances is found in the work of continental theorists and practitioners, and most of that is concerned ultimately with the illumination of the scenic, end-on stage, or elaborate festivals, indoors and out. Nevertheless, much of what was written can be (and clearly was) transferred to the English theatre, and, drawing on evidence from play-texts, records and occasional eyewitness reports, we can get at least a sense of what a visitor to an indoor playhouse would have experienced. To that written and occasional visual evidence I have added the invaluable findings from experiments by researchers at the Baroque Theatre Foundation at Český Krumlov in the Czech Republic[4] and the discoveries made from productions and exercises I have undertaken at the University of Bristol using a full-scale, candlelit reconstruction of the stage and auditorium of the unidentified playhouse shown on the drawings held in the Jones/Webb collection at Worcester College, Oxford (see Figure 1).[5]

Daylight

General illumination in the indoor playhouse came from two sources: daylight through windows and artificial light, mainly from candles. We cannot be sure how many windows gave on to the Blackfriars hall, nor how large they were, though five on each side, two lighting the tiring-house and the remainder the auditorium, is a reasonable suggestion. The Worcester College drawings, on the other hand, show no daylight at all entering at the ground-floor level apart from small slit windows that provided some illumination to the circulation passage (which might have been augmented with tapers).[6] At the level of the first-floor galleries there are six elliptical-headed windows, though these have been truncated by having the sills raised,

[3] The principal continental sources are Sebastiano Serlio, *Architettura*, in particular volume II (1545); the *Dialogues* of Leone di Somi (1556–65), but not published in full, in English, until 1927; Angelo Ingegneri, *Il discorso della poesia rappresentiva e del modo di rappresentare le favole sceniche* (1598); Nicolo Sabbattini, *Pratica di fabricar scene e machine* (1637–8); and Joseph Furttenbach, *Mannhafter Kunst-Spiegel* (1663). See Barnard Hewitt (ed.), *The Renaissance Stage: Documents of Serlio, Sabbattini and Furttenbach* (University of Miami Press, 1958).

[4] I am especially grateful to Dr Pavel Slavko, Castle Director, for his help with my research.

[5] Examples of these experiments are available on my DVD, *The Chamber of Demonstrations: Reconstructing the Jacobean Indoor Playhouse* (Bristol: University of Bristol and Ignition Films, 2009).

[6] Tapers were made of a thin piece of rope dipped in wax or tallow, but as they required less attention than candles they were often used in bedrooms and would have been equally appropriate as corridor

presumably to allow for the degrees of seating in front of them. It has been suggested that these windows would have contributed in no small measure to the illumination of the auditorium and stage.[7] However, I think this is to ignore the extent to which the daylight would have been reduced once the benches in front of the windows were occupied, and how the upper gallery itself would have significantly reduced even further the spill of the light on to the stage. Interestingly, records of performances at Oxford and Cambridge universities, where a similar relation of audience to windows pertained, contain repeated, but not explained, references to damage to the windows, which may have resulted from the proximity of bodies and glass.[8] However, there are also references in the Oxford and Cambridge records to windows being shuttered for afternoon performances,[9] and Thomas Dekker's description in chapter 3 of *The Seven Deadly Sins of London* ('Candle-light or, The Nocturnal Triumph') of the city of London looking 'like a private playhouse, when the windows are clapped down, as if some Nocturnal, or dismal tragedy were presently to be acted',[10] would suggest that the playhouses might have done something similar to control the amount of light through the windows. The German architect Joseph Furttenbach, who published various works on theatre between 1627 and 1663, wrote that before performances began, 'the windows . . . next to the spectators' benches must have their shutters closed so that everything is made dark again'.[11] The 'again' might imply that the windows let in light and air while the audience settled and were then shuttered to create more advantageous conditions for candlelight, but beyond Dekker's reference, and others to 'wooden windows' (i.e., shutters) at the Second Blackfriars,[12]

lighting. As Robert Graves points out, however, tapers were often called candles, and vice versa. Robert Graves, *Lighting the Shakespearean Stage 1567–1642* (Carbondale, IL: Southern Illinois University Press, 1999), pp. 22–3.

7 Ibid., pp. 130–57, *passim*. Five smaller windows at the same level provide backstage light.

8 For example, at Queens' College, Cambridge, February 1595, 'Item for repairing th' hall windowes after the plaies, xlv[s]', and in February 1598 at St John's College, Cambridge, 64 shillings and 4 pence was spent on replacing glass and repairing the windows 'after the Comedie', Malone Society, *Collections* (hereafter MSC), vol. 11, pt. 3, 'Dramatic Records: The Academic Drama at Cambridge' (Oxford: Malone Society Publications, 1931), pp. 191, 225.

9 When Charles I went to St John's College, Oxford, in 1636 he saw two plays, one in the afternoon and one at night. After lunch, his host, the chancellor of the university, Archbishop Laud, 'caused the windows of the Hall to be shut, the candles lighted, and all things made ready for the play to begin' (John R. Elliot Jnr, Alan H. Nelson, Alexandra S. Johnston and Diana Wyatt (eds.), *Records of Early English Drama: Oxford* (2 vols.; University of Toronto Press, 2004), vol. 1, p. 541), which I take to refer to using shutters to create darkness for the performance.

10 Thomas Dekker, *The Seven Deadly Sins of London*, ed. Edward Arber (London, 1879), p. 25.

11 *Mannhafter Kunst Spiegel* [*The Noble Mirror of Art*], in George W. Brandt and Wiebe Hogendoorn (eds.), *German and Dutch Theatre, 1600–1848* (Cambridge University Press, 1993), 27–8.

12 Irwin Smith notes that 'the window frames themselves were almost certainly of stone', *Shakespeare's Blackfriars Playhouse* (London: Peter Owen, 1966), p. 302.

there is no specific evidence of such a practice so far as English commercial playhouses are concerned. As they did at the outdoor theatres, plays indoors started around 2 or 3 o'clock in the afternoon (though sometimes much later) and generally appear to have lasted between two and three hours. But the Blackfriars operated only from September to April, and by 5 p.m., especially in the middle of winter, the amount of daylight through the windows would have been virtually non-existent.[13]

Artificial light

Candles suspended above the stage in chandeliers (often called 'branches') lit the stage, while it is likely that a smaller number of candles in wall sconces (or 'wallers' (simpler, often temporary devices to support a candle; see p. 120)) were attached to the fabric of the auditorium, possibly to the columns supporting the upper gallery, in order to provide some light in the auditorium. This uneven distribution of candles would have resulted in a concentration of light on the main acting area, an effect referred to by the Italian Leone di Somi, responsible for theatrical entertainments to the Mantuan court, in his *Dialogues on Stage Affairs*: 'It is a natural fact ... that a man who stands in the shade sees much more distinctly an object illuminated from afar ... Wherefore I place only a few lamps in the auditorium, while at the same time I render the stage as bright as I possibly can'.[14] The key point here is that the impact of artificial lighting in the playhouse lies precisely in the relationship between the darkness and the light.

But just how much artificial light was there? Unfortunately, it is not easy to answer this key question, as only one record exists that refers specifically to the number of candles used during commercial performances. In 1636/7, one Richard Heton became the 'housekeeper' (or manager) of the Salisbury Court indoor playhouse, which had opened in 1629. In September 1639, Heton drafted a document (now lost) setting out, in effect, his manifesto, the terms and conditions for his tenure. Heton's strictures on the players

[13] For example, working with Robert Graves at Shakespeare's Globe for a 'Winter Playing' exercise in February 2005, when the sun set at approximately 5.00 p.m., we observed that there was insufficient light by 4.30 p.m. to be able to distinguish any detail in a performer's actions, let alone facial expression, which suggests that the daylight entering the indoor playhouse at that time, with perhaps still half an hour of performance time remaining, would have had little effect. At the same time, artificial lights to the rear of the stage, and particularly those placed in the recess made by opening the central doors, were very effective.

[14] Leone di Somi, *Dialogues on Stage Affairs* (*c.* 1556–7), in Allardyce Nicoll, *The Development of the Theatre* (5th edn; London: Harrap, 1966), p. 275.

(the reformed company of Queen Henrietta's Men) were uncompromising, and clearly intended to secure a company at the playhouse and to 'avoid many differences and disturbances that happen both between the Company and housekeepers [and] amongst the Company themselves'.[15]

Heton began by asserting his right to hire and fire actors as he wished and to determine whether the company could perform anywhere other than Salisbury Court unless the Lord Chamberlain or Master of the Revels so ordered. He then set out the 'Instructions touching Salisbury Court playhouse' for the Company, heading it, 'The difference betwixt the first Articles and the last': in other words, what they could expect from him in return for these new draconian rules. Heton included a number of allowances that had not figured in the previous Articles, one of which was that, whereas the housekeeper had previously contributed nothing to the cost of lighting the theatre, he would from now on bear 'half' the cost of the 'lights, both waxe and Tallow, wch halfe all winter is near 5s a day', in other words, a total expenditure of somewhere near 10 shillings, and the only known *specific* reference to the expenditure on candles by an indoor commercial playhouse.[16] In his indispensable study of early modern lighting, Robert Graves uses this brief entry as a starting point to 'make a rough estimate'[17] of the candle-power likely to have been on show at Salisbury Court, using a late-Caroline *average* price of 2 shillings a pound for wax and sixpence a pound for tallow, and accepting that each candle, wax or tallow, weighed one-sixth of a pound, which produced a candle just over 10 inches long and three-quarters of an inch in diameter at its base – the same size as appears to be used in *The Wits* frontispiece image,[18] and which the surviving eighteenth-century candle-holders at Český Krumlov are also clearly designed to accommodate. Graves suggests that 'it is clear the articles were drawn up to convince the actors how generously the householders were going to treat them', but responds by assuming that 'near 5s a day'

[15] Transcribed in Peter Cunningham, 'The Whitefriars Theatre, the Salisbury Court Theatre, and the Duke's Theatre in Dorset Gardens', *Shakespeare Society Papers* 4 (1849), 95–100, though he gave neither the source nor the whereabouts of the documents. G. E. Bentley published them in *The Jacobean and Caroline Stage* (6 vols.; Oxford: Clarendon Press, 1941), vol. II, pp. 684–7, and they can also be read in full in Glynne Wickham, Herbert Berry and William Ingram (eds.), *English Professional Theatre, 1530–1660* (Cambridge University Press, 2000), pp. 664–7.

[16] Bentley, *Jacobean and Caroline Stage*, vol. II, p. 686. [17] Graves, *Lighting*, p. 184.

[18] Reproduced in R. A. Foakes, *Illustrations of the English Stage 1580–1642* (Stanford University Press, 1985), pp. 159–61. The size of candle shown in the two chandeliers above the stage, each with eight branches, appears to be the size produced by making 'six candles to a pound' of wax or tallow. In other respects, however, the image is unreliable; see note 47 below.

means a figure of 4 shillings a day, 'to allow for the householders' exaggeration',[19] resulting in a total daily spend of 8 shillings.

However, if, as the document appears to suggest, the actors themselves had until this point borne, if not the whole cost of the candles, certainly more than 50 per cent, it seems to me inconceivable that they would not know what that cost had been. So I am going to make my own assumption that Heton's 'near 5 shillings' is a truer statement than Graves allows, and to interpret it as 4s 9d, giving a total daily spend of 9s 6d. Next, Graves takes off a further 2 shillings for backstage and rehearsal lights, lanterns, 'general replacement and upkeep', and so forth, leaving a sum of 6 shillings per day available for candles. Heton refers only to the purchase of 'wax and tallow' (which could include torches as well as candles given the flexibility of terminology; see below),[20] but there would of course be some expenditure included in this sum for maintaining and buying or replacing equipment – a torch, for example, might cost around a shilling (depending on what type) while a dark lantern cost about 3 shillings – though such things were reusable and would be only an occasional purchase. As far as maintenance costs were concerned, records show that the chandeliers at court were more often repaired than replaced, although, as they were regularly transported from one royal palace to another (no palace appears to have had its own permanent lighting rig), that maintenance is more explicable. However, other lighting equipment used at royal entertainments appears to have been routinely replaced, such as wire to stretch across a hall from which to suspend the chandeliers and hooks with which to tighten it; wire or rope (the last with protective metal sleeves to stop it burning) used to hang the chandeliers and pulleys (metal and wooden) to raise and lower them, plus soap and resin to smooth their operation; candlesticks (metal and earthenware, often in considerable numbers); prickers (spikes to secure candles) and wallers; torches and the fuel for them; and metal 'candle plates' to protect ceilings from flame and smoke or plaster board to protect walls.[21] Graves argues that if Salisbury Court 'replaced its equipment as often as the court did, 2 shillings would not be sufficient'.[22] However, at court these things were presumably disposed of after the performances or damaged while being removed or transported, whereas equipment installed in a

19 Graves, *Lighting*, pp. 183–4.

20 If all the money went just on candles, it would have purchased 114 tallow at one penny each, or 28 wax at four pence each.

21 See, for example, the equipment listed in MSC, vol. XIII, 'The Jacobean and Caroline Revels Accounts, 1603–1642' (Oxford: Malone Society Publications, 1986), pp. 10–11, 83–4, 98, 122, 127–9, 141.

22 Graves, *Lighting*, p. 184.

permanent theatre space was a company asset and so likely to be carefully looked after. So I make another assumption, reduce Graves's figure, and across 'all winter' I deduct just a shilling a day, leaving 8 shillings and sixpence a day for the 'wax and tallow' rather than the 6 shillings Graves' calculation allows: the impact on the number of candles that could be bought and, within that number, the possible proportions of tallow to wax, is significant. For example, 8 shillings and sixpence would have bought 102 tallow candles (at a penny each)[23] to be distributed around the stage and auditorium. And if twelve wax candles were purchased at a cost of 4 shillings, sufficient to provide two wax lights in each of six wall brackets in the pit (such as were installed in the gallery at the Cockpit in Court), enough still remained to buy fifty-four tallow candles, nearly double Graves' upper limit of thirty.

A modern reconstruction of an indoor theatre, however, may reasonably decide that in order to respond to the unquestionably different expectations of Jacobean and modern audiences a higher level of illumination is required, one that can still capture the nature and 'feel' of the original practice without making what was a convention in Jacobean performance into a theme in ours. Furthermore, comparisons based on domestic use are not appropriate; a candle in the home to read by, or light the way to bed, makes it possible to see, whereas illumination in a theatre must make it possible for an audience to *watch*. So in all but the most 'authentic' reconstruction practices or a research exercise, a sensible balance must be made in order to avoid having the stage operate in one time period and the audience in another; the essential present tense of a theatrical performance must be preserved with the audience as participants, listening and watching, not as merely curious observers of an experiment.

Of course, Heton's document would be easier to interpret if we had details of the dimensions and other physical characteristics of Salisbury Court. As it is, we know little more about this playhouse other than that it stood on a plot of land probably bordered by Water Lane (now Whitefriars Street) and Tudor Street, and had been converted from a barn. Especially intriguing is the implication from Heton's document that there was little or no expenditure on candles during the summer months, when it appears from other records that this playhouse, unlike the Blackfriars, was in use.

23 In general terms, one penny in the 1630s was roughly equivalent to forty pence now, with a wax candle costing four times as much, which is not far from the cost of a hand-made, dipped wax candle today, for a comparatively small order for which I paid £1.50 each in 2011. The price difference between wax and tallow has narrowed however: unrefined sheep tallow candles cost me £1.00 each.

According to a document dating from 1660, it was 40 feet square,[24] and other references too suggest that it was indeed a small playhouse: in Thomas Nabbes' *Tottenham Court*, a 'pleasant comedy' acted there in 1633, the Hostess speaks the Epilogue, inviting the audience to return another day, promising them that 'When others [i.e., playhouses] filled rooms with neglect disdain ye, / My little house (with thanks) shall entertain ye'.[25]

Indeed, the evident variance in dimensions between different indoor theatres (just as we know there was between the Globe, Fortune and Rose outdoor playhouses) should warn us against drawing up too firm a template of lighting practice generally, and we must be equally wary of assuming that even at the same playhouse, each and every play, of all genres, would be lit in similar fashion, a point to which I will return. What we can be more certain of, however, is that the commercial companies would undoubtedly have wanted to keep their costs down as much as possible, especially at the Salisbury Court if the small box-office returns recorded by Bentley for the 'little' playhouse are typical, and it was not a high-earning venue.[26] But to what extent was the candle-power in use in playhouses governed by economics rather than artistic choice? We may be able to gain an idea of what were considered desirable, rather than only acceptable (or affordable) levels of illumination, by examining what was provided at court, where financial constraints were presumably not as significant an issue.

At the Cockpit in Court, a playhouse in a remodelled cockpit in the grounds of the palace at Whitehall, extensive renovations in 1629–30 included inserting a calico ceiling decorated with stars cut out of assidue[27] designed 'to cover all the room overhead', so blocking daylight from the roof lantern,[28] boarding over some of the windows, then painting them to resemble glass (probably to retain the outward appearance of the building).[29] In 1662 shutters were installed on some windows. It appears, therefore, that although the theatre was generally used for performances after dark, there was still a desire to reduce the daylight entering, so emphasizing the impact of the artificial light. The stage was evidently lit by ten small and

24 Bentley, *Jacobean and Caroline Stage*, vol. VI, pp. 91–3.

25 Thomas Nabbes, *Tottenham Court* (1639), p. 71.

26 Bentley, *Jacobean and Caroline Stage*, vol. VI, p. 93.

27 An alloy of copper and zinc, rolled into thin sheets and used in imitation of gold leaf; also known as 'arsedue', 'arsedine', 'orsedine', 'orsedue'. In 1604 it cost the Revels Office between 2 shillings and 2s 6d a pound, and they paid 2 shillings a pound for having it cut; MSC, vol. XIII, 'Revels Accounts', p. 10.

28 Though it appears it could be drawn back, presumably to provide daylight for rehearsals, maintenance, etc.; Bentley, *Jacobean and Caroline Stage*, vol. VI, p. 273.

29 Ibid., p. 272.

two large chandeliers, each holding three and fifteen candles respectively, but no document exists that specifies exactly how these were deployed in the space, nor how big the candles were. (Whether a candle is wax or tallow, but not its size, has some bearing on its light output, but obviously bigger candles burn for longer.) Nor is it clear whether they were all hung or some were attached to the walls, whereas in 1660 a specific order was placed for 'twenty fair gilt branches' each holding three candles and for six 'sconces for the passages that are dark'.[30] So for plays generally without scenery, this adds up to sixty candles in branches plus perhaps twelve in sconces which, added to the thirty in the two great chandeliers, would give a total of 102 (assuming that the 1660 purchase was a replacement for existing lighting equipment).

However, entertainments were frequently staged in a variety of court venues such as St James's Palace or Somerset House, which in the seventeenth century as the home, in turn, of masque-loving Queen Anne and enthusiastic amateur actress, Queen Henrietta Maria, became 'the centre of scenic drama in England'.[31] Court entertainments included masques and performances with scenery, where the number of candles and torches used were often counted in staggeringly high numbers: a note in Inigo Jones' hand, scribbled on a design for the masque, *Albion's Triumph* (1631), is an order for 48 torches, 36 'ordinary torches', 192 'good wax' candles and 200 'sises' (small, sometimes round candles).[32]

More relevant to a comparison with the commercial theatres are plays performed at court *without* scenery – in other words, plays transferred directly from the professional theatre, presented on stages erected just for that event and then dismantled, and with temporary lighting facilities. Again, the documented evidence is frustratingly patchy, but the Declared Accounts of the Office of Works for November 1633–4, for example, refer to 'making ready the presence chamber several times for plays to be acted'[33] at St James's Palace by the King's Men, which records of the Master of the Revels, Henry Herbert, list as Shakespeare's *Richard III*, Shirley's *The Young Admiral*, *The Taming of the Shrew* and, two days later, Fletcher's *The Tamer Tamed*.[34] The presence chamber at St James's

30 Ibid., p. 279.

31 John Orrell, *The Theatres of Inigo Jones and John Webb* (Cambridge University Press, 1985), p. 81.

32 Stephen Orgel and Roy Strong, *The Theatre of the Stuart Court* (2 vols.; London: Sotheby Parke Bernet, 1973), vol. I, p. 464.

33 MSC, vol. x, 'Dramatic Records in the Declared Accounts of the Office of Works 1560–1640' (Oxford: Malone Society Publications, 1975), p. 47.

34 N. C. Bawcutt (ed.), *The Control and Censorship of Caroline Drama: The Records of Sir Henry Herbert, Master of the Revels 1623–73* (Oxford: Clarendon Press, 1996), pp. 184–5.

measured approximately 20 feet by 40 feet, which compares closely to the internal dimensions of the stage and the pit in the Sam Wanamaker Playhouse at Shakespeare's Globe.

The Revels accounts for the same occasion show that John Watts, a wire-drawer employed in fashioning branches and other lighting fixtures and fittings, attended on each of those performance dates, presumably to oversee that all the technical aspects went smoothly.[35] The expenses incurred include the purchase of wallers and the repair (presumably by Watts) of eight branches (at a cost of £7). Assuming this reference to branches is to the November plays, as its position in the accounts would suggest, and if all eight were flown at the same time, and if each branch held between three and eight candles, this would give between twenty-four and sixty-four candles. (Interestingly, the installation of a raised stage is not mentioned, which suggests that its installation would have left insufficient height in the room to fly the chandeliers without staining the ceiling – there is no mention of ceiling plates – leaving the actors to perform on the floor.) The four separate purchases of wallers suggests they relate to each of the four plays. Each purchase amounted to 3 shillings, which (using more detailed figures elsewhere in the accounts) would buy eighteen wallers at 2 pence each, each holding one or two candles, which added to the branches gives a total between fifty and eighty-four candles, the lower figure well within the Salisbury Court range. Why the wall brackets were not reused is unclear. They may have been fragile and so easily broken (they were not expensive), or as the room was clearly used regularly and so needed to be put straight after each play, it might have simply been quicker to throw them away.

Positioning the lights

Illustrations of theatres in later periods often show no chandeliers at all, or, if they do, they are often hung so high above the stage that they would have had no noticeable effect beyond lighting the ceiling. In practice, chandeliers need to be suspended no higher than 8 feet (2.2m) above the stage: the French essayist, La Bruyère, writing in the late seventeenth century, describes (perhaps with some exaggeration) a court dandy getting his wig caught in a chandelier.[36] A particular feature of chandeliers is that they appear to cast their light 'behind' them, which suggests that they were hung further 'down stage' (i.e., away from the tiring-house wall) than we might at first imagine.

35 MSC, vol. XIII, 'Revels Accounts', p. 128.
36 Jean de La Bruyère, *Characters*, trans. Jean Stewart (Harmondsworth: Penguin, 1970), p. 183.

Indeed, the intriguing space between the front edge of the stage and the front row of benches shown on Worcester College drawing 7b may have been designed to allow the front pair of chandeliers to be hung slightly forward of the stage, the gap beneath ensuring the audience did not get wax dripped on them, but close enough when lowered to be brailed back to rest on the stage while being attended to in the intervals (see Figure 1).

The exact number of chandeliers above the stage of any early modern indoor theatre is not known, and may well have varied for different performances at the same theatre of different genres of play, and at theatres with stages of different sizes (see below).[37] Once raised, the chandeliers were for the most part likely to remain at a constant height above the stage throughout each act. However, as they were installed with gear that enabled them to be raised and lowered, it seems inevitable that the company would have noticed the variation in the light levels depending on their height above the stage and taken advantage of that to create different effects. There is no evidence prior to the Restoration to confirm (or challenge) this suggestion, but in experiments at Bristol we discovered that raising the chandeliers only a few feet reduced the light on the actors to a discernible extent, producing a distinct lighting change. Ben Jonson's *Catline* (*c.* 1611), staged at the Globe and Blackfriars, includes the stage direction, '*A darkness comes over the place*' (Act 1, line 312).[38] At the outdoor playhouse this must obviously have been achieved by the actors' performances, but when it was performed indoors, it may be a description of what actually happened on stage.

A 10-inch candle may burn for the duration of a play,[39] but to do so it needs regular trimming (or snuffing) and in some circumstances may need replacing, operations that took place during the act intervals, which became an integral part of virtually all plays after 1608. One frequently reads that tallow candles produced both smoke and unpleasant smells, but while any candle may smoke more than usual if it is left alone, or is in a draught (the

[37] In 1674 the Theatre Royal in Drury Lane was lit by four chandeliers (each holding twelve candles) with two more (again holding twelve) lighting the apron stage and the auditorium lit by approximately sixteen sconces on the pillars supporting the galleries, each holding two or four candles. There is no evidence that chandeliers were hung over the pit until Garrick's tenure at the Drury Lane theatre in the mid eighteenth century (Graves, *Lighting*, p. 183).

[38] Ben Jonson, *Catiline His Conspiracy*, ed. W. F. Bolton and Jane F. Gardner (Lincoln: University of Nebraska Press, 1972). The direction was included in the 1616 folio edition, but not in the 1611 quarto.

[39] Experiments at Český Krumlov show that a 10 1/2-inch wax candle loses 6 inches of wax in 4 1/2 hours, while a tallow candle of the same size loses nearly 10 inches. Candles placed higher in a chandelier can burn faster than those below.

candle's main enemy), experiments at the University of Bristol and those at the Baroque Theatre Foundation at Český Krumlov found that candles made from tallow (animal fat) did not produce significantly more smoke or an unpleasant smell, even at Bristol where a lower-quality sheep fat was used than the beef tallow used at Český Krumlov.[40] I think it is likely that both smoke and smell came more from the tobacco pipes, especially of the young gallants seated on the stage.[41] As with so many aspects of early modern performance practice, we must be careful to avoid establishing general principles. For example, there is no evidence that each interval in a performance was of equal duration. In Ben Jonson's *The Magnetic Lady* (Blackfriars, 1632), for example, the discussions about the play between two actors playing audience members – Damplay and Probee – that occupy the four act breaks are all of different lengths (seventy, eighty-five, thirty-eight and thirty-six lines).[42] Even more intriguing, because it represents an intervention in the very process of preparing a play in the theatre, is the autographed manuscript of Philip Massinger's *Believe As You List* (Blackfriars, 1631), a fair copy prepared by the King's Men's bookkeeper, Edward Knight. In it he wrote 'Long' in the margin at the beginning of Act 2 and Act 4.[43] Having directed the play myself and been involved with the RSC production in 2005, I can see no particular demands of stage-setting, changes of costume or character that would require an extended break at these points, and the play's acts are of more or less of equal length. But as the main purpose of intervals in the first place was to provide the necessary time to attend to the lights (not, as some have suggested, primarily to give opportunities for music),[44] was there something particular that needed to be done here? Could it be that these were the points at which any lights in the auditorium that had perhaps been burning before the actual play began were attended

[40] See Peter Perina, 'Candle Lighting in Theatres in the 17th and 18th Centuries', *The World of Baroque Theatre: A Compilation of Essays from the Český Krumlov Conferences 2004–6* (Antwerp: Cesky Krumlov, 2007), pp. 131–4. However, both experiments may have used a higher quality of tallow than that used in earlier theatres.

[41] At line 27 of Act 2 scene 6 of Jonson's *The Alchemist*, Subtle accepts a gift of a pipe of tobacco from Abel Drugger. By line 77 he is smoking and enjoying it, and I like to think the actor cadged a light from one of the stage-sitters.

[42] Ben Jonson, *The Magnetic Lady*, ed. Peter Happé (Manchester University Press, 2000).

[43] Philip Massinger, *Believe As You List*, in Philip Edwards and Colin Gibson (eds.), *The Plays and Poems of Philip Massinger* (5 vols.; Oxford: Clarendon Press, 1976), vol. III. The autograph manuscript of the play is held in the British Library, Egerton 2828.

[44] Gary Taylor, 'The Structure of Performance: Act-Intervals in the London Theatres, 1576–1642', in Gary Taylor and John Jowett, *Shakespeare Reshaped 1606–1623* (Oxford: Clarendon Press, 1993), pp. 3–50 (p. 31). Music was, of course, a central part of the indoor (and especially the Blackfriars) experience, but the prime function of the interval was to manage the lighting.

to in addition to the chandeliers? But this is pure speculation, and a further reminder of how difficult it is to recapture early staging practices.

With the chandeliers lit, casting sufficient general light for actors and audience, hand-held candles, lanterns and torches were the instruments most commonly used to articulate the general lighting state. Indoors and out, each of these pieces of equipment carried a conventional level of meaning (in addition to indicating night-time scenes). Apart from general domestic use, candles were commonly associated with funerals, religious settings, studies or banquets, while lanterns or lamps were often linked to clandestine behaviour, an association reflected in real life when Guy Fawkes was arrested in the cellars of Whitehall carrying a dark-lantern (now on display in the Ashmolean Museum, Oxford). As lanterns were not so prone to going out as candles, they could be moved about more vigorously, enabling points of action in lively scenes to be illuminated, or could be used by characters speaking from the upper level where some precise illumination was needed to draw the spectator's eye to them. Torches were the most striking of the hand-held instruments, particularly in the confined space of an indoor stage, and were equally popular in court entertainments. Torches (especially outdoors, such as those shown on the frontispiece to Kyd's *The Spanish Tragedy* being used on the Rose stage) may have been fuelled by rope or cotton wadding soaked in tar, whereas indoors the term might also have referred to a cluster of candles bound together, described in George Chapman's *The Memorable Masque* as 'torches of virgin wax, whose staves were great canes all over gilded'.[45] Torches made the greatest impact of all, introducing a sudden burst of light on stage, such as Vindice describes in *The Revenger's Tragedy*: 'last revelling night / When torchlight made an artificial noon' (1.4.27).

A brief word needs to be said about footlights. There are no records whatsoever to suggest that footlights were used on the early modern commercial theatre stage – the frontispiece of *The Wits* is often advanced to support the idea that they were used but in this respect, as in others, the drawing is an unreliable witness.[46] Footlights are not appropriate for a thrust stage with an audience in effect viewing from four sides, and would also be extremely unlikely to remain alight given the draught produced by the full-length dresses and cloaks moving close to them. Nicolo Sabbatini

[45] George Chapman, *The Memorable Masque*, in David Lindley (ed.), *Court Masques: Jacobean and Caroline Entertainments 1605–1640* (Oxford University Press, 1995). The torches are illustrated in Orgel and Strong, *Theatre of the Stuart Court*, vol. 1, pp. 250, 263. Examples of these survive at Český Krumlov.

[46] John H. Astington, 'The Wits Illustration, 1662', *Theatre Notebook* 47 (1993), 122–40.

employed them for his end-on staging, but quickly decided against them, believing that they made the stage appear darker rather than lighter, and disliking the screen of smoke the burning oil created between the audience and the stage.[47]

'The luster of Torches, the sparking of rich Jewells'

I am not going to discuss here the fundamental issue of the impact of lighting on the actors or their audiences, but I want to look briefly at its relationship to the costumes and decoration of the indoor theatres.[48] As cited elsewhere in this volume, in 1625, Sir Francis Bacon observed of fabrics that 'the colours that show best by candlelight are white, carnation, and a kind of sea-water-green'.[49] We can see the truth of this in the work of the eighteenth-century English painter Joseph Wright, who made his name with a series of 'Candle Light' pictures (he is perhaps most famous for his painting of 'An Experiment on a Bird in the Air Pump', 1768) that show his special interest in the contrasts of artificial and natural light, the effects of a single light source and the play of shadows that resulted. His painting *The Alchymist* of 1795 (which is as detailed in its depiction of the laboratory equipment as Jonson was in the alchemical terminologies in his text) captures the chiaroscuro that was undoubtedly characteristic of the 'look' of scenes on the indoor stage. The alchemist in Wright's painting wears a sea-green robe, and his two assistants in the background wear green and red respectively, while Romeo and Juliet – in a painting titled *Romeo and Juliet: The Tomb Scene*, exhibited in 1790 – wear white and carnation. Bacon also noted that 'rich embroidery' was 'lost and not discerned', but recommended the use of 'oes or spangs [what we would call sequins], as they are of no great cost, so they are of most glory'.[50] The silver thread in costumes was similarly designed to catch the light, as indeed were the actors' faces, gleaming with a lustre derived from their makeup.[51] The total effect must have been captivating.

47 See Gosta M. Bergman, *Lighting in the Theatre* (Stockholm: Almqvist & Wiksell International, 1977), pp. 75–6.

48 The title of this subsection is taken from a pamphlet, 'October 4, 1642, A Deep Sigh Breath'd Through the Lodgings at White-Hall', describing the deserted 'Cockpit and Revelling Rooms, where at a Play or Masque the darkest night was converted to the brightest Day that ever shin'd': Bentley, *Jacobean and Caroline Stage*, vol. VI, p. 284.

49 Francis Bacon, 'Of Masques and Triumphs', in John Pitcher (ed.), *Francis Bacon: The Essays* (Harmondsworth: Penguin, 1985), pp. 175–6 (p. 176).

50 These paintings and other 'candlelights' are reproduced and discussed in Judy Egerton, *Wright of Derby* (London: Tate Publishing, 1990).

51 See Farah Karim-Cooper, *Cosmetics in Shakespearean and Renaissance Drama* (Edinburgh University Press, 2006), and also Chapter 10 below.

Exactly how the candles were deployed at the Cockpit in Court is unclear from the records, but as I suggested above, it seems to me not impossible that the 'ten smaller' branches 'about . . . the stage'[52] might have referred to candle-holders attached to the walls of the *frons scenae*. In 1585, when Angelo Ingegneri staged the inaugural production at the Teatro Olimpico in Vicenza (which was designed by Palladio, constructed by Scamozzi, and visited twice by Inigo Jones in 1613–14), he placed candles in glass holders beneath sculptural details to highlight them,[53] and at the Italian Renaissance theatre in Sabionetta there remains evidence that small glass containers filled with wax (or possibly oil) were secured in iron brackets to the structure of the stage. We should not discount the possibility that something similar could have been done at the Blackfriars.[54] Indeed, one of the reasons that live candles are superior to electric imitations (despite real advances in the technology)[55] is that the uneven flicker of the burning wicks of dozens of candles plays with the surfaces on which the light falls, softening them and giving life and texture.[56] Graves suggests that for the indoor theatre audience, '[i]nsofar as the candles were few in number, the audience found itself in the dreary, dull light they saw every day in their homes, business and inns'.[57] But it is important that we consider the effect in the playhouse overall, including the (apparently) glamorous clothes worn by the actors and the richly decorated clothes and jewels of many in the audience, the effect of a ruff or collar reflecting light to an actor's face, and how the theatre was itself decorated. We have little direct evidence of the painterly treatment of the interior of the theatre. However, a major influence on the choice of paint colour would have been the candlelight which, to be as effective as possible, needs two things: pale surfaces to reflect the light and elements in the fabric of the theatre that are specifically designed and decorated to catch, reflect and play with the light. So far as the paint colour was concerned, this too appears to have been in line with Bacon's observations: light stone, pale green (such as were used in later candlelit Georgian theatres), pale grey and blue are

52 Egerton, *Wright*, p. 273.

53 Remo Schiavo, *A Guide to the Olympic Theatre*, trans. Patricia Ann Hill (2nd edn; Vicenza: Accademia Olimpica, 1985), p. 140.

54 Licisco Magagnato, *Il Teatro Olimpico* (Milan: Electra, 1992) includes Ingegneri's sketch of the stage with the positions of some lights and actors (p. 170).

55 Francis Reid, 'Historically Informed Lighting in Baroque Opera Staging', in Perina, *World of Baroque Theatre*, pp. 155–63.

56 On 5 October 1667 Samuel Pepys recorded in his diary that on a visit backstage at the Theatre Royal, Drury Lane, he was surprised by the contrast between the actors' costumes and the 'show they make on the stage by candle-light'; Samuel Pepys, *The Diary of Samuel Pepys*, ed. Mynors Bright (3 vols.; London: J. M. Dent, 1953), vol. III, p. 75.

57 Graves, *Lighting*, p. 195.

the shades most frequently described. It is interesting to note that when the second Banqueting Hall in Whitehall was completed in 1622, primarily to accommodate lavish entertainments, it was painted pale grey/white, but when that use came to an end in 1635 with the arrival of the long-awaited Rubens ceiling paintings, it was redecorated to resemble mahogany. And when the Cockpit in Court was remodelled in 1629–30, the painter Mathew Goodricke used mainly stone as the basic colour set off with a 'fayre blewe' picked out with gold, which was matched by the painting and gilding applied to the cornicing, chandeliers and other candle-holders, and by the calico ceiling 'garnished' with 'a great number of stars' cut from assidue).[58]

Carved features would be highlighted with gold leaf (or cheaper substitutes such as assidue, or even white and yellow paint), and the same effort to make the lights sparkle (especially to achieve the effect for comedy that di Somi describes) may well have included polished metal reflectors on the wall brackets and adding ground glass to the varnish, 'in the French way', to make the light, in John Ronayne's phrase, 'jump about'.[59] Bacon refers to coloured lights in court entertainments and, given the frequent traffic between the palaces and the playhouses, I see no reason to discount the possibility of having them on the professional indoor stage. Similarly, at court they had crystal chandeliers hung with silver wire,[60] and thin wires with fragments of glass or polished metal attached to reflect the light were often twined through the branches of the chandeliers, or they were sometimes decorated with tassels and fringes cut from assidue, effects which the playhouses may have been able to imitate at less expense.[61]

In the opening scene of Thomas Heywood's *Love's Mistress*,[62] which according to its title page was presented at court as well as being 'Publicly Acted by the Queens Comedians, at the Phoenix in Drury Lane' in 1634, one character speaks to another, and refers to the audience as 'this sphere

58 Bentley, *Jacobean and Caroline Stage*, vol. VI, pp. 272–3.

59 Private correspondence. Ronayne notes that coloured varnish was sometimes laid over tin, and also quotes a pamphlet, 'A Short Introduction to the Art of Painting and Varnishing' (London, 1685), held in the British Library, that includes instructions how 'to lay on your Mettle Speckles: First wet your work with Varnish, with a soft brush, then while 'tis wet dust your speckles upon it thro' a piece of Tiffany [a transparent gauze muslin], and then Varnish it twice, to keep 'em from rubbing off, 'tis enough' (fo. 14). I am very grateful to John Ronayne for his generous interest in this chapter.

60 Collections, vol. XIII, 'Revels Accounts', pp. 98, 122. In February 1633 at Denmark House the chandeliers were also 'garnished' with ivy, gathered from Greenwich and Hyde parks.

61 Ibid., 50, p. 64.

62 Thomas Heywood, *Love's Mistress, or The Queen's Masque*, ed. Richmond Shady (Salzburg: Edwin Mellen Press, 1977).

spangled with all these stars', and in Lewis Sharpe's *The Noble Stranger*,[63] acted at Salisbury Court in 1638, the Prologue says, 'Blest fate protect me! What a lustre's here? / How many stars deck this our little sphere'. Both images liken the view of the audience, whether viewed from the stage or anywhere else in the theatre, to a starlit sky, with the candles in their holders on the gallery fronts catching the colours of the auditorium, the decorated ceiling subtly illuminated by the sparkling chandeliers, and the light dancing and reflecting from the clothes and jewellery of the audience. As George Wither wrote in his poem, *Fair Virtue* (1622), describing a woman's clothes, 'You may liken every gem / To those lamps which at a play /Are set up to light the day'.[64]

Early commentators on the art and practice of lighting are as aware as lighting designers are today of the creative contribution lighting makes to an audience's responses to a play. I have discussed below the possible ways in which lighting would have contributed to the impact of performances of a tragedy at the Blackfriars, but the different needs of comedy may well have resulted in different numbers, disposition and nature of the lights. A spectator at a performance given for Elizabeth I at Christ Church College, Oxford, in 1565 recorded:

> Burning lamps, hanging lamps, and candles made a very bright light there. With so many lights arranged in branches and circles and so many torches providing flickering light here and there with unequal brightness, the place shone, so that like daylight [the lights] seemed to sparkle and help the splendour of the shows with the greatest radiance.[65]

The circumstances (and expenditure) were particular to a royal event, of course, but the link between lighting and mood is obvious and something of the same attitude and approach, if of less magnitude, is likely to have influenced commercial practice. Leone di Somi writes that when staging a comedy, as 'the author provides us with a pleasant, charming plot and . . . the actor gives to this a vivid interpretation, surely it is equally essential that the architect should represent gladness and joy on the stage'. And the key to achieving that, in di Somi's opinion, is to be led by the example of lighting 'bonfires and torches . . . as a sign of joy [from which] arises this theatrical

[63] Lewis Sharpe, *The Noble Stranger* (London: British Library, 2011), prologue.
[64] George Wither, *Fair Virtue; or, The Mistress of Phil'arete* (London, 1622), p. 68.
[65] *Records of Early English Drama: Oxford*, vol. II, 979. In fairness, however, it should be noted that the following entry is by another spectator who recalled that, in making this display, they burned in one night all the candles that were supposed to last for five.

convention of thus imitating festive occasions', of 'using lights . . . to imitate . . . this mood of gaiety'.[66]

Case study: *The Duchess of Malfi* at the Blackfriars, autumn 1614

John Webster's play was performed at the open-air Globe playhouse as well as at the indoor Blackfriars, by the King's Men, probably in 1614. The company had been using their indoor playhouse for five years, and (except for the time when the Globe was being rebuilt after the 1613 fire) continued to transfer plays from one venue to another, the implications of which practice are a major, yet neglected, area of exploration and discovery.

Two years before *The Duchess of Malfi* was staged indoors, Webster's *The White Devil* had been performed at the outdoor Red Bull playhouse, an experience that Webster found unacceptable at almost every level, complaining in his preface to the printed play that it had been 'acted, in so dull a time of winter [and] presented in so open and black a theatre, that it wanted [i.e., lacked] a full and understanding auditory' but got instead an audience mostly of 'ignorant asses'.[67] The implication was clear: the play needed to be performed in a warm, indoor theatre with a judicious audience capable of listening to and understanding it, in other words, at the Blackfriars. And among the many features of staging implied by the text of his follow-up play, features that are clearly designed for indoor performance, is the detailed use of light and darkness to create states that not only enhance the atmosphere of scenes but also reflect the shifting emotional moods of the play, so enriching the theatrical experience for the audience in ways unavailable on the daylit stage of the Globe. It is precisely this unique Blackfriars experience that the indoor Jacobean theatre – the Sam Wanamaker Playhouse – aims to create for today's audiences.

A character in Francis Beaumont's, *The Woman Hater*,[68] staged at the indoor Paul's playhouse in 1606, describes his extravagant arrival at the theatre:

> I'll after dinner to the stage, to see a play, where, when I first enter, you shall have a murmur in the house . . . all the gallants on the stage rise . . . offer me their places: then I pick out someone whom I please to grace among the rest, take his seat, use it, throw my cloak over my face, and laugh at him. (1.3.68)

66 Somi, *Dialogues*, p. 274.
67 John Webster, *The White Devil*, ed. John Russell Brown (London: Methuen, 1966), p. 2.
68 Francis Beaumont, *The Woman Hater*, ed. Alexander Dyce (Freeport, New York: Books for Libraries Press, 1970).

It appears that at least one spectator at the Blackfriars, Bulstrode Whitelocke, made if anything an even bigger entrance, as his own signature tune ('Whitelocke's Coranto', composed by himself) would be struck up when he arrived.[69] The 'Blackfriars Music', as the orchestra was known, was renowned in its own right and might play for an hour while the spectators found their seats, settled and chatted. During all this time it is possible that only the light from the windows, perhaps aided by the candles in wall brackets in the pit, illuminated the theatre, as it seems likely the company would have wanted to conserve their stage candles as much as possible.[70] The induction to John Marston's *What You Will*,[71] also performed at Paul's playhouse in 1601, dramatizes these moments before the play got under way: '*Before the music sounds for the act, enter* ATTICUS, DORICUS *and* PHYLOMUSE*; they sit a good while [on stools on the stage] before the candles are lighted, talking together*'. After a while, the Tireman (a stage manager) enters '*with lights*' (probably tapers) with which to light the candles in the chandeliers, which are presumably resting on the stage, and in the wall brackets attached to the pillars in front of the stage boxes. Here, and in Jonson's *The Staple of News*,[72] where the bookholder calls 'Mend your lights, Gentlemen – Master Prologue begin', it seems likely that the Prologue spoke while the candles were lit and raised while music 'sounded the act', and the play proper began. The moment when the fully lit chandeliers are raised and the whole nature of the stage is changed as it comes alive, provides a truly energizing opening to any performance.

For a play with no further demands on the lighting, the candles would remain in this position throughout, being lowered to the stage in the intervals to be trimmed and, where necessary, replaced. Should a candle begin to burn irregularly between intervals, the documented practice on the Continent was to extinguish it using a long pole with a wet sponge on the end manoeuvred by a stage-hand from the upper gallery, but although this technique might also have been used in London, no mention of it or any other method is made in any reference to English practice. It is this pattern

69 Andrew Gurr, *Playgoing in Shakespeare's London* (2nd edn; Cambridge University Press, 1996), pp. 210–12.

70 A visitor to the Leipzig theatre in 1783 recorded that he 'entered the pit . . . and nearly fell down the last few steps at the entrance because of the darkness': the pit was illuminated by only fifteen of the available candles, and with no daylight to augment them. Quoted in George W. Brandt and Wiebe Hogendoorn (eds.), *German and Dutch Theatre, 1600–1848* (Cambridge University Press, 1993), p. 96.

71 John Marston, *What You Will*, ed. M. R. Woodhead (Nottingham: Nottingham Drama Texts, 1968).

72 Ben Jonson, *The Staple of News*, ed. Anthony Parr (Manchester University Press, 1988).

that Webster's play follows for its first three acts. In the fourth, however, he may have taken the opportunity to alter the playhouse lighting to enhance the mood. In those indoor plays that appear to take advantage of changeable lighting states, these variations are often clustered to take advantage of points in the action – most notably act breaks – to adjust the height of the chandeliers: in *'Tis Pity She's a Whore*,[73] for example, much of the third act is played in increasing darkness which is integral to the plot before the interval is used to relight and possibly enhance the lighting for the fourth act that opens with a wedding feast, while the whole of Marston's *Antonio's Revenge*[74] traces an arc of increasing darkness, physically and metaphorically.

So, in the interval after the third act of Webster's play (perhaps one that would have been marked '*Long*' in the prompt-copy), some of the candles in the chandeliers may have been extinguished before being hoisted to their higher position, and *possibly* shutters on the windows closed, or at least on those nearest the stage. In any case, with the fourth act beginning at roughly 3.45 p.m. on a winter afternoon, the daylight outside would already be fading. The act opens with the servant, Bosola, reporting to the Duchess's mad brother, Ferdinand, who has come to visit her. He has, however, vowed never to *see* her and he exits as the Duchess enters. The servant, Bosola, informs her that her brother has ordered that 'neither torch nor taper / Shine in your chamber' (25–6), and removes what lighting there is: his own torch and her taper, and probably extinguishes the candles in the sconces either side of the stage. The stage will now not only appear, but of course actually *be*, darker than at any point in the play so far, and her exchange with her brother – 'FERDINAND: Where are you? DUCHESS: Here sir. / Ferdinand: This darkness suits you well' (29–30) – will be played in what we would term a naturalistic setting, with the audience able to see as little as the characters. They talk awhile, before Ferdinand offers his hand to the Duchess to kiss. Taking it, she realizes first that the hand is cold, and then that it is not attached to her brother's arm. Recoiling, she cries out: 'Hah! Lights! – O horrible' (53). The audience, in the near darkness, cannot of course know what is going on until Bosola, entering with a light, first illuminates for the Duchess, and the audience, the severed hand, before drawing back the curtains of the recess at the rear of the stage ('Look you: here's the piece from which was ta'en', 56) and, with the flame of the torch, showing what he tells us are the dead bodies of her husband and their

[73] John Ford, *'Tis Pity She's a Whore*, ed. Martin Wiggins (London: A&C Black, 2003).
[74] John Marston, *Antonio's Revenge*, ed. W. Reavley Gair (Manchester University Press, 1978).

children. A torch is used here, no doubt, not only because of its ability to focus the attention on specific things on stage, illuminating them surrounded by darkness, but also because its intensity fits the violence and horror of these moments. The remainder of the act sees the cruel mental and physical torture of the Duchess, the extraordinary dance of madmen, and finally the murder of the Duchess, all played on the darkened stage, with hand-held lights to pinpoint moments of action, and accompanied by music suiting the mood. Indeed, it may be that the stage was darkened further at the moment of her death by removing any other lights, rendering them almost entirely ineffective, so that when her brother comes to view her dead body, her face is caught in the light of a single candle, finally tipping him over the edge to complete insanity: 'Cover her face; mine eyes dazzle' (4.2.264). Leone di Somi describes a similar pattern in a tragedy he produced in which, 'as soon as the first unhappy incident occurred – the unexpected death of a queen – I contrived at that very instant most of the stage lights . . . were darkened or extinguished. This created a profound impression of horror amongst the spectators and won universal praise'.[75]

The interval at the end of the fourth act, while the audience recover from the terrible events they have witnessed, allows the tire-men to trim the candles, return the branches to their normal height and to relight the candles at the sides of the stage, the restored lighting matching the startlingly upbeat tone of the start of the final act. This mood is short-lived, however, and as much of the action of the fifth act refers to darkness, both real and metaphorical, a lower level of illumination might have been retained, or repeated so that in the closing moments of the play, using candles and lanterns (a 'dark lantern' is specified at 5.4.43) to act as small spotlights, including for those on the upper level in 5.5, the moments of death for the good and bad are caught in startling close-up, while torches may have lit the final tableau of 'this great ruin' (5.5.111).

The Duchess of Malfi was also performed in daylight at the Globe, and it provides an example of how a play might be radically changed depending on its venue. This is seen most acutely in the scene of the Duchess's torment by her brother discussed above. Indoors, as I have suggested, on the increasingly darkened stage the hand-held lighting would have been needed to illuminate the key moments in the action. At the Globe, however, these

[75] Somi, *Dialogues*, p. 274. Scott Palmer suggests the technique of extinguishing lights for tragic effect 'was borrowed from Tenebrae religious services where candles are extinguished one by one to create a solemn, sombre mood as the church gradually darken,' *Light: Readings in Theatre Practice* (Houndsmills: Palgrave Macmillan, 2012), p. 7.

instruments would have acted as signifiers of that darkness, aided by the verbal references to listening and to the difficulty the characters have in seeing each other (lines indeed that might have proved redundant at Blackfriars). The difference between the indoor and outdoor staging centres on how each version positions the audience. At the Blackfriars (certainly for all but those closest to the stage), it is likely that spectators would have been as uncertain as the Duchess as to what was going on, and so been as horrified and shocked as she at the revelation of the dead man's hand. In other words, the Blackfriars audience would have experienced Ferdinand's behaviour from the Duchess's point of view. At the Globe, however, where presumably the audience could see what Ferdinand was doing, they would observe the cruelty enacted upon her. No Jacobean theatre professional could surely have resisted the opportunities offered to stage this most terrifying of plays in an atmosphere that would have matched it perfectly, to create a thrilling experience that performances in the new indoor playhouse at Shakespeare's Globe will enable us to recover.[76]

[76] Many of the points made above can be seen in action in *Chamber of Demonstrations*.

CHAPTER 7

Acoustic and visual practices indoors

Sarah Dustagheer

In *Characters of Virtues and Vices*, Joseph Hall describes the attributes of a profane man: he 'comes to Church as to the Theater, saving that not so willinglie, for companie, for custome, for recreation, perhaps for sleepe, or to feed his eyes or his eares'.[1] In Hall's satire the theatre, alongside the church, could offer a feast for the eyes and ears. This chapter offers an examination of that feast, analyzing the acoustic and visual experience at indoor playhouses. The first part establishes the ways in which music was a dominant and integral aspect of the dramaturgy of indoor plays, as seen particularly in the work of Marston and Shakespeare. In the second part my focus turns to the visual aesthetic of one particular indoor playhouse. Contemporary accounts of the Blackfriars tell us that the audience 'glittered' and 'glistened' under the candle-light, using the playhouse to display the latest London fashion. In response to this distinct visual environment, I suggest that playwrights deployed props and costumes to create a rich, materialistic vision for their stage. Ultimately, the chapter will identify how playwrights created acoustic and visual practices which made effective use of the indoor playhouse environment.

Acoustic practices

Music, as many scholars have pointed out, was a dominant feature of indoor playing because of the instrumentation possible in an enclosed and small space; outdoor playhouses had a very different acoustic environment. Bruce R. Smith describes the Blackfriars Playhouse, with its building material mix of wooden galleries and stage, stone walls and glass windows, as 'a very "live" space'; sound waves would have dispersed and resonated around this theatre.[2] Before considering music in more detail, it is worth examining a

[1] Joseph Hall, *Characters of Virtue and Vice* (London, 1608), H1r.
[2] Bruce R. Smith, *The Acoustic World of Early Modern England: Attending to the O-Factor* (University of Chicago Press, 1999), pp. 214–15.

somewhat overlooked effect of the acoustic environments of indoor playhouses. When comparing the repertories performed at the Globe and the Blackfriars during the same time period (1600–08), we find at the indoor playhouse a lack of loud sound effects such as those heard outdoors. At the Globe there were staged storms (as in *Julius Caesar*, *King Lear* and *Pericles*), varied volume battle sounds (*Julius Caesar*, *Antony and Cleopatra* and *Hamlet*), bells (*Othello*, *Macbeth* and *The Devil's Charter*), chimes (*The Merry Devil of Edmonton*), hammers (*Thomas Lord Cromwell*) and clock chimes (*Julius Caesar* and *Twelfth Night*). None of these effects are deployed by playwrights writing for the Children of the Queen's Revels at the Blackfriars; under these terms, the repertory is quiet, even silent. It seems very possible that this absence exists because of the playhouse's acoustic environment. Put simply, deploying a series of loud sound effects was perhaps unsuitable for such a 'live' space, where sound bounced and travelled around the auditorium, and it seems playwrights avoided such effects in their work.

Instead the acoustic effect which dominated the repertory at the Blackfriars and other indoor playhouses was music. As David Lindley suggests, and Mariko Ichikawa's chapter in this book confirms, music became a 'key ingredient' of indoor playing.[3] Alongside the pre-show and inter-act music, the repertories of the Blackfriars and Paul's demonstrate the dominance of music within play-texts. Between 1599 and 1609 the Children of the Queen's Revels staged thirteen masques: two in *Cynthia's Revels* and *The Malcontent*, respectively, and single masques in *The Dutch Courtesan*, *The Fawn*, *The Gentleman's Usher*, *May Day*, *Poetaster*, *Sir Giles Goosecap*, *Tragedy of Byron*, *The Widow's Tears* and *Your Five Gallants*. At Paul's after the late 1590s, Michael Shapiro points out that '16 of the 21 plays . . . contain a total of 80 songs'.[4] The prevalence of music in these repertories owes something to the musical culture in which the companies existed. Formed originally from boy choristers, the early companies at Paul's and the Blackfriars were managed by or had long-standing associations with musicians such as Nathaniel Giles, Richard Edwards, Richard Farrant and Edward Pearce, to name a few.[5]

However, alongside this musical culture, playwrights were also taking advantage of the opportunities afforded by the indoor acoustic environment.

3 David Lindley, *Shakespeare and Music*, Arden Critical Companions (London: Thomson Learning, 2006), p. 92.

4 Michael Shapiro, *Children of the Revels: The Boy Companies of Shakespeare's Time and their Plays* (New York: Columbia University Press, 1977), p. 236.

5 Indeed, Tiffany Stern points out in Chapter 5 above the number of musicians and composers that inhabited the area around Blackfriars.

Music became far more than just an incidental or discrete presence, a pre-show or inter-act addition. Instead, it was integral to the dramaturgy of many indoor plays as playwrights began to weave music into narrative and character development. In the Blackfriars play *Your Five Gallants*, Middleton centres the play's narrative conclusion on the last scene's masque. Here his title characters perform a 'Strange-gallant and conceited maske' to impress Katherine, the wealthy virgin they hope one of them will marry.[6] Unfortunately, they have asked disguised rival suitor Fitzgrave to pen the masque and he seizes the opportunity to expose the gallants' immorality. Middleton's play is typical of boy companies' indoor repertories where masques 'form a backdrop to a climactic scene, in which a major conflict is resolved by the masque or in spite of it', according to Linda Phyllis Austern.[7] Indeed the plots of Jonson's *Cynthia's Revels* and Marston's *The Malcontent* and *The Fawn* also resolve in extended masque scenes.

In the Paul's play *Blurt Master Constable*, music does not resolve but rather establishes the play's central narrative dilemma. During dancing at the beginning of the play, French prisoner Fontinell watches his keeper Camillo dance with Violetta. While the betrothed couple '*dance a straine*', Fontinell falls in love with Violetta. After this dance is finished, in the next, Violetta '*stands by marking Fontinell*', as he moves around the stage and, of course, begins to feel attraction for him.[8] The love triangle between Camillo, Violetta and Fontinell drives the rest of the plot and is initially established through this opening dance sequence. As well as plot, music is used to expound characters' emotional situations: for example, in John Day's *Law Tricks* at the Blackfriars, the Countess is sung a song 'to beguile' her 'sad sorrow'.[9] Similarly, widower Earl of St Anne 'feedes his eares with soule-exciting musicke' in George Chapman's Blackfriars play *Monsieur D'Olive*.[10] And in Marston's *Antonio and Mellida* at Paul's, grief-stricken Antonio asks his page to sing and '[l]et each more breath the heart of passion, / The sad extracture of extreamest griefe'.[11]

Marston's work for Paul's and the Blackfriars particularly demonstrates the importance of music to indoor playwriting. I have mentioned several of

6 Thomas Middleton, *Your Five Gallants* (London, 1608), H2v.
7 Linda Phyllis Austern, *Music in English Children's Drama of the Later Renaissance* (Philadelphia: Gordon & Breach, 1992), pp. 96–7.
8 Thomas Dekker, *Blurt Master Constable* (London, 1602), A4v.
9 John Day, *Law Tricks* (London, 1608), E3v.
10 George Chapman, *Monsieur D'Olive* (London, 1606), A4v.
11 John Marston, *Antonio and Mellida* (London, 1602), G2v.

his plays already (*The Malcontent*, *The Fawn* and *Antonio and Mellida*) but it is *Sophonisba*, performed at the Blackfriars in 1605/6 which especially reveals Marston's engagement with music in his work. Music underscores many of the key narrative events of the play; a prime example is the entrance of Erichtho, a spirit from the underworld. Anti-hero Syphax evokes Erichtho with a dense, bewitching description:

> A loathsome yellowe leannesse spreades hir face
> A heavy hell-like palenes loades hir cheekes
> Unknowne to a cleare heaven
> . . . she bursts up tombes
> From half rot searcloaths then she scrapes dry gums
> For hir black rites.[12]

Just before Syphax begins this speech of jarring consonants and heavy monosyllabic words ('bursts up', 'scrapes dry gums', 'black rites'), a stage direction demands: '*Infernall Musicke plaies softly whilst* ERICHTHO *enters and when she speakes ceaseth*'. Music provides an atmospheric underscore to Syphax's words. Furthermore, when Erichtho abruptly stops the music (and the speech), the implication is that she has some control over the infernal sounds the audience have heard, adding to her otherworldly power. Indeed, this is confirmed later on in this scene when Erichtho promises she will force '[T]he ayre to musicke and the shad[e]s of night / To forme sweete sounds' and, a few lines later, '*Infernall Musique*' begins to play.[13] In this way, the cueing of music in *Sophonisba* has rich implications for the play's other-worldly atmosphere and characterization.

Of course the use of music – to inform narrative, character or atmosphere – was not exclusive to indoor playhouses. We only need think of the '*Musicke of the Hoboyes . . . under the Stage*', which sounded at the Globe, signalling Antony's demise the night before battle in *Antony and Cleopatra*.[14] But it is safe to say that music was a more dominant feature of indoor playhouse repertories, as contrasted with outdoor ones. This difference is exemplified in the King's Men's repertory before and after 1609. In this critical year, the company repossessed the Blackfriars and began using this indoor theatre as their winter space, performing at the Globe in the summer months. Although music had always been part of their repertory, post-1609 the amount of music – songs and masques – rapidly

[12] Marston, *Sophonisba* (London, 1606), E4r. [13] Ibid., F1r.

[14] *The First Folio of Shakespeare: The Norton Facsimile*, ed. Charlton Hinman(New York: W. W. Norton, 1968), TLN 2482. All further Shakespeare references to this edition are provided within the main text.

increased. For example, only two surviving plays performed before the company's Blackfriars acquisition contained masques (*The Revenger's Tragedy* and *Timon of Athens*) but post-1609 masques 'became a conspicuous feature of the King's Men's plays', such as *The Maid's Tragedy* and *Henry VIII*.[15] The repertory also begins to feature many songs in plays including *The Captain*, *Cymbeline*, *The Tragedy of Valentinian*, *Bonduca* and *The Witch*. What we see, therefore, is the conditions of indoor performance influencing repertorial practice.

The Tempest contains one of the King's Men's post-1609 masques, and this is just one component of the play's intense musicality.[16] On Prospero's island everyone 'shall have ... Musicke for nothing' (TLN 1502). Throughout the play characters frequently engage with and comment on music: 'Where shold this Musick be?' (TLN 530), 'I heard a humming' (TLN 1024), 'What harmony is this?' (TLN 1540), 'Marvellous sweet Musicke' (TLN 1541). In much the same way as the Children of the Queen's Revels' playwrights before him, Shakespeare intertwines music and narrative events in writing for the Blackfriars. Ariel's voice and sounds shape the action, such as when Ferdinand follows the sound of his music inland and so meets Prospero and his daughter; or when Caliban, Trinculo and Stephano follow Ariel's music and fall for the trap Prospero sets for them. Alongside the dominant presence of music in *The Tempest*, the very way in which characters experience music may quite specifically respond to the acoustic environment at the Blackfriars. Peter J. Seng notes that in the play Shakespeare 'puts ... emphasis on "dispersed" music, performed as if it came from all over the stage'.[17] Ariel appears invisible to others when he sings and so they frequently try to identify the source of the music they hear. Ferdinand wonders where the singing comes from; Gonzalo cannot identify the 'humming' in his ears; and Stephano and Trinculo are confused by the very sound of music. *The Tempest*'s characters are surrounded by dispersed and all-encompassing music: an acoustic experience, I suggest, which replicates that of the audience. As I have outlined, at the indoor playhouse sound bounced and dissipated around the auditorium. Smith points out that 'in its shape the Blackfriars theatre ... *dispersed* sound waves

[15] Andrew Gurr, Introduction to Francis Beaumont and John Fletcher, *Philaster or, Love Lies A-Bleeding* (Manchester University Press, 2003), pp. xxxiv–xl.

[16] For more on the masque, see David Lindley, 'Music, Masque and Meaning in *The Tempest*', in *The Court Masque* (Manchester University Press, 1984), pp. 47–59.

[17] Peter Seng, *The Vocal Songs in the Plays of Shakespeare: A Critical History* (Cambridge, MA: Harvard University Press, 1967), p. 252.

throughout the room'.[18] The dispersal of music in *The Tempest* – characters' comments that sound surrounds them – may well reflect the way in which music sounded at the indoor playhouse. Thus the 'emphasis on "dispersed" music' that Seng notes, could represent Shakespeare's implicit recognition of the aural opportunities found at the company's new theatrical space.

Certainly in other post-1609 plays Shakespeare seems to experiment with music in the new acoustic environment of the Blackfriars. In particular, he is especially interested in using music to underscore magic and otherworldly moments; most obviously we see this interest in Prospero's musical magic in *The Tempest*. But other otherworldly uses of music include *Cymbeline*, where music underscores Posthumus Leonatus's vision of his dead family. Towards the end of the play, '*Solemne Musicke*' plays while '*an Apparition*' of his father, and then his mother, appear on stage (TLN 3065–71). Similarly in *Henry VIII*, written in collaboration with Fletcher, '*Sad and solemne Musicke*' (TLN 2639) precedes Queen Katherine's heavenly vision. In *The Winter's Tale*, although not specifically a supernatural intervention, Shakespeare presents the 'awakening' of Hermione's statue as a magical miracle, one underscored by music, as Penelope Woods points out in Chapter 8 below. Paulina protests that her ability to make Hermione's statue move does not rely on 'wicked Powers' (TLN 3295) or 'unlawfull Businesse' (TLN 3302) but '[p]aradoxically these disclaimers work to persuade us . . . that we are in fact witnessing a marvel'.[19] Music is central to this marvel as Paulina instructs: 'Musick; awake her: Strike / 'Tis time: descend: be stone no more' (TLN 3306–7). It appears that 'the music itself causes the transformation of the statue into the living Hermione'.[20] In this way, after the acquisition of the Blackfriars, we see not only an increase in use but possibly a very particular development in Shakespeare's imaginative use of music.

In a study of modern architecture and acoustic experience, Barry Blesser and Linda-Ruth Salter argue, 'Individuals who use spaces for a particular purpose . . . often acquire a heightened sensitivity to particular aspects of aural architecture', that is, to the acoustic effects and experience of a particular building.[21] The repertories of indoor playhouses suggest that early modern playwrights appeared to have acquired a 'heightened sensitivity' to the acoustic environment of indoor spaces. Taking full advantage of the opportunities of the indoor playhouse, playwrights constructed character

18 Smith, *Acoustic World*, p. 216. 19 Lindley, *Shakespeare and Music*, p. 138. 20 Ibid.

21 Barry Blesser and Linda-Ruth Salter, *Spaces Speak, Are You Listening? Experiencing Aural Architecture* (Cambridge, MA: MIT Press, 2007), p. 8.

and narrative *through* music, and song, masque and dance were part of the dramaturgical vocabulary of indoor playwriting.

Visual practices

During the Prologue of *Cynthia's Revels*, Jonson observes that certain members of the Blackfriars audience know 'no other learning, than the price of Satten and Velvets; nor other Perfection, than the wearing of a Neate sute'.[22] He singles out for attack the materialistic and fashion-conscious theatregoers, but the play which followed probably appealed to those very audience members. Jonson packs *Cynthia's Revels* with moments in which various items of clothing and jewellery are on display. He turns the Blackfriars stage into an eye-catching shop window, and throughout the play courtiers covet each other's stylish attire. Amorphus approves of Asotus's hat: 'this Hat possest mine eye exceedingly; 'tis so prettie, and fantastique'; Moria admires Phantaste's 'new ruffe [which is] Intricately rare'; Philantia notes that Phantaste wears new head attire which is 'excellent . . . and rare' and based on an '*Italian print*'.[23] The courtiers flirt and exchange gifts which include a purse, a jewel, a pendant, a glove, a chain of pearl, a diamond, a watch, a pair of bracelets and a ruby. *Cynthia's Revels* requires a lot of on-stage properties and is typical of plays written for the Blackfriars. Characters on this indoor stage frequently refer to fashion, flaunt elaborate clothing and exchange or display gifts of jewellery. While such displays did occur on all early modern stages, the representation of material culture was particularly dominant at the Blackfriars (as Chapters 5 and 10 by Tiffany Stern and Farah Karim-Cooper also demonstrate), and I suggest was a response to the distinct visual environment of that playhouse.

The work of Ann Rosalind Jones and Peter Stallybrass demonstrates quite clearly that all early modern playhouses 'functioned as engines of fashion'.[24] Costume was an essential dramaturgical tool for actors, and audience members also used the space of the playhouse to dress up. Indeed, anti-theatricalist William Prynne complains of those who spend 'whole dayes . . . *attyring themselves in their richest robes*' for a playhouse visit.[25] But indoor playhouses had a particular reputation for fashionable

[22] Ben Jonson, *Cynthia's Revels* (1601), A4v. [23] Ibid., C3v, E1v–E2r and E2v, respectively.

[24] Ann Rosalind Jones and Peter Stallybrass, *Renaissance Clothing and the Materials of Memory* (Cambridge University Press, 2007), p. 187. Most recently, Catherine Richardson, *Shakespeare and Material Culture* (Oxford University Press, 2011) offers an excellent discussion of the importance of costume and props on Shakespeare's stage.

[25] William Prynne, *Histriomastix* (London, 1633), 2R1v.

exhibitionism. Audiences had more disposable income for higher (than outdoor playhouse) priced theatre tickets and, presumably, for the latest clothing. And while at outdoor playhouses one had to consider inclement weather in clothing choices, indoors, no such restrictions applied. Early modern writers frequently associate the fashion-conscious with indoor playhouses. Discussing '[h]ow a Gallant should behave himsefe [*sic*] in a Play-house', Thomas Dekker notes that the stage of an indoor playhouse was a place of 'conspicuous *Eminence* . . . which meanes the best and most essenciall parts of a Gallant (good cloathes, a proportionable legge, white hand, the Persian lock, and a tollerable beard) are perfectly revealed'.[26] The candlelit indoor space offered the perfect catwalk for fashionable early modern Londoners like Dekker's gallant. Several contemporary writers note the effect of this lighting on clothing. Nathaniel Richards satirizes a '*Glitering Smocke* Gallant sitting at a Play'; and Tiffany Stern has already drawn attention to Francis Lenton's apt description of the gallant's 'silken garments, and his sattin robe . . . his spangled rare perfum'd attires, / Which once so glistred in the Torchy Fryers'.[27] 'Glittering', 'spangled', 'glistered': this vocabulary gives us a sense of the visual effects of candles upon the well-dressed audience at the Blackfriars.

The auditorium itself also contributed to the dazzling visual aesthetic indoors. Several anti-theatricalists decried the seductive or rather 'sumptuous' and 'gorgeous' decor of outdoor playhouses, and there is no reason to suggest that indoor playhouses were any less decorated; though we must concede that there are no specific references to painted *indoor* stages.[28] Nonetheless, much like the audience who took advantage of sparkling candlelight, it is likely theatre companies also picked designs and colours for their indoor auditorium that were particularly spectacular in the unique lighting conditions indoors. A play from the Children of the Queen's Revels' repertory gives a possible insight into the types of hangings used on stage at the Blackfriars. In Day's *Law Tricks*, Polymetes, Julio and Emilia discuss 'verie faire hangings' which seem to be on stage before them; Emilia describes how they depict 'the Poeticall fiction of *Venus* killing *Adonis* in the violet bed'.[29] Day's play requires an on-stage hanging which is a vivid depiction of an infamous classical scene. It seems plausible that companies had several stage hangings, which could change from day to day, even in

[26] Dekker, *The Gull's Hornbook* (London, 1609), E2r and E2v, respectively.
[27] Nathaniel Richards, *The Celestial Publican* (London, 1630), L4v; and Francis Lenton, *The Young Gallants Whirligig* (London, 1629), C4v, respectively.
[28] Stephen Gosson, *Plays Confuted in Five Actions* (London, 1582), E1r. [29] Day, *Law Tricks*, D4v.

accordance with particular plays. Undoubtedly, well before any actor came on stage, the visual environment of the Blackfriars boasted a rich tapestry of colours and images: possibly a 'gorgeous' interior, hangings with classical narratives or other images/patterns and, of course, the well-heeled audience, all glittering under the candlelight (or, what Tiffany Stern has referred to as 'living decoration').[30]

It is little wonder, then, that when Henry Evans established the Children of the Queen's Revels he spent time and effort in securing costume for the boy actors, enabling them to match the rich clothing and decoration seen in the Blackfriars auditorium. Evans spent £200 on 'apparel and other playing materials', a significant amount of money in early modern terms.[31] Furthermore, Jones and Stallybrass note that in 1600 Evans 'joined up with Edward Kirkham, Yeoman of the Revels and in charge of the Revels wardrobe, to supply him with clothes'.[32] As Yeoman of the Revels, Kirkham had access to the spectacular costume used for revels and masques performed at court. The Great Wardrobe, which housed court revels clothing, was nearby, just east of where the playhouse stood. When it came to furnish the Blackfriars' tiring-house with costumes, it is likely that the Great Wardrobe was an obvious and, crucially, *local* resource to which the company had access through Kirkham and his connections to the Revels office. Other local resources or even influences on costuming at the Blackfriars were the many feather sellers, silk workers and other clothing-related craftsmen that populated this particular area of London.[33] Both within and without its walls, the Blackfriars Playhouse was surrounded by producers and consumers of London fashion.

Playwrights who wrote for the Blackfriars perhaps drew on and showcased the material resources Evans acquired. In doing so, they created a rich material on-stage aesthetic which mirrored and even excelled the surrounding auditorium. *Cynthia's Revels* was the first new play the company performed at the Blackfriars and, as already noted, it is filled with clothing and jewellery. It also contains two masques where the courtiers dress up to perform in front of Cynthia. In the first masque, Cupid draws

30 See Tiffany Stern, 'Taking Part: Actors and Audience on the Stage at Blackfriars', in Paul Menzer (ed.), *Inside Shakespeare: Essays on the Blackfriars Stage* (Selinsgrove, PA: Susquehanna University Press, 2006), pp. 35–53.

31 Andrew Gurr, *The Shakespearean Stage, 1574–1642* (4th edn; Cambridge University Press, 2009), p. 68.

32 Jones and Stallybrass, *Renaissance Clothing*, p. 179.

33 Anthony House's research demonstrates that a significant number of clothes workers made up the population of the Blackfriars' precinct in the sixteenth century. See 'The City of London and the Problem of the Liberties, *c.* 1540 – *c.* 1640', Ph.D. dissertation, University of Oxford, 2006.

attention to the costumes of the '*four fair Virgins from the palace of their Queene* PERFECTION': '*The first in Citron coullour*', '*The second, in Green, is* AGLAIA', '*The third, in the discolour'd Mantle spangled all over, is* EUPHANTASTE' and '*The fourth, in white, is* APHELEIA'.[34] Euphantaste's '*spangled Mantle*' might describe a piece of clothing that contained metallic thread and shimmered under the candlelight at the Blackfriars, much like the glittering audience. With this first play for the boy company, Jonson establishes that audiences at the Blackfriars could expect to see beautiful clothing shimmering in candlelight both on and off stage. Later plays follow suit as a few examples demonstrate. In Edward Sharpham's *The Fleer*, Antifront points out the material of Ruffles' fine courtly suit: 'O, my gallant ruffles it out in silke'.[35] In Francis Beaumont's *The Knight of the Burning Pestle*, Mrs Merrythought shows her jewellery, or 'fine knacks', to her son Michael, pointing out 'here's a Ring, and here's a Bruch & here's a Bracelet, and here's two Rings more, and here's mony and gold'.[36] In *The Coxcomb*, a Beaumont and Fletcher play probably performed at the Blackfriars in 1608, Viola rewards milkmaids Nan and Madge with 'trifles' and 'toyes'; Madge boasts about her gift 'all gold and painted, and pretious stone in't'.[37] It is clear that under the candlelight both company and wealthy audience flaunted jewellery and clothing. Marston explicitly refers to the conditions in *The Dutch Courtesan* when Caqueteur notices Tysefew's ring because 'it shewes well by candlelight' (A3v).

If the audience at the Blackfriars gave the auditorium a rich, eye-catching aesthetic, then the Children of the Queen's Revels' playwrights ensured that actors reflected this appearance. Yet more than just reflection, I suggest playwrights battled for visual dominance as playing company and audience both vied for the catwalk that was the Blackfriars stage. In *The New Inn*, Jonson attacks stool-sitting gallants on the stage who come 'To see, and to bee seene'; 'To make a generall muster of themselves in their clothes of credit: and possesse the Stage, against the Play'.[38] The gallants who sat on stage are the specific focus of Jonson's ire, they are '*Stage*-furniture' who distract from the play. Dekker also focusses on the behaviour of on-stage gallants in *The Gull's Hornbook*, satirically advising them to enter just as the

34 Jonson, *Cynthia's Revels*, K3r–K4v.

35 Edward Sharpham, *The Fleer* (London, 1607). This page is incorrectly labelled C3r; keeping with the order of the rest of the pages, it is in fact D3r.

36 Francis Beaumont, *The Knight of the Burning Pestle* (London, 1613), D2r.

37 Beaumont and Fletcher, *The Coxcomb*, in *Comedies and Tragedies Written by Francis Beaumont and John Fletcher* (London, 1647), 2O2v.

38 Jonson, *The New Inn* (London, 1631), (*)2v.

play begins 'as though [they] were one of the *Properties*'.[39] Although cynical in tone, Dekker and Jonson perceive the on-stage gallants as additional stage objects, furniture or props, an inherent part of the theatrical encounter indoors. Both actors and gallants entered from the tiring-house, sparkled under the candlelight, displayed clothing and presented actions which demanded attention. Jonathan Haynes proposes: 'The stage was a center of the social battlefield: the theatre was an arena for social display, especially by those sitting on the stage'.[40] Furthering this point, I argue that the spectacle of materiality in the Children of the Queen's Revels' repertory enabled the boys to gain visual attention, reclaim the space and to re-'possess' the stage.

Beyond reclaiming the stage, playwrights fought on this 'social battlefield' through satires of fashion, challenging those who used the playhouse as a catwalk. Fashion-followers preening under the Blackfriars candlelight were frequently met with sharp fictional portraits of superficial vanity. In *Cupid's Revenge*, lecherous duke Leontius dresses to impress widow Bacha and preens in front of '*a looking-glasse*'.[41] Although at this point in the play the dukedom is in crisis, Leontius vainly obsesses about his appearance. He complains that his 'Feather is not large enough' and gripes that his tailor 'has made [his] dublet so wide' and that 'the knave has put no points at [his] arme'. The duke's servant Timantius tries to reassure him, noting that the feather ''tis such a one as the rest of the yong Gallants weare'. Such young feather-wearing gallants, of course, sat on stage at the Blackfriars and feather sellers were located in the area just outside the theatre;[42] Beaumont and Fletcher have created here a very localized joke. Moreover, Leontius personifies a satiric character appearing regularly in printed accounts of the Blackfriars. In his satiric observations entitled 'Notes from Black-Fryers', Henry Fitzgeffrey mocks the 'plumed *Dandebrat*' who attends the theatre; and Richards describes a '*glitering Smocke* Gallant' who flaunts 'Hat and Feather'.[43] While Fitzgeffrey, Richards and others created derisive portraits of the stool-sitting gallant in print, Beaumont and Fletcher produced a live performance version in *Cupid's Revenge*. Timantius's comments about the feather suggestively align the vain duke with 'the rest of the yong gallants' sitting on stage; it is easy to imagine the actor gesturing to these audience members, raising a knowing laugh from the rest of the auditorium.

39 Dekker, *Gull's Hornbook*, E3v.

40 Jonathan Haynes, 'The Elizabethan Audience on Stage', in James Redmond (ed.), *Theatrical Space* (Cambridge University Press, 1987), p. 65.

41 Beaumont and Fletcher, *Cupid's Revenge* (London, 1615), E2r.

42 See Stern, 'Taking Part'.

43 Henry Fitzgeffrey, *Satires and Satirical Epigrams: With Certain Observations at Blackfriars* (London, 1617), F2r; Richardson, *Celestial Publican*, L4r.

In *Eastward Ho!* Chapman, Jonson and Marston satirize the social pretensions of those who dress to impress. When Gertrude, daughter of a goldsmith, becomes engaged to knight Sir Petronel, she organizes a change in clothing to reflect her shift in social status. Her obnoxious social aspirations manifest in an obsession with fashion as she makes demands of her tailor Poldavy: 'off with this gowne for shames sake . . . let not my Knight take me in the Citty cut in any hand . . . I must be a Lady'.[44] She wants to discard her '*Cittizens gowne*', which the stage directions note she is wearing, and adopt court clothing, to become 'a lady'. As in *Cupid's Revenge*, Gertrude represents a harsh satiric portrait of any of the vain gallants on stage, and her fate in *Eastward Ho!* is a sharp warning. Her pretensions, so intrinsically linked with materialism, are short-lived when she discovers that her husband Sir Petronel is a penniless fraudster. In one of the play's many bitter and comic ironies, she ends up pawning her clothes for money: 'my Jewels be gone, & my Gownes & my red velvet Petticote'.[45] The fashionable finery which Gertrude connects with her social climbing is merely a transient cash asset.

For Middleton, materialism is associated with the worst vices of London in *Your Five Gallants*. The dizzying circulation of clothing and jewellery throughout the play is central to his portrait of five greedy and vain gallants. For example, Goldstone steals Fitzgrave's cloak and pawns it to Frip who, in the first scene, decloaks to reveal he is wearing the luxurious and colourful stolen cloak underneath his own; when he is caught by Fitzgrave wearing the cloak it embodies both his vanity and Goldstone's thievery. Middleton links clothing with other vices in the character of Tailsby. This 'whore' gallant, and a favourite of the ladies, pawns his entire suit during a gambling game but, soon after, his various mistresses send him gifts of clothing to replace the items he loses. In *Your Five Gallants*, clothes and jewels move from thief to pawn-broker to gambler to prostitute to conman. A chain of pearls is the most elaborate instance of this circulation. Fitzgrave gives the chain as a gift to Katherine, the wealthy heiress who all the gallants want to impress and marry; Pursenet pick-pockets the chain and gives it to his courtesan; she then gives it to Tailsby as a love token. This exchange is just the beginning of the chain of pearls' flurried movement throughout the play as it is stolen, pawned, gifted, lost and sold. As with Gertrude's clothes in *Eastward Ho!*, Middleton's chain of pearl signifies, among other things, the transient and superficial nature of material value.

[44] Chapman, Jonson and Marston, *Eastward Ho!* (London, 1605), A4r. [45] Ibid., H2r.

It is notable that, when the King's Men began performing at the Blackfriars in 1609, similar displays and satires of material culture became a trend in their repertory, perhaps demonstrating a dramaturgical response to the company's newly acquired winter venue. We might think of the grand spectacle of *Henry VIII* – the elaborate costumes and props demanded for Anne Boleyn's coronation and Elizabeth's baptism – as an especially impressive material display under the Blackfriars' candlelight. In *The Tempest*, Shakespeare showcases an array of costumes: for instance, Prospero's 'Magick garment' (TLN 110) and Ariel's appearance dressed as a '*water-Nymph*' (TLN 453–4) and then a '*Harpey*' (TLN 1583). And of course there is the '*glistening apparel*' brought on to trick Caliban, Stephano and Trinculo – this stage direction may describe the intended appearance of these costumes under the lighting conditions at the Blackfriars. In a more macabre example of a glittering display, in Fletcher's *The Tragedy of Valentinian* the corrupt emperor tricks virtuous Lucina into his palace and then bombards her with an eye-catching exhibition of his wealth, showing off 'Jewells and . . . ropes of Pearle'.[46] But it is Jonson in *The Devil is an Ass* who provides the most direct and specific development of the more light-hearted satiric portrayals of fashionistas seen in the Children of the Queen's Revels' repertory. Performed by the King's Men in 1616, this play focusses on Fitzdottrell, a vain young gallant who revels in showing off at 'the Black-friers Play-house'.[47] As a satiric portrait of certain audience members at Blackfriars, Fitzdottrell represents the ultimate composite of fashion-conscious characters – such as Duke Leontius, Gertrude or Middleton's gallants – seen regularly on the indoor theatre's stage from 1600. The gallant rents out his wife to Wittipol in return for a cloak he can wear at the theatre, in order to make an elaborate show of himself there: 'Sit i'the view, salute all my acquaintance / Rise up betweene the *Acts*, let fall my cloake'.[48]

In the opening scene of *Bussy D'Ambois*, performed by the Children of the Queen's Revels in 1604, Bussy is reluctant to attend court in his 'thridbare . . . poore suit' (A3v). In the second scene, after a quick costume change, Bussy enters court 'something altered in attire' (B2r) and courtier L'Anou sarcastically comments, 'See what a Metamorphosis a brave suit can worke' (B3r). The Blackfriars was full of 'brave' suits both on and off stage; 'thridbare' or 'poore' attire was a rare commodity in this theatre. Many contemporary satirists, like Dekker, Overbury and Lenten, alert us

[46] Fletcher, *The Tragedy of Valentinian*, in *Comedies and Tragedies*, 7A4v.
[47] Jonson, *The Devil is an Ass* (London, 1641), C1v. [48] Ibid.

to this feature of the indoor playhouse. The last few pages have established that plays performed at the Blackfriars registered the stylish look of the audience as playwrights created a materialistic vision for the indoor stage. Furthermore, playwrights undermined those who might use the Blackfriars stage as a catwalk with unsettling portraits of preening, vain gallants, which exposed the corrupting side of materialism. I have focussed on the materialistic vision that playwrights created at the Blackfriars as it is the playhouse named in contemporary accounts of fashionable indoor audience members taking advantage of candlelight. But there is no reason to suggest that other indoor playhouses, which also housed well-dressed audiences using the candlelight to show off their clothing, were very different.

Indeed we can see some evidence of the visual practices seen at the Blackfriars – displays and satires of materiality – in plays written for other indoor playhouses. In *The Changeling* (first performed around 1622), De Flores appears to refer to the candlelight conditions of the Phoenix playhouse when he notices the ring on the finger of his murder victim, Alonzo: 'Ha! what's that / Threw sparkles in my eye? – Oh 'tis a diamond / He wears upon his finger'.[49] De Flores draws attention to the way in which this prop, which becomes a macabre love token later on in the play, sparkles in the candlelight of the playhouse. In *The Insatiate Countess*, performed at the Whitefriars in around 1610, Marston creates an elaborate visual presentation in a masque which involves painted shields delivered to several characters, who go on to display and describe the detail of the images on their masques.[50] Finally, writing for Paul's around 1604–6, Middleton opens *Michaelmas Term* with a personified 'Michaelmas Term' in a 'whitish Cloake' that must be changed – on the stage – for a 'civill, blacke' gown, more suitable and fashionable for city life.[51] Middleton's satiric focus for the majority of the play is the legal community of early modern London, and the lawyers who made up the audience at Paul's. But Theodore B. Leinwand, the play's most recent editor, points out that 'wealthy citizens often wore black' and so Michaelmas Term's switch of attire for metropolitan life may also take a swipe at those fashionable elite within the auditorium.[52]

49 Thomas Middleton and William Rowley, *The Changeling* (London, 1653), D4r.
50 Marston, *The Insatiate Countess* (London, 1613), C1r.
51 Middleton, *Michaelmas Term* (London, 1607), A2r.
52 Middleton, *Michaelmas Term*, ed. Theodore B. Leinwand, in Gary Taylor and John Lavagnino (gen. eds.), *Thomas Middleton: The Collected Works* (Oxford University Press, 2007), note to Induction, line 4, p. 337.

It is significant that many of the playwrights I have mentioned throughout this chapter wrote plays for the Children of the Queen's Revels or King's Men, who both performed at the Blackfriars at different times. Jonson and Fletcher contributed plays to the boy and adult companies, as did Middleton, who also wrote for Paul's and the Phoenix; and Marston wrote for companies who performed at Paul's, the Whitefriars and the Blackfriars. By understanding the visual and acoustic practices which marked indoor performance, it is possible to see the reportorial trends perhaps deriving from the creative influences of the indoor conditions. For instance we might compare Marston's early use of music in *Antonio and Mellida* at Paul's in 1602 to his particularly developed cueing of music in *Sophonisba* at the Blackfriars four years later. Or we could chart Jonson's first satire of materiality and vanity at the Blackfriars in *Cynthia's Revels* 1600 through to his most explicit metatheatrical effort in *The Devil is an Ass* in 1616 via his collaborative contribution to *Eastward Ho!* in 1605. I began this chapter with Hall's quotation, which suggested that the playhouse could 'feed' the ears and the eyes of audience members. Yet it is also apparent that indoor playhouses offered a feast for the senses of playwrights, fuelling creative practices that responded to the specific acoustic and visual environment of these early modern venues.

CHAPTER 8

The audience of the indoor theatre

Penelope Woods

Theatre has been defined as the interconnection of three features. Peter Brook proposed that 'a man walks across this empty space whilst someone else is watching him and this is all that is needed for an act of theatre to be engaged'.[1] However, in this chapter I want to re-evaluate this formula. I suggest that space is rarely if ever 'empty' but always negotiated through its cultural and social signifiers. P. A. Skantze points out the fine gradation available between the sense of space that is empty and that which is full and how the attuned audience member is conscious of the air in a theatre being '"full" when an audience is attending, receiving, and returning the performers' energy'.[2] I want to reconsider the 'man' in this equation, and pay attention to the female share in spectatorship at the Blackfriars Playhouse. Crucially, I want to evaluate the activity of 'watching', which I suggest is neither straightforward nor passive but nested in an ethical, reflexive and culturally specific framework. Finally, I want to shift the emphasis from the components of theatre – space, performer and audience – to the complexity of what happens *in between* them. Theatre, now and through history, is about what brings these components together and about what holds them apart; theatre is about what produces, sustains or punctures their relationships and reactions to one another. The theatrical in-between of the seventeenth-century indoor theatre needs to be historicized.

In 2012 a special edition of *Criticism* made some similarly bold claims for the ability of 'historical phenomenology' to historicize the in-between. Ten years on from Bruce Smith's first use of the term 'historical phenomenology', and the attention it received in *Reading the Early Modern Passions*,[3] editors Kevin Curran and James Kearney write of 'the dynamism and nebulousness

1 Peter Brook, *The Empty Space* (Cambridge, MA: Athenaeum Press, 1968), p. 9.

2 P. A. Skantze, *Stillness in Motion in the Seventeenth-Century Theatre* (London and New York: Routledge, 2004), p. 14.

3 Gail Kern Paster, Katherine Rowe and Mary Floyd-Wilson, *Reading the Early Modern Passions: Essays in the Cultural History of Emotion* (Philadelphia, PA: University of Pennsylvania Press, 2004).

of feeling and sensation' which requires new historical attention 'by thinking in terms of ecologies rather than artifacts, experiences rather than objects, and by abandoning neat distinctions between persons and things'.[4] Curran and Kearney propose that this field of enquiry 'emphasizes how meaning accrues from the way sensing bodies experienced and perceived objects'.[5]

A paucity of critical discourse to describe the phenomena of the in-between hinders this project. In this chapter I take some features of space, performance and reception at the Blackfriars Playhouse to investigate what difference this made to the in-between. Rhetoric and drama theory coined terms for operations of the in-between. Here, I consider the topoi of 'pity' and 'wonder'. Attempts today to elucidate the in-between employ terms such as 'intimacy' and 'atmosphere'. The term 'intimacy' seems particularly important to consider in relationship to this theatre, in uncovering what might be happening in between given the frequency of its use and its lack of exposition. Teresa Brennan identified a discursive and thematic gap in attending to how affect was transmitted and received. Brennan writes: 'The transmission of affect was once common knowledge; the concept faded from the history of scientific explanation as the individual, especially the biologically determined individual, came to the fore.'[6] She adds that 'while it is recognized freely that individualism is a historical and cultural product, the idea that affective self-containment is also a production is resisted'. In the early modern period selves and bodies were understood to be more open and porous, more plastic and liable to be changed by the affects of environment, society and performance; what happened in between at the theatre occurred within a different social perception of its effect and significance. Gail Kern Paster, Katherine Rowe and Mary Floyd-Wilson remind us that 'early modern Europeans had not yet separated the mind from this changeable body, or the body from the world'.[7] Historical phenomenology addresses a gap in the discipline of theatre history which has produced detailed and invaluable accounts of the measurements of historical performance sites without addressing the ways in which these spatial co-ordinates framed and produced relational exchanges and the essential in-between of performance.[8]

4 Kevin Curran and James Kearney, 'Introduction', *Criticism* 54.3 (2012), 353. 5 Ibid.

6 Teresa Brennan, *The Transmission of Affect* (Ithaca, NY: Cornell University Press, 2004), p. 2.

7 Kern Paster et al., *Reading the Early Modern Passions*, p. 16.

8 See for instance Irwin Smith's monograph on the Blackfriars, *Shakespeare's Blackfriars Playhouse* (New York University Press, 1964), and Richard Hosley's detailed work 'The Second Blackfriars (1596)', in *The Revels History of Drama in English*, vol. III, *1576–1613*, ed. Clifford Leech and T. W. Craik (London: Methuen, 1975), pp. 197–226.

I focus on three scenes staging 'tragic' female characters in indoor performances in 1610–11: Desdemona in *Othello*, the 'Lady' in *The Lady's Tragedy*, and Hermione in *The Winter's Tale*. For each of these plays an audience eyewitness account survives that I shall use to reconstruct the operation of the in-between. In a consideration of historical spectatorship, the trace of 'watching' that survives after the event in the form of an 'eyewitness' account is fortuitous. I use these scenes and these accounts to probe one aspect of performance practice that elicits a particular set of responses in order to evaluate whether and how this in-between might vary from the outdoor to the indoor ecology of performance and its reception. These are scenes in which the female character, played by a boy, remains on stage for a period of time pretending to be dead (or a statue). While this is not unique to plays performed in the indoor theatre, female characters on stage asleep, in a swoon or dead as the focus of tragic action and pity occurs frequently in earlier plays (*Much Ado About Nothing*, *A Midsummer Night's Dream*, *Romeo and Juliet* for instance); however, in the material and cultural context of the indoor theatre this figure produces a different theatrical in-between.

Looking at an actor's body on stage pretending to be dead disrupts the face-to-face encounter which was a predominant condition of performance in both the outdoor and indoor theatres. Instead, by playing dead (or a statue) the actor is rendered an object to be looked at (not a subject to be engaged with). This different, voyeuristic regime of looking produces a different affect. Voyeuristic looking in a small space in greater proximity to the actor's body, I suggest, has a more intense quality than in the amphitheatres.

Desdemona's face

In 1610 Henry Jackson, a student at Oxford, wrote an account of a performance of *Othello* given by the King's Men in one of the colleges. Corpus Christi Hall, built in 1516, measures 53 feet by 56.5 feet.[9] This is similar to the capacity, if not the shape, of the second Blackfriars Playhouse, which was a slightly longer and narrower rectangle.[10] (*Othello*, written around 1603, was also performed at the Globe and the Blackfriars.) Jackson's account is exceptional among surviving eyewitness accounts of early

[9] James Campbell Associates, Ground Floor Plan of Corpus Christi College, November 2012, gives the hall dimensions as 16.11 m x 17.22 m (roughly 53 feet x 56.5 feet).

[10] Glynne Wickham takes the Blackfriars' dimensions of 46 feet x 66 feet from a lawsuit, *Early English Stages: 1300 to 1660* (3 vols.; London and New York: Routledge, 1959–81), vol. II, p. 138. The measurement in square feet for Corpus Christi College Hall is just under 3000, and the second Blackfriars by these measurements was just over.

modern performance in its detailed description of the affective experience of attending an early seventeenth-century performance; Jackson articulates eloquently what happens in the in-between of this theatre event.

The performance was much applauded by the full house that day. Jackson writes that the audience had been 'moved to tears'. The audience wept not only in response to what the actors said, but, Jackson explains, in response to certain things that the actors did.[11] Jackson illustrates this with a description of the scene in which Desdemona dies:

> Desdemona, killed in front of us by her husband, although she acted her part excellently throughout, in her death moved us especially when, as she lay in her bed, with her face alone she implored the pity of the spectators.[12]

Jackson conflates the body of the boy actor with that of Desdemona (he uses the feminine pronoun 'illa' and feminine agreement throughout this description).[13] His account reflects a profound investment in the tragedy of Desdemona that culminates in her body, and face, on stage in the final scene. The account suggests that Jackson had been able to look long and hard at this face, perhaps that he had a good view or was fairly close to the action. Jackson's careful distinction between the effect of what the actors had said (*dicendo*), and of what they did (*faciendo*) serves as a reminder that this was an audience member whose frame of engagement was highly determined by his grammar school education. Jackson points us to the distinction between oratory, which calls up vivid images in the mind's eye (or *oculi mentis*), and action itself, which shortcuts rhetoric to put images directly before one's eyes. Richard Meek has recently speculated about the interrelationship of rhetoric and action on the early modern stage. He asks: 'Surely such acts of narration [in Shakespeare] would be redundant, given drama's ability to place things before the eyes of an audience?'[14] Meek, like other critics, answers this question with reference to the perceived limitations of the

11 'In quibus non solum dicendo, sed etiam faciendo quaedam lachrymas movebant' ['In which not only by saying but also by doing certain things they moved the audience to tears']. Cambridge, Corpus Christi College, CCCC, MS 304, fos. 83v–4. Latin text available in *Records of Early English Drama: Oxford*, ed. John R. Elliott, Jnr et al. (4 vols.; University of Toronto Press, 2004), vol. 1, p. 387 (with thanks to Yasmin Haskell for discussion of this letter and my translation).

12 'At vero Desdemona illa apud nos a marito occisa, quanquam optime semper causam egit, interfecta tamen magis movebat; cum in lecto decumbens spectantium misericordiam ipso vultu imploraret.' Translation by Antony B. Dawson, 'Performance and Participation', in *The Culture of Playgoing in Shakespeare's England: A Collaborative Debate* (Cambridge University Press, 2001), p. 19. I amended Dawson's 'audience' to 'spectators' since the point Jackson is making here is specifically one about the action and visual signifier of the boy actor's performing face. Jackson uses the term 'spectantium' here, from *specto spectare*, to look, or behold, rather than 'audiens'.

13 Ibid. 14 Richard Meek, *Narrating the Visual in Shakespeare* (Farnham: Ashgate, 2009), p. 10.

public theatre's bare stage for creating vivid images. I suggest that Jackson's account, and others in this chapter, perhaps proposes a complex condition of proximate voyeurism instantiated at the indoor theatres, in which doing *certain* things (rather than saying things) might move an audience to tears. Grammar school training in rhetoric provided boys with *schemata sententiae* or 'emotion scripts' (Katherine Rowe's useful term) through which to rehearse affective engagement and response.[15] Pity, the emotion most appropriately produced by spectatorial engagement with tragedy, is the topos Jackson employs to describe the affect of the boy's action in this scene. The object of Desdemona's living/dead face provided a charged conduit for the production of this affect in its indoor audience.

Jackson considers both Desdemona's performance in its entirety – 'she acted her part excellently throughout' – but he also considers the performance-in-time of her death scene. He uses a present participle clause to bracket out Desdemona's ongoing presence (and action) through this scene. The durational quality of this action (the imploring face) is almost certainly significant to its intensity. Desdemona remains on stage for three hundred lines after she has 'died' (she revives to speak to Emilia after thirty-three lines), while other characters enter, speak, accuse, wound, murder and die. What remained the compelling focus of attention for Jackson was Desdemona's static but 'imploring' face.

The second feature that is significant here is a different relationship of exchange between audience and performer set up by this face-to-face performance. Carol Chillington Rutter cites the 'wide-eyed, if glazed, gaze' of the many severed heads that appear in Shakespeare's plays, something which complicates their interpretation as subject or object on stage.[16] Did the youth performing Desdemona dead leave his eyes open in a fixed death stare? Or, killed in bed, was s/he the manifestation of 'sleep, death's counterfeit' (*Macbeth* 2.3.51) with eyes closed? For the actor, the last would certainly be easier over three hundred lines. Either way, the spectator was free to look long and hard at this tragic face without any likelihood of them looking back. This is a voyeurism that is not available in other moments of performance, either indoors or outdoors. The audience and performers shared the same lighting in both theatres and consequently spectators were always potentially implicated in a direct relationship with performers in which they had a certain

[15] Lynn Enterline's recent work on emotion and rhetoric in the grammar school education provides context to this reading, *Shakespeare's Schoolroom: Rhetoric, Discipline, Emotion* (Philadelphia, PA: University of Pennsylvania Press, 2012).

[16] Carol Chillington Rutter, 'Talking Heads', in Stuart Hampton-Reeves and Bridget Escolme (eds.), *Shakespeare and the Making of Theatre* (Basingstoke: Palgrave Macmillan, 2012), p. 107.

responsibility. How spectators responded, what they exchanged with the performer in return for a look or a line, made a difference to the nature of the performance. The dead body on stage offered a touchstone for a response and feeling of pity that was momentarily outside this condition of exchange.

Dead bodies, wax figures and statues

Tiffany Stern describes the proliferation of 'small-scale fixed aesthetics such as statues and tableaux' in the later plays by Shakespeare, surmising that in using a small space rather than the amphitheatre space, 'static arts were what worked best at Blackfriars'.[17] It is probable that the material constraints of the smaller stage space (evidently a concern for performers and playwrights)[18] prompted a more frequent use of the static spectacle. It has been found, by contrast, that in performance at the reconstructed Globe constant movement is a key tactic to compensate for the sightline limitations of the auditorium, and can be effectively employed as a means of directing focus and securing attention in a theatre with no lighting technologies. In a small indoor space where lots of movement is not feasible, this development of a performance practice of stillness – the use of static bodies present on stage for a sustained period of time – has its own particular dynamic force. The ambiguous tableaux and bodies performing statues, dead bodies, sleeping bodies or wax figures interact with the space and social dynamics in deliberate and precise ways. The list of these ambiguous dead/sleeping/statuesque bodies in the repertory of the indoor theatre includes, for instance, Desdemona's still body undressed by her maid, and then her murdered body; the Lady's dead body and monument which are wept over and then fondled in *The Lady's Tragedy*; the dead bodies of the Duchess's husband Antonio and children, and subsequently the Duchess herself in *The Duchess of Malfi*; the body of Imogen both asleep in bed and, disguised as Fidele, seemingly dead in *Cymbeline*; and the statue/body of Hermione in *The Winter's Tale*. In these scenes these characters are rendered objects which ask to be looked at but which cannot look back. This rare disequilibrium in the voyeuristic power of the audience's share in the indoor theatre is significant.

17 Tiffany Stern, 'Taking Part: Actors and Audience on the Stage at Blackfriars', in Paul Menzer (ed.), *Inside Shakespeare: Essays on the Blackfriars Stage* (Selinsgrove, PA: Susquehanna University Press, 2006), p. 47.

18 See for instance the descriptions offered in Ben Jonson's plays in particular, of the actors who claim the audience would 'thrust and spurn and knock us on the elbows' (*The Devil is an Ass*, ed. Peter Happé, Revels Plays (Manchester University Press, 1996)).

The problem of living actors performing dead bodies

There is a problem with modern sensibility and this dynamic of the dead body when presented on the proscenium arch stage. The complexity of the living body performing a dead body threatens a kind of absurdity. These spectacles in *Cymbeline*, for instance, in a production directed by Trevor Nunn at Cambridge Arts Theatre in 2007 were met with laughter the night I attended (the dummy standing in for Cloten's headless body in particular). On the way out an audience member behind me asked: 'Was that really Shakespeare? It was so funny!' Yukio Ninagawa's production of the same play at the Barbican in 2012 attempted to compensate for an absurd plot and its peculiar static (and non-static) spectacles with very grand and lavish set design. Nevertheless, Lyn Gardner describes the 'titter-generating eagle' of the production and registers a superficiality of affective engagement she felt this production had achieved in her review.[19] Today it is a rarely produced play. In the context of performance at the small Blackfriars Playhouse and with its particular audience, I suggest it may have been experienced very differently.

Contrary to these instances, I propose that experiencing the living actor's body pretending to be something it cannot be (dead/a statue/made of wax) can be profoundly affecting. But this affect is indexed by proximity. The closer the audience is to this living/dead body, the more potent the affect is. Furthermore, there is a temporal dimension to this affect as well as a spatial one, and this depends on how long the living body is being asked to be taken for a dead one. Curran and Kearney talked about how meaning might 'accrue' between sensing bodies; I think in this instance it is not a linear dynamic. Rather, the affect of a living person in close proximity being asked to be taken for a dead body in a tragic play, fluctuates and wavers. Bert O. States describes this as a kind of 'binocular' vision, where the thing being attended to oscillates between the immediate thing and the theatrical sign.[20] The 'shudder' that results from this intransigence of particular theatrical objects to be collapsed into that which they represent (such as living male bodies pretending to be female dead bodies or stone statues) charges these theatrical moments.[21] I am interested in the possibility that this was a deliberate performance strategy encounter in the theatre, a strategy that

[19] Lyn Gardner, '*Cymbeline* – review', *Guardian*, 30 May 2012. (The debate about the 'success' of the aesthetics of the production continues in audience comments online.)

[20] Bert O. States, *Great Reckonings in Little Rooms* (Berkeley: University of California Press, 1987), p. 37.

[21] Ibid.

might intrude or disrupt the affect of pity, and, as a durational practice, where the dead or otherwise static body remained on stage for a period of time. Since this traffics precisely with the force of the in-between and, particularly, the durational in-between, it is lost from historical accounts. The experience of time, or duration, resists reconstruction in ways that the materiality of theatre does not. However, traces of the significance of this aspect of indoor performance linger.

Blackfriars' auditorium and proximity

Stern, who suggests that the Blackfriars would have felt like a 'private hall' akin to college halls, such as Corpus Christi, and the Inns of Court,[22] has argued that the proximity of the 'high-paying audience' at the Blackfriars resulted in an increased emphasis on the details of performance: 'devices of the "close-up," like facial expression', Stern suggests, may have become 'more meaningful in a Blackfriars play'.[23] In Chapter 9 below, Paul Menzer also employs analogy with television and film to articulate the effect of a different proximity in the Blackfriars Playhouse.[24] The facial close-up is experienced as a condition of intimacy.

This term 'intimacy', one used by practitioners and academics, is both freighted with meaning yet rarely defined. Whenever it is used in theatrical contexts, a claim is being made about the nature of the in-between. For practitioners, 'intimate' is always a positive feature or description of a performance space. As Iain Mackintosh attests, it is the holy grail of modern theatre architecture and theatre production.[25] Theatre historians also use the term 'intimate' to articulate a particular quality of performance.[26] There is an assumption of a shared understanding of the intimate, with its overtones of privacy, proximity, familiarity, profundity, authenticity. However, this term is overdue attention and exposition, particularly from historians. Performance at the Globe's Sam Wanamaker Playhouse will be described in terms of its particular intimacy, and we might wisely take the opportunity to consider what that is.

Derived from the Latin *intimeo*, *intimare*, 'to put or bring into, drive or press into',[27] 'intimacy' is a term concerned with exchange and interrelationship

[22] Stern, '"Taking Part"', p. 48. [23] Ibid., p. 46. [24] See Chapter 9 below.

[25] Iain Mackintosh, *Architecture, Actor and Audience* (London and New York: Routledge, 1993), p. 106.

[26] John Russell Brown examines Jackson's account of *Othello* in a recent article in terms of the insight it gives us into the intimate nature of performance in indoor theatres. 'Staging Shakespeare's Plays: A Choice of Theatres', *New Theatre Quarterly* 26.2 (2010), 117.

[27] See: 'intimate, adj and v.', *Oxford English Dictionary Online*, accessed 3 December 2012.

linked to the in-between. In its semantic horizon of usage today (it was not used in the seventeenth century), the term has a euphemistic slipperiness. Menzer locates 'intimacy' in its operation of literal and metaphorical proximity – we are 'intimate' with those whom we are 'close' to – but he points to the ambivalence lurking in this condition. Intimacy is something to be enjoyed, but also 'suffered'.[28]

Practitioners have consistently described the quality of the performance at the reconstructed outdoor Globe in terms of its intimacy. Michael Holden, chief executive of Shakespeare's Globe from 1994 to 1998, articulated his surprise at finding that this was 'the largest intimate theatre in London'.[29] The term 'epic intimacy', coined by actor Ian Redford, has been used by Globe playwright Ché Walker to describe the in-between of performance at the Globe.[30] It has something to do with proximity (Redford identifies the privileged position of the 'groundlings' who experience the greatest proximity) but it is also to do with faces. Intimacy is about faces in the shared lighting of the Globe that are visible to one another and implicate performance within a direct social encounter that is confronting, exposing and potentially flirtatious. Artistic director Dominic Dromgoole has described this dynamic of intimacy in terms of its 'riskiness' and 'exposure'. The Globe is different, Dromgoole says, 'mainly and profoundly because of the shared light and the fact that everyone is in it together. The nature of exposure at the Globe makes you very vulnerable and it's that vulnerability that gives it life'.[31]

Interviews with audience members similarly attest to the riskiness and threat of this face-to-face interaction with some audience members enjoying it and others disliking it intensely. One audience member likened it to the risky experience of choosing to sit in the front row at a comedy show. She said: 'Do I go and look them in the eye? I do enjoy that experience. I like that.'[32] The self-consciousness, riskiness and embarrassment produced by eye contact are experienced differently from person to person. Another audience member was explicit about her dislike of this experience, saying: 'the thing with theatre is that you've got to lose yourself in it, and the minute they come to you and sort of look in your face then it's gone'.[33] This threat to 'absorption' posed by the direct encounter is worth attending to.

[28] See Chapter 9 below. [29] A. J. Gurr, personal email exchange.

[30] *Romeo and Juliet* company interview (1), 11 August 2009, End of Season Interviews, Shakespeare's Globe Library and Archives (SGLA).

[31] Penelope Woods, interview with Dominic Dromgoole, 22 January 2009, SGLA.

[32] Annette, Ian, Frank and Karen, pre-performance conversation, *The Frontline*, matinee, 23 May 2009, (11), Woods Audience Interview Archive, SGLA.

[33] Mary, post-performance conversation, *Romeo and Juliet*, matinee, 18 June 2009, (6).

The face-to-face encounter had potency and significance for the early modern audience also. In a rare account of spectatorship at the Blackfriars recorded in the satiric *Life of a Satyrical Puppy called Nim* by 'T. M.' (possibly Thomas May), Nim describes how 'About the beginning of the fourth *Act* my face withstood a fresh encounter'.[34] The antagonistic (embattled) social and flirtatious experience that Nim conveys here is significant within a consideration of an 'ecology' of look exchange and face-to-face encounter in the indoor theatre. Actors and audience experience themselves being accosted, pressed up against, pressed into, by the social- and play-world experience in this socially negotiated performance space that shimmered under candlelight.

Some female spectators at the Blackfriars held fans to protect their faces from these face-to-face encounters. Ladies might sit in boxes, perhaps with a 'lettice-window'[35] or lattice screening which further protected them from the prying eyes of both audience and actor, according them the privilege of seeing close up but not being seen.[36] I take this to be the (frustrated) implication of Jonson's description of the female indoor audiences, with caps and fans, 'rank'd in the darke';[37] able to obscure their reactions and seemingly disengaged from any reciprocal exchange with performers or audience. These female spectators perhaps took themselves out of the equation of the ethical and social face-to-face encounter at the Blackfriars, even as the tragic female characters offered themselves up to be voyeuristically looked at.

The move from a public, outdoor theatre to the private, indoor theatre has been read as a move to more 'intimate' conditions of reception. However, unravelling what is meant by 'intimacy' prompts a reconsideration of this description. The condition of proximity in the actor–audience exchange in the Blackfriars Playhouse heightened the need for social and performative strategies for dealing with the negotiation of the intimacy of the face-to-face encounter. A different in-between based on proximity, voyeurism and eroticism was established.

Blackfriars' auditorium and eroticism

In a book concerned with the erotics of the Renaissance stage, Celia R. Daileader considers the association of sexuality and death, highlighting the proliferation of deaths embedded in narratives of sexual anxiety and violence, including

34 See Andrew Gurr, *Playgoing in Shakespeare's London* (4th edn; Cambridge University Press, 2004), pp. 283–5.

35 See description in Thomas Goffe's *The Careless Shepherdess* cited ibid., p. 51.

36 See the discussion of latticed boxes in the Blackfriars in Chapter 6 above.

37 Ben Jonson, commendatory verse on *The Faithful Shepherdess*, by John Fletcher, 1608.

Desdemona, Bianca, the Duchess, Beatrice-Joanna, Evadne, and 'the "fake" deaths of Hero and Hermione', amongst others.[38] The performances of these deaths are implicated in the practice of static, durational spectacle under consideration here, and in its spectatorial regime of voyeurism.

The erotics of the small candlelit theatre require consideration. Stern offers the joke in a performance of a Braithwait play about dining at the 'Sign of The Hand in the Placket', in which the actor swiftly enjoined a fumbling audience member: 'prey sr holde thou still else wee shall lose our sign'.[39] The Blackfriars was a social space permeated with erotic possibility. Rather than detracting from engagement with the play-world, I suggest that this circulation of looks and longing and fumbling informed what has been described as itself a noticeably sexualized dramatic turn. The vulnerability of Desdemona's gradually undressed body in the scene preceding her murder was, I suggest, instrumental in the production of the keen voyeuristic pity felt by Jackson in response to the Corpus Christi *Othello*.

The Lady's Tragedy

I want to compare Jackson's account of 'pity' at the sight of the dead Desdemona to another eyewitness account of a moving death scene, this time offered by Daileader herself of a production of *The Lady's Tragedy* in 1994. It is not a contemporary eyewitness account; however, it attends to the affect of the spectacle of the actor playing dead in minute and revealing detail.

This was a rare production of this play by the theatre company Show of Strength, directed by Alan Coveny, in a reception room above the Hen and Chicken pub in Bedminster, England. This event room is even smaller than Corpus Christi Hall, measuring 14.8 metres by 8.8 metres.[40] The maximum capacity is two hundred spectators, although Daileader does not mention in this account how full the room was. What was illuminating about the production for Daileader was that the dead body of the Lady, who kills herself to avoid becoming the Tyrant's wife, was played by an actor, rather than represented by a dummy. 'The act of looking dead for a total of 344 lines', writes Daileader, 'is no inconsiderable feat'. The complexity of the living actor playing the dead body, a particular theatrical signifier and sign

[38] Celia R. Daileader, *Eroticism on the Renaissance Stage* (Cambridge University Press, 1998), p. 92.

[39] Braithwait, *Whimzies*, 52; Richard Braithwait, *The Honest Ghost* (1658), 25, cited in Stern, 'Taking Part', p. 48.

[40] For comparison, this is approximately 48.5 feet x 29 feet; the footprint is 1400 feet, about half that of Corpus Christi or the Blackfriars.

that resist being taken straightforwardly for one another, is highly affecting. Daileader writes:

> For, however convincing this performance of deadness, the audience of course recognized it as such; the Lady's limbs were too supple, her lips too moist; she might have been, like so many bashful maidens in courtly love lyrics, merely pretending to sleep. In fact, the Tyrant's fondling of this 'corpse' acquired a powerful eroticism that the use of a dummy would have prevented; even for those spectators seated too far from the stage to observe as I did, the actress' breathing, our ontological sense of her vitality, together with the Tyrant's insistence of the same, made it too tempting to look at the actress, not the role, and to imagine how it felt to play dead and be fondled.[41]

Daileader begins as Jackson had done, by asserting how 'the audience' felt and thought. However, she moves into an intriguing self-reflexive response that positions her as a spectator among others and factors their varying responses based on their varying spatially indexed spectatorial positions into her account. Finally, her account reflexively and sympathetically responds to the close-up experience of the details of the actor's living body, the ontology of this particular theatrical sign. Unlike Jackson, Daileader is not absorbed into the Lady's tragedy by her living/dead presence, but rather the fine, ontological detail of this female actress playing dead that is available through proximity prompts a curious reflexivity. Daileader wonders what it would be like if she herself were playing the dead Lady and being fondled by the Tyrant. An erotically charged capacity for sensing, after death, is accorded to the Lady in this reading.

Striptease

Desdemona remains on stage 'dead' for three hundred lines, the Lady, in Middleton's play, for three hundred and forty-four. There are other similarities in these two static staged female figures. The Tyrant has the dead body of the Lady, carefully dressed, brought on stage to have her face made up (*LT* 5.2).[42] Desdemona, on the other hand, is undressed by her maid Amelia on stage (*O* 4.3). Unpinning these layers was a voyeuristic, intimate insight (or intrusion) into a habitual domestic routine, that, in the context of the play's anxiety about sexual incontinence and the material context of the performance's of hungry-eyed spectators, was also erotically charged.

[41] Daileader, *Eroticism*, pp. 100–1.

[42] See *The Lady's Tragedy*, ed. Julia Briggs, in *Thomas Middleton: The Collected Works*, ed. Gary Taylor and John Lavagnino (Oxford University Press, 2007), p. 895. For a discussion of the implications of face paint in this scene, see Farah Karim-Cooper, *Cosmetics in Shakespearean and Renaissance Drama* (2nd edn; Edinburgh University Press, 2012).

Dekker suggests that the gallant on stage was sufficiently close to the performers that he could 'examine the play-suits lace, and perhaps win wagers upon laying tis copper'.[43] (The gallant here is attending to the sartorial performance with sufficient intensity to discover whether the luxurious metallic threads in the lace costume were really gold, in other words, genuinely precious, or were merely pretending to be gold when in fact they were inexpensive copper). These eager sartorial eyes would have scrutinized the elaborate undressing of Desdemona. In Chapter 7 above Sarah Dustagheer attests to the significance of dress and its detail for performers and spectators alike at the Blackfriars, while Tiffany Stern has suggested that the beautifully attired and sparkling visible and prominent audience themselves made the performance of tragedy unfeasible, concluding that 'Relentless, dark tragedies would be trivialized by such a setting'.[44] However, this hungry attention to sartorial detail was precisely the intensity of voyeuristic spectatorial attention which the tragic effects of these static moments sought to engage.

The Winter's Tale

Like *Othello*, *The Winter's Tale* is a play of male preoccupation with sexual continence and radical doubt. The epistemological crises in both these plays have much to do with theatre. *Othello*, written when the King's Men only had the open-air playhouse at the Globe, is concerned with 'ocular proof'. This epistemological regime in the theatre, we know, is inherently unstable, since everyone and everything is pretending to be something other than what they are. *The Winter's Tale*, on the other hand, is concerned with a kind of sensed and felt truth. This is the kind of truth that a 'sensorium' (to employ Michael Witmore's term)[45] such as the second Blackfriars, might make you long to feel. This too will prove not to be a stable epistemology in the theatre either. Leontes tells Antigonus:

> You smell this business with a sense as cold
> As is a dead man's nose. But I do see't and feel't

43 Dekker, *The Gull's Hornbook*, reproduced in E. K. Chambers, *The Elizabethan Stage* (4 vols.; Oxford: Clarendon Press, 1923), vol. 1, p. 367.

44 Stern, 'Taking Part', p. 43.

45 Michael Witmore, 'Phenomenology and Sensation: Shakespeare, Sensation, and Renaissance Existentialism', *Criticism* 54.3 (2012), 421.

As you feel doing thus[46] – and see withal
The instruments that feel. (*Winter's Tale* 2.1.151–4)

So vivid is Leontes's felt experience of the truth of his suspicions that it is as potent and as palpable as touch itself. This is the 'haptic or palpative' epistemological tradition, considered in Witmore's article, that operated particularly in a space indexed by proximity and nested within social practices of flirtation and eroticism, of hiding, and showing and prying.

The Winter's Tale culminates in the scene in which Hermione is presented as a statue of exquisite verisimilitude, and subsequently brought to life before our, and Leontes's, eyes. (Or else, *The Winter's Tale* culminates in a carefully staged piece of drama within a drama choreographed by Paulina, a scene in which Hermione pretends to be a statue that comes to life). The Lady, in *The Lady's Tragedy* written in the same year, has her stone monument broken into by the Tyrant's men to retrieve her body forcibly. Hermione's stone monument or statue, in Shakespeare's more strange and magical play, itself seems to transform into flesh.

When the Tyrant sees the Lady's stone monument, he says:
The monument woos me; I must run and kiss it.
Now trust me if the tears do not e'en stand
Upon the marble. What slow springs have I?
'Twas weeping to itself before I came.
How pity strikes e'en through insensible things
And makes them shame our dullness. (*Lady's Tragedy* 4.3, 9–14)

Leontes also figures his response to the cold stone version of his wife in terms of his desire to woo and kiss the stone, the contrast of warm life and cold stone, the sense of shame and the proposition of female stone that might *feel* more or more appropriately than the tyrannical male. Leontes says:

O, thus she stood,
Even with such life of majesty – warm life,
As now it coldly stands – when first I wooed her.
I am ashamed. Does not the stone rebuke me
For being more stone than it? (*Winter's Tale* 5.3.34–8)

Seeing her body taken out of the monument by moonlight, the Tyrant is moved to kiss her dead lips, to the horror of his attendants. Leontes, after staring at the statue for fifty-eight lines, cries: 'Let no man mock me, / For I will kiss her' (*WT* 5.3.78–9). Paulina warns him away saying: 'The

[46] Most editions include a stage direction here. John Pitcher adds: '[laying hold of Antigonus]', in the Arden edition, 2010.

ruddiness upon her lip is wet / You'll mar it if you kiss it, stain your own / With oily painting' (*WT* 5.3.81–3). The Tyrant, on the other hand, has the Lady's lips painted to look more lifelike and then kisses her again. While the painting on the Lady's lips, applied by her lover Govinus, is the poison that kills the Tyrant when he kisses her, Hermione's statue, unkissed, comes to life and voluntarily embraces Leontes. The juxtaposition of these two scenes permits an appreciation of the complexity of what is asked of the spectator. Looking at the pitiful objects of the dead Lady and the statue of dead Hermione, both wronged characters, establishes a regime of voyeuristic, pitying and erotic looking.

The eyewitness account of *The Winter's Tale* that is relevant here was written by Simon Forman. Forman saw the play at the Globe Theatre on 15 May 1611. It differs from Jackson's account, which was written for a friend, and Daileader's account, which was written to be published, since Forman's account was written for himself in his 'Book of Plays'. Like the other plays Forman writes accounts of (including *Macbeth* and *Cymbeline*), it offers a fairly detailed description. Each of the three sections begins with an imperative: 'Observe', 'Remember' and 'Remember'. Forman concludes with a sententious note-to-self: 'Beware of trusting feigned beggars or fawning fellows.'[47] Nowhere in the account does Forman mention Hermione or the statue. Perhaps he left before the end of the play, or perhaps the affective quality of the statue, a player remaining stone-still on stage for over eighty lines before being brought to life, was very different when it was not experienced in the same condition of proximate, intimate, voyeurism as the Blackfriars.[48]

There are two final points to be made about the case of Hermione. Unlike Desdemona and the Lady, Hermione returns to life and subjectivity. She is no longer an object to be looked at who cannot return the look. The strange and miraculous circumstances of her transformation are indexed, not so much by pity, as in the case of Desdemona and the Lady, as 'wonder'. This is a category of spectatorial experience exemplifying the concerns of the neo-Aristotelian drama theorists who 'argued that a play must present events that seemed impossible. It must stun the senses and overwhelm the rational mind.'[49] Wonder, like pity, existed within a horizon of rehearsed emotions for the audience educated in rhetoric at grammar schools.

47 Chambers, *Elizabethan Stage*, vol. II, pp. 340–1.

48 Farah Karim-Cooper also draws attention to this omission and comes to the same conclusion. See Chapter 10 below.

49 William Shakespeare, *The Winter's Tale*, ed. John Pitcher, Arden Shakespeare (London: Bloomsbury, 2010), p. 69.

However, wonder also belonged to the categories of philosophical and new scientific thought. Aristotle had argued that wonder was the cue for philosophical thought in the *Metaphysics*, while Francis Bacon describes wonder as 'the seed of knowledge'[50] in *The Advancement of Learning*. The experience of wonder is 'an impression of pleasure' that provokes learning and the desire for knowledge.[51] The proximate and highly affective experience of the statue scene, I argue, produced a particular captivating experience. The afterlife of this in-between may have been different from the cathartic release of pity for Desdemona and the Lady.

Finally, I offer an inadequate footnote on the role of music in these highly affecting static scenes. These scenes were implicated within a new musical tradition. It is not the still, dead/living figures alone that prompt the overwhelming sense of pity and wonder, but the choreography of these scenes with cued musical accompaniment. While the Tyrant and Leontes speak of silence, music plays a crucial role in the production of affect here. These are not piteous or wondrous silences, but very specifically wondrous soundscapes that interact with the heightened moments of scrutiny and voyeurism in a particular way. As other chapters in this volume testify, music plays a crucial role in the affect of indoor performance. A rehabilitation of *Cymbeline* in performance might benefit from confidence in the affect of the performance of these static scenes in conjunction with attention to the cues for wondrous music.

I began with a man who walks across an empty space while someone watched on, and I conclude having traced a series of tableaux in which the static body of the performer playing dead, unable to look back, is gazed at by a voyeuristic audience in a highly determined social, erotic space. Some of these spectators left ekphrastic accounts of their watching for us to puzzle over and decode. Others, like the female spectators in the dark, hidden behind fans, tantalize us with the possibilities of their response. Did they, perhaps, like Daileader, imagine themselves in the position of those boy actors? Without the same grammar school training were they also overwhelmed with pity at the tragedies of Desdemona and the Lady? What afterlife did their sense of wonder at Hermione's transformation have? Populating the historical account with a thick description of the horizon of possible response attempts to address the hitherto empty space of the historical in-between.

[50] 'Introduction', *The Winters Tale* ed. John Pitcher (London: Bloomsbury/Arden, 2010) p. 69.

[51] Aristotle, (θαυμάζω) *Metaphysica*, trans. W. S. Ross in *The Works of Aristotle*, vol. VIII (12 vols.; Oxford: Clarendon Press, 1908), 982b, 10–27. Francis Bacon, *The two books of Francis Bacon. Of the proficience and advancement of learning, divine and humane* (London, 1605), B3v.

CHAPTER 9

In the event of fire

Paul Menzer

Something odd used to happen before each show at the Blackfriars Playhouse in Staunton, Virginia. An actor would tell you to silence your cell. They would thank their sponsors. They would then outline what to do 'in the event of fire'. The directive to turn off your phone but remain on alert always seemed at least slightly at odds. What if someone's calling to tell you the theatre's on fire? In any event, the warning has thus far proved thankfully misplaced. In the first decade of its operation the Staunton Blackfriars has been disrupted by blizzards, hurricanes, power outages, vicious windstorms and even one earthquake. An actuarial table would indicate that you are 100 per cent more likely to experience an earthquake than a fire during a performance at the Blackfriars. And yet, no pre-show announcement ever warned what to do in the event of a tremor – sit quietly, perhaps, and vibrate.

The warning of what to do 'in the event of fire' is, however, more than a mere public safety announcement. It is a reminder of the history of theatre with fire, from the *ur*-immolation of the Bankside Globe to the mass conflagration at Chicago's Iroquois Theatre and even to juridical hypos concerning the limits we place on free speech. Theatre history is haunted by flames, and pre-show cautions of their impending event rehearse theatre's peculiar pyro-phobia. At the theatre today – as in modern sport, where the referee is undefeated – the fire marshal is the author of every event. After all, regardless of who wrote the play, it is the fire marshal who signs the wall. Pre-show cautions about impending fires are not just warnings, then; they are wagers with history, with which theatre is forever hedging its bets. And so before each performance actors offer an incantation to guard against imminent erasure and thus position each performance in the seam between the eternity it seeks and the mortality for which it has to settle.

Theatre is in love with loss, and so adores the idea of its own demise. When the fire curtain falls at a West End theatre, it is both a safety measure and a celebration, a precaution, certainly, again our immolation but a boast as well about the wrack we'll all come to. Today, the theatre-on-the-brink-of-doom trope is familiar enough to both fire marshals and fundraisers. But whether flirting with fire or courting contributors, theatre is always rehearsing its fatalistic – or, narcissistic – desire for its own destruction and its bid for survival. After all, theatre today relies largely on charity, and so many a play opens not just with a hymn to fire but a call for alms. (In the United States the axiom might be that once a phenomenon – theatre, jazz, the environment – is embraced by public radio, it is no longer public. By contrast, when the rare theatre piece *is* genuinely popular, it is commonly priced beyond most pockets. Once the *Times* tells you that you can't afford to miss it, what they mean is that you can't afford to see it.) Wherever we place the emphasis, however – on mortality or eternity, or the space in between – James Burbage's indoor playhouse represents a signal intervention in western theatre's anxiety about its demise and its chances for survival.

Drama takes time and drama takes place, and the playhouse is the axis where those dimensions meet. When the King's Men moved into the Blackfriars in 1609, it changed western theatre's relationship to both time and place for ever. This chapter therefore argues, first, that Burbage's Blackfriars reset the sensory norm for theatrical spectatorship in the seventeenth century. It did so by institutionalizing intimacy, as Penelope Woods details in Chapter 8 above. If the Blackfriars reset the sensory norm, however, it also reset the clocks, establishing the threnody of loss that permeates performance even today. This chapter ultimately argues that the Blackfriars was the first instance of museum theatre – an institution that braided preservation with ephemerality into a tight strand – because it was, among other things, the first playhouse with a historical consciousness, a consciousness characterized by all it had to lose.

Theatre inside out

The amphitheatre is architecture's answer to a question of design: what configuration enables the maximum number of eyes and ears to see the human figure and to hear the human voice? The circle and the steppe are the evident solutions. Surround a central figure with others and array them on banks to see over one another's heads. The Theatre, the Rose, the Globe and the Swan improved upon this arrangement by closing the circle and stacking the audience. For all their innovations, however, the Elizabethan outdoor playhouses were simple refinements of an ancient model. Howsoever simple, the 1599 Globe was the best that theatre technology had to offer until artificial projection and amplification came along (and the Globe was in its own right an analog amplifier, a timber projector). The amphitheatre is a design of such ruthless efficiency and brutal elegance that its dispositions obtain even today. What is the National's Olivier but the theatre at Epidaurus with indoor plumbing and a coat check?

The Olivier also has a roof, of course, as did the Blackfriars and other indoor theatres of the early modern era. In this respect, the indoor playhouses of Shakespeare's age answer a follow-up question to the one posed above: how to enjoy the benefits of the amphitheatre without having to stand in the rain? The answer seems simple: put a lid on it. The roof is simply a work-around to an elemental problem of the amphitheatre design. But simple alterations can produce complex consequences. For the amphitheatre answers to a problem of distance – how to make one form apparent to a multitude of others – but the indoor playhouse creates one. And the problem it produced was a problem of proximity.

In strictly material terms, of course, it is easy to think of Burbage's indoor playhouse simply as an inverted amphitheatre: private not public; coterie not populist; intimate not rowdy. Sure enough, indoor actors faced technical challenges that inverted those they faced outside. At the Globe, actors took a candle on stage to bring on the night; at the Blackfriars, lights could be dimmed for 'nocturnals'. At the Globe, voices and instruments fought London's din; at the Blackfriars, instruments were muted for the neighbours' sake. And while actors at the Globe played on a broad platform with the crowd at their feet and massed around them, at the Blackfriars they traded elbows with gallants, working in the 'compass of a cheese trencher' as Jonson barked (*Devil is an Ass*, Prologue line 8).[1] The Blackfriars, in these terms, compromised the Globe, inverted its disposition, practices and protocols. The Blackfriars was simply the Globe turned outside in.

And yet, to imagine the Blackfriars as an inverted Globe underestimates its historical significance. For the Blackfriars did not just invert the Globe; it ultimately supplanted it. That is, an inside–out architectural binary of theatre history leaves the early modern amphitheatre in place as the dominant term. The logic of this binary posits the Globe as the norm and the Blackfriars as a derogation of or compromise to the normative model of theatrical experience. This logic has some traction on the truth, but it obscures the extent to which indoor playing not only erased the slash between 'inside/out' but replaced the dominant term and remains in

[1] *The Cambridge Edition of the Works of Ben Jonson*, ed. David Bevington, Martin Butler and Ian Donaldson (7 vols.; Cambridge: Cambridge University Press, 2012).

place today. The Blackfriars was not a proscenium playhouse, but it introduced proscenium protocols, a 'prosceniumicity', which, as I develop below, refers to a variety of social relations more than a physical disposition. In short, a theatre does not need an arch to realize the aim of a proscenium house: the separation of actor and audience.

The Blackfriars struck the death knell not just for the Globe, not just for early English outdoor playing, but for a theatrical norm of outside theatre that was nearly two thousand years old. In these terms, the Blackfriars ultimately replaced not just the Globe, the Swan, the Rose, the Curtain; it and its descendants replaced the theatre at Epidaurus and those at El Djem, Rome and Nîmes. The Blackfriars, in short, was no mere winter haven for the shivering King's Men, glad enough to be inside during the frosty months but eager to return to the *al fresco* norm. Rather, its opening marked the beginning of the end for a long chapter in western theatre history, revising the sensory norm for theatrical attendance in which the experience of assembly has been thoroughly domesticated. In fact, the sensory norm of inside playing, of institutionalized intimacy, is only reinforced by the recent revanchism of theatrical reconstructionism. The novelty of the rebuilt Globe is that it is a novelty. In sum, the Blackfriars reconfigured not just what it meant to be live in 1610, but what it still means to be live today. Drama takes time and drama takes place, and the Blackfriars reset western theatre's disposition towards both by articulating a commitment to intimacy and an investment in loss that permeates the protocols of playmaking even today.

Extremely loud and incredibly close

When James Burbage first tried to 'move Shakespeare indoors', his attempt was rebuffed on account of the noise and the crowds. The famous petition of Blackfriars residents singles out the 'great resort and gathering' of all manner of unsavouries whose 'pestering and filling up of the same precinct' will, the petition's author adds almost as an afterthought, be downright dangerous when the plague descends. In addition, the 'noyse of the drummes and trumpetts will greatly disturbe and hinder both the ministers and parishioners in tyme of devine service and sermons'.[2] As many have noted, the petition is symptomatic of a probably timeless not-in-my-backyard (or not-in-my-liberty) principle of civic maintenance.

[2] Irwin Smith, *Shakespeare's Blackfriars Playhouse: Its History and Design* (New York University Press, 1964), pp. 478–9.

The Blackfriars residents had a good thing going and saw the actors as a threat to the quiet life. After all, you know what those people are like.

The petition intriguingly departs, however, from the tropic programme of the period's anti-theatrical literature. The petition does not focus on the inherent turpitude of playing or the immodest behaviours it might promote. The concern is not that plays might outdraw sermons – as it was for Philip Stubbes and William Prynne – but that they might outdrown them. Plays are noisy and a nuisance and so are the bodies that attend them. Running through the petition is a concern with proximate bodies, pestering, crowding and milling among and upon one another. The petition is, of course, concerned about the ambient noise and crowds *outside* the playhouse, but from the moment of its inception, the Blackfriars was perceived in terms of its aural and somatic intensification.

The petitioners were perceptive. Inside, the Blackfriars *was* pestered with people, filled with an audience that jockeyed with the players for room. In his prologue to *The Devil is an Ass*, Jonson poeticizes the Blackfriars complaint, rehearsing an irritation about attending 'grandees' who 'knock us o' the elbows' and 'thrust and spurn' and 'leave us no place' (Prologue lines 3–12). It is also a Blackfriars petition, this one from the players to the audience to give them room to play. Whether continuation or innovation, the practice of allowing gallants on stage altered theatrical practice for ever. It was, as Ralph Alan Cohen notes, the practice that 'distinguishes it most from the Globe', with Tiffany Stern agreeing that the 'closed audience . . . around and on the stage will have been strikingly different from the one around the Globe'.[3] The pressure the closed audience might have upon a play is comically dramatized in *The Knight of the Burning Pestle* where it is far from clear exactly who is in charge. What *is* clear is that it is unclear, a firm demarcation between actors and audience blurred by proximity.

While the Blackfriars evidently put pressure on bodies, it also apparently alarmed the ears. The Blackfriars petition is concerned about the impending racket, presuming that the Lord Chamberlain's servants will simply import the 'drummes and trumpetts' of the outdoor playhouse to the smaller confines of the quondam friary, once a place, we assume, of prayerful silence. Their fears were misplaced, however, since the Blackfriars evidently invested in a quieter soundscape – recorders, not shawms; cornets, not trumpets. Even the artillery was toned down. *Love's Pilgrimage*, which appeared at the Blackfriars in 1635, calls for a cannon to be discharged,

[3] 'The Most Convenient Place: The Second Blackfriars Theater and its Appeal', in Richard Dutton (ed.), *The Oxford Handbook of Early Modern Theatre* (Oxford University Press, 2009), p. 218.

which a bookholder has altered to 'Joh. Bacon ready to shoot off a pistol.'[4] In this respect, the Blackfriars offered up small-bore Shakespeare, its repertory a lesser calibre than an offer outdoors.[5]

Again, however, such a reading imagines the Blackfriars as an amphitheatre with a roof on it, keeping its audience dry but dampening the effects. Instead, we should see the move indoors as the radical break with theatrical protocol that it retrospectively represents. Indeed, to the extent that the on-stage audience broke with Globe practices, so did the Blackfriars' commitment to music. For when the King's servants moved indoors in 1609, the famed Blackfriars consort stayed put, playing pre-show concerts and the occasional interlude. Along with the practice of allowing an audience on stage, the King's servants' commitment to a mixed-media event of music and drama further differentiates their indoor practices from those at the Globe. The Blackfriars was not the Globe at a decreased order of magnitude. The Blackfriars experience was not a diminution; it was different.

Quite apart from the music and sound effects, the shift from outside to indoor had a significant impact on the human voice, not just in volume but also in quality. Bruce Smith points out that while we are used to thinking of the Globe as an aurally intimate space, its volumetric scale – which he estimates at 243,714 cubic feet – 'surpasses that of modern theatres'.[6] As Sarah Dustagheer also points out in Chapter 7 above, not only did the smaller Blackfriars turn down the volume, it dispersed sound quite differently – surprisingly, the move from the twenty-sided outdoor polygon to a rectilinear indoor space 'would have produced a "round" sound quite different from the "broad" sound of the Globe – just the reverse of the effect suggested by the physical shapes of the two structures'.[7] In sum, the Blackfriars represented a resituation of the theatrical experience, retuning the spatio-audio norm of attendance.

In modern terms the Blackfriars altered the 'aspect ratio' of spectatorship, introducing a new sensory norm. The idea of a 'sensory norm' is by no means restricted to the early modern period, of course; every historical moment has its own. Philip Auslander has taught us to understand ours as a televisual culture, one that grows out of a particular time, place and

[4] Andrew Gurr, *The Shakespearean Stage, 1574–1642* (Cambridge University Press, 1992), p. 177.

[5] See Sarah Dustagheer's discussion of the acoustic differences between indoor and outdoor repertories, Chapter 8 above.

[6] Bruce Smith, *The Acoustic World of Early Modern England: Attending to the O-Factor* (University of Chicago Press, 1999), p. 210.

[7] Ibid., p. 217.

technology. Today, mediated experience – on stage, on screen, in a concert hall or a stadium – adheres to the protocols of film and television. Even 'live' events are produced and dictated by the protocols of televisuality. American football is a television show, as anyone who has been to a professional match knows as they sit through yawning periods of inactivity as the viewers at home watch commercials or fetch more chips. Analogously, until the Blackfriars, the early modern era had its own sensory norm – not televisuality, of course, but 'amphitheatrics', characterized by a standing audience surrounding an outdoor platform. The Blackfriars, I argue, altered all that. In short, if the early modern period can be reductively seen to have witnessed so many other transitions – orality to print, feudal to merchant culture, a distributed to a centralized authority – we can read as well in the early seventeenth century a transition in the sensory norm of theatrical presentation and attendance. Viewed within a macro-historical scale, this theatrical transition represents a major break from a two-thousand-year history of outdoor, amphitheatre playing and the onset of the over four-hundred-year history of proscenium protocols – a transition we might describe as the move from distance to proximity, from amphitheatrics to prosceniumicity.

In these terms, it may be only a mild exaggeration to claim that the intimacy of performance we experience via television and film today finds its primitive origin on the Blackfriars stage (and as Penelope Woods argues in Chapter 8, 'intimacy' in performance is an under-theorized idea). The Blackfriars was not quite the first television, but it did introduce as a theatrical norm a proximity to the human face and voice we otherwise enjoy (or suffer) only with our intimates. While audiences may not actually sit on stages today, our ticket prices nonetheless reflect the priority we place upon proximity to the actor's face and form. The access to an imagined interiority that is, today, our default expectation from live performance depends to a great degree upon physical proximity, and that proximity results from certain technical and architectural developments that we can trace to the early 1600s.

We might anticipate that such a reliably intimate relationship between actor and audience allowed plays to explore interiority through the expressively nuanced voice and body of the actor. Oddly, however, the opening of indoor venues in seventeenth-century England brought, instead, flying machines, creaking trapezes, disappearing banquets and sputtering squibs. In addition to Shakespeare's quaint devices, we find, in the Jacobean playhouses, calls for extravagant effects like those in Middleton's *No Wit, No Help Like a Woman's* – '*A thing like a globe opens of one side of the stage and flashes out fire*' (9.65–66) – and in his *Lady's Tragedy*: '*On a sudden, in a kind of noise like a wind, the doors clatters, the Tombstone flies open, and a great light appears in the midst of the Tomb*' (4.4.44–5).[8] These few but representative examples help suggest that the indoor stage did prompt an innovation in performance technologies, but those technologies gestured away from the actor and towards gimcrack wonder. The commercial success of indoor playhouses brought about, in short, a counterintuitive move – not the close-up drama of psychological intimacy, but a theatre of wonder, distance, and deferral, a theatre of domesticate spectacle.

Much theatre-historical work has ascribed this spectacular turn to the fashion for court masques (considered below), but I want here to rehearse an alternative theory. We might rethink the physical proximity the Blackfriars enforced and conclude that communities who eliminate physical space reproduce it with what Guy Debord, in his Marxist reading of commodities of leisure, called 'spectacular separation'.[9] Such communities develop technologies of separation, or what, here, we might call 'theatre'. After all, it is only tolerable to gaze into the nostrils of today's film stars because of the 'technology of separation' that virtually distances us from them. In this case, the technology is film or digital recording, which captures an image and replaces real presence with its resemblance. Indoor playing developed its own arts of deferral, as proximity enforced a distribution of effects among theatrical technologies including, but not limited to, the actors' bodies. As argued above, the Blackfriars helped bring about an increase in spectacle, but the proximate cause was not decadence; it was proximity. This proximity, in turn, reverts to a problem raised at the outset of this chapter, one of distance. If the amphitheatre triumphed by conquering distance, then the indoor theatre reintroduced a distance it had conquered all too well.

The rise of the machines

I have argued elsewhere that acting is an art of indecent exposure.[10] This idea animates Henry Chettle in *Kind-Hartes Dream*, where, in a line he attributes to Tarleton, he diagnoses a phobia inherent to acting, that of being 'publike in everie ones eye, and talkt of in every vulgar mans mouth'.[11]

[8] *Thomas Middleton: The Collected Works*, ed. Gary Taylor and John Lavagnino (Oxford: Clarendon Press, 2007).

[9] Guy Debord, *Society of the Spectacle* (Detroit: Black & Red, 1983), p. 167.

[10] 'Crowd Control', in Jennifer A. Low and Nova Myhill (eds.), *Imagining the Audience in Early Modern Drama, 1558–1642* (Basingstoke: Palgrave Macmillan, 2011), pp. 19–36.

[11] Henry Chettle, *Kind-Harts Dream* (London, 1604), E4r.

Chettle's focus on the mouths of the vulgar introduces a queasy digestive metaphor implying that acting involves a reciprocal supply and demand between artistic production and the audience's appetite – consumer culture, in other words. A clown in Robert Wilson's *The Three Ladies of London* echoes the digestive figure introduced by Chettle. The actor worries aloud: 'But yonder is a fellow that gapes to bite me, or else to eat that which I sing.'[12] When Jonson complains about acting within the compass of a cheese trencher, the unstated but irresistible logic of the metaphor leads us to conclude that the actors are the cheese.

Chettle and Wilson were probably not thinking specifically about indoor playhouses, but they were nonetheless diagnosing something endemic to playing – a theatrical version of agoraphobia. The indoor playhouse, I would argue, exacerbated the occasions under which such phobia might thrive, bringing the crowd across the threshold that separated – in the amphitheatre – actor from audience, blurring the territories of us and them. When we recall that gallants entered from the tiring-house to take their place upon the Blackfriars stage, even backstage offered no refuge from the crowd.

An epidemiological perspective on this phobia might then diagnose the Blackfriars as an incubator for its spread, and prescribe spectacle as a preventative measure. As suggested earlier, spectacle creates virtual distance when architecture eliminates it. While Ben Jonson wrote plays that claustrophobically capitalized upon the Blackfriars' architecture and location in plays like *The Alchemist* and *Epicoene*, the King's servants' other playwrights – Shakespeare and Fletcher most notably – turned to the exotic peripateticism of tragicomedy to create virtual worlds elsewhere. If what you have got to play in is a cheese trencher, then it can create at least an illusion of distance to pretend you are on a distant island – perhaps even an 'uninhabited' one as the 1623 Folio nonsensically but perhaps wistfully adds to the end of *The Tempest*.

Such an agoraphobic theatrical environment might seem – as noted above – an opportunity for players and playwrights to consolidate character, capitalizing on proximity to explore interiority. Yet, perversely, proximity further fractured character, distributed it among an array of effects, which gathered around the actor's form. Claire Colebrook, paraphrasing Giles Deleuze, has suggested that '[c]haracters are not harmonious and unified substances but assemblages or "refrains": a

[12] Robert Wilson, *Three Ladies of London* (London, 1590), D3r.

collection of body-parts, gestures, desires and motifs'.[13] They are also, we might add, the costumes and properties they wear and handle. Hamlet provides, as so often, a signal example. Hamlet begins by insisting that it is not alone his inky cloak that can denote him truly, and he is right. It is not alone, though it is in part, his inky cloak that exhibits his grief, his central 'character'. For it is also his commonplace book, in which he habitually writes; his sword, which he employs as both weapon and cross; the trap he leaps into to wrestle Laertes; the arras he perforates to kill Polonius; the recorder he governs; the text he recites; the skull he most famously stares at. The paradox is plain. Renaissance drama's most characteristic representative of a complex interiority is partly the product of a complex of exteriority. Interiority is the affect, exteriority the percept, in Deleuzian terms. In other words, subjectivity is distributed among a range of theatrical accessories that the Hamlet actor must skilfully manage. 'Hamlet' is the effect of a range of theatrical technologies, including but not limited to the performer's body and its interaction with its physical environment.

In these terms, the actor is the principle of organization in the proliferation of effects, the centre around which costumes, properties, architecture and text increasingly were made to coalesce by a theatre growingly reliant upon them. As before, I would suggest, via Debord, that these spectacles of separation responded to the proximity of bodies, faces and elbows. Thunder sheets, smoke effects and trapeze descents are the actor's revenge against proximate bodies, a way of carving out space where none exists. In other words, the relationship of machinery to the theatre in general and the Blackfriars in particular is symptomatic, not causal.

Spectacle, then, can create distance, but in doing so it alters the ontology of the live. For, if the actor was the principle of organization, he also became a principle of reliability. The on-stage life of material resources points to the off stage system of personnel, materials and timing – everything in its right place at exactly the right time. Hamlet's recorder, for instance, just seems accidentally to be there – what are the odds? – but it would be an accident if it were *not* there, just as it would be an accident if it were a skull rather than a recorder that the player handed Hamlet or if the gravedigger threw up a commonplace book rather than a skull for Hamlet to meditate upon. All of this requires co-ordination of men and materials, of inventorying and planning, of pulling and restocking – it takes, in short, a lot of skill to make the causal look casual, to make the incidental appear to be

[13] Claire Colebrook, *Giles Deleuze* (London and New York: Routledge, 2002), pp. 106–7.

accidental. In a theatre that relies on materiality and 'special effects', the actors play a moving part in a complex theatrical machine.

Theatre machines are built for reproducibility – to produce sameness – and a theatre that relies on them has entered into a new ontology, a new variety of reproducibility. As Philip Auslander points out, 'The audience's inevitable curiosity about how technical effects are achieved makes them centers of attention.'[14] Thunder sheets, flying machines, coloured lights, black drapes are designed to produce the same effect each time regardless of the particularities or personnel of a performance. A thunder sheet will thunder be it during the tragedy of *King Lear* or the romance of *Cymbeline*, for a rumble of thunder is generic only in the non-literary sense. Theatre machines are designed to be reliable, and they draw the viewer's attention to the spectacle of reproduction that implicates its human agents as well. As Walter Benjamin observed of a different medium at a different time, 'To an ever-increasing degree, the work reproduced becomes the work designed for reproducibility.'[15] Well before the photographs that prompted Benjamin's famous remarks, the Blackfriars took the first steps towards a kind of art 'designed for reproducibility'.

In retrospect, the Blackfriars might be seen as a pilot product of a new phase of spectatorship. To push this idea into a proto-Marxist reading, we might read this phase not just as a redistribution of theatrical audiences but a redisposition of social relations. In Debord's reading, 'the spectacle is not a collection of images, but a social relation among people, mediated by images'.[16] Early modern theatre through its reliable scheduling and purpose-built places entered theatre into the economy of repetition, in which live events are produced by the determinants of the schedule. On the surface, there may seem something paradoxical about scheduled liveness – at two-of-the-clock of a Wednesday afternoon, the Globe theatre will sell you ephemerality for the cost of a penny and your patience. If there seems something at least slightly contradictory about planned spontaneity, however, we need to recall that 'liveness' is not synonymous with spontaneity. Because these 'live' events took place at predetermined times, places and prices, they are no longer 'ephemeral' in the sense that we so often claim for theatre. We should, instead, understand early modern theatre within a particular cultural context, one in which meanings are mobilized within a

[14] Philip Auslander, *Liveness: Performance in a Mediatized Culture* (London and New York: Routledge, 1999), p. 41.

[15] Walter Benjamin, *The Work of Art in the Age of its Technological Reproducibility and Other Writings on Media* (Cambridge, MA: Harvard University Press, 2008), p. 24.

[16] Debord, *Society of the Spectacle*, p. 4.

climate with an emergent sense of a theatre that offers up everyday drama instead of the occasional event. The extent to which the period cared or was concerned about this is hard if not impossible to determine from an historical remove, but anxieties about the Blackfriars that express themselves as worries about proximity and amplification seem nagged into life by a new consciousness about 'the live'.

The Blackfriars was not just loud and crowded, of course; it was also expensive. That expense was surely also a part of the sensory norm of the Blackfriars experience. The period's euphemism for this experience was 'private' as opposed to 'public', a legal nicety to be sure but one that also implied that accessibility (and its inverse) came at a price. In other words, institutionalized intimacy and the rise of the spectacle also implied certain economic relations. The Blackfriars quite literally left no space for the penny groundlings. When a gallant rose at an interval to show off a gown or doublet or boot, he was making a spectacle of himself and revealing the true commodity exchange that the Blackfriars enabled and that Broadway and the West End honours today: money watching money.

Museum theatre

The argument that the Blackfriars reset 'the sensory norm' of theatrical spectatorship serves up old wine in new skins, of course. After all, theatre historians are in general accord that the Blackfriars changed theatre for good. Or, rather, theatre history agrees that the Blackfriars changed theatre for the worse. The indoor fireworks of increased spectacle are, after all, usually described in terms of loss, the pernicious pressure of courtly masquing. For instance, Ralph Alan Cohen notes that the second Blackfriars seemed increasingly influenced by the masque, writing:

> the work of Inigo Jones and the other scene innovators in designing lavish mise-en-scènes for the masque had also engendered a competing aesthetic, one in which technological advances would privilege the capacity of theater to create the illusion of different and separate worlds, and in that aesthetic the visual presence of the audience would become a hindrance.[17]

I have argued above that the desire for 'different and separate worlds' arises out of the anxiety of intimacy. More often, however, the blame is placed elsewhere. For instance, Jacalyn Royce writes: 'After Heminges died in 1630, the company finally gave priority to the Blackfriars over the Globe and

[17] Dutton, *Early Modern Theatre*, p. 224.

allowed their repertory to succumb to the fashion of fantastic visual scenery that appealed to the physical eye over verbal scenery that spoke to the mind's eye.'[18] Helpless in the face of such pressure, the King's servants finally 'succumbed' to elitist fashion for facile wonder, giving way before the pampered pressure of courtly elites.

This is theatre history as melodrama with Inigo Jones as its mustachioed villain, his foreign first name so unlike honest William, Henry and Dick (its near rhyme with 'Iago' not helping his case). This notion is probably wrong. First, the bareness of the 'bare' platform of the early modern amphitheatre is greatly overstated, as though – in Alan Armstrong's terms – an elegant thin line can be drawn from James Burbage to Mies van der Rohe.[19] We know the outdoor theatres to have been, themselves, invested in wonder. This is the story that Henslowe's inventory has been trying to tell us for some time now. Second, the rise of spectacle once theatre shifted indoors, the lamented transition from ear to eye, is no doubt overstated as well. Gabriel Egan, for one, has demonstrated that Hamlet's idiom to 'hear a play' (2.2.538) is far surpassed by early modern references to seeing one.[20] Theatre has always been a place to see. That is what the word means. There was almost certainly no wholesale conversion in the seventeenth century of acoustically alert audiences to optically anaesthetized spectators. So treasured is this fable that no mere plurality of information seems likely to shake it.

But the notion that the King's servants 'succumbed' to a sinisterly Italianate influence is also at odds with one of theatre history's other most cherished fables. Early modern playmakers are often celebrated as bluff men of business – one eye on their scripts, the other on the bottom line. We would have to believe that they somehow lost their touch around 1610, embracing court spectacle over the vehement protests of their audience. We should allow instead that the Blackfriars audience may have voted with their purses. In any event, a consistent reading of the King's servants' business acumen would find them giving the people precisely what they wanted: a show.

Howsoever melodramatic, this version of theatre history is no less revealing for its diagnostic imprecision. For this version of theatre history enacts the phenomenon it purports to describe, one of loss. This is the inverse of Whig history – with its relentless commitment to progress – and tells instead the

[18] 'Early Modern Naturalistic Acting: The Role of the Globe in the Development of Personation', in Dutton, *Early Modern Theatre*, p. 494.

[19] Quoted from a lecture delivered at the NEH Institute, 'Shakespeare Inside/Out', summer 2008.

[20] Gabriel Egan, 'Hearing or Seeing a Play?: Evidence of Early Modern Theatrical Terminology', accessed http://gabrielegan.com/publications/Egan2001k.htm

'Persian version', in the words of Robert Graves, of theatre history, a history of loss told by the losers. The Blackfriars, as I exaggeratedly posited above, was the first theatre with a historical consciousness, a consciousness of loss, to be precise. One of the ways in which that is an exaggeration is that there was another theatre with an historical consciousness built some quarter of a century earlier by the same man who built the Blackfriars. That theatre was called 'The Theatre'. While the name may strike us as unimaginative, it was, in fact, an astonishing act of the imagination. (Consider by contrast the fashion for naming playhouses as if they were pubs: The Hope, The Rose, The Globe, The Swan, The Red Bull – 'The Theatre' was an extraordinary anomaly.) But what Burbage and Brayne must have had in mind were the theatres of classical antiquity, and the Latinate name broadcast their ambitions (or pretensions). 'The Theatre', then, was a playhouse with a very precise idea of theatre history and even about how the theatrical past might be reawakened. In these terms, the Shoreditch 'Theatre' was the first Original Practices playhouse, and James Burbage was the first theatrical reconstructionist. It is his legacy, in more ways than one, that the twentieth-century Globe and Blackfriars honours.

The Theatre, in other words, celebrated the triumphs of theatrical antiquity and tried to resurrect its spirit through the medium of architecture. If James Burbage's most famous amphitheatre honoured by name an idea of theatrical triumphalism, however, his indoor playhouse honoured theatrical loss. However unwittingly, by building the Blackfriars upon the ruins of the Reformation, Burbage's playhouse articulated a version of theatre history haunted not by triumph but by ruin. The fact that it was the protocols of indoor playing – what I have called a kind of 'proscenium-icity' – that ultimately survived rather than the 'amphitheatrics' of the Globe means that the theatre history we inherit and inhabit is a history of loss, of spectacles of ruin emblematized by fire.

It is impossible to tell how intentional was the linguistic slip when the Lord Chamberlain's servants rechristened their 'theatre' and called it a 'globe'. Prank or pretension, the name took the *theatrum mundum* metaphor about as far as it could go. The 'Blackfriars', by contrast, celebrates reversion, ennobles the dissolution of the Dominicans, whose ruined choirs were filled first by choristers and, later, by men flogging fables. The Blackfriars celebrates, by name, the past, turns away from the ambitions of the Globe to install an idea that we act upon ruins. From the fourteenth century to the twenty-first, the name 'Blackfriars' honours a long history of mendicant institutions. It may seem a long way from a monastic order to a company of players, but both institutions are charity cases.

The Blackfriars was not an outlier, however. By accident or design, all the indoor stages of the age were what developers today would call 'creative reuse' as opposed to purpose-built. Probably for reasons of engineering or expense, no theatrical entrepreneur in the age ever purpose built an indoor playhouse from the ground up. Unlike the amphitheatres, the indoor playhouses were all retrofits – of inns, of cockpits, or friaries – and in so being, inevitably implicated their operations within the history the building conveyed, as Tiffany Stern explores in Chapter 5 above. As the King's servants may have worried in 1613 when they staged *Henry VIII* on the same grounds where Henry's divorce took place, history can be a drag.

Makes time shapely. That is how Bert States defines what drama does. It gives to temporality a temporary coherence, allows us, for a fleeting instant, to watch time at work and in time's apprehension discover comprehension. A playhouse is a place that provides room to watch time at work. In this regard, a playhouse is a museum to time. Of course, theatre makers get nervous at the term 'museum theatre', places like Williamsburg in America that restage colonial life right down to the buttons on your bonnet. That nervousness is probably symptomatic of the fact that, far from the oxymoron they imagine it to be, 'museum theatre' may be redundant (but then so is 'modern drama'). In many respects, for all its innovations, the Blackfriars was the first museum theatre, or the first museum *to* theatre, or, at least, to theatre's fundamental material, time, and it gave a name to the kind of time that theatre thereafter honoured: loss.

I have argued above that the Blackfriars reset the aspect ratio of the theatrical experience, institutionalizing intimacy. At the same time, it inaugurated theatre's relationship with time, with its own theatre history. Drama takes time and drama takes place – and the playhouse is where those dimensions meet. This was true for the theatre at Epidaurus, the Teatro Olimpico in Vicenza, the Curtain in Shoreditch, and James Burbage's playhouse in Blackfriars. The Blackfriars, however, profoundly departed from those others, and not simply because it had a roof. It was the first theatre to be simultaneously about the idea of theatre; it articulated a new idea of time and place, an idea we inherited and are still largely beholden to today. The idea of the past enshrined in its name is about loss and displacement, about 'acting in ruins', or remains, for by building a playhouse within a dissolved priory, James Burbage invested simultaneously in a bold new entrepreneurial venture that also obligated his audience to remember the past.

Coda: revisions

The end of this chapter remembers its beginning and in doing so revises it. When I consult the archive, where theatre keeps its memory, the phrase 'In the event of fire' is not, precisely, what the actors at Staunton Blackfriars said, since such a phrase might seem to suggest that the fire will certainly come eventually, 'in any event', though just not now. The phrase was, in fact, 'In the *unlikely* event of fire'. A cynic might question the theatrical gamesmanship of starting each performance with intimations of apocalypse – of considering as a constitutive quality of performance today a promised fire that never arrives. The live event, like the fire itself, is faithfully invoked but constantly deferred. The fire arrived for the King's Men, of course, and the Blackfriars must have seemed a blessing while they rebuilt their Globe. It was, however, ultimately the Blackfriars that survived the fire, at least figuratively so, since theatre history has proved its model to be the enduring one after the erasure we call the 'closing of the theatre'. If the first Blackfriars was a museum to time, and spectacles of its loss, then Staunton's Blackfriars honours a related but different idea about the possibility of recovering from history, the singular realization upon which metaphysicians and meteorologists both agree: lightning doesn't strike twice.

CHAPTER 10

To glisten in a playhouse: cosmetic beauty indoors

Farah Karim-Cooper

In 1608/9 when the King's Men occupied once and for all the Blackfriars Playhouse, it must have become clear to the company and their audiences that, during the winter months, their repertory, stagecraft and range of effects would have to be adapted to accommodate the very different architectural conditions in which they would be performing, specifically, the same conditions with which the boy companies were more familiar. Indeed contributors to this volume have already shown the many ways this may have happened. Even if dramatists and actors did not really see the need to create new repertories for a new space as some have argued, it is undeniable that the open-air Globe Theatre (and other amphitheatres), with its large thrust stage, 800 to 1,000 groundlings and 2,000 gallery sitters, was starkly different from the indoor, candlelit space that had a stage roughly half the size of the Globe and seated only 600. The audience was less diverse in the Blackfriars than the Globe, with the admission at six pence, and crucially, the visual tone and acoustic would have differed from the Globe's in exciting and challenging ways. It was not that the King's Men had not performed in indoor, candlelit spaces to exclusive audiences, as John Astington reminds us in Chapter 1 above; on the contrary, their performances at inns, private homes, at court and the Inns of Court would have already given them a taste of the unique indoor aesthetic to which, for years, they desired to claim for their own exclusive use. What I would like to do here is imagine the visual tone of the Blackfriars Playhouse, focussing primarily on the aesthetic created by the convergence of elements that affected the reception of performance in the indoor space. One of the unique effects of performance in the Blackfriars Playhouse to which this chapter will attend is the interplay between textual imagery, faces, cosmetic materials and candlelight.

I will explore the social and ideological questions raised by the philosophy of beauty, early modern cosmetic practices and their representation in Jacobean drama, and I will show how cosmetic materiality and the special effects produced by candlelight have a particular linguistic and thematic resonance with some of the plays in the King's Men's repertory that are known to have been performed in the Blackfriars Playhouse.

Beauty in Jacobean England

The ideal of female beauty in Jacobean England, it should be said, was hardly different to the ideal just decades before. It was one inherited from the Continent and which had origins in the classical ideology of bodily beauty. Typically, a pale complexion, an apparent blush in the cheeks, ruby lips, golden hair and dark eyes featured in the period's poetic and courtly discourse as the primary attributes of beauty. What is not commonly observed, however, is the fact that words such as 'lustre', 'shine', 'glow', 'glisten' and 'shimmer' frequently accompany idealized descriptions of female beauty, referring to what was viewed as perhaps the most essential quality of a woman's complexion. Classical definitions of beauty (as I have shown elsewhere)[1] heavily influence Renaissance formulations, particularly in their emphasis on the qualities of proportion, symmetry and chromatic harmony. The Aristotelian influence assured that the proportion of parts was seen as a prerequisite for beauty. Proportion soon became a very important Renaissance value that was crucial to art, poetry and architecture. The English writer George Puttenham says in *The Arte of English Poesie*: 'all things stand by proportion, and without it nothing could stand to be good or beautiful'.[2] What Puttenham suggests here is that proportion had to be a defining principle when judging goodness *and* beauty, and this applied to art as well as to the human body. Plato, by contrast, found that it was not necessary for beauty to be associated with the tangible object nor tied merely to symmetry and proportion. Instead, it is more abstract. Plato, therefore, personified beauty, declaring it 'the goddess who presides at childbirth', and deigning it a privilege given only to some; he also distinguished between absolute beauty and divine beauty, both being associated with purity and virtue.[3] When we look to the continental Renaissance, it is the Neoplatonist Marsilio Ficino who reshapes Plato's philosophy of beauty and gives it its Christian significance.

[1] See Farah Karim-Cooper, *Cosmetics in Shakespearean and Renaissance Drama* (Edinburgh University Press, 2012) and 'Performing Beauty on the Renaissance Stage', in Christine Dymkowski and Christie Carson (eds.), *Shakespeare in Stages: New Theatre Histories* (Cambridge University Press, 2010), pp. 93–106.

[2] George Puttenham, *The Arte of English Poesie* (London. 1589), p. 53.

[3] Plato, *Symposium*, in John M. Cooper and D. S. Hutchinson (eds.), *Plato: Complete Works* (Indianapolis: Hackett, 1997), p. 489.

He suggests that 'beauty is a kind of force or light, shining from Him through everything'. For Neoplatonists such as Ficino, then, beauty itself should originate from the light of the soul; this visible glow is imagined as God's image radiating from beneath the surface of the body, and is therefore a powerful manifestation of virtue.[4] The causal link between virtue and bodily lustre is sustained well into the Caroline period, as Eleanor Collins shows in Chapter 12, in her discussion of the dramatic female heroines of the 1630s.[5] A few Elizabethan and Jacobean examples of this imagery of shining reveal that the connection between lustre and virtue was well ingrained in the cultural imagination. John Bodenham's *Belvidere, or the Garden of Muses* (1600), imagines 'vertue' repeatedly as that which shines forth: 'Like to the sunne, so virtue lights the world . . . Vertue will shine though ne're so much obscur'd . . . / . . . Vertue makes women seeme to be diuine . . . / . . . Vertue in beauteous bodies shineth best . . .'[6]

By the seventeenth century the philosophy of beauty continued to develop, but the key precept remained constant: a pale, glistening complexion. An English translation of Thomas Buoni's *Problemes of Beautie* (1606) offers up further definitions in the form of a dialogue, with questions posed about beauty and its uses. Like many before him, Buoni celebrates an idealized form which should reflect 'the white in the snow and red in the rose'. He invokes the Neoplatonic discourse, suggesting that women's faces should correspond to the cosmos, that is, the celestial and radiant beauty of the heavens: 'who beholds & rests not astonished at the clear light of the Moone, the bright beams of the sun, the whiteness of siluer, the splendour of gold'.[7] Like the heavens, the ideal woman should glisten and sparkle like silver or gold, like the sun or the moon. A few years on, William Austin goes so far as to declare that a woman's face is the very 'epitome of heaven'.[8] The etymological registers in 'cosmos' and 'cosmetic' may become apparent when we consider the poetic and prescriptive discourses that attributed a celestial quality to female beauty. In the continental descriptions, the rhetoric associating female beauty with the cosmos and with the quality of shining or glistening was also prevalent earlier. Florentine poet Agnolo Firenzuola's disquisition on beauty provides an itemized description of

[4] Marsilio Ficino, *Commentary on Plato's Symposium*, in Albert Hofstadler and Richard Kuhns (eds.), *Philosophies in Art and Beauty: Selected Readings in Aesthetics from Plato to Heidegger* (University of Chicago Press, 1964), p. 213.
[5] See p. 233. [6] John Bodenham, *Belvidere, or the Garden of Muses* (London, 1600), p. 18.
[7] Thomas Buoni, *The Problemes of Beautie and humane affections*, trans. S. L. Gent (London, 1606), sig. A2v.
[8] William Austin, *Haec Homo, Wherein the Excellency of the Creation of Woman is described by way of an Essay* (London, 1639), p. 105.

the ideal woman. In addition to describing the proportions of her body down to the length of her fingers, Firenzuola also spends a great deal of time commenting on the importance of chromatic harmony in a woman's face. He insists that 'the cheeks must be fair. Fair is a colour that besides being white, also has a certain lustre, as ivory does'.[9] The distinction that Firenzuola makes here between white and ivory is subtly discernible in the physical 'lustre' apparent in the latter. As I have argued elsewhere, 'it would seem that the terms "fair" and "white" are not always to be taken as interchangeable'; fairness conveys a 'lustre that is comparable to silver' or, more to the point, pearl.[10] To cite Thomas Buoni again, he also notes the distinction between colour and lustre when he insists that 'Beauty consisteth not so much on colour as on illumination or illustration of those colours, which giveth grace, and lustre to every countenance, and without which all Beauties are languishing'.[11] Cosmetic recipes from the sixteenth and seventeenth centuries, such as William Warde's translation of the Italian recipe manual *The Secrets of Alexis of Piemont* (by Girolamo Ruscelli), also take up this idiom of fairness, frequently offering concoctions that suggest ways of producing recipes that 'maketh a faire skinne', for example, or 'a water that maketh the face white and shining'. There are facial cleansers that require 'the milke of an asse, and egge shelles, and make thereof distilled water, and wash your face with it, and it will be white, faire and glistering'.[12]

A significant paradoxical question arises, however, and one that I raised in my book-length study of cosmetics: how is a so-called 'virtuous' woman meant to achieve a lustre in her complexion? How does the Neoplatonic ideal of virtue 'shine' through her skin without cosmetic compounds, such as silver foil, crushed pearl or a simple egg glaze? While Firenzuola is quick to comment that, although the prescriptions for the ideal beauty are quite specific, such beauty should be no less than natural. He 'said fair because it should not be a washed-out white, without any lustre, but shiny like a mirror; not shiny because of lotions or polishes or powders'.[13] Of course, Neoplatonists might argue that a woman's virtue would create a luminescence that would naturally be visible upon her cheeks. This familiar fantasy of female virtue constructs the ideal woman, however, through metaphorical abstractions; thus, the introduction of material cosmetics

[9] Agnolo Firenzuola, *On the Beauty of Women* (1541), trans. Konrad Eisenbichler and Jacqueline Murray (Philadelphia: University of Pennsylvania Press, 1992), p. 15.

[10] Karim-Cooper, *Cosmetics in Shakespearean and Renaissance Drama*, p. 11.

[11] Buoni, *Problemes of Beautie*, p. 27. [12] Girolamo Ruscelli's *The Secrets of Alexis of Piemont*, p. 121.

[13] Firenzuola, *On the Beauty of Women*, pp. 51–3.

would inherently destabilize, though ultimately help to reformulate, the ideal portrait of beauty. The arousing glisten of a 'fair' face is something that is also detectable in Renaissance portraiture – a medium which visualized and enabled a wider transmission of this beauty standard. Brian Steele notes that in sixteenth-century paintings of Venetian beauties, 'the erotic imagery parallels themes in Petrarchan lyrics; visual details constitute analogues to poetic metaphors; and both arts catalog identical standards of beauty'.[14] Portrait painting was conducted with similar, if not, at times, the same materials with which faces were painted: white lead, mercury, turpentine, pearl. Equally intriguing is the fact that Elizabethan poetic blazons consistently use metaphors that emphasize the importance of a 'lustre' and 'shine' to female beauty. Robert Greene's 'Samela', for instance, says:

As fair Aurora in her morning grey,
Deck'd with the ruddy glister of her love,
Is fair Samela;
Like lovely Thetis on a calmed day,
Whenas her brightnes Neptune's fancy move,
Shines fair Samela;
Her tresses gold, her eyes like glassy streams,
Her teeth are pearl, the breasts are ivory
Of fair Samela;[15]

Glass, pearl, ivory – these are all materials with a shiny or glistening surface; they are also common poetic tropes and two are actual ingredients either used to bejewel a body or found within a cosmetic compound. Greene invokes classical divinity as well as the physical heavens when he describes the beauty of Samela. The last line cited here, 'fair Samela', then, summarizes the poem's argument when we consider the word 'fair' in the light of Firenzuola's precise designation of its meaning: lustre. In Elizabethan and Jacobean poetry, the many apostrophes to beauty invoking Cynthia or Phoebe refer to the glittering or silvery moon, purposely drawing attention to images of brightness or lustre in order to praise an archetypal mistress. Ubiquitous are phrases such as 'heavenly grace', 'glistering glosse of bewtie's blaze', for example.[16]

14 Brian Steele, 'In the Flower of their Youth: "Portraits" of Venetian Beauties ca. 1500', *Sixteenth Century Journal* 28.23 (summer 1997), 481–502 (494).

15 Robert Greene, 'Doron's Description of Samela' from Menaphon (1589), in Revd Alexander Dyce (ed.), *The Dramatic Works of Robert Greene* (London, 1831), vol. 11, p. 22.

16 George Gascoigne, 'Gascoigne's Praise of his mistress', in William Carew Hazlitt (ed.), *The Complete Poems of George Gascoigne* (London, 1869), vol. 1, p. 54.

The moon represented chastity, but it was also an image that many satirists and poets used to mock cosmetic vanity, since the very source of the moon's shine or glow was thought to be borrowed light; Jonson's satirical portrait of courtly vanity, *Cynthia's Revels*, performed by the Children of Queen's Revels at the Blackfriars Playhouse in 1600, is centred upon this motif. In this play, Jonson portrays the Elizabethan court as a vain and over-effeminate cosmetic pageant; he has Crites observe: 'There stands a neophyte glazing of his face, / Pruning his clothes, perfuming his hair (3.4.35–6).[17] Here Jonson seems to participate not only in the discourse that satirizes the court, but also in the anti-cosmetic arguments of his day. Polemicists had argued that face paint, lip colours, wigs, perfumes and the wide variety of other accoutrements and ingredients used to beautify the body actually changed the body and interfered with the workmanship of God himself. Philip Stubbes's infamous excoriation of the luxurious practices of his day rebukes women for overindulging in cosmetic beauty: 'Doo they think thus to adulterate the Lord his workmanship, and to be without offence?' Stubbes deliberately undermines the autonomy of women when fashioning their own physical appearances: 'Thinkest thou that thou canst make thyself fairer then God, who made us all?'[18] Some anti-cosmetic writers even associated cosmetic adornment with witchcraft, Catholicism and the devil, referring to it as the 'the devil's craft'.[19] I have argued elsewhere that what is clear from the anti-cosmetic discourse is that materiality is often pitted against the spiritual. An anxiety about transformation and self-determined female mutability underpins most of the opposition to cosmetics. Playwrights like Jonson, for example, echoed these discursive attacks through their portrayals of early modern cosmetic culture and practices. But it is ironic in most instances when we consider the fact that cosmetic spectacle was crucial to theatrical performance in this period; indeed, it was an essential technology of theatre production as it enabled boys to play women, actors to play ghosts and witches and could be deployed in a variety of ways to achieve the illusions upon which early modern theatre traded.

Cosmetic practices reflect a dialectical response to the textual and visual media of the period that identified particular physical attributes as desirable. What we have to take into account are the material connections between language and cosmetic practice. As is well known, women were often

17 Ben Jonson, *The Fountaine of Selfe-Love, or Cynthia's Revels* (London, 1601), sig. F2r.

18 Philip Stubbes, *The Anatomie of Abuses*, ed. F. J. Furnivall (London, 1877), p. 64.

19 Roger Edgeworth, sermon, in *Sermons and Society: An Anthology*, ed. Paul A. Welsby (Harmondsworth: Penguin, 1970), p. 51.

described as having cheeks like lilies and roses, or complexions like ivory or silver, teeth like pearls, necks like ivory or alabaster and so on. Some recipes actually call for these materials in a range of compounds.[20] Not just natural ingredients, but precious minerals and gems that were gleaned for their cosmetic properties: silver foil, and even gold, and we know now that pearl was a popular cosmetic ingredient in the Jacobean period especially. A basic concoction of white lead and vinegar – known as ceruse – would have created a somewhat silky pigment and formed the basic facial foundation, upon which pearl or various other embellishing ingredients, including poppy or almond oil, could be applied. Problematically, as I have already suggested, using cosmetics was seen by many as immoral and even sinful. Puritans and satirists argued that face paints, lip colours, wigs, perfumes and other accessories that altered the body destroyed God's workmanship. Much of this opposition is discussed in my book-length study, but the crucial point for the purposes of this chapter is that the face was viewed as a map to the self; once painted, it could no longer be read, thus hypocrisy, vanity and corrupt sexuality (usually female) were all linked to the painted face – at once epitomized by the iconic notion of the painted harlot. But we know that women of all social ranks, especially nobility, used facial cosmetics, including, notoriously, Queen Elizabeth I. In *Cynthia's Revels*, Ben Jonson had already begun to strip away the layers of cosmetic covering from the court to reveal a society addicted to and obsessed with vanity and the display of wealth. The epistle to the court provides the initial warning that the rest of the play carries further:

> It is not pould'ring, perfuming, and euery day smelling of the taylor, that conuerteth to a beautiful obiect: but a mind, shining through any sute, which needs no false light either of riches, or honors to helpe it (13–17)

The Neoplatonic admonition for a shining virtue, here expressed as the intellect/mind, has not escaped Jonson, and it reflects the playwright's tendency to privilege the intellectual over the visual. The moral imperative of the play is evident in the bitter denunciations of effeminacy and the cosmetic taint of the court, as Crites puts it:

> . . . I have seene
> The strangest pageant, fashion'd like a court,
> (At least I dream't I saw it) so diffus'd,
> So painted, pyed and full of rainbow straines . . .
>
> (3.3)

[20] See Karim-Cooper, *Cosmetics in Shakespearean and Renaissance Drama*, pp. 22–5.

Here, we can see that cosmetic artifice is metaphorical, not just material, and it is applied in this context as a signifier of vanity. Jonson gets his cues from the wealth of anti-cosmetic writers of the time, including William Averill, Philip Stubbes and Barnabe Rich, among many others, who couched their anti-cosmetic rhetoric within bitter diatribes against the vanity of the age.[21] As I argued earlier, irrespective of the anti-cosmetic arguments expressed in Jonson's satirical drama, makeup was crucial to performance, and, at times at the Blackfriars, its effects were contingent upon the beautified faces of the elite spectators.

Beauty in the indoor playhouse

It would not be unreasonable to assume that a prolific reader like Ben Jonson would have read continental recipe manuals such as *The Secrets of Alexis of Piemont*, which went through several reprintings throughout the seventeenth century. Extremely popular in its day, both on the Continent and in England, Ruscelli's 'Secrets' brought together well over a thousand recipes and remedies, including the oddities 'Against the Stinking of the Breath', 'To know whether a Woman shall ever Conceive' and 'To make the Skin Stretch, and Return again into his place'. But among this eclectic collection are hundreds of recipes for beautifying the body. These include recipes for perfumes, face paints and sweet waters, exfoliants, soaps, hair dyes and tonics for hair removal and hair growth. There are roughly over fifty recipes for face paints or 'fucuses'. Jonson's city comedies consistently demonstrate an interest in the politics, economics and poetics of ingredients, which seems to be part of his wider preoccupation with, as Ian Donaldson suggests, 'projectors':

> In the years 1613–1616 projecting in England was at its zenith. Money was plentiful everywhere except in the royal treasury, interest rates were low, and foreign trade was flourishing; proposals for new and lucrative ventures, such as those ironically floated in The Devil is an Ass – for trading in raisings, bottle-ale, forks, dog-skins, cosmetics, toothpicks, etc. – were being regularly canvassed. The projectors promoting these (often dubiously viable) schemes were successfully amassing their private fortunes.[22]

[21] See William Averill, *A Dyall for Dainty Darlings, roct in the cradle of securitie* (London, 1584); Philip Stubbes, *The Anatomie of Abuses* (London, 1583); Barnabe Rich, *The Excellency of good women* (London, 1613).

[22] Ian Donaldson, *Ben Jonson: A Life* (Oxford University Press, 2011), p. 343.

In Ben Jonson's comedy *The Devil is an Ass* performed at the Blackfriars by the King's Men in 1616, Wittipol disguises himself as a Spanish lady, pretending to be a 'tutor' to Madam Fitzdotterel (the wife of a country aristocrat determined for his wife to learn the fashions and ways of the city women) in the arts cosmetic. Wittipol, by this point in the play, is well versed in the cosmetic technology of the day and specifies the use of 'oils of lentisco; zucche, mugia-make / The admirable varnish for the face, / Gives the right lustre' (4.4.35–6).[23] This brief example of Jonson's well-known fetish for jargon provides a mere taster of the extensive satirical cataloguing of ingredients that takes place in this play and that occurs elsewhere in his canon, such as in *The Alchemist* (1610). But Jonson was not the only one interested in cosmetic materiality and the spectacle it produced indoors. There are a few plays that were performed at Blackfriars that exploit this visually appealing theme in addition to Jonson's *Epicoene* (acquired by the King's Men in 1609) and *The Devil is an Ass*; Thomas Middleton's *The Lady's Tragedy* (1611); Shakespeare's *The Winter's Tale* (1611) and Philip Massinger's *The Duke of Milan* (1626) all linger upon cosmetic materiality in some form.

At this point we might ask ourselves what was it about the performance conditions in the Blackfriars that sparked an interest in cosmetic themes. Several chapters in this volume paint a portrait of the visual properties of the indoor theatres. Tiffany Stern and Martin White discuss the impact of candlelight upon the atmosphere of the playhouses and Sarah Dustagheer discusses the further implications candlelight has on the repertory's emphasis upon material culture. As others have already cited, in 'Of Masques and Triumphs', Francis Bacon notes: 'The *Colours*, that shew best by Candle-light, are; White, Carnation, and a Kinde of Sea-Water-Greene; And *Oes*, or *Spangs*, as they are of no great Cost, so they are of most Glory'.[24] During indoor performances, the visual tone was created by the coming together of light, colour and sequins or jewels. In the same essay, Bacon later observes that scenes should 'abound with light'. We know too that the use of torchbearers in performance at court was a staple of early Tudor interludes, thus it is not unlikely that they were used in the indoor stages as well. Taking into account Bacon's instructions, Stern also reconstructs the atmosphere at Blackfriars when

[23] Ben Jonson, *The Devil is an Ass*, ed. Peter Happé, Revels Plays (Manchester University Press, 1996).

[24] Francis Bacon, 'Of Masques and Triumphs', in *The Essayes or Counsels* (1625), p. 225; see Chapters 5 and 6 above.

she suggests, 'Spectators at indoor playhouses were adorned with jewels that sparkled in the artificial light. Sir John Harington writes an epigram in which a lady goes to the theatre with "Cloathes in seemly, & most sumptuous fashion: / Wearing a border of rich Pearle and stone"; Lenton, more tellingly, writes of the "spangled rare perfum'd attires" in which a gallant "glistred" in the "Torchy Fryers"'.[25] I would add to this description the notable glister from painted and bepearled faces in the audience and, indeed, on stage. These conditions of performance demonstrate why plays written for the indoor venue exploit themes that indulge the eye and attempt to cater to a female spectatorship.

As was shown earlier, Firenzuola's prescriptions for beauty emphasized the powerful connection between illumination and the face. Shakespeare's actors would have known that a glow from within was not enough to stage these connections or the 'face-to-face' encounters discussed in this collection by Penelope Woods; however, an external glow worked to great effect. Robert Graves thinks that, in the indoor playhouse, 'the audience sat in window light, while candles were placed as near the actors as possible to emphasize the splendour of their costumes' and, I would add, their faces.[26] I am interested in the ways in which artificial light in the Blackfriars would work hard to illustrate the many instances in the repertory where the stage directions call for the luminous display of female beauty. At this point, I want to consider the relationship of these unique performance conditions to the repertorial preoccupation with themes of female chastity and the beauty ideal. The material link between these two phenomena is pearl. Pearl in solid, liquid or powdered form, as a jewel adorning a woman's hair, ears or dress, as a metaphor, as a poison (e.g. in the cup of wine in *Hamlet*), as a transformative agent of beauty, would have been seen and heard of frequently in the Blackfriars. Pearl was also a cosmetic ingredient. A woman with a dusting of pearl on her face might want to sit very near candles, so that she appears, magically, to exude the Neoplatonic lustre of virtue. Seventeenth-century moralist Thomas Tuke, in his *Treatise Against Painting* (1616), tells us: 'all painting or colouring of the face is not of one kind, nor by one meane. The more artificiall and sumptuous is by tincture, the skinne being dried and stained with artificial colours. This the wealthier sort performe by the help of pearle.'[27] Tuke's account suggests

[25] See Chapter 6 above.

[26] Robert Graves, *Lighting the Shakespearean Stage 1567–1642* (Carbondale: Southern Illinois University Press, 1997), p. 176.

[27] Thomas Tuke, *A Treatise Against Paint[i]ng and Tincturing of Men and Women* (London, 1616), p. 30.

that pearl could be used to stain the face itself or give the face its lustre or 'sumptuousness', as he calls it. Thus some plays performed in the Blackfriars highlight, at times, not only the luxurious materiality of costume, jewels and candlelight but cosmetic ingredients as well. Moreover, the thematic preoccupation with female chastity and beauty is registered through this material referencing, visually and textually.

In Thomas Middleton's *The Lady's Tragedy*, performed at Blackfriars in the winter of 1611/12, the exhumed body of 'the Lady' is brought in state back to court; she is dressed as a saint and will shortly be painted by her disguised lover – Govianus– to satisfy the usurping Tyrant's necropheliac desires. The stage directions read:

> *They bring the body in a chair, dressed up in black velvet which sets out the paleness of the hands and face, and a fair chain of pearl cross her breast and the crucifix above it. The Tyrant stands silent awhile, letting the music play, beckoning the soldiers that bring her in to make obeisance to her, and he himself makes a low honour to the body and kisses the hand.*[28]

Here we have a chaste female body, depicted as a saint through a mixture of iconic clothing and jewels, and soon she will have her face painted. The painted face, normally associated in the period with corrupt female sexuality, coupled with her saintly status makes The Lady a paradoxical emblem of early modern perceptions of womanhood. She is at once saintly and sexually provocative, erotic flesh and cold marble. The actor playing her would probably be painted with a fucus of white lead and fake pearl. As a staged event at the Blackfriars, the entire scene would be illuminated with artificial light combined with the decreasing natural light through the windows towards the end of the performance as day descends into night. The dimmer but warm luminescent glow of the candlelight would, in this moment, draw a spectator's gaze to the glistening features of the Lady, creating a stunning stage picture of female beauty that is at once saintly and sexually provocative. It is tempting to consider that the spectators sitting on stage, the 'living decoration',[29] would also be glittering in their own rich apparel, creating a joint performative spectacle of actor and audience, and sitting elsewhere would be the female spectators who presented themselves as the most fashionable while watching boys dressing and performing a parody of them.

[28] Thomas Middleton, *The Lady's Tragedy*, ed. Julia Briggs, in Gary Taylor and John Lavagnino (eds.), *Thomas Middleton: The Collected Works* (Oxford University Press, 2007).

[29] Tiffany Stern, 'Taking Part: Actors and Audience on the Blackfriars Stage', in Paul Menzer (ed.), *Inside Shakespeare: Essays on the Blackfriars Stage* (Selinsgrove, PA: Susquehanna University Press), pp. 35–53.

Such parody becomes relentless in Jonson's comedies; his mockery of strong female bonds is evident in plays like *Epicoene* and *Volpone*, but more so in *The Devil is an Ass*. Here we meet the Ladies Tailbush and Eitherside; in Act 4 scene 3 they are comparing their complexions, as they discuss the most fashionable ingredient in London:

TAILBUSH What vile fucus is this
Thou hast got on?
EITHERSIDE 'Tis pearl.
TAILBUSH Pearl? Oyster-shells:
As I breathe, Eitherside, I know't (61–5)[30]

This intended humorous exchange reveals quite a lot about the beauty industry and women's engagement with it, but it also reveals something about a theatre company's cosmetic practices. What we learn is that pearl was a desirable and valuable cosmetic ingredient but that faux pearl, in the form of oyster shell, in this case, though a substitute can have an unwelcome effect on the complexion, as Tailbush mockingly suggests. It shows too how the quest for beauty is a point of divisive contention between women. But what would have been the desired effect of pearl on one's face? Glistening is an effect that is significantly more spectacular under artificial lighting conditions, conditions very different from those in outdoor theatres, as Martin White has pointed out. It seems unlikely that real pearl was used as a cosmetic tincture by acting companies, even the fairly well-to-do King's Men. But I do think they tried to replicate it, as the clues in the above excerpt from *The Devil is an Ass* show. Linguistic signifiers in other plays suggest that as a poetic trope, too, pearl had a sustained presence in the repertory: in *Othello*, the *Merchant of Venice* and others, pearls are referenced as decorative jewels with exotic significance; sometimes they are apt images used to describe the tears of a woman; sometimes a woman herself is described as a pearl – reflecting her virtue. In *A Midsummer Night's Dream* it is the moon that 'decks the bladed grass with liquid pearl' (1.1.211). In addition to its beauty in the verse, it would have been a highly visible decorative jewel adorning the clothing, hair and makeup of the female spectators in the Blackfriars. What Thomas Tuke highlighted in his reference to the 'wealthier sort' using pearl was the fact that the materials of makeup, like clothing, had social and economic significance.

30 Ben Jonson, *The Devil is an Ass*, ed. Peter Happé, The Revels Plays (Manchester University Press, 1994, 1996).

What meaning different cosmetic ingredients held raises important questions when considering the politics of performance at the socially encoded Blackfriars. What we know about these spectators is that they were significantly wealthier than a majority of amphitheatre audiences. We assume that there was an increased number of female spectators in the Blackfriars, and, if so, that the dominant presence of a fashionable female audience would indeed have been a factor in the stylization or the aesthetic of performance in this playhouse. The private indoor playhouses, such as Blackfriars, provided an exclusive environment for the display of the most current fashions in clothing, accessories, hairstyles, head-dresses and makeup. The smallest details were of the utmost importance and could create exaggerated effects when in close proximity to others and under the glimmering glow of candles. By the same token, people cared about ingredients and materials that were worn on or applied to the body and each ingredient held meaning, physical and metaphorical; just like any other object or prop you find on stage. So how do we read meaning in something like pearl? The pearl, for early moderns, actually had a rich network of symbolic associations. In addition to being a sign of wealth, it had long been considered a symbol of virtue, truth and chastity. Culturally, there was a long-standing tradition of a pearl as a healing agent linked with the imperfections and ailments of the human body. Midwifery texts and medical manuals from the seventeenth century refer to pearl as an ingredient in various recipes: it is used in a recipe to cure a barren womb – in which it can be dissolved or beaten to a powder and made into a confection. In another it aids in a cure for illnesses such as the French pox or syphilis (in this recipe, one must extract the essence of pearl and mix it with the tincture of coral to make a perfect cordial). As jewels, pearls were popular hair adornments throughout Europe during the Renaissance; in Shakespeare and Fletcher's *Henry VIII* Act 4, scene 1 Queen Anne enters with her hair adorned with pearl, evidence that boy actors simulated current fashions on stage. In some European cities, sumptuary laws limited the number of pearls that could be worn at once in a woman's hair, suggesting that the practice had become widespread and was perhaps becoming a tad overindulgent. Pearls could be worn in singles or in clusters combined with various other jewels or goldwork to create elaborate pieces. As contemporary portraits show, they were sometimes sewn on to clothing and worn as earrings, necklaces, particularly carcanets (chokers) and on pendants. However, the booming fashion for pearls gave rise to the false or faux pearl trade.

Several publications from the fifteenth and sixteenth centuries provided instructions to make false pearls, using small shells and fish scales to effect the sought-after glistening jewel. Fake pearls could also be sewn on to clothing and worn in clusters as jewels as well. Imitation pearls might only have cost a penny a piece, the same amount one paid to be a groundling at the Globe. Fake pearls could also be made using powdered glass, egg whites and snail slime; this type of faux pearl, like the authentic one, could be crushed or liquefied, thus providing a cosmetic varnish for flesh as well as for canvas. Thus the judgement of painted faces as false has added significance when the materials in the paint are as inauthentic as the face itself appears to be. If pearl represents virtue or purity and in some circles was thought to have healing powers, false pearl, if used widely (as a cosmetic as well as a jewel), complicates the Neoplatonic philosophy of beauty – even while it undermines the elitist fantasy of a privileged access to it. Therefore, I would argue, pearl had dichotomous meanings on stage: sometimes virtue or chastity – but when it was used on the face, its meaning may have blended with the widely accepted reading of painted ladies – corrupt female sexuality. The use of glistering makeup on statues such as the Lady and Hermione in *The Winter's Tale* suggests that theatrical appropriations of cosmetic materiality produced a redefinition of female virtue and how it could be represented through paint.

***The Winter's Tale*: a Blackfriars spectacle**

In his essay 'Ekphrasis in *The Rape of Lucrece* and *The Winter's Tale*', Richard Meek identifies Shakespeare's 'ekphrastic' strategy in these two works, seeing it as an opportunity for the playwright to explore the 'relationship between the visual and verbal modes of representation'.[31] Meek examines the relationship between the literary and its depiction of the visual (in the form of events that have occurred) in *The Winter's Tale* and argues that more so in this play than anywhere else in Shakespeare, 'we are asked to believe in happenings that are only described to us'.[32] What this creates is a relationship to the play that is unstable, because the reliability of sight and second-hand sight is called into question. Meek is right to note that the statue scene materializes the deceptive nature of the sense of sight; the complex layers of meaning – the painted statue, which is not a statue, nor is it actually Hermione, as it is an actor who happens to be a boy – is evidence of the fact that, as Meek puts it, 'visual proof is something that is open to interpretation: both hearing and seeing have their limitations'.[33]

[31] Richard Meek, 'Ekphrasis in *The Rape of Lucrece* and *The Winter's Tale*', *Studies in English Literature, 1500–1900* 46.2 (spring 2006), 390.

[32] Ibid., 395. [33] Ibid., 399.

But what we must also consider are the performance conditions that shaped the dramaturgical strategy and the complex patterns of poetic description that provoke the tension between the visual and narrative. While this play, as well as most of Shakespeare's repertory after 1609, would have been performed at the Globe as well as Blackfriars, I want to focus on the Blackfriars performance, as the statue scene seems to be a rich and complex advertisement for the King's Men's indoor playhouse, its spectacular effects and its dialogic engagement with women. When reading Simon Forman's description of the play's performance in the spring of 1611, it strikes as odd that there is no mention of the statue scene, which is, no doubt, the moment of the play that defines its genre, and it seems to be the scene that has had the strongest emotional impact upon readers and spectators ever since.[34] But why does Forman not mention it? Is it because he was at the outdoor Globe and that it may not, in fact, have packed the visual punch it was designed to pack in the Blackfriars, lit with candles and with a close-sitting audience? It is not a question that can be answered here, but it makes me pause upon the visual emphasis in that scene and ponder Shakespeare's performance rather than literary strategy as a way of demonstrating the crucial impact that the move indoors had on the visual and material constituents of theatre.

It is undeniable that the sense of sight in this play is vulnerable. People see things that are not there; illusions are easily achieved and seeing seems to disentangle itself from knowing. Stuart Clark suggests that the metaphors associated with 'the process of visual cognition', in Renaissance culture, 'notably those of mirroring, painting, and the making of impressions in wax, evoke an expectation of representational accuracy'.[35] According to visual theorists, 'the mind had direct access to accurate pictures of the world; the world was what it appeared visually to be'.[36] This idea, broadly speaking, imparts some power to visual theatre, suggesting that its constituents are able to achieve illusion with very little question. But in Shakespeare's plays there is a continuous interrogation of the idea that what you see is what you get, and *The Winter's Tale*, especially, dramatizes what happens when visual mistakes are made. George Hakewill wrote in 1606 that sight is 'an immediate instrument, not only

[34] See *The Case Books of Simon Forman: Sex and Society in Shakespeare's Age* by A. L. Rowse (London: Pan Books, 1976).

[35] Stuart Clark, *Vanities of the Eye: Vision in Early Modern European Culture* (Oxford University Press, 2007), p. 2.

[36] Ibid.

of wantonness, but of gluttony, covetousnesse, theft, idolatry, jealousie, pride, contempt, curiosity, envy, witchcraft, & in a maner of the whole rebelion & apostasie, as well of the body, as the minde'.[37] Leontes misinterprets a gesture Hermione makes towards Polixenes, which provokes the near tragic consequences of her banishment and supposed death. In 1.2 he questions Camillio, who insists Leontes is mistaken:

> Ha' not you seen, Camillo?
> (But that's past doubt: you have, or your eye-glass
> Is thicker than a cuckold's horn) or heard?
> (For to a vision so apparent rumour
> Cannot be mute) or thought? (267–71)

Leontes trusts the unstable theory that his own mind has 'direct access' to what is seen and thus questions the sensory ability of Camillo instead. Shakespeare's performance strategy seems to be to undermine sight, paradoxically, by placing theatrical emphasis on spectacle. In the final moments of the play the sense of sight is invoked again. Throughout Act 5 words like 'marvel', 'look', 'visible', 'see', 'looks', 'mark', 'gaze', 'eye', 'looker', 'behold', 'perceive' create a vocabulary of vision to guide the spectators towards the final and perhaps Shakespeare's most illusionistic moment – the painted appearance and physical movement of Hermione's statue:

> 'Tis time; descend; be stone no more; approach;
> Strike all that look upon with marvel. Come!
> I'll fill your grave up: stir, nay, come away:
> Bequeath to death your numbness; for from him
> Dear life redeems you. You perceive she stirs:
> [*Hermione comes down.*]
> Start not; her actions shall be holy as
> You hear my spell is lawful (5.3.99–105)

This moment performed at Blackfriars would involve those visible elements of theatre practice in that space that I (and others in this volume) have been discussing: cosmetic ingredients, including either pearl or faux pearl, costume designed to dazzle under candles, actor–audience proximity and the numerous candles themselves. Significantly, the candles perform a unique function in this moment. As Meek reminds us, *ekphrasis* is a literary motif, a verbal form of representing the visual, but he also points out that ekphrastic description produces spectacle, enhancing and creating a

[37] George Hakewill, *The Vanitie of the Eie, First Beganne for the Comfort of a Gentlewoman Beareaved of Her Sight, and Since vpon Occasion Enlarged and Published for the Common Good* (1606) (Oxford, 1615), p. 10.

'powerful illusion of presence'.[38] The candles in this scene from *The Winter's Tale* perform the same function, a kind of lighting *ekphrasis*. It is a visual process that highlights, paradoxically, the deceptive nature of spectacle even while it works to elevate it. What we see under the glow of candles is a painted lady coming to life; the very thing the Tyrant wants to see happen in *The Lady's Tragedy*. In the Middleton play, the consequence of kissing the saintly corpse, however, is death, as Penelope Woods also points out. In Shakespeare's play, Paulina's admonition to Leontes to refrain from kissing the 'oily' statue enables the illusion to come to fruition and the result is reconciliation. The two plays discussed here demonstrate their absolute dependence upon the ingredients of cosmetics, the special effects of seventeenth-century theatre lighting and the intimate conditions at Blackfriars. Female beauty and virtue are thus articulated and redefined in relation to each other through these material representations on the indoor stage.

38 Meek, 'Ekphrasis in *The Rape of Lucrece*', 400.

PART III

The new fashions for indoors

CHAPTER 11

The new fashion for indoor plays

Andrew Gurr

Necessary adjustments for transferring plays from big stage to small

The difference between staging a play at the Globe and doing the same one at the Blackfriars may not have been a problem for the King's Men. They were quite used to switching their venues (as John Astington also points out in Chapter 1 above). They routinely took their plays away from their home base for performance at court, or to one of the Inns of Court such as Middle Temple, where they played *Twelfth Night* at Candlemas in 1602, or around the country. In most seasons they would take a few plays on tour, playing in local taverns, guildhalls or in the great halls of country castles and estates. Each venue would have been different. They would have to adjust to different acoustics, different auditoria, varying backstage provision, including the number of entry doors onto the temporary stages, variable lighting (candle-light for evening shows), and most frequently a markedly smaller space to act on. The major problems in transferring plays between the Globe and the Blackfriars arose far less for the players than they did for their audiences.

We are familiar with the Globe's repertory, and the way all the earlier plays in it were written to allow for the broad spread and depth of the Globe stage. Duels, physical tussles like Orlando's wrestling at the beginning of *As You Like It*, large-scale battles on stage such as Shrewsbury in *1 Henry IV*, scenes where one character conceals himself from the others on stage while he tells the audience how he thinks about what he hears them say, as in *Much Ado*, would all have to be scaled down at the smaller indoor venues. Each season from 1609 onwards plays written for the Globe were transferred to the Blackfriars, yet the texts of these older plays written before the company gained use of the Blackfriars show little sign of much being done to the texts to facilitate the transfer. Sometimes the Folio versions of the earlier plays, such as *Henry V*, *The Tempest* and *A Midsummer Night's Dream*, have act breaks marked (though the Folio *Henry V* gets them wrong). On the whole such built-in pauses were a late development. The breaks were necessary to halt the action at the Blackfriars so that the candles could be trimmed or replaced. Other small changes might be made. *Dream* has a stage direction telling us that the four young lovers '*sleepe all the Act*', meaning that they are to remain on stage pretending to be asleep for the duration, two minutes at most, of the interact pause between Acts 3 and 4. This direction is not in the quarto text of 1600.

Theatre audiences are deeply influenced by the auditorium they occupy. Outdoor settings, whether for a play or a sporting event, help you to feel you are part of a crowd. You are all gathered for the same purpose; you respond to what you came to see, influenced by everyone else's reactions. In a more confined and roofed enclosure, on the other hand, you are free from the weather outside; you can enjoy your own space and feel yourself an individual, separate from the others around you. At the Globe the crowd standing in the yard generated emotion that everyone else shared. At the Blackfriars, with your own seat, you were conscious of your separate identity, a free and perhaps sceptical observer of the events you had paid for. Outdoor venues feel public, whereas being indoors feels more intimate, more like a private house or a private gathering of kin. For decades the indoor playhouses were called 'private' in contrast to the outdoor venues, always called 'public'. That was a social distinction, marked by the snobbery of the view that the indoor venues were more exclusive than the Globe or the Fortune. Long after the King's Men took the Blackfriars back from the boy company, publishers of plays and others continued to insist that the indoor playhouses were private and exclusive, in contrast to the 'public' venues. Both types of venue reflected that social distinction. After 1609, whenever playgoing gentry attended a play by the Shakespeare company in the summer months at the Globe, their choice meant that they knew they had to share their pleasures in the company of more populist, noisy and lower-class people.

At an indoor venue the all-seated audience is likely to be more docile in its responses to the play than an audience half of which is on its feet surrounding the stage. That is still evident today when you compare audiences at the National Theatre with those at the new Globe. If to this difference you add the fact that for Jacobean and Caroline audiences, access to the much smaller indoor venues cost their customers at least six times more than 'understanding' at the Globe, the division intensifies. The groundlings who got to know their Shakespeare at the Globe had a different mindset from those who came to enjoy his plays at the indoor Blackfriars. That difference is significant.

The differences were many, not all of them obvious. The more material ones, such as the tighter acoustics and the effect of the surrounding hard-walled surfaces behind the gentry at the Blackfriars, plus the dozen or more visible gallants, sword at side, who sat there on stools around the sides of the stage itself surrounding the players, flaunting their grandeur with their jewels and bright attire, these features, the candles augmenting the daylight and making the audience's costumes glitter, all made it pretentiously affluent-looking. Off-stage music played overtures to the play for a long time while the auditorium was filling up. On 18 September 1602 a courtier who accompanied the Duke of Stettin-Pomerania to see a play at the Blackfriars reported that they were entertained with a concert lasting nearly an hour before the play started. *The Tempest*, the first of Shakespeare's plays clearly composed for the Blackfriars, makes much more use of off-stage music and on-stage songs than any of his other plays. This innovation to the Shakespeare range came from knowing that the King's Men had acquired the Blackfriars consort of musicians along with the theatre. The sudden fury on stage of the storm that opens the play would have made a drastic and startling contrast after the harmonious music that had preceded it. Later in the play music comes back into its role, serving to soothe the wildness of the characters hostile to Prospero's peace.

Features of the indoor stages that affected performances

Two major differences between the Globe and the Blackfriars must have had an impact on staging. One, most obviously, was the markedly smaller size of the indoor stage, with its cluster of gallants sitting round the edges making the acting space still smaller. The other was the absence at Blackfriars and the other indoor venues of any stage posts. We know little directly about how the posts were used at the Globe except for pretended acts of concealment, but their position on the stage does help to give such a large space an architectural shape that affects such movements as entrances and exits to and from the three stage doors.

Other devices that we know about at the Globe must have created difficulties for staging at the Blackfriars. In a scene at court, when the king is making a speech, as Claudius does in the second scene of *Hamlet*, he would sit centre stage on his throne, known as the chair of state (in Denmark Marcellus calls it rotten). This substantial seat was placed on a small dais, with the royal insignia visible on a cloth behind it and a small canopy over it. Courtiers would group themselves around the throne, all facing it, their hats off in deference to royal authority. Blue-coated attendants would stand by the exit doors of the stage, ready to dash off if ordered to deliver a message, or to intervene and confront any new arrivals on stage.

Such scenes had to be crowded, since kings are very rarely left alone. At the indoor venue for such scenes, the players would have been most distinguishable from the gallants on their stools around them because they had to stand, hat in hand, facing the throne, while the audience on the same stage remained sitting on their stools behind them. Anyone speaking to the throne's occupant, Hamlet aside (literally), would have had to stand at what we would call the centre front of the stage, facing inward to the throne while addressing the ruler.

This fake representation of the reality of life at the royal court would have had clear resonances for any gallants at the Blackfriars who had actually attended at court and had seen the behaviour of their peers in that far more august setting. To be seated on such occasions would have intensified their awareness of the players' pretension to imitate the familiar reality.

The other and more frequent feature of stage choreography at the two types of playhouse was controlled and limited by the two main entry doors on stage and the distance between them and the main speaking area at front centre stage. Making an entrance has always been a feature of actors' self-presentation. In the Japanese kabuki theatre, entrances are made along a lengthy passageway extending across one side of the whole spread of the auditorium. In such a theatre the entering actor takes at least a minute to make his way from his first appearance until he has reached the stage where he speaks. That gives the audience ample time to survey and savour him, his costume, his mannerisms, and from those his obvious role in the play. At the Globe, the time taken between appearance at a stage door and walking up to join a group already on stage was much shorter, but it does seem to have lasted for at least two lines of dialogue. This time was often built into the earlier plays written for enactment at the Rose or the Globe. Often the speakers at centre stage would comment on the new arrival.

Like the kabuki characters, entrances provided a splendid opportunity for the newcomer to establish his or her distinctive features. Malvolio, when he first appears in his garters and yellow stockings, shows himself simultaneously to be adopting a wholly different pose from his former severe steward's role, and to have been gullible enough to fall for Maria's ingenious plot. Moreover, since when he makes his entrance Olivia has been speaking of her love, the moment of his arrival is wonderfully comic because it is both opportune, literally colourful, and an occasion for him to misunderstand what he has just heard her saying.

Entrances were great opportunities for comic body language. In the second scene of *Measure for Measure*, when the '*Bawd*' enters and waddles up to join the speakers at centre stage, Lucio proclaims her entry, first calling 'Behold, behold, where Madam *Mitigation* comes.' He and the gentry enjoy ten sarcastic exchanges about her before Lucio first addresses her directly. He then tells her, 'thy bones are hollow; Impiety has made her feast of thee'. His companion amplifies this: 'How now, which of your hips has the most profound Ciatica?' She was evidently meant to use the ten lines that accompany her entry by hobbling towards them arthritically, to exhibit her distinctive character. Sciatica was commonly thought to be a consequence of venereal disease. Such a lengthy ploy with body language could have featured on the indoor stage, too, though with some difficulty, and less distance for her to walk. At the Globe there was ample space, including perhaps a circuit round a stage post, before she meets the folk she then addresses. At the Blackfriars the boy playing Mistress Overdone (her name given in the Folio list of characters at the play's end) would have been required to somehow make a complete tour in front of the gallants on their stools before ending up with the gentlemen who stood at centre stage.[1]

Along with its smaller space between entrance and front stage, the absence of the two major posts on the stage at the Blackfriars removed one of the Globe stage's most valuable features. The two eavesdropping scenes in *Much Ado*, where first Benedict conceals himself to overhear the teasing story that Beatrice is madly in love with him, and then Beatrice does the same to hear that Benedict loves her, would have been done far more easily at the Globe than at the Blackfriars because of the Globe's pair of large posts. The two eavesdroppers could pretend to conceal themselves behind them while still being in full view of almost all the audience.

On the larger stage of the Globe, too, the posts provided a useful marker for stage movements. In many ways they served to identify how its parts functioned for differing roles. The so-called *platea*, or marginal area around the flanks, where clowns and other solo people could speak directly to the audience, was separated from the central authority localities by the stage posts. Action in stage centre or front, where the royal throne or chair of state would be located, and where sometimes a canopied bed was put out, so that Juliet could fall on it after taking her poison, was the *locus*, or authority place, the site for major actions. Subversive and more intimate activities took place round the flanks of the stage closest to the yard. The stage posts clarified these opposed sites.

[1] An admirable assessment of the time taken at the Globe for entrances and exits is by Mariko Ichikawa, *Shakespearean Entrances* (Basingstoke: Palgrave Macmillan, 2002), chapter 2.

The consequences of music indoors

One of the major influences of the move indoors had little to do with the King's Men, though it had vast and permanent effects on London's theatre generally. It affected the staging of plays, though not in any of the familiar ways discussed in this book. What really determined this change was first the Blackfriars music, and eventually its effect on some audiences (and certain writers of court staging) through the extensive use of song and dance. In the later years, the royal control of theatre had rather more impact than just to guarantee its closure by Parliament in 1642.

By the 1630s William Davenant was trying to turn plays into musicals. During the long plague closure of 1636–8 he even planned a wildly ambitious scheme to build a new theatre in St Bride's parish in Fleet Street, on the western flank of the city, not far from the indoor Salisbury Court theatre and the Blackfriars. His new theatre was to be indoors, with scenery, a music room and a huge stage fitted out for dancing. On 26 March 1639 he petitioned for leave to erect a 'Theatre or Playhouse with necessary tireing and retiring Rooms and other places convenient', the aim being 'to exercise Action, musical Presentments, Scenes, Dancing and the like'.[2] His licence, printed by Thomas Rymer in *Foedera*, specifies that the land to be used for it was to be 'forty yards square at the most' – a huge space compared with the thirty or fewer yards spread of the outdoor playhouses, or the twenty-two yards in length and thirteen in width of the Blackfriars.

This project, although backed by one of the king's favourites, Endymion Porter, failed thanks to some peculiarly covert interference. And not long after this thwarted venture, Davenant became embroiled in the first of the civil wars. After a decade of gun-running for the Royalists during the Interregnum and a brief period with the exiled king theatregoing in Paris, he was caught by the Cromwell government en route to Virginia, trying to convert the colonists there. However, after a period in the Tower he was allowed to make a new beginning with his new kind of play. They immediately became notable for their colourful scenic staging and their music and dance.

At first Davenant called his new works 'opera', a word borrowed from Italian, a term he used because the old idea of a 'play' (as the opposite to work) was still viewed with disfavour. These innovations embodied all his former ambition to feature music, dance and scenery on the stage, in imitation of the extravagant staging done for the court before the war.

[2] See G. E. Bentley, *The Jacobean and Caroline Stage* (7 vols.; Oxford: Clarendon Press, Oxford, 1940–68), vol. IV, pp. 304–9.

The most famous of his novelties was *The Siege of Rhodes*, staged indoors, first at Rutland House and then at the old Cockpit. John Evelyn the diarist reported that in 1659 'I went to visit my brother in London; and, next day, to see a new opera, after the Italian way, in recitative music and scenes.' Evelyn, reacting coldly to its colourful novelty in a time of great political stress, found it 'much inferior to the Italian composure and magnificence; but it was prodigious that in a time of such public consternation such a vanity should be kept up, or permitted'.[3]

Once the monarchy was restored in 1660, Davenant became manager of one of the two new theatre companies, along with Thomas Killigrew. The two men introduced scenic staging, female actors, and as much as they could of the panoply from Italian and French theatre that the returned King Charles had relished during his long exile in Paris. Davenant took care to introduce to the new stages scenic and other features of court masques that he had helped to create in the 1630s. For *The Siege of Rhodes* he used spectacles taken from his own masque, *Salmacida Spolia* of 1640, in which the king and queen had acted, and which featured designs invented by Inigo Jones.

Through the next two decades Davenant's musical and operatic versions of Shakespeare and other earlier writers for the one company easily came to prevail in fashion over Killigrew's more old-fashioned productions for the other. He converted quite a few plays into operas. *Macbeth*, Fletcher's *The Beggar's Bush* and *The Tempest* became full-scale operas in the 1670s, mostly in versions that Davenant altered drastically. Shadwell in 1674 made *The Tempest* into an opera, or more accurately a musical. Orchestral help for such productions was soon to hand. The king very quickly revived the royal music, setting up a group known as the King's Musick in 1660. Chiefly it was a string orchestra, imitating Louis XIV's famous group of twenty-four royal violins. By early 1664 the two London theatres shared them, one set of twelve musicians playing *en ensemble* at each. That was more than double the number of musicians the King's Men had maintained at the Blackfriars, which was a mixed or broken consort of five or so woodwinds and strings.

Besides this group of musicians, Davenant's company also appointed a dancing master in November 1664. It is difficult to avoid the view that Davenant, a lively relic of the indoor theatres from the 1630s, was chiefly responsible for, or guilty of, the bulk of the changes in staging that came with the Restoration of 1660. We should not underrate how much his

[3] Quoted by Mary Edmond, *Rare Sir William Davenant* (Manchester University Press, 1987), p. 134.

influence must have thrust in the same direction at the Blackfriars through the 1630s.

Tragicomedy and novelty at the indoor theatres

The mixed genre of tragicomedy, with its dangers but not deaths, invented at the beginning of the century, developed immensely in the indoor playhouses. One of its versions, usually known to Shakespeare critics as romance, or more simply the 'late plays', has been rather too abruptly or absolutely differentiated from the earlier comedies among the sequence of what we know Shakespeare wrote. *Twelfth Night* contains some major perils, but is always called a comedy. The two comedies that followed it, *Measure for Measure* and *All's Well That Ends Well*, are usually thought of as 'problem plays', though still set in the comedy genre that the Folio editors assigned them to. The turning-point for when Shakespeare is seen to have started writing romances is *Pericles*, written and staged in 1607, in collaboration with a rather murky figure, George Wilkins, who soon disappeared from any involvement in the King's Men's activities. This play remained among the most popular in the company's repertory for the next three decades. That it precipitated Shakespeare's later 'romances' is not in question. What is still at issue is which came first, and which affected which, the romance genre or access to the Blackfriars?

Other chapters in this collection have looked at the old theory that the King's Men's acquisition of the Blackfriars, thirteen years later than originally planned, affected the kind of play Shakespeare was writing. I am old enough to have heard Gerald Eades Bentley lecture about his theory that company pressure impelled Shakespeare to write all of his 'romance' plays from 1608 onwards for the new Blackfriars audience, not the Globe.[4] As a very junior lecturer, I recall challenging him about it, citing as evidence the fact that *Pericles* was written well over a year before possession of the Blackfriars began to loom on the company's horizon. Bentley's answer was to push the question aside by saying that nobody knows enough about *Pericles* to use it as hard evidence for anything.

Understandably, that left me and many others less than satisfied, though the debate goes on. A recent book by Jeffrey Knapp, for instance, asserts that Shakespeare was always supremely aware of his own identity as author and playwright, and that this self-knowledge was always inherent in his plays. On *Pericles*, written in collaboration with the disreputable Wilkins, he

[4] G. E. Bentley, 'Shakespeare and the Blackfriars Theatre', *Shakespeare Survey* 1 (1948), 38–50.

ventures a wholly novel theory.[5] 'I want to argue', he writes, 'that, by opting to cowrite *Pericles* with Wilkins, Shakespeare purposely sought to diminish his honor and his sovereignty as a playwright – in particular, to end a uniquely triumphant run of tragedies that he had come to view as a self-limiting success.' In other words, *Pericles* was a calculated piece of fanciful poppycock intended to release him from the aura he had acquired with the great tragedies. That is indeed an original speculation, though it does ignore the subsequent arrival of both *Antony and Cleopatra* and *Coriolanus*. It gives a neat twist to the old idea that Shakespeare went through a period of depression, and that he wrote the tragedies as an expression of that mood. The fact that *Pericles* proved to be his most popular play after *Hamlet* merely proves, according to Knapp, what a clever fellow he still was in 1607.

While this might prompt some fanciful new thoughts about what was going through Shakespeare's mind in 1607 and after, it leaves us still to wonder what influenced theatrical form at this time, and the accompanying development of the 'romance' genre. Shakespeare's radical shift in fashion with *Pericles* (in some degree preceded by *Measure for Measure* and *All's Well*, both of which, although firmly based in real settings, possess features not unrelated to romance) invites further consideration now, when we are looking at the effects of the company's move indoors. The move is still thought in some quarters to have impacted on the late plays, even though the romance trend can be traced in earlier texts. Shakespeare's innovations in league with Wilkins and later collaboration with Fletcher have led to claims that they reflect a radical shift in Shakespeare's own work. Material knowledge about the move indoors, not least Bentley's theory, has deeply influenced thinking about his shift to writing in collaboration. So we need to consider what, besides our expectation that audiences expected a different mode of writing for the Blackfriars, might have prompted this. On one side of the timing, both *All's Well* and perhaps *Measure for Measure* seem to anticipate features of *Pericles* and its successors. On the other, we should ask just how far might the company's acquisition of the indoor venue in 1608 have influenced the subsequent writing of *Cymbeline*, *The Winter's Tale*, *The Tempest* and *Two Noble Kinsmen*. Did the addition of Beaumont and Fletcher to the company influence Shakespeare, or did the change work the other way round? Calculating how far 1609's innovations relate to the Blackfriars could either heighten the apparent impact of the indoor theatre or shrink its influence and make it less distinctive.

[5] Jeffrey Knapp, *Shakespeare Only* (University of Chicago Press, 2009).

We know that when the King's Men first got use of their indoor venue they brought most of the plays from their existing repertory there. They may have commissioned new plays designed to suit the more affluent new audiences at the Blackfriars, but their chief author was still Shakespeare, and the evidence about his changing pattern of composition is, to say the least, elusive. We can be sure that *The Tempest* was designed specifically for the Blackfriars, if only because it both makes far more use of off-stage music, a new facility that the Blackfriars musical consort brought to the company, and because it has act breaks built into it. They were necessary at the candlelit Blackfriars to give time for candle trimming, unlike the Globe and the other outdoor venues, where the action could be continuous. In *The Tempest* the actors who leave to finish Act 4, Prospero and Ariel, re-enter to begin Act 5. The Globe did not use such breaks until well after the Blackfriars take-over. But we cannot be certain even that *The Tempest*'s companion piece, *The Winter's Tale*, and its other 'late' sibling, *Cymbeline*, were written before or after *The Tempest*. All three might be called romances or tragicomedies, like the undoubtedly earlier *Pericles*, but the sequence of their composition cannot be ascertained with certainty.

One thing we can be fairly sure of is that *The Tempest* was written around the same time as Jonson's *The Alchemist*, both of them specifically for the Blackfriars. Jonson's play is actually set inside a house in the Blackfriars precinct, and its owner, Lovewit, is the figure who gets away with all the profit from the games of trickery going on there. I have suggested before that his success in the play features Jonson's not entirely private joke against Shakespeare, who, having become one of the company owners of the playhouse, was taking its profits from the actors who gained them for him.[6] In that light, it is also easy to see Shakespeare's immaculate observation of the unities in *The Tempest* as his own joke against Jonson's concern to maintain them, as he does in *The Alchemist*, and as Shakespeare so outrageously omitted doing in *The Winter's Tale*. If the company had recently staged *The Winter's Tale*, its sixteen years and two remote countries ridiculing the unities, the tight conformity to the unities in both the new plays augmented the games the two writers were playing with each other.

Erica Sheen views the contrasts between Jonson's and Shakespeare's pair of Blackfriars plays as expressing rival ideas about their different concepts of what theatre should be. That is bound to be true. Jonson, she maintains, was showing his preference for a few intelligent readers over the ignorant

[6] See Andrew Gurr, 'Who is Lovewit? What is he?', in Richard Allen Cave, Elizabeth Schafer and Brian Woolland (eds.), *Ben Jonson and Theatre* (London and New York: Routledge, 1999), pp. 5–19.

masses who saw the plays in the theatre. Her case, endorsing Zachary Lesser's well-justified view,[7] is based on the Latin epigram Jonson set on the title page of *The Alchemist*, entered in the Stationers' Register in 1610 and printed in 1612. It declares '*Neque, me ut miretur turba, laboro: / Contentus pucis lectoribus*': 'I do not toil for the masses, but am happy just to have good readers.' The printed play's address 'To the Reader' complains of plays where '*the Concupiscence of Daunces, and Antickes . . . so raigneth, as to runne away from Nature, is the onely point of art that tickles the* Spectators.' Sheen reckons that in reply Shakespeare brought up the value of royal authority. In her *Shakespeare and the Institution of Theatre*, she claims that

> Shakespeare's apparent aim, and achievement, in *The Tempest* was not simply to answer *The Alchemist*: it was to turn the mirror of Shakespearean theatre on the social and political framework by which the play's contempt for popular theatre legitimated itself. If, within 45 lines, Jonson's spectators knew that what they were looking at and thinking about were the Blackfriars and the King's Men, by the end of 1.2 Shakespeare's spectators could have been in no doubt that the object of their gaze was the very image of Jonsonian monarchy. *The Alchemist* begins with a parodic account of theatrical labour undertaken in absence of the owner of the house. The Tempest responds with a spectacular contrast between sovereignty and collective labour which proceeds to a comprehensive vindication of that labour.[8]

I am not sure that the two openings do quite or only what Sheen says they do, but it is true that each of the two plays demonstrates its own distinct view of good theatre. In the last play he wrote for some years, *Bartholomew Fair* of 1614, Jonson renewed his mockery of the values behind *The Tempest* and Shakespeare's other late plays. Like *The Alchemist* with its setting in the current Blackfriars, and unlike *The Tempest* or *Cymbeline*, *Bartholomew Fair* was firmly located in contemporary London's Smithfield market. The two writers were certainly at odds over what was best for making theatre.

The most obvious extension of this game came from Shakespeare's subsequent involvement with John Fletcher. When writing *The Tempest* Shakespeare was familiar with Fletcher's *The Faithful Shepherdess*. Bart van Es in Chapter 13 below cites parallels between the two plays. What is most odd about this is how Shakespeare came to choose one of Jonson's own acolytes as his new collaborator. Fletcher's previous plays were all written

[7] Zachary Lesser, *Renaissance Drama and the Politics of Publication* (Cambridge University Press, 2004).

[8] Erica Sheen, *Shakespeare and the Institution of Theatre* (Basingstoke: Palgrave Macmillan, 2009), pp. 134–5.

for the boy company at the Blackfriars, so not far in the background must have been the thought in company minds that he would be useful writing plays for the King's Men's new playhouse. In the event, after writing several plays in collaboration with Shakespeare, Fletcher took over the retiring author's role as resident playwright permanently. Between 1611 and his death in 1625 he wrote or shared in the writing of more than thirty plays for the company.

Of Shakespeare's new collaborator, we do know that with his partner Francis Beaumont, and the boy company's leading player Nathan Field, Fletcher had once been Jonson's most faithful follower. He and Beaumont both wrote poems for the publication of *Volpone* in 1607, obviously having read the play beforehand in manuscript. In turn Jonson wrote a verse commendation for Fletcher's *Faithful Shepherdess*, as did Beaumont and the other chief 'son' of the time, Nat Field. Beaumont also wrote prefatory verses for *Catiline* in 1611 and *Epicoene* in 1612, and Fletcher wrote a poem for the publication of *Catiline*.

The close relationship between Jonson and these early 'sons' is evident in the fact that they were all in the habit of exchanging copies of their plays in manuscript. *The Alchemist* echoes features that appear in *The Knight of the Burning Pestle*, only staged once in 1607 and not printed until 1613, and of *The Coxcomb* (1609, not printed till the Folio of 1647), while *Epicoene* and *The Alchemist* echo two of Beaumont and Fletcher's earlier plays, *The Scornful Lady* and *The Woman's Prize*. Such instances of interchanging their manuscripts show each writer reading and discussing the other's plays before any of them were published.

Perhaps knowing what was to come, while writing *The Tempest* Shakespeare must have got hold of a copy of Fletcher's *The Faithful Shepherdess*, either in manuscript or in print (it was printed probably in 1610, though without any date on its title page). His own play contains distinct echoes of Fletcher's, as Bart van Es demonstrates. In return, Shakespeare's influence on Beaumont and Fletcher seems evident in their *Philaster*, written by the two while *Cymbeline* was also composed, with significant parallels. Fletcher's dependence on Shakespeare is also apparent in the plays he wrote subsequently. *Bonduca* in 1613–14 and *Valentinian* in 1614 both copy *Cymbeline* by taking their stories from early British history, when England was invaded by the Romans. The shared interests and species of play the three writers produced are evident in all the plays they wrote between them from 1610 to 1614. What is more, they all diverged markedly from Ben Jonson's preferred species. Clearly Fletcher chose to divorce himself from his former allegiance to the other bard.

We have already looked, by means of *The Tempest*'s first scene, at the impact on what audiences expected after the concerts that preceded the King's Men's shows at Blackfriars. The expectations of any theatre audience are hard to define, but some attempt at identifying what the indoor playgoers went to see and hear should certainly be made. Some would have read the playbills advertizing that afternoon's play's title. Many of them would have gone simply through habit, or to show themselves and their costly clothing off to their peers. Jonson's *The Devil is an Ass* in 1616 offered his usual acerbic description of playgoers at the Blackfriars. Fitzdottrell tells his wife,

> Heere is a cloake cost fifty pound, wife,
> Which I can sell for thirty, when I ha' seene
> All *London* in't, and London has seene me.
> To day, I goe to the *Black-fryers Play-house,*
> Sit i' the view, salute all my acquaintance,
> Rise up between the *Acts*; let fall my cloake,
> Publish a handsome man, and a rich suite
> (As that's a speciall end, why we goe thither,
> All that pretend, to stand for't o' the *Stage*)
> The ladies aske who's that? (For, they doe come
> To see us, *Love*, as wee doe to see them)[9]

This was far from being the only comment on how fashionable it had become to display yourself there, and flaunt your handsome dress. Sadly, it says nothing of the mentality of such people, and what they might expect from the performance. Possibly a better idea might be gained from considering some of the special groupings of the known playgoers. Nothing exists to suggest that the grouping of companionable types known to go to the Blackfriars was equally evident at the Globe.

Audiences at the Blackfriars and possibly other indoor playhouses included numbers of gallants who knew each other well, and who assembled there in intimate coteries. Such assemblies of like-minded wits would bond by exchanging mock-serious verses and group jokes. The self-styled Order of the Fancy, for instance, was first formed as a drinking club at a London tavern. Some time before 1629 it began regular meetings at Blackfriars. The Order's members included the poetaster Sir John Mennes, perhaps Robert Herrick, John Smith and John Weeks, all would-be poetic wits, plus the King's Men's player Thomas Pollard. Besides Pollard, on his home territory, came two King's Men's writers, Philip Massinger and William Davenant.

[9] Act I scene 6. Jonson, *Works*, ed. C. H. Herford, Percy and Evelyn Simpson (11 vols.; Oxford: Clarendon, Press, 1925–52), vol. VI, p. 178.

Clearly, poets and players together in such gatherings could share their minds over far more than the play itself while they mingled at the playhouse.

The Order's members all seem to have written verses to each other, mostly satirical comments on current topics. Inevitably, too, they shared their comments on the King's Men's plays. One of Mennes's verses was an attack on Queen Henrietta Maria's love for romantic Platonism, which Davenant and Thomas Carew had been fostering (and themselves quietly mocking) in the plays they contributed to the Blackfriars repertory through the 1630s.[10] Other such groups, bonded into their own intimate coteries, shared the same social status as this self-styled order. It was a natural consequence of the fact that throughout the period when the Blackfriars was run by the King's Men the indoor playhouses were the only venues other than Paul's Walk where such people could gather in numbers to exchange their pleasantries. There was ample room for them to sit and talk, they were more comfortable than they could be at the outdoor playhouses, and the experience was bound to last longer than a chat on meeting friends during a long stroll through the cold walks of St Paul's. The price of entry to the Blackfriars bought them, socially, far more than the Globe's penny.

[10] See Timothy Raylor, *Cavaliers, Clubs, and Literary Culture. Sir John Mennes, James Smith, and the Order of the Fancy* (Newark: University of Delaware Press, 1994), pp. 71–110.

CHAPTER 12

Changing fashions: tragicomedy, romance and heroic women in the 1630s hall-playhouses

Eleanor Collins

By the 1630s the indoor playhouse had long been part of the theatrical landscape of early modern London. The adult company of King's Men had been performing in the Blackfriars for twenty years, while various of Christopher Beeston's companies had enjoyed success at the Cockpit since 1616/17. By 1629 it appears that Queen Henrietta's Men, the company of longest tenure at the Cockpit, had come to rival the King's Men.[1] Unlike Shakespeare's company, they performed at their hall-playhouse all year round, exploiting the economic advantages that the more expensive entry fee afforded and, presumably, catering to a demand for indoor theatre experience that was not bound by the seasons. When Richard Gunnell built and then opened the smaller Salisbury Court in Whitefriars in 1629, the indoor playhouse must have seemed an attractive financial investment: a permanent fixture in early modern cultural life. Yet though the hall-playhouses were now relatively established, this is not to suggest that their repertories became settled or staid. On the contrary, the indoor venues continued to inspire experimental and challenging drama to draw new audiences and entertain regular patrons, and during the 1630s new fashions and theatrical trends emerged, encouraged by the spaces of the indoor theatres as material sites of performance, and by their new-found cultural status.

This chapter will explore the genres of tragicomedy and romance that were developed and revived on the Caroline stages of the hall-playhouses, and which have become, in many critical accounts, characteristic or distinctive of drama in this later era. In particular, it will focus on the figure of the heroic woman in 1630s drama, and the carefully negotiated representation of female characters in the plays throughout a period that

[1] If the number of times the companies were called to perform at court can be read as an indicator of success; see also Andrew Gurr, *Playgoing in Shakespeare's London* (2nd edn; Cambridge University Press, 1996), p. 183.

both Sophie Tomlinson and Julie Sanders argue underwent a 'sea change' in the way that 'female cultural agency' was perceived.[2] It will begin with an account of the specific cultural and practical influences, largely deriving from the court, that encouraged this shift in attitude within tragicomic drama of the Caroline years, and go on to explore two plays that are exemplars of its defining characteristics: Davenant's *Love and Honour* and Killigrew's *The Prisoners*. Although Fletcher's Jacobean drama for the Blackfriars, including *Philaster* (1608–10) and *Bonduca* (*c.* 1613), had already worked to shift attention towards the power of female agency, this chapter examines how courtier playwrights appropriated the genres of romance and tragicomedy to explore new ideas about the status of women and establish new dramatic possibilities (and limits to those possibilities) for female characters on stage.

The discussion goes on to consider the broader emergence of strong female roles on the Caroline stage, and the extent to which theatrical revivals complicated or contributed to a growing appreciation of heroic women and their theatrical appeal in this time of cultural transition. It grounds the established theatres' encounters with the courtiers as productive and generative in negotiating the representation of women in this period, and concludes by raising a series of practical questions relating to the theatrical experience of both acting and watching such 'women' – still played by boys – in the indoor playhouses. I aim to provide a sense of the interwoven factors – ideological, theatrical, economic, material – that contributed to the representation of women on the stage of the indoor playhouse, and give an account of the specific set of conditions that led the repertory in this particular direction over the 1630s.

Contexts: the theatrical queen, the playwriting court and the cult of platonic love

Theatrical activity of the late 1620s and 1630s is widely acknowledged to have been remarkable in terms of the recalibration of the relationship between women and theatre that it effected. Sophie Tomlinson has argued that drama in the 1630s bears witness to 'a fresh valuation' of the 'intellectual and moral qualities' of women, 'the playwrights' new awareness of women as active subjects', and a 'new vocality and visibility of women in Caroline

[2] Sophie Tomlinson, *Women on Stage in Stuart Drama* (Cambridge University Press, 2005), p. 11; Julie Sanders, *Caroline Drama: The Plays of Massinger, Ford, Shirley, and Brome* (Plymouth: Northcote House, 1999), p. 39.

culture'.[3] This was a cultural shift so profound that it contributed, in Tomlinson's narrative, to the emergence of the first female actors on the English public stage in the Restoration, and it was directly linked to the performances of Queen Henrietta Maria and her women in court masques. Though Queen Anne had performed in masques over the Jacobean reign, it was Henrietta Maria's contributions to court theatre – which were to include speaking roles and the performance of male roles by women – that have been credited as direct interventions into the renegotiation of female agency: literary, political and social.[4] The deliberate example that was made of William Prynne's unfortunately timed *Histriomastix* (published 1633), which referred to women actors as 'notorious whores' and lost him the tips of his ears in the pillory, has proved an enduring lynchpin in the narration of the debate over female performance. The vitriolic language in Prynne's (more widely anti-theatrical) text, and the reactionary justice meted out by the court, underscores the sensitivity around the theatrical capacity of women and has provided an important focal point for critics.[5] Yet as Tomlinson has helped to demonstrate, Prynne's was just one voice, strained and conspicuously zealous, that spoke from the edges of an arena of debate which became dominated by the practitioners and personnel of the theatres themselves. In a vigorous, imaginative and remarkably public dialogue which took place both on courtly and public stages and amidst the pages of printed playbooks, the attributes of female theatricality, subjectivity and intellect were worked over and revalued.

This cultural shift was owed not only to Henrietta Maria's theatrical activities and the attention they may have drawn from audiences, however (including those removed spectators who could envisage female performance by reading the printed masques and accounts of courtly entertainment). It was also partly dependent on social and political developments within the established conditions of play production, visible from the late 1620s, with the emergence of the courtier playwrights. As new producers of drama, 'fostered' by Henrietta Maria, and often writing for reputation and

[3] Tomlinson, *Women on Stage*, pp. 81, 114, 118.

[4] Sophie Tomlinson, 'She that Plays the King: Henrietta Maria and the Threat of the Actress in Caroline Culture', in Gordon McMullan and Jonathan Hope (eds.), *The Politics of Tragicomedy* (London and New York: Routledge, 1992), p. 192.

[5] *Histriomastix* was released for sale in London bookshops at the same time as Henrietta Maria was immersed in rehearsal for Walter Montagu's masque *The Shepherd's Paradise*. See Tomlinson, *Women on Stage*, pp. 23–4; Kim Walker, 'New Prison: Representing the Female Actor in Shirley's *The Bird in a Cage* (1633)', *English Literary Renaissance* 21, 285–400; and the introduction to *The Bird in a Cage* in Hero Chalmers, Julie Sanders, and Sophie Tomlinson (eds.), *Three Seventeenth-Century Plays on Women and Performance* (Manchester University Press, 2006).

favour rather than from a more strictly professional investment in theatre, the courtier playwrights were in a position to reinvent and renegotiate theatrical traditions and use them to ends that were motivated, in part, by the interests of their royal patrons. Playwrights associated with the Court include William Davenant, John Suckling, Thomas Killigrew and Lodowick Carlell, and between them they made a significant contribution to the repertories of the Caroline indoor playhouses. Their emergence as writers of professional drama was related to the cultural ascendancy of the hall-playhouses in the 1630s. The reputation of the indoor playhouses as fashionable destinations for a gentrified audience and performance venues of social prestige was endorsed and augmented by Henrietta Maria's several visits to the Blackfriars theatre in the 1630s.[6] Her trips physically (albeit momentarily) repositioned part of the court within the indoor playhouses, and Tomlinson argues that they bear witness to 'the greater cross-fertilization between the cultures of the court and the metropolis in the Caroline period'.[7] Royal interest in the theatre was further instanced by the giving of clothes and gifts of money – most notably in the queen's gift of costumes to dress a revival of *The Faithful Shepherdess* in 1634.[8] These conditions, in which both the reputation of the indoor playhouses and the pursuit of literary interests were explicitly endorsed by the queen, combined in the work of courtier playwrights. And their intervention in the professional theatrical marketplace signalled not only an appreciable shift in the relationship of the theatre to the court, but invited the creation and development of repertories under new terms. In particular, the courtiers' dramatic output represented a scenario in which former audience members and aristocratic patrons of drama actively participated in its composition and shaped plays according to prerogatives that differed from those of the established writers of commercial repertories – some of whom, like Thomas Heywood, had been writing for the professional theatre for over thirty years.

The influence of royal patronage on drama has long been observed. It has played an important role in theatre history, from the anecdotal (Queen Elizabeth I's love of Falstaff as causally connected to *The Merry Wives of Windsor*) to the historically rigorous and specific (Scott McMillin and Sally Beth MacLean's analysis of the Protestant politics of the first Queen's Men's repertory in the 1580s; the influence of royal patronage on the repertory of the

[6] Rebecca Bailey, *Staging the Old Faith: Queen Henrietta Maria and the Theatre of Caroline England* (Manchester University Press, 2009), pp. 134–5.

[7] Tomlinson, *Women on Stage*, p. 11.

[8] N. W. Bawcutt, *The Control and Censorship of Caroline Drama: The Records of Sir Henry Herbert, Master of the Revels 1623–73* (Oxford: Clarendon Press, 1996), p. 186.

King's Men as traced by Andrew Gurr).[9] But the social and cultural conditions of the Caroline reign led to the widespread performance of drama before London audiences that was produced from within court circles – specifically from within the queen's feminized court. As many critics have demonstrated, the ideological grounding of the new playwrights' drama is easily traced back to courtly origins – and is most explicit in its appropriation of a Caroline conception of platonic love, which was exploited by Henrietta Maria as a resonant trope at court. The queen's notion of platonic love – which idealized the chaste admiration and spiritual worship of women – derived from her exposure to the doctrine at the French court, and writers and playwrights in her immediate circle were quick to entertain her intellectual appetite with literary and dramatic renderings of its central tenets. Yet platonic love, with its clearly delineated gender roles and emphasis on metaphysical purity over sexual fulfilment, had a political as well as an aesthetic function. As Lesel Dawson has described, it meant that 'women were able to extend the time of their courtship, the liminal period during which they exercised control over their suitors',[10] and as such it could be pressed to work as a rich metaphor in narratives of sovereignty and servitude. Martin Butler has defined this construction of female authority as part of the 'politicization of love',[11] and Henrietta Maria capitalized on the opportunities it afforded in the masques she acted in, the art she commissioned, and the deliberate fashioning of her own image and sovereign reputation. As this chapter will show, the representation of one type of heroic woman on the Caroline stage – an awe-inspiring, exemplary princess, whose beauty is often described as (spiritually) illuminating, radiating light – owes much to the cultural agenda that Henrietta Maria deployed at court.

This is not to suggest that the drama of the 1630s indoor playhouses adhered to an explicitly royalist agenda. The idea of the court's tyranny over drama, and the 'suspiciously teleological' relationship that has held in criticism between theatre and royal patronage, was closely interrogated by Martin Butler. His work has been instrumental in discrediting the causal link that was assumed between the 1642 closure of the theatres and a performance tradition that had associated itself closely, in its decadence, with the declining English court, and as such was 'inevitably . . . swept

9 Scott McMillin and Sally Beth MacLean, *The Queen's Men and their Plays* (Cambridge University Press, 1998); Andrew Gurr, *The Shakespeare Company, 1594–1642* (Cambridge University Press, 2004).

10 Lesel Dawson, '"New Sects of Love": Neoplatonism and Constructions of Gender in Davenant's *The Temple of Love* and *The Platonick Lovers*', *Early Modern Literary Studies* 8.1 (2002), 4.1–36 (para. 2), accessed 30/01/2012, http://extra.shu.ac.uk/emls/08-1/dawsnew.htm

11 Martin Butler, *Theatre and Crisis, 1632–1642* (Cambridge University Press, 1984), p. 35.

towards a disastrous and unavoidable collapse'.[12] Though the representation of female dramatic characters was greatly influenced by ideologies filtering down from the court, the courtiers' drama was by no means uncritical or blithely accepting of the queen's doctrine of platonic love.[13] The emergence of the courtier playwrights and the ideologies of Henrietta Maria had a discernible influence on 1630s drama, as the following discussion of Davenant's *Love and Honour* and Killigrew's *The Prisoners* will show. But the case for the legitimacy of female performance and, more widely, the acceptance of women's potential heroicism – even upon the stage – was by no means straightforwardly won.

Love and Honour: the 'hope of endlesse glory'

William Davenant's *Love and Honour* was first performed in 1634 at the Blackfriars by the King's Men and was written contemporaneously with his masque, *The Temple of Love*, presented early in 1635 by the queen and her ladies at Whitehall. The masque is exemplary in its articulation of Henrietta Maria's conception of platonic love, celebrating the Temple of Chaste Love, the beauteous Queen and the 'lesser lights' of her train, who 'raise strange doctrines, and new sects of Love: / Which must not wooe or court the Person, but / The Mind; and practise generation not / Of Bodies but of Soules'.[14] *Love and Honour*, a tragicomedy set in Italy, draws on much of the same imagery and discourse in its depiction of Evandra, the heroic princess around whom the dramatic narrative revolves. She is associated with images of light and regeneration: 'hasty flowers' are imagined to spring from 'their cold rootes', 'Invited by her eye-beames', and at one point her suitor Alvaro, the prince of Savoy, invokes her to 'rise, break from this thick / And silent darknesse, like the eldest light', at which point the stage trap opens and she is lifted from the underground cave in which she has been concealed.[15] When she returns to the cave she is explicitly figured as the sun, and 'Descend[s] like the bright officer of day' (B2). Evandra's feminine qualities are also figured as divinely calming: she 'softens' Alvaro's spirits and draws his thoughts from war, away from the rash masculinity of military action that Prospero embodies within the drama (B2). And in contrast to Prospero, Alvaro adopts a chivalric code indebted to platonic love, and makes recourse to the 'sober checks / Of sweet

[12] Ibid., pp. 7–11 (p. 10). [13] See ibid., pp. 55–83, and Dawson, '"New Sects of Love"'.

[14] William Davenant, *The Temple of Love: A Masque* (London, 1634), printed for Thomas Walkley. A2, B2.

[15] William Davenant, *Love and Honour* (London, 1649), A3v, B1v.

Philosophy', 'cold / And holy temper', and sacred vows (A3v, B2). When, in Act 5, Alvaro discovers that he has gained a rival in love in the character of Leonell, the men become bound in their mutual adoration of Evandra, in language that melds the discourse of religion and of servitude: 'heaven affects plurallitie / Of worshipers, t'adore and serve' (D3v).

Davenant's positive representation of women and female influence in the play is not limited to mere description, but powers the dramatic narrative itself, which begins promisingly with the prioritization of women's choice and autonomy. The women prisoners held in Savoy are permitted to return to Milan after a year if they do not marry in that time, and the men of Savoy must earn their marriage by 'wooing' them 'to consent': as the circumspectly named Frivolo says, 'wee have no power to use constraint, nor to / Inforce a maidenhead, on paine of death' (A4v). And in order to save Alvaro's life, Evandra and her female companion, Melora, set out to 'suffer [his penance] our selves' – a deed that will 'confer / A dignity for ever on our Sexe' (C3). The women lock Alvaro out of the way in the cave and thwart a duel by imprisoning Prospero with him, thus displacing outdated, masculine codes of honour. They forcibly take control of the action – Evandra says to Melora that ''tis *thou and I* that must / Take solemne leave, and never meete in this / Our beauty, colour, or our warmth agen' (C3v; my emphasis). Leonell, the Prince of Parma, is left, 'blushing', obedient, and emasculated, to watch the cave door and slip the prisoners food each hour (C4). Evandra and Melora then embark on their quest, which is set out explicitly in terms of an 'obligation on our sex' (C3v), 'An act as will outlive all history', while Leonell remarks: 'this sure is such / A great example of a female fortitude / As must undo all men' (C4) – a clear reference to *femme forte*, the French construction of female valour and bravery that was popularized in England during the 1630s.[16]

Davenant's celebration of female wit and courage is clear – Evandra is, in Rebecca Bailey's words, a 'transforming power' of beauty.[17] But as Bailey notes, the closing of the play 'curbs such heroic female aspirations' and denies the women their 'hope of endlesse glory' (E2).[18] In a series of farcical revelations which involves the discarding of two false beards, the senior patriarchs of the play wrest control of the action from Evandra, who asks, dismayed, 'why would / You with this danger on your selfe destroy / That noble fame I vertuously pursu'd?' (E2). The men resolve the near-tragic feud which has dominated the action, and a series of reconciliations ensues, while

[16] Bailey, *Staging the Old Faith*, p. 159; Tomlinson, *Women on Stage*, p. 115.
[17] Bailey, *Staging the Old Faith*, p. 159. [18] Ibid., p. 162.

Evandra's marriage to Alvaro is forestalled by the bizarre revelation that he is already promised to Melora, a fact that has remained unremarked upon until now. In the restoration of traditional gender roles, Evandra is conveniently and 'worthily bestow'd' upon the meek Leonell (E3); she speaks only once more following her puzzled response to the unfolding of events, and that is compliantly to accept her father's wishes.

Furthermore, any serious potential for the exemplification of sincere courtly wooing, according to the temperate doctrine of platonic love, is deflected in the subplot that sees the colonel Vasco attempt to win the hand of his Milanese prisoner. This strand of the play is relegated to a comic diversion, countering the tragic plot of the main action, in which the female prize in question is a rich, old widow with a chronic cough – 'Her Grandameship' (Bv) – who 'looks as she had / Been long buried' (C). Vasco relies on 'cleaneness and good looks' to woo her (Bv); he does not need to court her at her window with 'rare musick' for 'she's very deafe, so that cost is sav'd' (B3). He appears 'fantastically accouterd' (C), and manipulates her into marriage in the space of only a few lines of dialogue: his officer Altesto exclaims: 'Provide us musick, wee'l dance her to death: / Thou shalt be her husband ere night, and her / Executor before morning' (Cv).[19] The morbid humour makes a mockery of the necessity of sentimental wooing that is gestured towards at the play's opening, and thwarts the romantic promise of the plot line. The widow is ridiculed throughout, a figure of fun whom Vasco tries to persuade to die, and then plots to divorce. It is as though Davenant deliberately takes the metaphor of beauty in the doctrine of platonic love too literally – the powerful and mysticized 'influence of . . . beauty' of which he wrote in *The Temple of Love*. The plain woman, the elderly, the unbeautiful remains in the shadows, cast aside, and her value is reduced to a monetary tally. She is also anonymous; Davenant does not assign her a name. In Davenant's emphasis on the widow's grotesque physicality – describing one of her 'cheek teeth' that has 'dropt under the wanscore bed' (C2); her skin like 'Parchment' (C), the 'stitch' in her side, her 'cough' of 'great antiquity' (Cv) and 'shrinking' eyes (D) – she is the polar opposite of the metaphysical, rarefied beauty that is Evandra and her neoplatonic ideals. Davenant hints elsewhere at the effects of passing time on feminine beauty: when Alvaro accepts Melora as his betrothed, he makes the strangely ambiguous comment that 'although / Thy beauty's chang'd, it is not lost' (E2v). Compare this to Alvaro's reference to Evandra earlier, when imploring Leonell to 'keep Evandra safe': he asks him to 'use

[19] See Chapter 8 above, on the use of sumptuous costuming in the indoor playhouses.

her / With such respective holinesse as thou / Wouldst do the reliques of a Saint inshrind' (C3), deploying a metaphor which depends on ideas of the unchanging and the sacred, but which also makes disturbing reference to the interred, the corpse.

It is important to note that the ambiguous treatment of the widow, and of Evandra at the close of the play, is dependent in part on Davenant's choice of genre – the comic subplot and the tragicomedy's conventional, narrative requirement of closure and resolution. By the 1630s there existed a relatively large canon of tragicomic drama that set the precedent for certain plot devices and established a number of theatrical conventions. Fletcherian tragicomedy had been performed on the Blackfriars stage for over a decade. Andrew Gurr describes how these 'plot-driven dramas of love, danger, and the peril of death . . . became almost a defining characteristic of the company repertory', whereas Lucy Munro writes that it was 'probably the genre's dominant Caroline form'.[20] This subgenre of tragicomedy typically explored anxieties centred on the female body, containing plays in which 'the body of the heroine also frequently carries the weight of the narrative' – and drama of the 1630s, including *Love and Honour*, bears witness to the continuation of that emphasis.[21] Fletcher had also set a precedent for the staging of heroic female agency in the tragedy *Bonduca* (*c.* 1613), which follows the heroics of the warrior queen, and (with Beaumont) *Philaster* (1608–10), featuring the virtuous Arethusa and cross-dressing Eufrasia. As Bart van Es notes in Chapter 13 below, *Philaster*, *The Maid's Tragedy* and *A King and No King* all 'focus on the trials of virtuous women', and he traces the influence of Beaumont and Fletcher, as 'young up and coming writers', on the drama written from the late 1600s – including Shakespeare's 'late' plays, which were to affirm this style of drama's links to the romance tradition.[22] *The Tempest*, *Pericles*, *Cymbeline* and *The Winter's Tale* feature the exotic locations, heroic quests, themes of wandering and loss, close encounters with death, wondrous resolutions and near divine revelations that characterize the romance, elements of which are echoed in Davenant's plot.[23] Evandra and Melora escape the 'inchanted house', the Italian cave and secret, underground corridors in which they are passively concealed (or imprisoned: there is a lock on the gate);

[20] Lucy Munro, 'Dublin Tragicomedy and London Stages', in Subha Mukherji and Raphael Lyne (eds.), *Early Modern Tragicomedy* (Cambridge: D. S. Brewer, 2007), pp. 175–92 (p. 156).

[21] Ibid., p. 181. [22] P. 249.

[23] To modern critics, the differentiation between the categories of romance and tragicomedy is now often considered 'anachronistic and unnecessary': Mary Ellen Lamb and Valerie Wayne (eds.), *Staging Early Modern Romance: Prose Fiction, Dramatic Romance, and Shakespeare* (London and New York: Routledge, 2009), p. 6.

they embark on their quest; and Evandra embraces her pending execution with tragic gravity. The narrative trajectory also illustrates the specific freedoms and 'opportunities' that the romance tradition could afford female characters, 'through action and especially through speech'.[24]

Yet while writers of tragicomedy could use the genre to explore new avenues for the representation of women, they continued to be influenced by long-standing conventions of the stage. The comic treatment of the decaying widow in the subplot may be absurd and farcical in performance, but it also betrays an intense sexual anxiety over the elderly female body that is barely masked; and it subtly foretells and cruelly mocks the realities of physical ageing and decline in would-be heroic women, valued as they are according to conceptions of beauty. In a similar vein, the series of unlikely resolutions at the close of Davenant's play conforms to dramatic conventions that had been developing for decades within the theatre profession, and shores up traditional gender roles and social codes. Evandra may exemplify female heroism in the main action, but at the play's close she takes her place, obediently, beside an unchosen husband, returning to silence. Though *Love and Honour* explores and (ostensibly) champions female agency, its formal requirements for closure forestall a more radical statement. This is a moment that realizes, in potential, the 'discordant juxtaposition of convention and values' that Mary Beth Rose has described in relation to tragicomedy.[25] The safe subordination of Evandra and Melora ends up as a function of the choice of dramatic genre – perhaps conveniently, given that female agency was still a highly contested notion on a stage that remained all male.

'A womans breast in a doublet': *The Prisoners*, cross-dressing and the culture of revival

A similar scenario occurs in Killigrew's seafaring romance *The Prisoners*, which was written around the same time as *Love and Honour* (*c.* 1633) but performed on the Cockpit stage by Queen Henrietta's Men. The 'glorious' and 'Beautious' Cecillia inspires devotional worship in Pausanes, who exclaims that he is sure such women are 'more then man, for I never saw

[24] Ibid., p. 13.
[25] Mary Beth Rose, *The Expense of Spirit: Love and Sexuality in Renaissance Drama* (Ithaca, NY: Cornell University Press, 1988), p. 182.

/ Any of that sex that made me tremble'.[26] Pausanes's language is inflected with platonic love – he 'philosophises' upon 'her diviner part' (A6v) – while other male characters in the play respond to her beauty with threats of sexual violence: particularly the pirate Gallippus, who frames his love for Cecillia in terms of martyrdom. Though Cecillia's body is objectified as precious cargo in the play, bound and carried to Gallippus's galley and fought over in chivalric duels, the roles are quickly – and visually – reversed, when Cecillia is freed and Pausanes and his friend Hipparchus are taken prisoner and themselves bound by the king, her brother. It falls to Cecillia to rescue them, fitting them with disguises and then dressing herself as a boy as she sets out in hot pursuit. It is not only her participation in an established theatrical tradition of cross-dressing heroines that defines Cecillia, but also her intellect and articulacy. When Philon tries to talk her out of such passionate pursuit of Pausanes, arguing that 'You have with your sex throwne off your modestie', Cecillia gives a lucid and eloquent account of her motives, which confidently asserts her position and works to inspire Philon's loyalty – 'I know my Cozen is full of honour, And / I know with all that honour he loves me' – and builds to a rousing call to arms: 'now I conjure thee / Fellow and Obey mee' (B12v–Cv). Shouting into the storm that breaks during the final lines of her speech, she gallantly continues: 'I'me resolv'd / And this night I'le to Sea, and in her greatest depth / Dive to finde that rich pearle' (Cv). As Julie Sanders has noted in relation to other plays of the period, the trope of the cross-dressing woman illustrates the competence and agency of women, while at the same time their persuasive impersonation of male roles can be read as a supportive commentary on Henrietta Maria's interest in acting and female performance.[27]

Though Killigrew glorifies and heroicizes Cecillia in this scene, her swash-buckling bravado is thwarted when her physical strength is overcome in the storm and necessitates her own rescue by Pausanes, who heroically 'leapes' into the sea to save 'the youth / That strikes the water with unskilfull oars' (C7v). The next time the audience sees her she is insensible – an unconscious body to be carried on stage beside that of her near-dead lover. At this point she has only twelve lines remaining to speak in the play. In the

[26] *The Prisoners and Claracilla: Two Tragae-Comedies* (London, 1641), duodecimo printed by T. Cotes for Andrew Crooke. A6, A6v. The duodecimo appears to contain an insert of six, ²A–²A6, after A2; A5 is missigned (B5). I am indebted to Sarah Wheale and Paul W. Nash at the Bodleian for their assistance in this matter. Note that the *Early English Books Online* electronic version is missing A4 (signed), on which is printed a Dramatis Personae. A4v is blank. The physical copy consulted is held at the Bodleian Library (Mal. 262).

[27] Sanders, *Caroline Drama*, pp. 40–2.

final act the shipwrecked characters are brought together on the same shore, guided by the light of a hermit's fire, and experience a sequence of fantastical revelations which identify Pausanes and Hipparchus as long-lost princes, reunite the banished ruler, Theogines, with the brother from whom he has been 'Divided' by 'strange accident' (C3v), and reconcile various fathers, sons, daughters, brothers and sisters (notably no mothers). The calm after the destructive violence of the storm and a series of chaotic scenes set aboard sinking ships emphasizes 'this our miraculous deliverance' (C7v) – both from the raging seas and the wider turmoil of a family history cursed by the consequences of broken vows. Cecillia's identity beneath her boy's clothes is revealed on the surprising discovery of 'a womans breast in a doublet' (C9v), and she wakes to be reunited with Pausanes, who is revived by the hermit's restorative ministrations: her extraordinary behaviour goes unrecognized amidst the events unfolding around her and is barely acknowledged. Though Cecillia triumphs in the 'heroics of marriage', her story becomes subsumed by the unravelling plot lines of Killigrew's play and the genre-determined priorities of its conclusion.[28] Cecillia represents the promise of an archetypal heroic woman, but also an implicit denial of its full realization: like Evandra, the closing moments of the drama return her to a traditional role of passive femininity, and she 'hide[s]' her 'blushes' in her royal brother's 'bosome' (C10v), having received royal sanction for her marriage at last.

Yet though Davenant and Killigrew's courtly princesses may fail to live up to the full promise of their heroism, the Caroline stages of the indoor playhouses abound with the fashion for female fortitude. The Blackfriars and Cockpit stages were populated by an array of incarnations of such wilful, intelligent and excellent women, linked implicitly or explicitly with the Queen's circle of platonic love. From Davenant at the Blackfriars came the satirical tragicomedy *The Platonic Lovers*, while Killigrew went on to write another tragicomedy based on French romance sources for the Cockpit around 1636, named after its leading heroine: *Claracilla*. Like Cecillia, Claracilla embodies the female virtues endorsed by platonic love, and her legendary beauty inspires servitude among a host of male courtiers. Killigrew's decision to name the play after its leading female role sparked a mini-vogue for a genre that Lucy Munro has described as 'she-tragicomedy', the plays 'focusing as they do on the trials faced by their exemplary heroines'.[29] In the next year the courtier John Suckling wrote *Aglaura* as a

[28] For the 'heroics of marriage', see Mary Beth Rose on tragicomedy and the 'reconfiguration of private life', *Expense of Spirit*, pp. 178–235.

[29] Munro, 'Dublin Tragicomedy', p. 178.

tragedy for the Blackfriars, its titular heroine 'conquering' the hearts of the court (and especially the king) with 'prettie ambushes and traps for hearts', while in a subplot the 'antiplatoniques' poke fun at 'Platonicke Ladies' who adhere to 'the new religion in love': 'a meere tricke to inhance the price of kisses'.[30] *Aglaura* is a revealing example of the direct influence that courtiers could have over professional drama, as its Blackfriars performance was subsidized by the author, who supplied the company with sumptuous costumes for its performance. Furthermore, the genre of tragicomedy appears to have been so popular at court that he rewrote the very end of the play to give it a tragicomic ending, radically altering the original sequence of events in the final act, which had seen the stage melodramatically strewn with bodies. The professional playwright James Shirley also capitalized on the trend for naming plays after female characters with *Rosania*, one of his Irish plays for Ogilby's Men which was licensed for the London stage in 1640 and performed at the Globe, and probably then the Blackfriars, as *The Doubtful Heir*.[31] In his choice of play title, Shirley was participating in 'the most fashionable of contemporary experiments with tragicomedy', though, as Munro has argued, he 'reworked' the genre in order to focus anxiety on the male, rather than female, body.[32] The female focus of the 1630s was sustained, though, in Rosania's 'simultaneous chastity and desirability', her pivotal role in the narrative, and in her success as a cross-dressing woman navigating the treacherous sexual politics of the Spanish court.[33]

The work of the professional playwrights not only perpetuated, but in cases anticipated, the courtiers' dramatic strategies when addressing increased female visibility in a theatrical culture. John Ford's romantic tragicomedy *The Lover's Melancholy*, licensed for the Blackfriars in 1628, is a case in point; his characters behave in accordance with the fashionable cult of courtly love, while the play's cross-dressing heroine, Eroclea, performs her part so persuasively, and is so central to the action, that Julie Sanders posits the theme of 'women and acting' as a 'central concern in designing this play'.[34] Philip Massinger's tragicomedies *The Emperor of the East* (1631) and *The Bashful Lover* (1636) also engage explicitly with the exemplary or heroic qualities of their female characters and were performed within the

30 John Suckling, *Aglaura* (London, 1638), printed by John Haviland for Thomas Walkley. Bv, B2v, D2v.

31 The prologue to the play's performance at the Globe indicates that it premiered at the amphitheatre, but Roslyn Knutson's work on repertory in performance suggests that popular plays were revived into the next consecutive season: Roslyn L. Knutson, *The Repertory of Shakespeare's Company, 1594–1613* (Fayetteville: University of Arkansas Press, 1991), pp. 32–40.

32 Munro, 'Dublin Tragicomedy', pp. 179–81. 33 Ibid., p. 178. 34 Sanders, *Caroline Drama*, p. 41.

same few years as *Love and Honour*, *The Prisoners* and *Claracilla*. The plays of the professionals and the courtiers were in dialogue with each other on the public stage, and each contribution to London's wider repertory of hall-playhouse drama enacted a new version of the debate over female agency, offering theatre audiences fresh theatrical contexts from which to approach and interpret the fare on offer. As Suckling's original version of *Aglaura* shows, the interest in female agency and performance spilled out into the genres which tragicomedy hybridized, in Ford's tragedy *Love's Sacrifice* (1633), for instance, and two comedies of particular note: Jonson's *The New Inn* (1629), which Sanders describes as 'an agitation on behalf of female theatricals', and Shirley's *Bird in a Cage*, performed at the Cockpit in 1633.[35] Both plays feature either female cross-dressing or performance and play an active part in the broader cultural focus on women that the tragicomedies and romances helped to define.[36]

Importantly, this account of the indoor repertories does not necessarily entail the critical binary that has long held between the 'courtiers' and the 'professional' playwrights. This opposition has been endorsed in part by the 'second war of the theatres' – an exchange that began in 1629 between the courtiers affiliated with the Blackfriars, and Shirley and the 'professionals', including Massinger, associated with the Cockpit. Any straightforward reading of the 'war' is complicated by the cross-company associations of both categories of dramatist at this time, but – more widely – professional and courtly influences were to be found in every indoor theatre in London. Changes in fashion were occurring not just on one stage but across many, in the collaborative model of competition described by Roslyn Knutson.[37] Yet while the intersection between professional and courtier drama could be generative, the relationship was also at times unstable and unresolved – even within the drama itself. The fault line between the court and the city was one that Massinger exploited in comic fashion in *The City-Madam*, performed at the Blackfriars in 1632. This play, in which the wife of a merchant assumes a hyperbolized governance over her husband's estate and extols absolute sovereignty in women, sees a set of female characters conventional to Jacobean city comedy adopt the queenly airs and attributes associated with Henrietta Maria's courtly ideologies. Massinger's comedy dramatizes the dispossession, humiliation and eventual subordination of the wife and

35 Ibid., p. 35.

36 See Kim Walker, 'New Prison', and the introduction to *The Bird in a Cage* in Chalmers et al., *Three Seventeenth-Century Plays on Women and Performance*, for detailed readings of the play.

37 Roslyn Lander Knutson, *Playing Companies and Commerce in Shakespeare's London* (Cambridge University Press, 2001), pp. 35–8.

her two daughters, emphasizing the need for 'City dames' to confine themselves to 'their own spheres' and maintain the 'distance twixt the City and the Court' required by decorum.[38] Yet even as Massinger works to separate the court and the city, his play travels along that imagined division to engage directly with behavioural norms and expectations of 'London Ladies' and the sense of female agency that was taking hold in theatres – and outside them, on the city's streets, as this play might suggest. While the plays of both courtiers and professionals may have been connected in varying degrees to the influence of Henrietta Maria and the questions that her dramatic performances laid at the theatres' doors, the sense of a general movement over an extended period of time – beginning in the late 1620s and gathering momentum through the 1630s – is tangible. And while private and court drama appears to have gone further in staging more explicit endorsements of female performance and heroism – in Davenant's *Temple of Love*, for instance, or William Cartwright's *The Lady-Errant* – positive representations of heroic women on the London stages, however qualified they were, contributed to an identifiable shift in the construction of female characters as subjects.[39]

The change in dramatic fashions that the 1630s witnessed was further complicated by the culture of theatrical revival on which the indoor repertories continued to depend – a practice that remained advantageous for companies, in economic terms, given the cost of licensing and staging new plays. The hall-playhouse repertories were not isolated or, at times, particularly distinct from those of the amphitheatres, and it is dangerous to draw too sharp a line between the types of venue and the theatre they produced. As Bart van Es has shown, the direct, causal link that is often assumed between Beaumont and Fletcher's 'new and amazingly popular kind of drama' and Shakespeare's romances, on the one hand, and the King's Men's occupancy of the indoor playhouse, on the other, is not as straightforward as might be supposed.[40] He attributes Shakespeare's 'late' style to a broader 'merging of traditions' in theatre, and it is this sense of the co-mingling of different influences and styles, collaboration between dramatists and the convergence of indoor and amphitheatre repertories that is fundamental here. For the broader genres of romance and tragicomedy were not new or distinct, in themselves, to the indoor playhouses: the romance tradition reached back to

38 Philip Massinger, *The City-Madam* (London, 1658), printed for Andrew Pennycuicke. L4v.

39 See Tomlinson's discussion of *The Lady-Errant* in *Women on Stage*, pp. 105–13.

40 Barbara Mowat, 'What's in a Name? Tragicomedy, Romance, or Late Comedy', in Richard Dutton and Jean E. Howard (eds.), *A Companion to Shakespeare's Works*, vol. IV, *The Poems, Problem Comedies, Late Plays* (Oxford: Blackwell, 2005), pp. 131–2.

the medieval period, and tragicomedy also took a popular form on the amphitheatre stage, such as in the Red Bull's 'remarkable cluster of tragicomic saints' plays' to which Munro has drawn attention. Tragicomedy was, more widely, an extraordinarily diverse and versatile genre: as Gordon McMullan and Jonathan Hope have observed, it encompassed 'an astonishing variety of forms, from formulaic popular drama to courtly romances based on wonder, from formal Italianate pastoral to plays which close with an uneasy combination of marriage and death'.[41] As such, Caroline audiences and dramatists could draw on an extensive variety of traditions and styles when experiencing and envisaging new plays, found within drama of the decades that had come before: plays which not only took their place within a broader cultural memory but that could be newly licensed and revived. The development of fashion in this period thus became a complex negotiation of styles and influences, necessitated by the bringing together of old and new drama as the spectres of past theatrical roles were embodied and resurrected by a new generation of actors, years later, in the indoor playhouse auditoriums.

Negotiation between tradition and innovation was a reciprocal process. I have written elsewhere on the effect that Thomas Heywood's serialization *The Fair Maid of the West* may have had upon Killigrew's tragicomedies for the Cockpit,[42] but the courtier drama of the 1630s also tuned into and 'refreshed' the concerns of old Jacobean drama, casting its female characters in new light. Heywood wrote the first part of *The Fair Maid* around 1601, and then added a sequel in 1631, which appears to have accompanied a revival of the old play. The sequel capitalizes on the newly popular mode of romantic tragicomedy, and revives its seafaring, heroic, cross-dressing heroine Bess in ways that reposition her fortitude in the light of the exploration of female autonomy in the 1630s. In this way, old plays were drawn into the ongoing renegotiation of both theatrical tradition and the drama's gender politics, and, when performed alongside Killigrew and Davenant's plays, resonated with current heroic portrayals of women. Alongside this was the development of more particular subgenres in theatre which appealed specifically to the queen's dramatic taste for pastoral tragicomedy – with Joseph Rutter's translation of *The Cid* in two parts (1637–8) and the (lost but pastorally named) revival of *Hymen's Holiday* for the Cockpit (1633), the revival of Thomas Goffe's *The Careless Shepherdess* at Salisbury Court

[41] Gordon McMullan and Jonathan Hope, Introduction to *The Politics of Tragicomedy* (London and New York: Routledge, 1992), p. 1.

[42] Eleanor Collins, 'From Court to Cockpit: *The Prisoners* and *Claracilla* in Repertory', in Philip Major (ed.), *Thomas Killigrew: Collected Essays* (Farnham: Ashgate, 2013), pp. 21–44.

(around 1638), and the revival of Fletcher's *Faithful Shepherdess* at the Blackfriars in 1634. The popularity of romance appears to have led to the appearance of Shirley's *The Arcadia* (1640) on the Cockpit stage, which followed on the heels of Kirke's old-fashioned play on chivalrous heroics, *The Seven Champions of Christendom* (1638). Both plays are often assumed to be revivals, but are as likely to have been newly written for the 1630s. There are also a number of lost plays that belong to this period which may, on the speculative basis of their titles, have contributed more widely to the trend for romance over the period, including the *Invisible Knight* (anon., 1632), *Princely Lovers* (anon. for the Cockpit, 1638), Ford's *Beauty in a Trance* (1638), *The Chevaliers* (anon. for the Cockpit, 1641) and *The Doge and the Dragon* (anon., 1641).[43] These repertory choices signal a concerted response to changing fashions, in the interplay between new work that courtier playwrights brought to the stage and an established corpus of extant drama; they can be seen as the result of a specific set of conditions in the 1630s that helped determine the fare on offer in London's theatres.

Heroic 'women' on stage

As a final consideration, I wish to turn to the question of how these heroic women might have appeared on stage in the indoor playhouses, and what the experience of seeing them performed might have been like to an audience. For however heroic the depiction of female characters may have been, these roles continued to be played by boys throughout the period: the heroic 'success' and credibility of each female character depended on men in the most practical, as well as ideological or narrative, terms. As we have seen in Davenant and Killigrew's creations, the extent of female heroism could be curbed by genre-induced resolutions of the romantic tragicomedies. But in play the boy actor's performance has an even more direct power to ridicule, send up or satirize the woman he portrays in real time – as well as flatter or idealize her. Dympna Callaghan has written that the male actor's body 'repeatedly and ritually enacts the displacement, exclusion, and discipline of its female counterpart', and she challenges the casual assumption that in early modern drama 'there must be women on stage, at least in every notion that counts, because there are representations of women' on stage.[44] Callaghan's appeal to the critic to recognize the continued mediation of

[43] The Lost Plays Database, accessed 31/10/2012, www.lostplays.org.

[44] Dympna Callaghan, *Shakespeare without Women: Representing Race and Gender on the Renaissance Stage* (London and New York: Routledge, 1999), p. 9.

women, and above all their essential *absence* from the professional stage, is a prudent reminder when considering the construction of heroic women in this time of transition. At the same time, it is possible that the impersonation of women by boy actors functioned as something of a safety device within early modern culture; their overt theatricality might have diminished female power on stage and tempered social anxiety over actors' representations of female bodies. Andrew Gurr has suggested that the 'strangeness' of players' 'counterfeiting their imitations of reality' may underpin the 'readiness to tolerate boy players' in London in the earlier periods of playing.[45] The overly theatrical performance of heroic women may have safely removed these representations from reality; they may also have rendered such representations palatable, and more socially acceptable.

These considerations point towards the impossibility of knowing how audiences would have received theatrical portrayals of heroic women – particularly, perhaps, in the case of women playgoers, who were most acutely subject to the difficulties inherent for playwrights in 'appealing to women while excluding them from the work of representation'.[46] Penelope Woods' chapter suggests how the different and greater female presence at the hall-playhouses was a new feature of indoor performance that did not go unremarked by playwrights and poets.[47] But how far the playwrights attempted to recognize rather than construct women playgoers' tastes and reactions is unclear: Callaghan has cogently argued that we should not read the 'consumption' of particular types of women on stage as indicative or suggestive in any way of their approval or acceptance by off-stage counterparts.[48] As Sanders has suggested, Shirley's juxtaposition in *A Bird in a Cage* of the farcical impersonation of women by men, and the convincing male performances of women, 'must have called to mind for contemporary audiences the equally successful performances of Henrietta Maria and her court women'.[49] But what we can learn of early modern audience's attitudes to this is very limited, even if the dramatists' own stance can be traced with any confidence within the play-texts in question. Any interpretation of the heroic woman on the early modern stage must be offset against such historical difficulties in the evidence – or lack of evidence.

A number of questions relating to the experience of watching the male performance of women in the indoor theatres also arise when we consider the practical effects of staging on interpretation and performance. In the

[45] Andrew Gurr, *The Shakespearian Playing Companies* (Oxford: Clarendon Press, 1996), p. 9.
[46] Callaghan, *Shakespeare without Women*, p. 164. [47] See Chapter 8 above.
[48] Callaghan, *Shakespeare without Women*, p. 15. [49] Sanders, *Caroline Drama*, p. 40.

quietened interiors of the hall-playhouses, with the relatively static positioning of its audience, did actors find that the ways in which they were watched by audiences differed from the kinds of spectatorship they encountered in the outdoor amphitheatres? Might the performances have been more studied, more staged and deliberate – or would they have grown in subtlety and naturalism in these years? Would the altered acoustics of the amphitheatres have affected delivery and encouraged actors to speak more softly, or did the need to be heard in the theatre continue to override such acoustic nuance? Did the enclosed space tend to encourage certain types of behaviour – in the actor as well as the audience? Or is it likely – or even possible – that Shirley's heroic Rosania transferred from the Globe to the Blackfriars stage with little discernible adjustment to characterization or acting style? Questions relating to the use of cosmetics – one of the 'visual tricks of the theatre', 'part of and crucial to the art and design of early modern theatrical production' – also come into play here.[50] Farah Karim-Cooper has written that in the outdoor amphitheatres, male actors 'required a vivid splash of paint' on their faces 'to create a spectacular image of visibility'.[51] Yet as she shows in Chapter 10 above, the conditions of performance in the Jacobean indoor playhouse allowed for a very different 'visual tone', which relied in part on the 'interplay between . . . cosmetic materials and candlelight' and enabled the material representation of 'the luminous display of female beauty'. The proximity of the audience to the boy actors, their faces adorned with glistening makeup beneath 'luminescent candlelight', could affect the representation of female characters – rendering them 'at once saintly and sexually provocative'. In a similar manner, in Chapter 7 above Sarah Dustagheer has shown that the 'glistering' costumes and jewellery, which clad and adorned the bodies under scrutiny on the Blackfriars stage, were used to specific effect in the indoor playhouses. Finally, it is worth considering the theatrical possibilities for lighting effects on the stage of the indoor playhouses – particularly in reference to those plays that appropriate light as a metaphorical emblem for the purity and beauty of heroic women. As lighting levels were variable in the indoor playhouse, theatrical moments such as Evandra's ascents from her underground cave offered rich opportunities for visual effect, which may have been realized by filling the stage with light on her appearance, lending a visual focus to the trope of platonic love: her presence might literally illuminate the theatre. In Chapter 6 above

[50] Farah Karim-Cooper, *Cosmetics in Shakespearean and Renaissance Drama* (Edinburgh University Press, 2006), pp. 137–8.
[51] Ibid., p. 137.

Martin White has explored the influence of light on atmosphere and mood: perhaps the 'sudden burst of light on stage' provided by a hand-held torch might carry with it a symbolic meaning, akin to the connection between light and 'gladness and joy' that Leone di Somi described. In the hybrid genre of tragicomedy, lighting may have proved a distinctive way of exploiting and adding texture to the plays' chequered moods. Similarly, the guiding light of Killigrew's on-stage fire in *The Prisoners* might offer a kind of hypnotic, soothing theatrical effect that serves to bind the narrative together and create a memorable indoor playhouse experience. The staging opportunities that the Caroline repertories provide, and the means by which effects and interpretations could be achieved within the indoor venues, would have affected the ways in which romantic tragicomedy as a genre was experienced. Modern-day revivals may have much to tell us about the performance of female heroism in these smaller, enclosed, significantly quieter venues.

This chapter has explored some of the ways in which the drama of this period evolved within the spaces and performance venues of the indoor theatres, and was written with its practical and cultural opportunities, and limitations, in mind. While Davenant and Killigrew's treatment of heroic women ultimately works to contain any truly radical conclusions, the idealized representation of women on the Caroline stage came to be, and remained, an active theatrical trope and fashionable trend over this period. As such, the indoor playhouse was a venue in which particular ideologies related to gender and politics came to be discussed and played out in an intensive and extended negotiation of the relationship between theatre and women. At once specific, in the courtier playwrights' focus on the discourse and tenets of platonic love, and more broadly suggestive through revivals of old romances and adventure dramas, the role that the theatre took upon itself in addressing the major cultural debates of the time comes through as strongly as ever through the Caroline years.

CHAPTER 13

Reviving the legacy of indoor performance

Bart van Es

The year 1608, in which the King's Men made a commitment to playing at Blackfriars, is widely recognized as a point of stylistic transition for Shakespeare. Plays such as *The Winter's Tale*, *Cymbeline* and *The Tempest*, which are written after this point, have qualities that divide them from the rest of the canon. They are less concerned with the interaction of characters; they are more evenly lyrical, tend towards abstraction, and have a distinctive focus on the generic qualities of romance. Across the late plays there is an emphasis on grand, last-minute revelations and the artifice of such moments is made conspicuous to the audience. As Anne Barton has observed, there is a curious tendency for those on stage to assert the truth of what they are seeing even as they and the onlookers are confronted with what seems palpably unreal.[1]

At first sight it seems logical to connect this distinctive late style with the company's adaptation to a new venue. There are many elements in Shakespeare's final phase of artistic development that match closely with the established tastes of the indoor audience, which had long been watching the Children of the Chapel Royal at Blackfriars. Boy players had performed at this venue since 1600. Music, visual artifice and an emotional distance from the performers were characteristic features of their repertory, and these effects seem to correlate closely with the technical capacities of a space in which sound and light could be more easily controlled. Plays performed at Blackfriars in the years preceding the King's Men's residence, such as *Cupid's Revenge* and *The Faithful Shepherdess*, had already exploited these physical characteristics, as Sarah Dustagheer points out in Chapter 7 above. In other ways too (especially in its self-conscious literary quality) there are continuities between the boys' repertory at Blackfriars and the new qualities of Shakespeare's work after 1608.

1 Anne Barton, '"Enter Mariners Wet": Realism in Shakespeare's Last Plays', in *Essays, Mainly Shakespearean* (Cambridge University Press, 1994), pp. 182–203.

On closer inspection, however, the connection between the late style and the indoor playhouse becomes problematic. First, the chronology is not straightforward. *Pericles* of 1607, which shares most of the features of the late plays, was completed before the company could have given any serious thought to Blackfriars. Shakespeare's change of dramatic technique thus seems at least in part an independent development. Recent critics of the late style (such as Russ McDonald) discover its origins in works as early as *Macbeth* of 1606.[2] Second, the late plays look less like indoor work than they ought to. They are filled with spectacular effects, cannon fire and hoisted descents from the ceiling that have no counterpart in the earlier children's repertory and that were technically ill-suited to the smaller indoor stage.[3] Such tricks would have limited appeal for a coterie audience. If Shakespeare were targeting the fashionable young men of Blackfriars, then the obvious option would have been humoural comedy or politically resonant tragedy of state. Third, and most fatally, 1608 did not in fact see the beginning of adult performance at the newly acquired playhouse. From the end of that year onwards a severe outbreak of plague brought restrictions on playing, which probably lasted until 1610.[4] Even when the pestilence finally abated there are few signs that the Globe had lost its primacy. It was the outdoor playhouse that saw the first performance, for example, of *Henry VIII*. On that occasion the use of stage cannons famously set fire to the building, but it was quickly rebuilt.

The repertory, then, provides little secure evidence for Shakespeare's having adapted his style to the new venue. In addition, the poet's institutional connection to Blackfriars is also less solid than the conventional shorthand of 'Shakespeare's indoor playhouse' or even 'the King's Men's indoor playhouse' implies. Blackfriars was built by James Burbage and it always remained a Burbage property. In August 1608 it was rented out on a

[2] Russ McDonald, *Shakespeare's Late Style* (Cambridge University Press, 2006), pp. 42–6.

[3] Revealingly, the autograph play manuscripts of William Percy indicate that this playwright thought spectacle ill-suited to indoor performance. Percy generally offers alternatives for the two types of venue. In one case, for example, he writes that 'if for actors [i.e. for the outdoor amphitheatre]' there should be 'a huge globe of fire pendant from the roof of the house, with ever and at one a chatting, howling, singing, and laughing between, [and] within the globe, on either side, . . . two angels'. For the indoor stage he recommends instead 'a full moon only appearing aloft on one side through the cloth'. Admittedly, his plans here are for the smaller children's stage at St Paul's, but the contrast applies in a more general sense. See Alnwick Castle MS Plays 507, 'Mahomet and His Heaven', fol. 38b. Effects like storms and the descent of gods were certainly much prized on the outdoor stages. Worcester's/ Queen Anne's Men, for example, seem to have made extensive use of stage machinery for Thomas Heywood plays, such as *Fortune by Land and Sea* and or his dramatizations of classical myth.

[4] See Leeds Barroll, 'Shakespeare and the Second Blackfriars Theater', *Shakespeare Studies* 33 (2005), 164.

long-term basis to Shakespeare and other investors (many of whom were King's Men). Yet no up-front payment was required of the new tenants.[5] The situation was thus very different from that which occurred nine years earlier, when 'housekeepers' directly committed their money to the construction of the Globe. Quite possibly, Shakespeare dropped out of this rental agreement quite quickly, because his name is not listed among those of the other 'housekeepers' in the legal documents relating to occupancy in February 1610.[6] Shakespeare alludes on numerous occasions to the physical fabric of the Globe playhouse, but there is nothing to compare with this at Blackfriars.[7] In various ways the indoor theatre looks like an arm's length connection for the playwright, quite different from his earlier embrace of the public stage.

This might seem like a sour note on which to end a book about Shakespeare and the indoor playhouse. As is generally the case with the late plays, however, nothing is quite what it at first seems. The time that the playwright spent working at Blackfriars was certainly limited, but this does not mean that he was unaffected by its earlier repertory or by the authors who had established their reputations there. Indeed, from a different perspective, the impact of the indoor stage was much stronger and more protracted than the old narrative of sudden conversion in 1608 allows. The rental partnership of August 1608 is not irrelevant to this story. Ironically, becoming a housekeeper in Blackfriars may have made Shakespeare more distant rather than closer to the working actors of his company. The many new men who had joined the fellowship in the Jacobean period were not asked to partake in the rental contract. These individuals were less familiar to Shakespeare and he seems not have written for them with the level of personal adaptation that had marked the early phases of his association with the Chamberlain's/King's Men. That distance from the actors could itself have been a driver in Shakespeare's continuing evolution: pushing him closer to poet-playwrights like John Fletcher and Ben Jonson, who would prove a major influence in the final phase of his career.

5 On the issue of a housekeeper's shares 'for nothing', see Cuthbert Burbage's replies to the petition of Swanston et al., transcribed in C. C. Stopes, *Burbage and Shakespeare's Stage* (London: Alexander Moring, 1913), p. 132.

6 For a discussion of this possibility, see E. K. Chambers, *William Shakespeare: A Study of the Facts and Problems* (2 vols.; Oxford: Clarendon Press, 1930;. Oxford University Press, 1988), vol. II, p. 68.

7 Cases where there is at least a strong likelihood of allusion include *Henry V*'s 'wooden O' (Prologue line 13), *Hamlet*'s 'Hercules and his load' (Folio, 2.2.359–60), *As You Like It*'s 'all the world's a stage' (2.7.140), and *The Tempest*'s 'the great globe itself' (4.1.153).

Shakespeare and the 'little eyases'

By 1608 Shakespeare would have been unusual as a playwright in lacking experience of the indoor houses (whether Blackfriars or St Paul's). Productions there had been running for the best part of a decade. Jonson, Chapman, Daniel, Marston, Middleton, Webster, Dekker, Beaumont and Fletcher had all written for the children, many of them showing a marked preference for their more socially exclusive audience. Shakespeare's commitment as attached playwright of the King's Men had effectively barred him from involvement in this new form of theatre. More than simple inexperience, there are signs of Shakespeare's hostility to what Rosincrance calls the 'late innovation' of child performance. In the Folio text of *Hamlet* the players are forced to travel to Elsinore because of the bad influence of 'an eyrie of children' that has set out to 'berattle the common stages'.[8] Following these insults emanating from St Paul's and Blackfriars, gentlemen 'wearing rapiers' are said to have abandoned the outdoor theatre. In its early years Blackfriars was thus a commercial and artistic threat.

The children had a style of performance that contrasted with that of the adult playhouse and their appetite for controversy had been the primary cause of the so-called Poet's War. It is true that the repertories were not as radically opposed as Alfred Harbage suggested in his influential study, *Shakespeare and the Rival Traditions*. Nevertheless, they were distinctive in a number of ways. First, plays for the children tended to emphasize the autonomy of their authors: allusions to poetic craft were common; many prologues explicitly recorded the intentions of the playwright; and the artifice of the drama as a whole tended to place emphasis on the 'written' quality of these plays. Second, the children's repertory was politically cynical. There was a suspicion of populist sentiment and a total exclusion of plays depicting national triumph. Third, plays at St Paul's and Blackfriars had a youthful, masculine bias. They did not take marriage very seriously and were especially scornful of emotional outpourings from non-aristocratic women; sympathy tended to centre on impecunious gallants in opposition to the merchant class. For these reasons certain staples of the outdoor repertory (such as the history play, citizen comedy and domestic tragedy) were fundamentally ill-suited for child performance. These genres were

[8] The phrase appears in both Q2 and the Folio, but the explanation of the 'little eyases' attack on the 'common stages' appears only in the latter. Compare William Shakespeare, *Hamlet*, ed. Ann Thompson and Neil Taylor, Arden Shakespeare (London: Bloomsbury, 2006), 2.2.296, and *Hamlet: The Texts of 1603 and 1623*, ed. Ann Thompson and Neil Taylor, Arden 3 (London: Arden/ Cengage, 2006), 2.2.331.

mocked in plays like *Histriomastix* (1599), *Jack Drum's Entertainment* (1600) and *The Knight of the Burning Pestle* (1607).[9] As well as satirizing adult productions, such works also derided the lowly, artisan, origins of the players themselves.

In the early years of the decade the King's Men offered a counterblast to this new repertory and to the insults emanating from Blackfriars. At the most obvious level, they mocked Jonson in person through *Satiromastix* (1601), the satire by Thomas Dekker, in which it was jokingly claimed that rivalry from across the river had made the adult players 'custom starved'. While there is nothing in the Shakespeare canon that is as clearly allusive to individuals as *Satiromastix*, there is plenty of evidence that the plays produced by Shakespeare in the first half of the decade involved a deliberate riposte to the kind of work being performed at St Paul's and Blackfriars. Prince Hamlet's attitude to the common players is one aspect of this picture: he eulogizes the passion of the player's description of Hecuba, supports the performers' moral function, and will have them 'well used' because 'they are the abstract and brief chronicles of the time'.[10] At a deeper level, the play itself is also a pointed contrast to the kind of drama that was popular on the indoor stages. Richard Burbage in the lead role was widely heralded by contemporaries for the emotional impact of his performance, something very different from the parodic style favoured by the children in the same genre, for example in Marston's *Antonio's Revenge* (1600).

Many plays written by Shakespeare in the first half-decade of the seventeenth century can be said to tilt at the indoor repertory. In the *Second Part of the Return from Parnassus* (a vacation comedy written in 1601 by students at St John's, Cambridge) it is reported that he had given Jonson 'a pill' in revenge for his calumnies. Some critics have identified coded attacks in *As You Like It* (1600) and *Troilus and Cressida* (1602).[11] The case for these specific references remains speculative, but, looking more widely, an oppositional element is difficult to deny. *Henry V* (written as St Paul's Boys was preparing its first season) could be said to provide a defence of what Harbage called 'Theatre of a Nation': it presents unity across English classes, patriotic endeavour, and its chorus repeatedly invokes traditional audience loyalty for the history plays. Dramas like *Othello*

9 Marston's *Histriomastix* was probably first written for the Middle Temple's Christmas Revels of 1598, but it transferred to St Paul's the following year. For a recent overview, see James P. Bednarz, 'Writing and Revenge: John Marston's *Histriomastix*', *Comparative Drama* 36 (2002), 21–51.

10 *Hamlet* Q2 2.2.461–2.

11 One especially well-documented example of this kind of reading is James P. Bednarz's *Shakespeare and the Poets' War* (New York: Columbia University Press, 2001).

(1603–4) and *All's Well That Ends Well* (1604–7) present faithful and passionate wives of a kind entirely opposite to the women presented on the indoor stages (who tend to be either vulnerable and childlike or cynical in the extreme). Whereas many works written for Blackfriars (including *May Day*, *Michaelmas Term* and *The Dutch Courtesan*) mock husbands who trust in their wives as deluded coxcombs, Shakespeare (alongside others writing for the amphitheatres) tends to present the opposite case. Although there was overlap and although plays occasionally transferred from one kind of playhouse to another, the competing repertories of the so-called 'public' and 'private' playhouses were (at least for the first few seasons) reasonably distinct. Shakespeare's first Globe plays, then, were already influenced by the indoor repertory, but only in the sense that it provided a challenge to which the adult company replied.

Yet, even before the collapse of the Children of the Chapel, the distinction between the Globe and Blackfriars was fading and Shakespeare himself had come much closer to the style of writing that was practised on the indoor stage. *Pericles* of 1607 bears comparison with plays that were performed at Blackfriars in the same period, notably Beaumont and Fletcher's *Cupid's Revenge*. As well as bearing a stylistic closeness to the works of other writers, this play seems to mark the return of co-authorship to Shakespeare's working practice. This method of composition had not been used by him for more than a decade, but *Pericles* can be shown in part to be Robert Wilkins's work.[12] *Timon of Athens*, of around the same period, is likewise co-authored; this time with Thomas Middleton, whose *Five Gallants* (*c.* 1607) had already been a success on the children's stage.[13] *Timon* was written between 1605 and 1607 and shares many of the characteristics of the indoor repertory of that

[12] The definitive study of Wilkins's contribution remains MacDonald P. Jackson, *Defining Shakespeare:* Pericles *as Test Case* (Oxford University Press, 2003). No major study finds evidence of collaboration in Shakespeare plays from 1594 till about a dozen years after. Arguments for the presence of another hand in *Measure for Measure* (1603), *Macbeth* (1606), and *All's Well That Ends Well* (1604–7) do not contradict this statement. In the first two cases, any alterations to the text would have occurred after Shakespeare departed from the company and arguments for co-authorship in *All's Well* are tied to a post-1606 date for this play. Relevant scholarship is found in Gary Taylor and John Jowett, *Shakespeare Reshaped: 1606–1623* (Oxford: Clarendon Press, 1993) and Laurie Maguire and Emma Smith, 'Many Hands: A New Shakespeare Collaboration?', *TLS*, 19 April 2012. Brian Vickers, *Shakespeare, Co-Author: A Historical Study of Five Collaborative Plays* (Oxford University Press, 2002) still provides an authoritative baseline of works in which co-authorship can be detected with confidence.

[13] See MacDonald P. Jackson, *Studies in Attribution: Middleton and Shakespeare* (University of Salzburg Press, 1979); John Jowett, 'The Pattern of Collaboration in *Timon of Athens*', in Brian Boyd (ed.), *Words that Count: Essays on Early Modern Authorship in Honor of MacDonald P. Jackson* (Newark: University of Delaware Press, 2004), pp. 181–205.

period. At a later stage Shakespeare would come to collaborate with Fletcher on *Henry VIII*, *The Two Noble Kinsmen* and possibly *Cardenio*. But even before 1608 it is likely that he had worked together with a playwright who had experience of Blackfriars. In the years immediately before making a financial commitment to the indoor theatre, therefore, Shakespeare was already becoming more connected, both personally and stylistically, to playwrights accustomed to producing witty, intellectually self-conscious material for this space. By this point the boys had also grown substantially older and had acquired a more diverse repertory. In some respects, therefore, the two distinct styles of production had begun to merge.

The Blackfriars repertory and Shakespeare's late style

It is still sometimes said that Shakespeare's late plays are distant and dreamy – the product of rural retirement in Stratford during old age. As Gordon McMullan has argued, however, such thinking is largely a product of romantic dogma about artistic and spiritual development. In the nineteenth and early twentieth century, critics like Dowden attributed the late style to a new contemplative wisdom in the poet.[14] Having suffered the spiritual crisis evinced in the tragedies, Shakespeare was deemed to have reached 'the heights' at the end of his life when he discovered the truths that poets such as Wordsworth and Coleridge would also uncover about a theistic connection between nature and man. To think of late Shakespeare as retired and philosophical is, as McMullan argues, a hang-over from this unwarranted assumption that Shakespeare presents a philosophy of life in his plays. A better explanation for the ethereal, visionary tenor of the late plays might be to stress *connectedness* instead of removal. Dramatic romance, masque and artistic self-consciousness were fashionable. It was not the wise contemplative elder statesmen of the theatre but young up-and-coming writers like Beaumont and Fletcher who were writing this way.

Shakespeare's late plays are close in spirit to existing work in the Blackfriars repertory (and to new plays written by Blackfriars playwrights for the King's Men). They are marked by increasing artistic self-consciousness and by a

[14] Edward Dowden, *Shakspere: A Critical Study of His Mind and Art* (London: 1875; London: Routledge, 1948). G. Wilson Knight's *The Crown of Life: Essays in Interpretation of Shakespeare's Final Plays* (Oxford University Press, 1947; London: Methuen, 1965) and Derek Traversi's *Shakespeare: The Last Phase* (New York: Harcourt, 1953) are developments of this approach.

tendency to make allusion to generic convention conspicuous. This makes them more explicitly 'literary' than the majority of plays written previously for adult companies. On this front, closeness to Jonson and Marston is readily apparent, but it is Fletcher, because of his direct collaboration with Shakespeare, who offers the most telling point of comparison for Shakespeare's late work.

In the past, enquiry into Fletcher's influence on Shakespeare proved inconclusive because it was impossible to determine a reliable sequence of play composition. Beaumont's *The Knight of the Burning Pestle* (1607), Beaumont and Fletcher's *Cupid's Revenge* (1607–8) and Fletcher's *The Faithful Shepherdess* (1608–9) were written around the same time as *Pericles*, which was performed up to a year before the lease of Blackfriars.[15] Beaumont and Fletcher's *Philaster* (1608–9), *The Maid's Tragedy* (1610) and *A King and No King* (1611) sit in a window of composition that overlaps with *Cymbeline* (1610), *The Winter's Tale* (1610) and *The Tempest* (1611).[16] Many works by Fletcher, therefore, could have been preceded by a comparable Shakespeare play. This is a problem for traditional source study. When one comes to consider the wider indoor repertory, however, exact notions of precedence are of less consequence. Shakespeare and Fletcher were closely connected on an institutional level, collaborating together and with other playwrights to produce work for the King's Men. The decision of King James to dissolve the Children of Blackfriars pushed playwrights from different traditions together; firstly, because the King's Men were now the primary employer of literary playwrights, and, secondly, because there was no longer a distinctive indoor repertory for Shakespeare to resist. These pressures moved Shakespeare closer to his playwright contemporaries, above all to Fletcher. At times one poet can be proved beyond doubt to have influenced another, but often it is more a case of simultaneous development along parallel lines.

In recent years critics have examined the closeness between Shakespeare and Fletcher principally through their late collaborations: *Henry VIII*, *Two*

15 For the dates of Fletcher's plays, I here use the table provided by McMullan, *Politics of Unease*, pp. 267–9, although I have also consulted Harbage, *Annals* and the relevant editions and scholarship. For Shakespeare I am using the most recent Arden edition (in this case William Shakespeare and George Wilkins, *Pericles*, ed. Suzanne Gossett, Arden 3 (London: Methuen, 2004), 2), again in consultation with relevant other authorities. The dates cited are a matter of consensus.

16 See note 16. Arden references here are *Cymbeline*, ed. J. M. Nosworthy, Arden 2 (London: Methuen, 1955), p. xv; *The Winter's Tale*, ed. John Pitcher, Arden 3 (London: Methuen, 2010), pp. 88–9; William Shakespeare, *The Tempest*, ed. Virginia Mason Vaughan and Alden T. Vaughan, Arden 3 (London: Methuen, 1999), p. 1. As Nosworthy's text is an old one, consistent comparison has also been made with Roger Warren's more recent edition, William Shakespeare, *Cymbeline* (Oxford University Press, 2008).

Noble Kinsmen and *Cardenio*. Yet connections were established at a literary level much earlier. The two playwrights experimented independently and learnt from each other as they developed a new lyrical mode of drama, one that drew heavily on the vogue for court masques. Fletcher's *The Faithful Shepherdess* was a pioneering work in this genre. Although the play was not a success on its first performance at Blackfriars, it was highly regarded among poets, with the second edition featuring commendatory verses by Chapman, Beaumont and Jonson as well as Nathan Field.

The play anticipates numerous features of later Shakespearean drama. Most obviously, its situation and plot bears comparison with *The Tempest*. The action takes place in a remote pastoral forest in which Fletcher's lead character (a magical healer named Clorin) sets out to reform a cast of sinful men and women through a series of carefully orchestrated theatrical shows, through which figures thought to be dead are revived. Clorin is assisted by a satyr. The words and actions of this pair are remarkably similar to those of Shakespeare's Prospero and Ariel:

> SATYR Shall I dive into the sea
> And bring thee corral making way
> Through the rising waves that fall
> In snowy fleeces? Dearest, shall
> I catch thee wanton fawns or flies
> Whose woven wings the summer dyes
> For many colours? Get thee fruit
> Or steal from heaven old Orpheus's lute?
> All these I venture for and more
> To do her service, all these woods adore.
> CLORIN No other service satyr but thy watch
> About these tricks, lest harmless people catch
> Mischief or sad mischance.[17]

There is little to distinguish the satyr's mastery of the elements and quickness to follow instructions from that seen in Ariel's later responses to Prospero:

> ARIEL All hail, great master; grave sir, hail! I come
> To answer thy best pleasure, be't to fly,
> To swim, to dive into the fire, to ride
> On the curled clouds. To thy strong bidding, task
> Ariel and all his quality.
> PROSPERO Hast thou, spirit, performed to point the tempest

[17] John Fletcher, *The Faithful Shepherdess*, in *The Dramatic Works in the Beaumont and Fletcher Canon*, ed. Fredson Bowers (10 vols.; Cambridge University Press, 1966–89), vol. III, 5.5.250–62. Subsequent references are to this edition and appear in the text.

That I bade thee?
ARIEL To every article.
I boarded the King's ship: now on the beak,
Now in the waist, the deck, in every cabin
I flamed amazement. Sometime I'd divide
And burn in many places – on the topmast,
The yards and bowsprit would I flame distinctly,
Then meet and join.

(*The Tempest* 1.2.189–93)

This is not simply a case of Shakespeare borrowing a plot and set of characters from an earlier drama; there is a much more comprehensive effort here to emulate a theatrical style. Pastoral songs throughout *The Faithful Shepherdess* may be said to provide a template for Shakespeare's. The shepherd song to Pan – 'All ye woods and trees and Bowers, / All ye virtues and ye powers, / That inhabits in the lakes, / In the pleasant springs or brakes' (5.5.218–21) – for example, sounds almost exactly like the verses spoken by Ceres in *The Tempest* three years later on the same stage:

You nymphs, called naiads, of the windring brooks,
With your sedged crowns and ever-harmless looks,
Leave your crisp channels, and on this green land
Answer your summons, Juno does command. (*The Tempest* 4.1.128–31)

Not just for brief stretches but over many hundreds of lines, Fletcher's rhetoric anticipates that of Shakespeare's late plays. Such close parallels with contemporary practice had not been evident in Shakespeare's writing in the preceding decade and a half.

What is true of rhetoric also applies to dramaturgy. Clorin's secluded cabin in *The Faithful Shepherdess*, for example, involves a very similar use of the 'discovery space' at the back of the playhouse to that found later in Prospero's cell or in Paulina's secluded villa in *The Winter's Tale*. The correspondence exists not only at a technical level but also in terms of mood and plotting. In the final act of *The Faithful Shepherdess* '*the curtain is drawn*' (s.d. 5.5.1) to reveal Clorin with the miraculously saved Cloe and Alexis. That action is echoed in *The Tempest*, where 'PROSPERO *discovers* FERDINAND *and* MIRANDA *playing at chess*' (s.d. 5.1.171), and also in *The Winter's Tale*, where Paulina draws a curtain and reveals Hermione, standing like a statue (s.d. 5.3.21).[18] Although *The Tempest* and *The Winter's*

[18] Neither *The Winter's Tale* nor *The Tempest* has stage directions that are directly authorial: for the former, the book was lost and had to be reassembled from actors' parts; for the latter, the Folio text

Tale also played at the Globe, it is revealing to picture these reconciliations as performed at Blackfriars, where they would have exploited the controlled light and intimacy of the venue in exactly the same way. The dramaturgical qualities of *The Faithful Shepherdess*, which were highly innovative, are exploited and extended in Shakespeare's later drama. The use of music, formal dance and visionary tableaux all overlap. If, as Fletcher reports, the indoor audience had failed to understand these effects when they were first used by him for boys' performance, things had certainly moved on a few years later for Shakespeare's plays at the same space. Unsurprisingly, the King's Men took *The Faithful Shepherdess* into their repertory for a successful revival at Blackfriars.

Overlap between *The Faithful Shepherdess* and *The Tempest* extends widely and is one concrete instance of the influence that Fletcher had on Shakespeare's late work. Numerous other examples of such imitation could be cited, including explicit allusion to Beaumont and Fletcher's *Philaster* in Perdita's speech on 'Whitsun pastorals' in *The Winter's Tale*.[19] The real story, however, is more complex than this one-way influence: it is one of close correspondence of plot, scenic effect, characterization and thematic focus across works that joined the repertory at the same time. Here it is the affinities between *Philaster* and *Cymbeline* that are most telling, because there is no absolute certainty about the relative dating of these plays. Their setting, plots, cast of characters and style of verse have much in common, but there is little direct verbal overlap between the two. Rather than homage or plagiarism, this looks simply like closeness between individuals working together for the same company in the same place.

Ashley Thorndike more than a century ago called the plays 'remarkably similar' and described a large number of parallels. As with *The Faithful Shepherdess* and *The Tempest*, the similarity is there at a conceptual level in the world that the dramatists have created. In both cases the action takes place in a vaguely drawn period of classical antiquity that is pitted with anachronistic detail, including dastardly Spaniards and Italians. The

was based on a presentation copy written up by Ralph Crane (see John Jowett, 'New Created Creatures: Ralph Crane and the Stage Directions in *The Tempest*', *Shakespeare Survey* 36 (1983), 107–20). These interventions, however, cannot have altered the nature of the reported action; indeed, being based on report, they are likely to be especially accurate. Although Paulina's action in revealing Hermione is not reported as a stage direction in the Folio, it is evident that this has happened because in the subsequent dialogue both she and Leontes refer to the curtain that has been drawn (*Cymbeline* F, TLN 3255, 3267).

19 Compare Beaumont and Fletcher, *Philaster* 4.6.2–6 and Fletcher's 'Preface to the Reader' in *The Faithful Shepherdess* to *The Winter's Tale* 4.4.129–34. Quotations from *Philaster* are sourced in Francis Beaumont and John Fletcher, *Philaster, or Love Lies a-Bleeding*, ed. Andrew Gurr (Manchester University Press, 2003).

political world of the two plays is decidedly early modern. In spite of references to classical gods, oracles and temples, these are stories about a seventeenth-century island nation that faces a continental threat. Beaumont and Fletcher's Sicily and Shakespeare's Britain are interchangeable most of the time.

Although marked by Jacobean politics, *Philaster* and *Cymbeline* show the influence of earlier Elizabethan literature, above all of Sir Philip Sidney's *Arcadia*. The final acts of these plays are particularly conspicuous in the way they foreground romance convention: a shared concern with sexual purity and corruption; stark reversal and revelation; a focus on nobility of blood. This closeness of purpose results in frequent overlap between the two dramas. Having married against the wishes of the king, the noble Philaster, of Beaumont and Fletcher's play, is easily duped into doubting the virtue of his wife, Arethusa. In exactly the same way as Shakespeare's Posthumus, he decides to murder the heroine (who, as a consequence of defying her father, ends up wandering alone through the wilderness). Both plays then exploit the potential of this shift away from a courtly setting to explore the tension between two different kinds of civility: on the one hand, that which comes from education; on the other, that which is natural and innate. This congruence produces comparable moments of reflection. For example, when the guilt-ridden Philaster is driven off by a 'country fellow', he marvels at this reversal:

> The gods take part against me, could this boor
> have held me else? (Beaumont and Fletcher, *Philaster* 4.5.103–4)

These thoughts are close to those of Shakespeare's Iachimo in the same situation, when apparently worsted by a peasant in British garb:

> I have belied a lady
> The princess of this country; and the air on't
> Revengingly enfeebles me, or could this carl,
> A very drudge of Nature's, have subdued me
> In my profession?' (*Cymbeline* 5.2.2–6)

The similarity here is really a consequence of the depth of thematic overlap and closeness of purpose: in both plays disguise and deception, male and female honour, and court and country are set against each other in a variety of ways.

Because the creators of both plays are concerned with such patterns of contrast, they tend to use characters to a practical purpose, thinking little about 'distinctiveness' or 'interiority' as such. The irascible Cymbeline (just as quick to pass sentences of death and banishment as he is to offer gestures of reconciliation) is thus likewise almost interchangeable with the King of Sicily in Beaumont and Fletcher's play. The two men treat their daughters and unlooked-for sons-in-law with the same wild oscillation between love and disdain. The young men of these plays, in turn, flit between jealous rage and a self-recriminating death wish. Philaster's fatalistic 'it is a joy to die, / I find a recreation in't' (*Philaster* 5.3.102–3) mirrors the statements of Posthumus, who declares himself 'merrier to die than live' (*Cymbeline* 5.4.173). The plays' denouements – a string of confessions overturned finally by the discovery that a dutiful pageboy is really a long-lost daughter – are of a piece.

Whatever their order of composition, *Cymbeline* and *Philaster* must have shared a stage during the 1610 season, both at Blackfriars and at the Globe. By this point the authors of both plays would have been conscious of working for a company that was in the unprecedented position of occupying two playhouses, with subtly different audiences and different characteristics as performance spaces. Attention naturally fixes on Shakespeare and the way he responded to Blackfriars. But it is useful to remember that Fletcher would have made adjustments in the opposite direction, adding amphitheatre production to his thinking whereas previously he had written only for the Chapel boys. It is evident that he and Beaumont did make a careful assessment of this change in circumstance. The high artifice of *Cupid's Revenge* and *The Faithful Shepherdess*, composed exclusively for Blackfriars, gives way to a somewhat more naturalistic mode in *The Maid's Tragedy*, *Philaster* and *A King and No King*. These plays, which accompanied Shakespeare's final productions, are also, in subtle ways, more sympathetic in their portrayal of female characters. All of them focus on the trials of virtuous women in a romance/pastoral setting, much in the way of *Pericles*, *Cymbeline* and *The Winter's Tale*. The effect is different from the more parodic bent of compositions exclusive to Blackfriars, and it is very close in emotional range as well as dramaturgy to that of Shakespeare's 'late style' plays.

The Globe and Blackfriars combined

What all of this suggests is a merging of traditions. Shakespeare gradually incorporated aspects of Blackfriars convention at the same time that indoor poets, notably Fletcher, expanded their focus to incorporate the capacities of adult players. Although this development was accelerated by the King's Men's acquisition of the new venue, it was (for a variety of reasons) already under way before 1608. The fact that Fletcher wrote *The Tamer*

Tamed, a sequel to Shakespeare's *Taming of the Shrew*, at this point further demonstrates this integration of repertories. Shakespeare and Fletcher were working alongside one another, attuning their respective specialisms. This period also sees a closer correspondence between Shakespeare and other playwrights, such as Middleton and Wilkins, with whom he seems to have co-written in the final half-decade of his life. The preponderance of co-authorship tessellates with other indications that Shakespeare was becoming more integrated with the body of professional playwrights and more distant from the actors in the years after 1606.

Blackfriars as a building, then, was not the decisive element that precipitated Shakespeare's change of style around 1607. The alteration came too early to be traced to the new venue and in any case Shakespeare's late plays have only a limited amount in common with those of the Blackfriars children's repertory. All the same, the playwright's late phase of development does bear the stamp of the indoor theatre. In the first few years of the 'innovation' of child performance Shakespeare had responded to the boy actors as competition, but later in the decade his working conditions came closer to those experienced by the playwrights of Blackfriars. In 1604 the number of sharers in the King's company expanded from eight to a dozen and around this time a number of the company's founding sharer-performers retired or died. It is very likely that Shakespeare himself also stopped performing at this juncture.[20] The weight of authority within the company thus moved away from 'mere' players and towards the more exclusive group of 'housekeepers' in the Globe. Control of playhouses became increasingly important in the new century and the lease of Blackfriars in 1608 pushed things further in this direction. The new men in what had become an expanded King's fellowship were not invited to join in the lease agreement. These actors (two of whom had been boy performers under the playhouse's previous managers) never got close to Shakespeare and are left unmentioned in his personal business documents and will. At a later stage some would demand legal redress for being excluded from the select group of playhouse proprietors. Quite possibly there were already expressions of resentment from these working actors when the original agreement was made. If Shakespeare was less close to these players, then this was another factor pushing him into the ambit of playwrights. Poets such as Middleton, Jonson and Fletcher had been employed to write for the

[20] Shakespeare's last recorded appearance as a player is in the acting list that prefaces *Sejanus* (1603) in Jonson's 1616 Folio. Other members of the King's Men are recorded as performers in later plays in the same volume (for example *Volpone* and *Sejanus*), so Shakespeare's absence is significant.

children, but after 1608 they increasingly came to write for the King's Men. Shakespeare was likely to feel the influence of contemporary playwrights more strongly as the repertories of the indoor stage and the amphitheatres converged.

Reviving the legacy of performance at Blackfriars thus has a complex, layered, significance in understanding Shakespeare, not just at the indoor playhouse but also at the Globe. We need to think of Shakespeare as having had a protracted and changing relationship with Blackfriars, stretching from early hostility, through accommodation, to absorption. In tracking this relationship it is important to note his changing institutional connections: with actors, with playwrights and with the physical buildings of the London theatre world. Shakespeare's final play, *The Two Noble Kinsmen*, provides a neat ending to this story. Its title page refers solely to performance at Blackfriars and, in all likelihood, the Prologue's reference to 'our losses' (line 32) laments the destruction of the Globe by fire. This, then, was the only play in the Shakespeare canon written for indoor performance alone. In every way it marks the culmination of elements that we associate with Shakespeare's Blackfriars period: it is co-authored, stylized and lyrical, and highly dependent on theatrical ceremony. It was also highly modish, picking up on the taste for Cervantean irony that was being catered to by a swathe of professional playwrights at this time.[21] Judging from the state of the script, Shakespeare may well have been absent from London when he composed his portions of it, but this too is appropriate.[22] A physical and institutional removal from the business of playing was itself a contributory factor in the development of a more normative mode of writing. Paradoxically, it was Shakespeare's distance from Blackfriars as much as his closeness to it that helped to create the late style.

21 For an exploration of this trend, see Bart van Es, 'Late Shakespeare and the Middle Ages', in Helen Cooper, Ruth Morse and Peter Holland (eds.), *Shakespeare's Middle Ages* (Cambridge University Press, 2013).

22 See William Shakespeare, *The Two Noble Kinsmen*, ed. Lois Potter, Arden 3 (London: Cengage, 1997), 32, on reasons for believing the playwrights were working apart and the hypothesis that Shakespeare was in Stratford at this time.

Appendix: list of plays performed at indoor playhouses, 1575–1642

Sarah Dustagheer

This appendix focusses on the six longest-running indoor professional playhouses of the early modern period: Paul's, the first Blackfriars, the second Blackfriars, Whitefriars, the Phoenix and Salisbury Court. It includes extant plays whose *first performance* (rather than composition) can be ascribed, with some confidence, to a particular playhouse. The list for each playhouse does not include plays that were originally performed elsewhere and subsequently revived at that playhouse. The information for all playhouses has been derived from E. K. Chambers, *The Elizabethan Stage* (4 vols.; Oxford, 1953); G. E. Bentley, *The Jacobean and Caroline Stage* (7 vols.; Oxford, 1941–68); Alfred Harbage, *Annals of English Drama, 975–1700*, revised by S. Schoenbaum and Sylvia Stoler Wagonheim (3rd edn; London: Routledge, 1989); and Andrew Gurr, 'Appendix: A Select List of Plays and their Playhouses', *The Shakespearean Stage, 1574–1642* (4th edn; Cambridge University Press, 2009). The following studies have been consulted for specific playhouses: Reavley Gair, *The Children of Paul's: The Story of a Theatre Company, 1553–1608* (Cambridge University Press, 1982); Irwin Smith, *Shakespeare's Blackfriars Playhouse* (New York University Press, 1964); Lucy Munro, *Children of the Queen's Revels: A Jacobean Theatre Repertory* (Cambridge University Press, 2005); Roslyn L. Knutson, *The Repertory of Shakespeare's Company, 1594–1613* (Fayetteville: University of Arkansas Press, 1991); Andrew Gurr, *The Shakespeare Company, 1594–1642* (Cambridge University Press, 2004); Mary Bly, *Queer Virgins and Virgin Queans on the Early Modern Stage* (Oxford University Press, 2000); and Eleanor Collins, 'Queen Henrietta's Men and the Cockpit Repertory, 1625–1637', unpublished doctoral thesis, University of Birmingham, 2009. Although the King's Men performed both at the Globe *and* the Blackfriars from 1609, I list all their post-1609 plays and do not attempt to identify which plays were or were not transferred between the two spaces. For each play I have given the approximate earliest year for first performance rather than composition or printing. In some cases, the names of the authors are debatable, but I have followed general consensus. All plays are listed in an approximate chronological order. The companies who performed at each playhouse are listed in chronological order of occupation and each play is given a company attribution if multiple companies have used one playhouse.

PAUL'S (PAUL'S CHILDREN)

Play	Playwright	Date
Gallathea	Lyly	1585
Endimion	Lyly	1588
Midas	Lyly	1589
Love's Metamorphosis	Lyly	1589
Mother Bombie	Lyly	1589
Antonio and Mellida	Marston	1599
Jack Drums Entertainment	Marston	1600
The Wisdom of Doctor Dodypoll	Anon.	1600
The Maid's Metamorphosis	Anon.	1600
Antonio's Revenge	Marston	1600
Blurt Master Constable	Dekker	1601
What You Will	Marston	1601
Satiromastix	Dekker	1601
Arabia Sitiens	Percy	1601
The Cuckqueanes and Cuckolds Errants	Percy	1601
A Forest Tragedy in Vacunium	Percy	1602
The Aphrodysial	Percy	1602
The Faery Pastorall	Percy	1603
The Phoenix	Middleton	1603
Westward Ho!	Dekker and Webster	1604
A Trick to Catch the Old One	Middleton	1605
Northward Ho!	Dekker and Webster	1605
Michaelmas Term	Middleton	1605
A Mad World my Masters	Middleton	1606
The Woman Hater	Beaumont and Fletcher	1606
The Puritan	Middleton	1606

FIRST BLACKFRIARS (CHAPEL CHILDREN)

Play	Playwright	Date
The Wars of Cyrus	Anon.	1576
The Arraignment of Paris	Peele	1581
Campaspe	Lyly	1583
Sappho and Phao	Lyly	1583
Dido Queen of Carthage	Marlowe	1585

SECOND BLACKFRIARS (CHILDREN OF THE QUEEN'S REVELS AND KING'S MEN, 1609–42)

Play	Playwright	Date
Cynthia's Revels (CQR)	Jonson	1600
Poetaster (CQR)	Jonson	1601
May Day (CQR)	Chapman	1601
Sir Giles Goosecap (CQR)	Chapman	1601
The Gentleman Usher (CQR)	Chapman	1602
The Malcontent (CQR)	Marston	1602
Law Tricks (CQR)	Day	1603
The Dutch Courtesan (CQR)	Marston	1604
Bussy D'Ambois (CQR)	Chapman	1604
The Fawn (CQR)	Marston	1604
Philotas (CQR)	Daniel	1604
The Widow's Tears (CQR)	Chapman	1604
Monsieur D'Olive (CQR)	Chapman	1605
Eastward Ho! (CQR)	Chapman, Marston and Jonson	1605
The Fleer (CQR)	Sharpham	1605
The Isle of Gulls (CQR)	Day	1606
The Knight of the Burning Pestle (CQR)	Beaumont	1607
Your Five Gallants (CQR)	Middleton	1607
Cupid's Revenge (CQR)	Beaumont and Fletcher	1607
The Faithful Shepherdess (CQR)	Beaumont and Fletcher	1608
The Coxcomb (CQR)	Beaumont and Fletcher	1608
The Conspiracy and Tragedy of Charles Duke of Byron (CQR)	Chapman	1608
Philaster (KM)	Beaumont and Fletcher	1609
Cymbeline (KM)	Shakespeare	1609
The Maid's Tragedy (KM)	Beaumont and Fletcher	1610
Valentinian (KM)	Beaumont and Fletcher	1610
The Winter's Tale (KM)	Shakespeare	1610
Bonduca (KM)	Beaumont and Fletcher	1610
Catiline (KM)	Jonson	1610
A King and No King (KM)	Beaumont and Fletcher	1611
The Tempest (KM)	Shakespeare	1611
The Lady's Tragedy (KM)	Middleton	1611
The Captain (KM)	Beaumont and Fletcher	1612
Henry VIII (KM)	Shakespeare and Fletcher	1612
The Duchess of Malfi (KM)	Webster	1613
The Two Noble Kinsmen (KM)	Shakespeare and Fletcher	1613
The Witch (KM)	Middleton	1613
More Dissemblers Besides Women (KM)	Middleton	1614
Love's Pilgrimage (KM)	Beaumont and Fletcher	1615
Thierry and Theodoret (KM)	Fletcher and Massinger	1615
The Laws of Candy (KM)	Ford	1615

Beggar's Bush (KM)	Fletcher	1615
The Devil is an Ass (KM)	Jonson	1616
The Queen of Corinth (KM)	Fletcher	1616
The Widow (KM)	Middleton	1616
The Loyal Subject (KM)	Fletcher	1616
The Knight of Malta (KM)	Fletcher, Field and Massinger	1616
The Fatal Dowry (KM)	Field and Massinger	1616
The Chances (KM)	Fletcher	1617
The Mad Lover (KM)	Fletcher	1617
The Bloody Brother (KM)	Fletcher and Massinger	1617
The Humourous Lieutenant (KM)	Fletcher	1618
The Little French Lawyer (KM)	Fletcher and Massinger	1618
The Duke of Milan (KM)	Massinger	1618
Sir John van Olden Barnavelt (KM)	Fletcher and Massinger	1619
Women Pleased (KM)	Fletcher	1619
The Custom of the Country (KM)	Fletcher and Massinger	1619
The Double Marriage (KM)	Fletcher and Massinger	1619
The False One (KM)	Fletcher and Massinger	1619
The Island Princess (KM)	Fletcher	1619
The Pilgrim (KM)	Fletcher	1621
The Wild Goose Chase (KM)	Fletcher	1621
The Prophetess (KM)	Fletcher and Massinger	1622
The Sea Voyage (KM)	Fletcher and Massinger	1622
The Spanish Curate (KM)	Fletcher and Massinger	1622
Osmond the Great Turk (KM)	Carlell	1622
The Wandering Lovers (KM)	Fletcher (and Massinger?)	1623
The Maid in the Mill (KM)	Fletcher and Rowley	1623
Rule a Wife and Have a Wife (KM)	Fletcher	1624
A Wife for a Month (KM)	Fletcher	1624
The Unnatural Combat (KM)	Massinger	1624
A Game at Chess (KM)	Middleton	1624
The Elder Brother (KM)	Fletcher and Massinger	1625
The Fair Maid of the Inn (KM)	Fletcher (and Massinger, Webster, Rowley and/or Ford?)	1626
The Staple of News (KM)	Jonson	1626
The Roman Actor (KM)	Massinger	1626
The Cruel Brother (KM)	Davenant	1627
The Lover's Melancholy (KM)	Ford	1628
The Deserving Favourite (KM)	Carlell	1628
The Soddered Citizen (KM)	Clavell	1628
The Northern Lass (KM)	Brome	1629
The Just Italian (KM)	Davenant	1629
The New Inn (KM)	Jonson	1629
The Picture (KM)	Massinger	1629
The Inconstant Lady (KM)	Wilson	1629
The Broken Heart (KM)	Ford	1630
The Queen's Exchange (KM)	Brome	1631
Believe As You List (KM)	Massinger	1631

The Emperor of the East (KM)	Massinger	1631
The Swisser (KM)	Wilson	1631
The Novella (KM)	Brome	1631
The Magnetic Lady (KM)	Jonson	1632
The City Madam (KM)	Massinger	1632
The Guardian (KM)	Massinger	1633
The Late Lancashire Witches (KM)	Brome	1634
Love and Honour (KM)	Davenant	1634
The Wits (KM)	Davenant	1634
Albertus Wallenstein (KM)	Glapthorne	1634
A Very Woman (KM)	Massinger	1634
A Challenge for Beauty (KM)	Heywood	1634
News from Plymouth (KM)	Davenant	1635
The Platonic Lovers (KM)	Davenant	1635
The Conspiracy (KM)	Killigrew, Henry	1635
1 and 2 Arviragus and Philicia (KM)	Carlell	1635
The Bashful Lover (KM)	Massinger	1637
The Lost Lady (KM)	Berkeley	1637
The City Match (KM)	Mayne	1637
Aglaura (KM)	Suckling	1637
The Goblins (KM)	Suckling	1637
The Passionate Lovers I and II (KM)	Carlell	1637
The Doubtful Heir (KM)	Shirley	1638
The Fair Favourite (KM)	Davenant	1638
The Unfortunate Lovers (KM)	Davenant	1638
The Distresses/Spanish Lovers (KM)	Davenant	1639
Brennoralt (KM)	Suckling	1639
The Country Captain (KM)	Cavendish and Shirley	1639
The Variety (KM)	Cavendish	1639
The Imposture (KM)	Shirley	1640
Queen of Aragon (KM)	Habington	1640
The Sophy (KM)	Denham	1641
The Brothers (KM)	Shirley	1641
The Cardinal (KM)	Shirley	1641
The Sisters (KM)	Shirley	1642

WHITEFRIARS (CHILDREN OF THE KING'S REVELS AND CHILDREN OF THE QUEEN'S REVELS)

Play	Playwright	Date
The Two Maids of More-Clacke (KR)	Armin	1606
The Turk (KR)	Mason	1607
Cupid's Whirligig (KR)	Sharpham	1607
The Dumb Knight (KR)	Markham and Machin	1607
The Family of Love (KR)	Barry	1607

Ram Alley (KR)	Barry	1608
Humour Out of Breath (KR)	Day	1608
A Woman is a Weathercock (CQR)	Field	1609
Epicoene (CQR)	Jonson	1609
The Revenge of Bussy D'Ambois (CQR)	Chapman	1610
The Scornful Lady (CQR)	Beaumont and Fletcher	1610
A Christian Turned Turk (CQR)	Daborne	1611
Amends for Ladies (CQR)	Field	1611
The Insatiate Countess (CQR)	Marston	1611

THE PHOENIX (QUEEN ANNE'S MEN, PRINCE CHARLES' MEN, LADY ELIZABETH'S MEN, QUEEN HENRIETTA MARIA'S MEN AND BEESTON'S BOYS)

Play	Playwright	Date
The Martyred Solider (QA)	Shirley, H.	1618
All Lost by Lust (QA)	Rowley	1619
The Witch of Edmonton (PCM)	Dekker, Ford and Rowley	1621
The Changeling (LE)	Middleton and Rowley	1622
The Spanish Gypsy (LE)	Middleton and Rowley	1623
The Welsh Ambassador (LE)	Dekker	1623
The Bondman (LE)	Massinger	1623
The City Night-Cap (LE)	Davenport	1624
The Sun's Darling (LE)	Ford and Dekker	1624
The Renegado (LE)	Massinger	1624
New Trick to Cheat the Devil (LE)	Davenport	1624
A New Way to Pay Old Debts (LE)	Massinger	1625
Love Tricks, or, The School of Compliment (LE)	Shirley	1625
A Maidenhead Well Lost (QHM)	Heywood	1625
The Maid's Revenge (QHM)	Shirley	1626
The Wedding (QHM)	Shirley	1626
The English Traveller (QHM)	Heywood	1627
The Great Duke of Florence (QHM)	Massinger	1627
King John and Mathilda (QHM)	Davenport	1628
The Witty Fair One (QHM)	Shirley	1628
The Grateful Servant (QHM)	Shirley	1629
The Fair Maid in the West II (QHM)	Heywood	1630
The Humourous Courtier (QHM)	Shirley	1631
Love's Cruelty (QHM)	Shirley	1631
The Traitor (QHM)	Shirley	1631
Love's Sacrifice (QHM)	Ford	1631
'Tis Pity She's a Whore (QHM)	Ford	1631
The Ball (QHM)	Shirley	1631
Hyde Park (QHM)	Shirley	1632
Perkin Warbeck (QHM)	Ford	1632

The Prisoners (QHM)	Killigrew	1632
A Tale of a Tub (QHM)	Jonson	1633
Covent Garden (QHM)	Nabbes	1633
The Bird in a Cage (QHM)	Shirley	1633
The Gamester (QHM)	Shirley	1633
The Young Admiral (QHM)	Shirley	1633
The Shepherd's Holiday (QHM)	Rutter	1633
Love's Mistress (QHM)	Heywood	1634
The Example (QHM)	Shirley	1634
The Opportunity (QHM)	Shirley	1634
The Antiquary (QHM)	Marmion	1634
Fancies Chaste and Noble (QHM)	Ford	1635
Hannibal and Scipio (QHM)	Nabbes	1635
The Coronation (QHM)	Shirley	1635
The Lady of Pleasure (QHM)	Shirley	1635
Claracilla (QHM)	Killigrew	1635
The Hollander (QHM)	Glapthorne	1636
The Duke's Mistress (QHM)	Shirley	1636
Wit in a Constable (BB)	Glapthorne	1636
I The Cid (BB)	Rutter	1637
Argalus and Parthenia (BB)	Glapthorne	1637
The Lady's Privilege (BB)	Glapthorne	1638
The Cunning Lovers (BB)	Brome, Alexander	1638
The Lady's Trial (BB)	Ford	1638
The Bride (BB)	Nabbes	1638
The Bloody Banquet (BB)	Drue	1639
The Court Beggar (BB)	Brome	1639
The Arcadia (BB)	Shirley	1640
A Jovial Crew (BB)	Brome	1641

SALISBURY COURT (KING'S REVELS, PRINCE CHARLES'S II, QUEEN HENRIETTA MARIA)

Play	Playwright	Date
The Rebellion (KR)	Rawlins	1629
The City Wit, or The Woman Wears the Breeches (KR)	Brome	1630
Amyntas (KR)	Randolph	1630
The Muses Looking Glass (KR)	Randolph	1630
Changes, or Love in a Maze (KR)	Shirley	1631
Holland's Leaguer (PC II)	Marmion	1631
A Fine Companion (PC II)	Marmion	1632
Messallina (KR)	Richards	1634
The New Academy, or The New Exchange (KR)	Brome	1635
The Lady's Mother (KR)	Glapthorne	1635
The Queen and the Concubine (KR)	Brome	1635
The Sparagus Garden (KR)	Brome	1635

The Antipodes (QHM)	Brome	1636
The English Moor (QHM)	Brome	1637
Microcosmus (QHM)	Nabbes	1637
The Noble Stranger (QHM)	Sharpe	1638
The Fatal Contract (QHM)	Heminges	1638

Bibliography

The references in this section have been organized in alphabetical order. The archives used by each author are listed first, followed by early books and current scholarly books and articles. With the plays, in some cases both the original text (available through Early English Books Online) and a recent edition are cited. All three of the current Jonson editions are cited, although the Cambridge edition came out too late to be used by our authors. For the earlier English books, no publisher is cited.

ARCHIVES

Calendar of State Papers Relating to English Affairs in the Archives of Venice, Volume 15: 1617–1619 (1909), 'Venice: January 1618, 21–31', ed. Allen B. Hinds, pp. 108–26

Ground Floor Plan of Corpus Christi College, November 2012. James Campbell Associates

Jackson, Henry, Letter, Cambridge, Corpus Christi College, CCCC, MS 304

Malone Society. *Collections, vol. II. Pt 1.* 'Blackfriars Records', ed. Albert Feuillerat (Oxford: H. Hart, 1913)

Vol. II. Pt. 3. 'Records: The Lord Chamberlain's Office', ed. E. K. Chambers (Oxford: Malone Society Publications, 1931)

Vol. X. 'Dramatic Records in the Declared Accounts of the Office of Works 1560–1640', ed. F. P. Wilson and R. F. Hill (Oxford: Malone Society Publications, 1977)

Vol. XIII. 'Jacobean and Caroline Revels Accounts, 1603–1642', ed. W. R. Streitberger (Oxford: Malone Society Publications, 1986)

Public Record Office (PRO) E 315/3242, /3243. National Archives, Kew

SCGL/PHO/C/023/1/2–7; SC/GL/NOB/C/023–023/1; SC/GL/NOB/C/023/1–9. London Metropolitan Archive

Shakespeare's Globe Archive, Academic Committee correspondence

Transactions of the Royal Historical Society, n.s. 6 (1892), 26–81 (29)

BOOKS AND ARTICLES

Airs, Malcolm. *The Tudor and Jacobean Country House: A Building History* (Stroud: Allan Sutton, 1995)

Anon. *King Leir*. Q1 (London, 1605)

Anon. *A Warning for Fair Women*. Q1 (London, 1599)

Astington, John H. *Actors and Acting in Shakespeare's Time* (Cambridge University Press, 2010)

'Counterweights in Elizabethan Stage Machinery', *Theatre Notebook* 41 (1987), 18–24

English Court Theatre 1558–1642 (Cambridge University Press, 1999)

'The Wits Illustration, 1662', *Theatre Notebook* 47 (1993), 122–40

Auslander, Philip. *Liveness: Performance in a Mediatized Culture* (London: Routledge, 1999)

Austern, Linda Phyllis. *Music in English Children's Drama of the Later Renaissance* (Philadelphia: Gordon & Breach, 1992)

Austin, William. *Haec Homo, Wherein the Excellency of the Creation of Woman is described by way of an Essay* (London, 1639)

Averill, William. *A Dyall for Dainty Darlings, roct in the cradle of securitie* (London, 1584)

Babington, Caroline, Tracy Manning and Sophie Stewart. *Our Painted Past. Wall Paintings of English Heritage* (London: Heritage Books, 1999)

Bacon, Francis, James Spedding, Robert Leslie Ellis and Douglas Denon Heath (eds.). 'Of Masques and Triumphs', *The Essayes or Counsels* (1625)

'Of Masques and Triumphs', in John Pitcher (ed.), *Francis Bacon: The Essays* (Harmondsworth: Penguin, 1985)

The Works of Francis Bacon (Boston, MA: Riverside Press, 1860)

Bailey, Rebecca. *Staging the Old Faith: Queen Henrietta Maria and the Theatre of Caroline England* (Manchester University Press, 2009)

Barlow, G. F. 'Wenceslas Hollar and Christopher Beeston's Phoenix Theatre in Drury Lane', *Theatre Research International* 13.1 (1988), 30–44

Barnwell, P. S., and A. T. Adams. *The House Within: Interpreting Medieval Houses in Kent* (London: Historical Monuments Commission, 1994)

Barroll, J. Leeds. 'Shakespeare and the Second Blackfriars Theater', *Shakespeare Studies* 33 (2005), 156–70

Barroll, J. Leeds, Alexander Leggatt, Richard Hosley and Alvin Kernan. *The Revels History of Drama in English*. Vol. III, *1576–1613* (4 vols.; London: Routledge, 1975)

Barton, Anne. '"Enter Mariners Wet": Realism in Shakespeare's Last Plays', in *Essays, Mainly Shakespearean* (Cambridge University Press, 1994), pp. 182–203

Bateman, Stephen. *A christall glasse of christian reformation wherein the godly maye beholde the coloured abuses used in this our present tyme* (London, 1569)

Bawcutt, N. W. *The Control and Censorship of Caroline Drama: The Records of Sir Henry Herbert, Master of the Revels 1623–73* (Oxford: Clarendon Press, 1996)

Beaumont, Francis. *The Knight of the Burning Pestle* (London, 1613). Ed. Sheldon P. Zitner (Manchester University Press, 1984)

Beaumont, Francis, and John Fletcher. *The Coxcomb*, in *Comedies and Tragedies Written by Francis Beaumont and John Fletcher* (1647)

Cupid's Revenge (London, 1615)

The Dramatic Works in the Beaumont and Fletcher Canon, ed. Fredson Bowers (10 vols.; Cambridge University Press, 1966–89)

Philaster. Q1 (London, 1620), Q2 (London, 1622). Ed. Andrew Gurr (London: Methuen, 1969); ed. Suzanne Gossett (London: A&C Black, 2009)

Bednarz, James P. *Shakespeare and the Poets' War* (New York: Columbia University Press, 2001)

'Writing and Revenge: John Marston's *Histriomastix*', *Comparative Drama* 36 (2002), 21–51

Behn, Aphra. *The Rover* (1677)

Benjamin, Walter. *The Work of Art in the Age of its Technological Reproducibility and Other Writings on Media* (Cambridge, MA: Harvard University Press, 2008)

Bentley, Gerald Eades. *The Jacobean and Caroline Stage* (7 vols.; Oxford: Clarendon Press, 1940–68)

'Shakespeare and the Blackfriars Theatre', *Shakespeare Survey* 1 (1948), 38–50

Bergman, Gosta M. *Lighting in the Theatre* (Stockholm: Almqvist & Wiksell International, 1977)

Berry, Herbert. 'Playhouses, 1560–1660', in Glynne Wickham, Herbert Berry and William Ingram (eds.), *English Professional Theatre, 1530–1660* (Cambridge University Press, 2000), pp. 287–674

'The Stage and Boxes at Blackfriars', *Studies in Philology* 63 (1966), 163–86

Blesser, Barry, and Linda-Ruth Salter. *Spaces Speak, Are You Listening? Experiencing Aural Architecture* (Cambridge, MA: MIT Press, 2007)

Bodenham, John. *Belvidere, or the Garden of Muses* (London, 1600)

Bowsher, Julian, and Pat Miller. *The Rose and the Globe – Playhouses of Shakespeare's Bankside, Southwark. Excavations 1988–91* (Monograph 48; London: MOLA, 2009)

Brandt, George W., and Wiebe Hogendoorn (eds.). *German and Dutch Theatre, 1600–1848* (Cambridge University Press, 1993)

Brennan, Teresa. *The Transmission of Affect* (Ithaca, NY: Cornell University Press, 2004)

Brett-James, Norman G. *The Growth of Stuart London* (London: Allen and Unwin, 1935)

Bristow, Ian C. *Architectural Colour in British Interiors, 1615–1840* (New Haven, CT: Paul Mellon Centre Publications, 1996)

Brown, John Russell. 'Staging Shakespeare's Plays: A Choice of Theatres', *New Theatre Quarterly* 26.2 (2010), 115–20

Bruyère, Jean de La. *Characters*, trans. Jean Stewart (Harmondsworth: Penguin, 1970)

Buoni, Thomas. *The Problemes of Beautie and humane affections*, trans. S. L. Gent (London, 1606)

Burnell, Henry. *Landgartha*. Q1 (Dublin, 1641)

Butler, Martin. *Theatre and Crisis, 1632–1642* (Cambridge University Press, 1984)

Callaghan, Dympna. *Shakespeare without Women: Representing Race and Gender on the Renaissance Stage* (London: Routledge, 1999)

Carson, Christie, and Farah Karim-Cooper (eds.). *Shakespeare's Globe: A Theatrical Experiment* (Cambridge University Press, 2010)

Chalmers, Hero, Julie Sanders and Sophie Tomlinson (eds.). *Three Seventeenth-Century Plays on Women and Performance* (Manchester University Press, 2006)

Chambers, E. K. *The Elizabethan Stage* (4 vols.; Oxford: Clarendon Press, 1923)

William Shakespeare: A Study of the Facts and Problems (2 vols.; Oxford: Clarendon Press, 1930; reprinted Oxford University Press, 1988)

Chapman, George. *The Memorable Masque*, in David Lindley (ed.), *Court Masques: Jacobean and Caroline Entertainments 1605–1640* (Oxford University Press, 1995)

Chapman, George, Ben Jonson and John Marston. *Eastward Ho!* (London, 1605)

Monsieur D'Olive (London, 1606)

Charles, F. W. B., with Mary Charles. *Conservation of Timber Buildings* (London: Taylor & Francis, 1995)

Chettle, Henry. *Kind-Harts Dream* (London, 1604)

Chettle, Henry, Thomas Dekker and William Haughton. *Patient Grissil*. Q1 (London, 1603)

Chitham, Robert, *The Classical Orders of Architecture* (2nd edn; London: Architectural Press, 2005)

Clark, Stuart. *Vanities of the Eye: Vision in Early Modern European Culture* (Oxford University Press, 2007)

Colebrook, Claire. *Giles Deleuze* (New York: Routledge, 2002)

Collins, Eleanor. 'From Court to Cockpit: *The Prisoners* and *Claracilla* in Repertory', in Philip Major (ed.), *Thomas Killigrew: Collected Essays* (Ashgate: Farnham, 2013)

Colvin, H. *The History of the King's Works* (6 vols.; London: HMSO, 1963–83)

Corkhill, Thomas. *A Glossary of Wood* (London: Stobart & Son, 1979)

Courtenay, L. T., and R. Mark. 'The Westminster Hall Roof: A Historiographic and Structural Study', *Journal of the Society of Architectural Historians* 46 (1987), 374–93

Cunningham, Peter. 'The Whitefriars Theatre, the Salisbury Court Theatre, and the Duke's Theatre in Dorset Gardens', *Shakespeare Society Papers* 4 (1849), 95–100

Daileader, Celia R. *Eroticism on the Renaissance Stage* (Cambridge University Press, 1998)

Davenant, William. *The Cruel Brother*. Q1 (London, 1630)

Love and Honour (London, 1634)

The Temple of Love: A Masque (London, 1634)

The Wits. Q1 (London, 1636)
Davies, John. *The Poems of Sir John Davies*, ed. Robert Krueger (Oxford University Press, 1975)
Davies, Phillip. *Lost London, 1870–1945* (London: English Heritage Publishing, 2009)
Dawson, Anthony B. 'Performance and Participation', in *The Culture of Playgoing in Shakespeare's England: A Collaborative Debate* (Cambridge University Press, 2001), pp. 11–38
Dawson, Lesel. '"New Sects of Love": Neoplatonism and Constructions of Gender in Davenant's *The Temple of Love* and *The Platonick Lovers*', *Early Modern Literary Studies* 8.1 (2002), 4.1–36. Accessed 29/10/2013. http://extra.shu.ac.uk/emls/08–1/dawsnew.htm
Day, Barry. *This Wooden 'O'. Shakespeare's Globe Reborn* (London: Oberon Books, 1996)
Day, John. *Law Tricks* (London, 1608)
De Vries, Jan Vredeman. *Perspective* (Amsterdam, 1604)
Debord, Guy. *Society of the Spectacle* (Detroit: Black & Red, 1983)
Dekker, Thomas. *Blurt Master Constable* (London, 1602)
The Gull's Hornbook (London, 1609)
The Seven Deadly Sins of London, ed. Edward Arber (London, 1879)
Dessen, Alan C. *Recovering Shakespeare's Vocabulary* (Cambridge University Press, 1995)
Digges, Leonard. 'Upon Master WILLIAM SHAKESPEARE, the Deceased Authour, and his POEMS', in William Shakespeare, *Poems* (1640)
Donaldson, Ian. *Ben Jonson: A Life* (Oxford University Press, 2011)
Douglas, Audrey, and Peter Greenfield (eds.). *Cumberland, Westmorland, Gloucestershire* (University of Toronto Press, 1986)
Dowden, Edward. *Shakspere: A Critical Study of His Mind and Art* (London, 1875; London: Routledge, 1948)
Dutton, Richard. 'Mastering the Revels', in *The Regulation and Censorship of English Renaissance Drama* (London: Macmillan, 1991)
Dutton, Richard, and Jean E. Howard (eds.). *A Companion to Shakespeare's Works.* Vol. IV, *The Poems, Problem Comedies, Late Plays* (4 vols.; Oxford: Blackwell, 2005)
The Oxford Handbook of Early Modern Theatre (Oxford University Press, 2009)
Eccles, Christine. *The Rose Theatre* (London: Nick Hern, 1990)
Edmond, Mary. *Rare Sir William Davenant* (Manchester University Press, 1987)
Egan, Gabriel. 'Hearing or Seeing a Play?: Evidence of Early Modern Theatrical Terminology'. Accessed http://gabrielegan.com/publications/Egan2001k.htm
Egerton, Judy. *Wright of Derby* (London: Tate Publishing, 1990)
Elliot, John R., Jnr, Alan H. Nelson, Alexandra S. Johnston and Diana Wyatt (eds.). *Records of Early English Drama: Oxford* (2 vols.; University of Toronto Press, 2004)
Enterline, Lynn. *Shakespeare's Schoolroom: Rhetoric, Discipline, Emotion* (Philadelphia: University of Pennsylvania Press, 2012)

Es, Bart van, 'Late Shakespeare and the Middle Ages', in *Medieval Shakespeare: Pasts and Presents*, ed. Helen Cooper, Ruth Morse and Peter Holland (Cambridge University Press, 2013)

Evans, Henry. Lawsuit against Richard Burbage, John Heminges and others, 1600. Quoted in Frederick Fleay, *A Chronicle History of the London Stage, 1559–1642* (London: Reeves & Turner, 1890)

Fennor, William. *Pluto his Travailes* (London, 1612)

Ficino, Marsilio. *Commentary on Plato's Symposium*, in *Philosophies in Art and Beauty: Selected Readings in Aesthetics from Plato to Heidegger*, ed. Albert Hofstadler and Richard Kuhns (University of Chicago Press, 1964)

Field, Nathan, and Philip Massinger. *The Fatal Dowry*. Q1 (London, 1632)

Finlay, Roger. *Population and Metropolis: The Demography of London 1580–1650* (Cambridge University Press, 1981)

Firenzuola, Agnolo. *On the Beauty of Women* (1541), trans. Konrad Eisenbichler and Jacqueline Murray (Philadelphia: University of Pennsylvania Press, 1992)

Fitzgeffrey, Henry. *Satires and Satirical Epigrams: With Certain Observations at Blackfriars* (London, 1617)

Flecknoe, Richard. *Miscellania* (London, 1653)

Fletcher, John. *Bonduca*, in *Comedies and Tragedies written by Francis Beaumont and John Fletcher*. F1 (London, 1647)

The Tragedy of Valentinian, in *Comedies and Tragedies written by Francis Beaumont and John Fletcher*. F1 (London, 1647)

Fletcher, John (with Francis Beaumont?). *The Captain*, in *Comedies and Tragedies written by Francis Beaumont and John Fletcher*. F1 (London, 1647)

Fletcher, John, and Philip Massinger. *The Little French Lawyer*, in *Comedies and Tragedies written by Francis Beaumont and John Fletcher*. F1 (London, 1647)

Fletcher, John, and William Shakespeare. *The Two Noble Kinsmen* Q1 (London, 1634)

Fletcher, John, Nathan Field and Philip Massinger. *The Knight of Malta*, in *Comedies and Tragedies written by Francis Beaumont and John Fletcher*. F1 (London, 1647)

Foakes, R. A. (ed.). *Henslowe's Diary* (2nd edn; Cambridge University Press, 2002)

Illustrations of the English Stage: 1580–1642 (Stanford University Press, 1985)

Ford, John. *'Tis Pity She's a Whore*, ed. Martin Wiggins (London: A&C Black, 2003)

Forgeng, J. L. *Daily Life in Elizabethan England* (Santa Barbara, CA: ABC-CLIO, 2010)

Furttenbach, Joseph. *Mannhafter Kunst Spiegel*, trans. George Kernodle [*The Noble Mirror of Art*], *The Renaissance Stage: Documents of Serlio, Sabbattini and Furttenbach*, ed. Bernard Hewitt (Oxford, OH: University of Miami Press, 1958)

Gair, W. Reaveley. *The Children of Paul's: The Story of a Theatre Company, 1553–1608* (Cambridge University Press, 1982)

Galloway, David (ed.). *The Elizabethan Theatre II* (Toronto: Macmillan of Canada, 1970)
Norwich 1540–1642 (University of Toronto Press, 1984)
Gardner, Lyn. '*Cymbeline* – Review', *Guardian*, 30 May 2012
Gascoigne, George. *The Complete Poems of George Gascoigne*, vol. I, ed. William Carew Hazlitt (London, 1869)
Girouard, M. *Elizabethan Architecture: Its Rise and Fall, 1560–1640* (New Haven and London: Yale University Press, 2009)
Robert Smythson and the Elizabethan Country House (New Haven and London: Yale University Press, 1983)
Gosson, Stephen. *Plays Confuted in Five Actions* (London, 1582)
Graves, Robert. *Lighting the Shakespearean Stage 1567–1642* (Carbondale, IL: Southern Illinois University Press, 1999)
Gravett, Kenneth. *Timber and Brick Building in Kent* (Chichester: Phillimore, 1971)
Greene, Robert. 'Doron's Description of Samela' from Menaphon (1589), in *The Dramatic Works of Robert Greene*, ed. Revd Alexander Dyce, vol. II (London, 1831)
Gurr, Andrew. 'The Date and the Expected Venue of *Romeo and Juliet*', *Shakespeare Survey* 49 (1996), 15–25
The Shakespeare Company, 1594–1642 (Cambridge University Press, 2004)
The Shakespearean Stage: 1574–1642 (4th edn; Cambridge University Press, 2009)
The Shakespearian Playing Companies (Oxford: Clarendon Press, 1996)
'*The Tempest*'s Tempest at Blackfriars', *Shakespeare Survey* 41 (1989), 91–101
'*The Tempest*'s "Top"', *Notes & Queries* 257 (2012), 550–2
'Who is Lovewit? What is He?', in *Ben Jonson and Theatre*, ed. Richard Allen Cave, Elizabeth Schafer and Brian Woolland (London: Routledge, 1999), pp. 5–19
Gurr, Andrew, with John Orrell. *Rebuilding Shakespeare's Globe* (London: Weidenfeld & Nicolson, 1989)
Hakewill, George. *The Vanitie of the Eie, First Beganne for the Comfort of a Gentlewoman Beareaved of Her Sight, and Since upon Occasion Enlarged and Published for the Common Good* (London 1606; Oxford, 1615)
Hall, Joseph. *Characters of Virtue and Vice* (London, 1608)
Harington, Sir John. 'Of the Lady that lookt well to her borders', in *The Most Elegant and Witty Epigrams* (London, 1618)
Harris, John, and Gordon Higgott. *Inigo Jones: Complete Architectural Drawings* (London: Royal Academy Publishing, 1989)
Harris, John, Stephen Orgel and Roy Strong. *The King's Arcadia: Inigo Jones and the Stuart Court* (London: Arts Council of Great Britain, 1973)
Haynes, Jonathan. 'The Elizabethan Audience on Stage', in James Redmond (ed.), *Theatrical Space* (Cambridge University Press, 1987), pp. 59–68
Henke, Robert. *Pastoral Transformations: Italian Tragicomedy and Shakespeare's Late Plays* (Newark, DE: University of Delaware Press, 1997)

Hewett, Cecil A. *Church Carpentry* (Chichester: Phillimore, 1982)
English Historic Carpentry (Chichester: Phillimore, 1980)
Hewitt, Bernard (ed.). *The Renaissance Stage: Documents of Serlio, Sabbatini and Furttenbach* (Miami University Press, 1958)
Heywood, Thomas. *Love's Mistress, or The Queen's Masque*, ed. Richmond Shady (Salzburg: Edwin Mellen Press, 1977)
Hodges, C. Walter. *The Globe Restored: A Study of the Elizabethan Theatre* (London: Ernest Benn, 1953)
Holder, N. 'The Medieval Friaries of London: A Topographic and Archaeological History Before and After the Dissolution', Ph.D. dissertation, University of London, 2011
Hosley, Richard. 'A Reconstruction of the Second Blackfriars', in David Galloway (ed.), *The Elizabethan Theatre II* (Toronto: Macmillan of Canada, 1970), pp. 74–87
'The Second Blackfriars (1596)', in C. Leech and T. W. Craik (eds.) *The Revels History of Drama in English*, vol. III, *1576–1613* (London: Methuen, 1975), pp. 197–226
House, Anthony. 'The City of London and the Problem of the Liberties, *c.* 1540–*c.* 1640', Ph.D. dissertation, University of Oxford, 2006
Ichikawa, Mariko. *Shakespearean Entrances* (Basingstoke: Palgrave Macmillan, 2002)
The Shakespearean Stage Space (Cambridge University Press, 2012)
Jackson, MacDonald P. *Defining Shakespeare:* Pericles *as Test Case* (Oxford University Press, 2003)
Studies in Attribution: Middleton and Shakespeare (University of Salzburg Press, 1979)
Jones, Ann Rosalind, and Peter Stallybrass. *Renaissance Clothing and the Materials of Memory* (Cambridge University Press, 2007)
Jonson, Ben. *The Alchemist*, ed. Elizabeth Cook, New Mermaids (London: Methuen, 2004)
The Cambridge Edition of the Works of Ben Jonson, ed. David Bevington, Martin Butler and Ian Donaldson (7 vols.; Cambridge University Press, 2012)
Catiline His Conspiracy, ed. W. F. Bolton and Jane F. Gardner (Lincoln, NE: University of Nebraska Press, 1972)
The Complete Plays of Ben Jonson, ed. G. A. Wilkes (4 vols.; Oxford University Press, 1981–2)
The Devil is an Ass (London, 1641). Ed. Peter Happé, Revels Plays (Manchester University Press, 1996)
Epicoene, in Ben Jonson, *Works*, F1 (London, 1616)
The Fountaine of Selfe-Love, or Cynthia's Revels (London, 1601)
The Magnetic Lady, ed. Peter Happé (Manchester University Press, 2000)
The New Inn (London, 1631)
The Staple of News. Folio printed in 1631 and included in Ben Jonson, *Works*, F2 (London, 1640). Ed. Anthony Parr (Manchester University Press, 1988)
Works, ed. Percy C. H. Herford and Evelyn Simpson (11 vols.; Oxford: Clarendon Press, 1925–52)

Jowett, John. Introduction to *Measure for Measure*, in Thomas Middleton, *The Collected Works* (Oxford University Press, 2007)

'New Created Creatures: Ralph Crane and the Stage Directions in *The Tempest*', *Shakespeare Survey* 36 (1983), 107–20

'The Pattern of Collaboration in *Timon of Athens*', in Brian Boyd (ed.), *Words that Count: Essays on Early Modern Authorship in Honor of MacDonald P. Jackson* (Newark, DE: University of Delaware Press, 2004), pp. 181–205

Karim-Cooper, Farah. *Cosmetics in Shakespearean and Renaissance Drama* (Edinburgh University Press, 2012)

Kiefer, Frederick. 'Curtains on the Shakespearean Stage', *Medieval and Renaissance Drama in England* 20 (2007), 151–86

Killigrew, Thomas. *The Prisoners and Claracilla: Two Tragae-Comedies* (London, 1641)

Knapp, Jeffrey. *Shakespeare Only* (University of Chicago Press, 2009)

Knight, G. Wilson. *The Crown of Life: Essays in Interpretation of Shakespeare's Final Plays* (Oxford University Press, 1947; London: Methuen, 1965)

Knutson, Roslyn L. *Playing Companies and Commerce in Shakespeare's London* (Cambridge University Press, 2001)

The Repertory of Shakespeare's Company, 1594–1613 (Fayetteville: University of Arkansas Press, 1991)

Lamb, Mary Ellen, and Valerie Wayne (eds.). *Staging Early Modern Romance: Prose Fiction, Dramatic Romance, and Shakespeare* (London: Routledge, 2009)

Lancashire, Anne. *London Civic Theatre* (Cambridge University Press, 2002)

Leacroft, Richard, and Helen Leacroft. *Theatre and Playhouse: An Illustrated Survey of Theatre Buildings from Ancient Greece to the Present Day* (London: Methuen, 1985)

Lenton, Francis. *The Young Gallants Whirligig* (London, 1629)

Lesser, Zachary. *Renaissance Drama and the Politics of Publication* (Cambridge University Press, 2004)

Lindley, David. 'Music, Masque and Meaning in *The Tempest*' in *The Court Masque* (Manchester University Press, 1984), pp. 47–59

Lindley, David (ed.). *Shakespeare and Music,* Arden Critical Companions (London: Thomson, 2006)

The Tempest (Cambridge University Press, 2013)

M, T., *The Life of a Satyrical Puppy Called Nim* (London, 1657)

McDonald, Russ. *Shakespeare's Late Style* (Cambridge University Press, 2006)

Mackintosh, Iain. *Architecture, Actor and Audience* (London and New York: Routledge, 1993)

'Inigo Jones – Theatre Architect', *TAB* 31 (1973), 99–105

McLuskie, Kathleen. '"A Maidenhead, Amintor, at my yeares": Chastity and Tragicomedy in the Fletcher Plays', in Gordon McMullan and Jonathan Hope (eds.), *The Politics of Tragicomedy: Shakespeare and After* (London: Taylor & Francis, 1992)

'The Shopping Complex: Materiality and the Renaissance Theatre', in Edward Pechter (ed.), *Textual and Theatrical Shakespeare: Questions of Evidence* (Iowa University Press, 1996), pp. 86–101

McMillin, Scott, and Sally Beth MacLean. *The Queen's Men and their Plays* (Cambridge University Press, 1998)
McMullan, Gordon. Introduction to William Shakespeare, *King Henry VIII* (London: Thomson, 2000)
The Politics of Tragicomedy (London: Routledge, 1992)
The Politics of Unease in the Plays of John Fletcher (Amherst: University of Massachusetts Press, 1994)
Shakespeare and the Idea of Late Writing: Authorship in the Proximity of Death (Cambridge University Press, 2007)
Magagnato, Licisco. *Il Teatro Olimpico* (Milan: Electra, 1992)
Jack Drum's Entertainment (London, 1601)
Maguire, Laurie, and Emma Smith. 'Many Hands: A New Shakespeare Collaboration?', *Times Literary Supplement*, 19 April 2012
Marston, John. *Antonio and Mellida* (London, 1602)
Antonio's Revenge, ed. W. Reavley Gair (Manchester University Press, 1966)
The Dutch Courtesan, ed. D. Crane (London: A&C Black, 1997)
The Insatiate Countess (London, 1613)
Sophonisba (London, 1606)
What You Will, ed. M. R. Woodhead (Nottingham: Nottingham Drama Texts, 1968)
Massinger, Philip. *Believe As You List*, ed. Philip Edwards and Colin Gibson, *The Plays and Poems of Philip Massinger*, vol. III (5 vols.; Oxford: Clarendon Press, 1976)
The City Madam. Q1 (London, 1658)
The Renegado. Q1 (London, 1630)
The Roman Actor. Q1 (London, 1629)
Matthew, H. C. G., and B. Harrison (eds.). *The Oxford Dictionary of National Biography* (61 vols.; Oxford University Press, 2004)
Meek, Richard. 'Ekphrasis in *The Rape of Lucrece* and *The Winter's Tale*', *Studies in English Literature, 1500–1900* 46.2 (spring 2006), 389–414
Mercer, Henry C. *Ancient Carpenters' Tools* (London, 1929)
Middleton, Thomas. *Father Hubburd's Tales* [1604], in *Thomas Middleton: The Collected Works*, ed. Gary Taylor and John Lavagnino (Oxford University Press, 2007)
The Lady's Tragedy, ed. Julia Briggs, in *Thomas Middleton: The Collected Works*, ed. Gary Taylor and John Lavagnino (Oxford University Press, 2007)
Michaelmas Term (London, 1607)
The Revenger's Tragedy, ed. R. A. Foakes (Manchester University Press, 1966)
The Second Maiden's Tragedy, ed. W. W. Greg (Oxford: Malone Society Reprints, 1909)
Your Five Gallants (London, 1608)
Middleton, Thomas, and William Rowley. *The Changeling* (London, 1653)
Mills, P., and J. Oliver. *The Survey of Building Sites in the City of London after the Great Fire of 1666* (5 vols.; London Topographical Society, 1962–7)
Mowl, Timothy, *Elizabethan and Jacobean Style* (London: Phaidon, 1993)

Mullaney, Steven. 'Affective Technologies: Toward an Emotional Logic of the Elizabethan Stage', in Mary Floyd-Wilson and Garrett A. Sullivan (eds.), *Environment and Embodiment in Early Modern England* (Basingstoke: Palgrave Macmillan, 2012), pp. 71–89

Mullin, Donald C. 'Lighting on the Eighteenth-Century London Stage', in *The Development of the Playhouse: A Survey of Theatre Architecture from the Renaissance to the Present* (Berkeley: University of California Press, 1970), p. 74

Mulryne, J. R., and Margaret Shewring (eds.). *Shakespeare's Globe Rebuilt* (Cambridge University Press, 1997)

Munro, Lucy. *Children of the Queen's Revels* (Cambridge University Press, 2005)

'Dublin Tragicomedy and London Stages', in Subha Mukherji and Raphael Lyne (eds.), *Early Modern Tragicomedy* (Cambridge: D. S. Brewer, 2007), pp. 175–92

Nabbes, Thomas. *Tottenham Court* (London, 1639)

Neill, Michael (ed.). *The Renegado* (London: A&C Black, 2010)

Nelson, Alan H. (ed.). *Cambridge* (2 vols.; University of Toronto Press, 1989)

Early Cambridge Theatres (Cambridge University Press, 1994)

The Plays of Henry Medwall (Cambridge: D. S. Brewer, 1980)

Nelson, Alan H., and John R. Elliott, Jnr (eds.). *Inns of Court* (3 vols.; Woodbridge: Boydell & Brewer, 2010)

Orgel, Stephen (ed.). *The Tempest* (Oxford University Press, 1987)

Orgel, Stephen, and Roy Strong. *The Theatre of the Stuart Court* (2 vols.; London: Sotheby Parke Bernet, 1973)

Orrell, John. *The Human Stage* (Cambridge University Press, 1988)

The Theatres of Inigo Jones and John Webb (Cambridge University Press, 1985)

Oxford, City of, A Survey and Inventory (London: Royal Commission on Historic Monuments, 1939)

Paster, Gail Kern, Katherine Rowe and Mary Floyd-Wilson. *Reading the Early Modern Passions: Essays in the Cultural History of Emotion* (Philadelphia: University of Pennsylvania Press, 2004)

Pearson, Sarah. *The Medieval Houses of Kent* (London: Royal Commission on Historical Monuments, 1994)

Pearson, Sarah, P. S. Barnwell and A. T. Adams. *A Gazetteer of Medieval Houses in Kent* (London: Royal Commission on Historical Monuments, 1994)

Penoyre, John, and Jane Penoyre. *Decorative Plasterwork in the Houses of Somerset. A Regional Survey* (Taunton: Somerset County Council, 1994)

Pepys, Samuel. *The Diary of Samuel Pepys*, ed. Mynors Bright (3 vols.; London: Dent, 1953)

Perina, Peter. 'Candle Lighting in Theatres in the 17th and 18th Centuries', in *The World of Baroque Theatre: A compilation of Essays from the Český Krumlov Conferences 2004–6* (Antwerp: Český Krumlov, 2007), pp. 131–4

Pevsner, Nikolaus, and D. Neave. *Yorkshire: York and the East Riding* (New Haven and London: Yale University Press, 1995)

Potter, Lois (ed.). *The Two Noble Kinsmen* (Walton-on-Thames: Thomas Nelson, 1997)

Potts, A. 'The Development of the Playhouse in Seventeenth-Century London', Ph.D. dissertation, University of Cambridge, 1998. Accessed 23/10/2012, http://playhousehistory.co.uk
Prynne, William. *Histriomastix* (London, 1633)
Puttenham, George. *The Arte of English Poesie* (London, 1589)
R. C. 'To Mr Alexander Gough upon his publishing The excellent Play call'd the Queen', in Alexander Goughe, *The Queen or the Excellency of her Sex* (London, 1653)
Raylor, Timothy. *Cavaliers, Clubs, and Literary Culture: Sir John Mennes, James Smith, and the Order of the Fancy* (Newark, DE: University of Delaware Press, 1994)
Reid, Francis. 'Historically Informed Lighting in Baroque Opera Staging', in *The World of Baroque Theatre: A Compilation of Essays from the Český Krumlov Conferences 2004–6* (Antwerp: Český Krumlov, 2007), pp. 155–63
Richards, Nathaniel. *The Celestial Publican* (London, 1630)
Richardson, Catherine. *Shakespeare and Material Culture* (Oxford University Press, 2011)
Rose, Mary Beth. *The Expense of Spirit: Love and Sexuality in Renaissance Drama* (Ithaca, NY: Cornell University Press, 1988)
Rowan, D. F. 'A Neglected Jones/Webb Theatre Project, Part II: A Theatrical Missing Link', in D. Galloway (ed.), *The Elizabethan Theatre II* (London: Macmillan, 1970), pp. 60–73
Rowse, A. L. *The Case Books of Simon Forman: Sex and Society in Shakespeare's Age* (London: Macmillan, 1976)
Ruscelli, Girolamo. *The Secrets of Alexis of Piemont: Containing Many Excellent Remedies Against Divers Diseases*, trans. William Warde (London, 1615)
Rutter, Carol Chillington. 'Talking Heads', in Stuart Hampton-Reeves and Bridget Escolme (eds.), *Shakespeare and the Making of Theatre* (Basingstoke: Palgrave Macmillan, 2012), pp. 102–27
Sanders, Julie. *Caroline Drama: The Plays of Massinger, Ford, Shirley, and Brome* (Plymouth: Northcote House, 1999)
Schiavo, Remo. *A Guide to the Olympic Theatre*, trans. Patricia Ann Hill (2nd edn; Vicenza: Academia Olimpica, 1985)
Schofield, John. *The Building of London: From the Conquest to the Great Fire* (London: British Museum Publications, 1984)
Medieval London Houses (London: Paul Mellon Foundation, 2003)
Scott, Thomas. *Exod. 8.19. Digitus Dei* (London, 1623)
Seltzer, Daniel. 'The Staging of the Last Plays', in John Russell Brown and Bernard Harris (eds.), *Later Shakespeare* (London: Edward Arnold, 1966), pp. 127–66
Seng, Peter. *The Vocal Songs in the Plays of Shakespeare: A Critical History* (Cambridge, MA: Harvard University Press, 1967)
Serlio, Sebastiano. *The Five Books of Architecture: An Unabridged Reprint of the English Edition of 1611* (New York: Dover Books, 1982)
Shadwell, Thomas. *Bury-fair* (London, 1689)
The Virtuoso (London, 1676)

Shakespeare, William. *The Norton Facsimile: The First Folio of Shakespeare*, ed. Charlton Hinman (2nd edn; New York: W. W. Norton, 1996)

Shakespeare's Plays in Quarto: A Facsimile Edition of Copies Mainly from the Henry E. Huntington Library, ed. Michael J. B. Allen and Kenneth Muir (Berkeley: University of California Press, 1981)

The Winter's Tale, ed. John Pitcher, Arden Shakespeare (London: Bloomsbury, 2010)

Shapiro, Michael. *Children of the Revels: The Boy Companies of Shakespeare's Time and their Plays* (New York: Columbia University Press, 1977)

Sharpe, Lewis. *The Noble Stranger* (London: British Library Publishing, 2011)

Sharpham, Edward. *The Fleer* (London, 1607)

Sheen, Erica. *Shakespeare and the Institution of Theatre* (Basingstoke: Palgrave Macmillan, 2009)

Sherlock, D. *Prior's Hall Barn, Widdington, Essex* (London: English Heritage, 1991)

Shirley, James. *The Sisters* (London, 1652)

Skantze, P. A. *Stillness in Motion in the Seventeenth-Century Theatre* (London and New York: Routledge, 2004)

Smith, Bruce R. *The Acoustic World of Early Modern England: Attending to the O-Factor* (University of Chicago Press, 1999)

Smith, Irwin. *Shakespeare's Blackfriars Playhouse: Its History and Design* (New York University Press, 1964)

Smith, John. *A Short Introduction to the Art of Painting and Varnishing* (London, 1685)

Somerset, J. Alan B. '"How Chances It They Travel?": Provincial Touring, Playing Spaces and the King's Men', *Shakespeare Survey* 47 (1996), 45–60

Somerset, J. Alan B. (ed.). *Shropshire* (2 vols.; University of Toronto Press, 1994)

Somi, Leone di. 'Dialogues on Stage Affairs (*c.* 1556–7)', in Allardyce Nicoll (ed.), *The Development of the Theatre* (5th edn; London: Harrap, 1966), pp. 252–78

States, Bert O. *Great Reckonings in Little Rooms* (Berkeley: University of California Press, 1987)

Steele, Brian. 'In the Flower of their Youth: "Portraits" of Venetian Beauties ca. 1500', *Sixteenth Century Journal* 28.23 (summer 1997), 481–502

Stephens, John. 'To his worthy Friend, H. F. upon his Notes from Black-Fryers', in Henry Fitzgeffrey, *Satyres and Satyricall Epigrams: The Third Booke of Humours: Intituled Notes from Black-Fryers* (London, 1617)

Stern, Tiffany. 'Taking Part: Actors and Audience on the Stage at Blackfriars', in Paul Menzer (ed.), *Inside Shakespeare: Essays on the Blackfriars Stage* (Selinsgrove, PA: Susquehanna University Press, 2006), pp. 35–53

Stopes, C. C. *Burbage and Shakespeare's Stage* (London: Alexander Moring, 1913)

Stubbes, Philip. *The Anatomie of Abuses* (London, 1583). Ed. F. J. Furnivall (London, 1877)

Sturgess, Keith. *Jacobean Private Theatre* (London: Routledge, 1987)

Suckling, John. *Aglaura* (London, 1638)

Summerson, J. *Architecture in Britain 1530–1830* (New Haven and London: Yale University Press, 1993)

Inigo Jones (Harmondsworth: Penguin, 2000)

Symonds, E. M. 'The Diary of John Greene (1634–57)', *English Historical Review* 43 (1928), 385–94

Taylor, Gary. 'The Structure of Performance: Act-Intervals in the London Theatres, 1576–1642', in Gary Taylor and John Jowett, *Shakespeare Reshaped: 1616–1623* (Oxford: Clarendon Press, 1993), pp. 3–50

Thomson, Leslie. 'Playgoers on the Outdoor Stages of Early Modern London', *Theatre Notebook* 64 (2010), 3–11

'"With patient ears attend": *Romeo and Juliet* on the Elizabethan Stage', *Studies in Philology* 92 (1995), 230–47

Thurley, S. *Whitehall Palace* (London: Merrel Publishers and Historic Royal Palaces, 2008)

Tomlinson, Sophie. 'She that Plays the King: Henrietta Maria and the Threat of the Actress in Caroline Culture', in Gordon McMullan and Jonathan Hope (eds.), *The Politics of Tragicomedy* (London: Routledge, 1992), pp. 189–207

Women on Stage in Stuart Drama (Cambridge University Press, 2005)

Traversi, Derek. *Shakespeare: The Last Phase* (New York: Harcourt, 1953)

Tuke, Thomas. *A Treatise Against Paint[i]ng and Tincturing of Men and Women* (London, 1616)

Turner, Robert Kean (ed.). *The Little French Lawyer*, in Fredson Bowers (gen. ed.), *The Dramatic Works in the Beaumont and Fletcher Canon*, vol. IX (10 vols.; Cambridge University Press, 1966–96; 1994), pp. 323–459

Turner, Robert Kean, and Patricia Tatspaugh (eds.). *The Two Noble Kinsmen* (Cambridge University Press, 2012)

Vaughan, Virginia Mason, and Alden T. Vaughan (eds.). *The Tempest* (Walton-on-Thames: Thomas Nelson, 1999)

Vickers, Brian. *Shakespeare, Co-Author: A Historical Study of Five Collaborative Plays* (Oxford University Press, 2002)

Waith, Eugene M. (ed.). *The Two Noble Kinsmen* (Oxford University Press, 1989)

Walker, Kim. 'New Prison: Representing the Female Actor in Shirley's *The Bird in a Cage* (1633)', *English Literary Renaissance* 21 (. . .), 385–400

Webster, John. *The Duchess of Malfi*. Q1 (London, 1623)

'Induction' to John Marston, *The Malcontent* (London, 1604)

The White Devil, ed. John Russell Brown (London: Methuen, 1966)

Wells-Cole, Anthony. *Art and Decoration in Elizabethan and Jacobean England. The Influence of Continental Prints, 1558–1625* (New Haven and London: Yale University Press, 1997)

Welsby, Paul A. (ed.). *Sermons and Society: An Anthology* (Harmondsworth: Penguin, 1970)

White, Martin. *The Chamber of Demonstrations: Reconstructing the Jacobean Indoor Playhouse* (University of Bristol and Ignition Films, 2009)

Renaissance Drama in Action (London: Routledge, 1998)

Wickham, Glynne, *Early English Stages, 1300–1660* (3 vols.; London: Routledge & Kegan Paul, 1959–81)

Wickham, Glynne, Herbert Berry and William Ingram (eds.). *English Professional Theatre, 1530–1660* (Cambridge University Press, 2000)
Williams, George Walton (ed.). *The Knight of Malta*, in Fredson Bowers (gen. ed.), *Dramatic Works in the Beaumont and Fletcher Canon*, vol. VIII (Cambridge University Press, 1992), pp. 345–482
Wilson, Jean. *The Archaeology of Shakespeare* (Stroud: Allan Sutton, 1997)
Wilson, Robert. *Three Ladies of London* (London, 1590)
Wither, George. *Fair Virtue; or, The Mistress of Phil'arete* (London, 1622)
Witmore, Michael. 'Phenomenology and Sensation: Shakespeare, Sensation, and Renaissance Existentialism', *Criticism* 54.3 (2012), 419–26
Wright, James. *Historia Histrionica* (London, 1699)
Yates, Frances. *The Theatre of the World* (London and New York: Routledge & Kegan Paul, 1969)
Yeomans, D. T. *The Trussed Roof: Its History and Development* (Aldershot: Scolar, 1992)

Index

Lightning Source UK Ltd.
Milton Keynes UK
UKHW02f0618091117
312447UK00003B/76/P

9 781108 438759